Hildegard von Bingen

To Pina

Sara Salvadori

Hildegard von Bingen

The Fountain of Wisdom
Arithmetic Geometry Music Astronomy

Beyond the Images

Scivias
Liber Divinorum Operum

SKIRA

This book was produced thanks to the contribution of

Fondazione
Cassa di Risparmio
di Lucca

This book has been translated thanks to a translation grant awarded by the Italian Ministry of Foreign Affairs and International Cooperation

The research was supported by

FONDAZIONE
PASQUINELLI

Cover
Liber Divinorum Operum, c. 132r
Biblioteca Statale di Lucca, ms. 1942

Head of Business Development
Edoardo Ghizzoni

Managing Editor and Head of Production
Manuela Calandra

Cultural Project Manager
Giulia Bassoli

Design
Luigi Fiore

Editorial Coordination
Emma Cavazzini

Copy Editing
Scriptum, Rome

Layout
Barbara Galotta

Translations
Susan Ann White for Scriptum, Rome

First published in November 2025 by
Skira editore srl
via Agnello, 18
20121 Milano, Italy
skira-arte.com

ISBN: 978-88-572-5417-3

This book has been printed by GPS Group on FSC®-certified paper

MIX
Paper | Supporting responsible forestry
FSC® C118234

Distributed in the USA, Canada, Central & South America by ARTBOOK | D.A.P., 75 Broad Street, Suite 630, New York, NY 10004, USA.
Distributed elsewhere in the world by Thames and Hudson Ltd., 181A High Holborn, London WC1V 7QX, United Kingdom.

The reproduction of the miniatures (c. 1v, 9r, 28v, 88v, 132r, sec. XIII) of the *Liber Divinorum Operum* was authorized by Sabrina Maria La Pusata, director of the Biblioteca Statale di Lucca where codex 1942 with the illuminated manuscript of the *Liber Divinorum Operum* is kept.
By permission of the Ministry of Culture – Biblioteca Statale di Lucca

The reproduction of the miniatures of *Scivias* was authorized by Sister Philippa Rath of the Abtei St. Hildegard – Eibingen, where the copy/facsimile of the Rupertsberg Codex Hs 1 is kept

The reproduction of the miniatures (c. 7v, 9v, 10v, 11v, 18v, 27v, 29v) of the *In honorem Sanctae Crucisof* was authorized by Bibliotèque national de France where codex Latin 2422 is kept

The translations of the Latin of the *Liber Divinorum Operum* are by Nathaniel M. Campbell, in *St. Hildegard of Bingen, The Book of Divine Works*, The Catholic University of America Press, Washington D.C. 2018

The translations of the Latin of *Scivias* are by Mother Colombia Hart and Jane Bishop, in *Hildegard of Bingen, SCIVIAS*, Paulist Press New Jersey, USA, 1990

Processing of the images
Sara Salvadori

Graphic design of the images
Patrizia Elena Bertini

Construction of the models
Sofia Basilissi
Plastici SB

Photographs
Enos Mantoani
Carlo Prevosti

Acknowledgments
Giuseppina Antognini once said to me, "your books are important, but what strikes me is the story behind them." Pina had grasped the force of the journey between the visible and the invisible, a constellation of encounters and extraordinary events, and she clearly saw its far-reaching implications. A personal journey shared with a group of people gathered around the touching beauty of Hildegard's images. Some of them have been the roots, others faithful companions, others passing meteors, and still others have provided loving care allowing me to collect, organize, and display the fruits of this work, and that of the two preceding volumes. To all of them, I extend my gratitude. Here, in particular, I wish to acknowledge those who worked on and supported the creation of this volume. Maria Stella Curti for her relentless pursuit of the light of the spirit and for her sisterly welcome. Giuseppina Antognini for always having been in love with life, art, and humanity. Their friendship and Pina's generosity, thanks to the Francesco Pasquinelli Foundation, which she established, were indispensable. Marcello Bertocchini for his visionary and immediate embrace of this second volume among the projects of the Cassa di Risparmio di Lucca Foundation, highlighting Hildegard's manuscript in the Lucca State Library, one of the city's most precious gems. Pietro Della Lucia for seeing the potential of a publishing project in the raw initial materials, which he brought to Skira, entrusting it to the excellent team led by Emma Cavazzini. Patrizia Elena Bertini, without whom none of the images in the books would have come to life. Caitlin Swanson for infusing the days with fragrant lightness and for reading the excellent translation by Scriptum on my behalf. Franco Lisi for sharing with me the journey into Hildegard's cosmos. Sofia Bassilisi for creating the three-dimensional models with the images of the visions, carefully photographed by Enos Mantoani and Carlo Prevosti. Anna for teaching me every day to go with the flow. Lorenzo for reminding me that the earth exists. Finally, a profound thank-you to Michela Pereira and Giorgio Mazzanti for their presence, solid pillars of the Temple of Wisdom. And to Sister Dorothea of the Abbey of St. Hildegard for her shining eyes and her joy in watching me work on the images in the Codex.
Sara Salvadori

The limpid and astonishingly modern voice of Hildegard von Bingen rose amid the fiery seasons of medieval spirituality, when European culture was defining new horizons of thought and faith. A nun and founder, mystic, composer, and advisor to kings and popes, Hildegard was a luminous presence in a time of great transformation.
I prefer the form Opus Divinorum *to the traditional* Liber Divinorum Operum *because, beyond the undoubted philological accuracy of the title, the word* Opus *highlights the comprehensive and unified nature of Hildegard's spiritual enterprise. The term* Liber *emphasizes the work's literary and codicological dimension;* Opus *enhances its theological, visionary, and cosmological significance, evoking the "great divine work" that the saint contemplates and interprets. It is therefore not simply a book, but a work of revelation and creation, a mirror of the* Opus Dei *itself.*
In these pages, contemplation and observation, revelation and the study of nature, poetry and doctrine meet. For Hildegard, the world is not the place of the fallen human race, but a sacred garden inhabited by the life-giving breath of God: a cosmos to be loved, understood, and protected. Her voice speaks to us of light, of balance, of a wisdom that permeates all creatures and calls them to unity.
Hildegard's words do not close, but open: they invite us to knowledge as a path to elevation, to song as prayer, to care of the body and soul as participation in the creative work. It is a spirituality that does not flee the world, but investigates and transfigures it.

A precious piece of this wisdom transmission is the so-called Lucca Codex, one of the oldest and most refined manuscript testimonies of Hildegard's work. With its illuminations, annotations, and textual variations, the codex reflects not only the theological depth of the Rhineland saint, but also the keen attention with which Italian monastic communities welcomed, preserved, and disseminated her revelations. This codex is not a simple relic: it is a channel through which Hildegard's voice continues to flow and regenerate, in dialogue with the incessant stream of time. Sara Salvadori has successfully conveyed, with philological accuracy and critical acumen, its complex and intricate web of words and miniatures, proportions and measurements, concepts and experiences, the vitality of an organic vision, constantly evolving and unfolding.
It is to her therefore that the Fondazione Cassa di Risparmio di Lucca would like to extend its deepest gratitude for the tireless and profound gaze with which Sara Salvadori has penetrated the Liber *and the* Opus, *delivering to the reader the luminous voice of Hildegard, that invites us to rediscover harmony lost and recognize, in everything, the trace of the divine that allows it to exist.*

Massimo Marsili
President of the Fondazione
Cassa di Risparmio di Lucca

A great legacy of wisdom and spirituality is passed on in this new book by Sara Salvadori, who guides us through the fascinating, multifaceted world of medieval mystic and theologian Hildegard von Bingen. With her profound sensibility and knowledge, the author conveys the essence of Hildegard's complexity and richness to us all.
During the four years it took to realize the project, this volume always enjoyed the enthusiastic interest and support of Giuseppina Antognini, founder and president of the Fondazione Pasquinelli, whose passing in April 2025 sadly prevented her from seeing it completed.
The chance encounter between Giuseppina and Sara triggered an exchange of correspondence and reflections, a dialogue that enabled them to explore and engage with not only Hildegardian thought, but also the research methods and passion that have guided the author throughout her research.
The contemplation and study of the image—seen not as decoration or illustration of the text but as representation of the vision—and the symbolic, all-embracing interpretation of each one, enable readers to immerse themselves in Sara's experience.
With her rigorous, dedicated approach, Sara Salvadori has made a complex figure like Hildegard accessible to a wide public, shining a light not only on her spirituality, but also on her unique gift of combining science, music, and nature in a harmonious whole.
For Hildegard, every discipline is interconnected and can be explained through the divine plan. Her life and works, experienced and created in a medieval context that apparently imposed strict limitations on women, are shown to be remarkably modern and timely. The saint's vision of the world and of spirituality bridges the human and the divine, heaven and earth, representing an unceasing quest for truth, on both a spiritual and scientific level. Sara Salvadori invites us to discover Hildegard's relevance today and to appreciate her capacity to look beyond the confines of time and space.
In memory of Pina's friendship and respect for Sara.

Alberto Fossati
President of the Fondazione Francesco Pasquinelli

Contents

Giorgio Mazzanti

A Prophecy for Today

Today, the "Sybil of the Rhine" is more alive than ever. Centuries later, Hildegard von Bingen still speaks to us with all the power of her feeling and breadth of her views. Her prophetic nature was understood by her contemporaries, as was the significance of her message. Preserved in time, it is also a prophecy for our times.

A prophet is not just someone who presents himself as such, but one who is enraptured, sequestered by God. Like Jacob, when he wrestles with the Angel of God at the River Jabbok, and bears the stigma as a limping gait; Jeremiah, who knows that God did violence to him; Amos, who is taken from the fields; and Saul, the future Paul, who is told: *It is hard for you to kick against the goads* (Acts 26:14).

The same thing happens when love is experienced. This is evident in the Song of Songs: You have stolen my heart… with one glance. I am my Beloved's. I held him and would not let him go. For Love is as strong as death.

Prophecy requires complete self-surrender, indeed it demands the death of the self, so that God may enter in and perform his action. The prophet is marked by the stigma of death. The author of Revelation falls as though dead upon beholding Christ in glory. Only when there is total self-surrender can the spark of prophecy be embedded and burst into flame in a human being, bestowing the gift of a gaze that can embrace and penetrate the twists and turns of human history from beginning to end, and thus engage with the complex reality of its time.

On the Lord's Day I was in the Spirit, and I heard behind me a loud voice like a trumpet, which said: "Write on a scroll what you see and send it to the seven churches" (Rev 1:10–11).

When I saw him, I fell at his feet as though dead. Then he placed his right hand on me and said: "Do not be afraid. I am the First and the Last. I am the Living One; I was dead, and now look, I am alive for ever and ever! And I hold the keys of death and Hades. Write, therefore, what you have seen, what is now and what will take place later" (Rev 1:17–19).

No one is seemingly more removed from the current reality than the prophet, yet he is deeply rooted in the historic present and its dynamics. He does not stop at superficiality, but penetrates the heart where human drama and destiny are decided. The prophet embraces the present because, enlightened by God's vision that encompasses the Alpha and the Omega of the unfolding of history, he knows its proper place and its ultimate destination. Completely surrendered to the Divine, even after moments of resistance and flight, of rigidity in body and mind, like Hildegard, the prophet becomes the mouth and eyes of God.

It was in this prophetic environment and dimension that Hildegard von Bingen, who herself experienced the gift of prophecy, was active. Her life was a continuous encounter and engagement with God, a process of deliverance to God, who through Hildegard reached her contemporaries, but also humankind in the following centuries until the present-day.

She also found it useless to put up resistance, which led to a rigidity of being also in the physical sense. She was asked to deliver herself so that God might deliver himself to her. It was the moment of *Fiat lux*, of God's act of creation, and of the womb of Woman, who became a handmaiden through the mystery of the flesh and of the weave of human life. Thus prophecy, ancient yet always modern, occurs within the constant dynamics of the relationship between God and the human; dynamics that do not preclude the innovative. Within the unchanging, God always does new things.

Hildegard had a highly individual, resolute personality and wide-ranging culture. She did not deny these, but aware of the infinite divide between her creatural nothingness and the absolute abyss of God, she knew that "God" was beyond human comprehension. The confession of her poverty was not a feminine affectation or fawning gesture, but statement of fact. No matter how many similarities are revealed between human realities and the world of God, their dissimilarity remains infinite. Although God communicates with human beings, He always transcends them. God acts *with* and *in* the human, who makes himself freely available to do his will, but He also infinitely surpasses them. That is why the Voice says: Write. Record what you see. And this is what Hildegard does. It is no coincidence that in one miniature the nun is represented in a small room, while she records on a tablet what she has seen and entrusts it to the monk who is her scribe.

What must be written? It must only be *described.*

The world of divine being and action presents itself to Hildegard through images, through partial views; in this case, the Word acts as a guide to a correct and coherent reading of the visions. The images are not a didactic aid, they are the message itself.

Other important figures have had instantaneous visions, like St. Benedict of Nursia, as recounted by Gregory the Great in *The Dialogues*, II, 35: *Benedict, being diligent in watching, rose early before the time of matins (his monks being yet at rest) and came to the window of his chamber where he offered up his prayers to almighty God. Standing there, all of a sudden in the dead of the night, as he looked forth, he saw a light that banished away the darkness of the night and glittered with such brightness that the light which shone in the midst of darkness was far more clear than the light of the day. Upon this sight a marvellous strange thing followed, for, as he himself did afterward report, the whole world, gathered together, as it were, under one beam of the sun.*

Unlike her teacher Benedict, Hildegard was entrusted with a whole series of figurative visions. These appeared in sequence and covered the entire arc of the adventurous relationship between God and Humanity. Within this vast horizon, man is called upon to take his place and to live, to experience the moment, the limited period of his existence, in the context of the combined history of the human and divine.

The miniatures, proposed by Hildegard and reproduced by some of her fellow nuns, fix the action of God in sequential scenes. They are like succinct parables, the means of conveying a long parabolic narrative. There is nothing superfluous in them, no purely decorative element. The numbers, divine and human figures, geometric forms, musical notations, and reprised and recurrent motifs, always send a message, providing a complete and detailed description of God's plan of salvation and of the way every single human being is called upon to follow.

The miniatures describe the dramatic unfolding of the story of salvation: God creates man, chooses a people, and inspires prophets and saints, so that each period will have the appropriate figures to shed light on the situations in which humanity finds itself and to indicate the right path.

God has shown himself not to be a solitary, but triadic being, *Tres/unitas*: God is Trinity. Not coincidentally, He is ingeniously represented as three interconnected concentric circles: a single "embrace" made up of those circles.

At a certain moment, Christ appears in the heart of the Trinity: the Word become flesh, the complete Man, *Ecce Homo*, the one who recapitulates all things in himself. He who is also the Lamb slaughtered for humanity at the beginning of the world, and who appears as the slaughtered Lamb upright on the throne at the end. The ultimate bridegroom toward whom humankind moves together with the multiple and diversified virtues that unfold and dance through history, and who finally enters into eternal Marriage with the celestial Jerusalem that descends from on high dressed in a white gown fashioned from the works of the just.

Thus, the miniatures fix the visions. These visions occurred in broad daylight and Hildegard saw them clearly, remembering every detail and the various colors. Hues that were appropriate for each individual, each place, each earthly and human reality; but also for expressing negativity, evil itself. The sequence of miniatures tells a figurative story, as do the Easter *Exultet* scrolls, for example those in Bari (11th-century works on parchment), which show, in illustrations placed upside down in relation to the text read from the pulpit, the figures and scenes described in the piece that is being sung or recited.

Sara Salvadori has studied the miniatures with keen insight and love, reading them not as a didactic element serving to support and convey oral teaching, but as windows on the divine sphere, prophetic visions deciphered through language. This has enabled her to grasp the specific meaning of each miniature, while also showing the various relationships between them and the coherence of the content of the different images, even ascertaining that the measurements of the spaces and the buildings, and their placement, are all exact. In the same way, the colors have a specific meaning, since they are not used simply to fill in, but to signify aspects of the beings who wear them; for example, there is no relationship between the black of the devil and the aurora of the Virgin Mary, while green has a positive connotation, an importance, because it symbolizes and conveys *viriditas* (viridity).

Colors and forms, people and buildings, are the figurative means through which God reveals himself and his part in the human story. They are intended to reach every human being so that they might move toward their ultimate destiny, but without alienating them from concrete life. The vision does not eschew either the earth or human bodies. Matter also derives from God who formed the body of man.

This shows us that Hildegard is not detached from life. The cosmic universe, the stars and stones, the grass and flowers, the forest and rivers, human construction and the celestial Jerusalem... none of these things are foreign to the nun. Nor does she shun the social and political reality of her time.

And she accepts them as a woman. Hildegard embraces her womanhood. Her perception of the necessity to keep bodies healthy and of their ultimate destination is typically feminine. And it is as a woman that she acts in the ecclesiastical and social worlds. At the same time, the "Sybil of the Rhine" denies her company to no one.

She intervenes authoritatively and forcefully, with state and ecclesiastical authorities as well as common folk, because she is delivered to God, who acts and speaks through this woman who has placed herself at his disposal.

The Divine speaks to her in a singular way, also through the scenes that it places before her. And this is where Sara Salvadori's gaze comes in, as she leads and guides readers through the meanders of the images and provides them with a reliable and precious Ariadne thread. At first glance the host of visions seems completely indecipherable, confused. But then one finds the way in and starts to see. Forms and transitions begin to emerge.

It is like coming out of a lighted room into the open country at night, when you are assailed by the darkness and everything seems black. But if you wait awhile you begin to see not only individual stars but also their configurations, the multiple constellations. The same thing happens with these miniatures: when tackled and described in fine detail, they become clear and can be interpreted and appreciated.

The images convey the message sent to humanity by God through the prophecy of a woman. A nun with a wide-ranging knowledge and contemporary culture, who delivers herself to the eternal, to the action and will of God. The Almighty who knows the heart of man and the dynamics of social relationships, the action and words appropriate to his condition, so that he might arrive at the truth that satisfies intelligence and heart. This is the prophetic action and content transmitted to us through Hildegard.

True prophecy never dies. It can cross vast divides and remain alive also by disappearing and resurfacing, to finally come down to us. To people today, who have the technologies and possibility to enter those visions and to recreate them in their entirety, but also their movements.

Hildegard's visionary universe appears to us in an unhoped-for way, in all its splendor and dynamism, its relationships and connections. The clearly presented pages of the book attract and astonish the reader. The factual accuracy in no way lessens the amazement and wonder they arouse.

The notes of music and the colors are of limited number and of a certain measure, but they constantly lend themselves to new compositions and new pictures. Measure does not preclude the infinite, the astonishing. The background does not prevent the rose from shining in all its splendor; on the contrary, it enhances that splendor.

As we get into the book, we get into Hildegard's overall vision. The prophetess also has something to say about our historic times, or rather *precisely* about our conflictual, whirlwind times, in which various aspects of the Sybil's personality are coming to light and emerging more and more clearly.

We are seeing the emergence of a strong, authoritative woman in the social and ecclesiastical environments, but a woman not without inner joy and happiness.

The emergence of a love for the cosmos and for nature, not because this is "healthy" but because they are gifts and revelatory acts of God, of the Divine. They are the first book of God.

The emergence of a concern with stones and flowers, for their beauty and their healing properties.

The emergence of a woman open to culture in all its various expressions, including music.

The emergence of a woman who considers the body and all its various components without false modesty.

The emergence of a woman who grasps the sacramental aspect of life and of the person of Christ. Between cross and altar there is a presential continuity.

The emergence of a woman who knows that evil is present in the heart of man and woman, in the relationships between people and faiths; who knows of the drama of the Synagogue and of Jerusalem torn between the historic and the celestial city, the place longed for by man the traveler, a stranger in this world, journeying toward the ultimate goal.

All these things combine to bring to light a message that is also appropriate for today's world, which can grasp it by embracing its profound and complete meaning. Not as a reductive or commandeering posture, but by resonating and harmonizing with it.

From this derives the astonishing affinity and empathy between Hildegard and our times, between her message and our present condition.

The author has the merit of introducing and revealing to us the prophetic charge of Hildegard's message for contemporary society—a message received, and conveyed, by women. Woman's visions, woman's interpretive reading. A marriage of humility and pride, joined together by a sacred and intense modesty, to bring together the heart of God and the heart of man. *Cor ad cor loquitur*. Woman to woman in empathic understanding.

Michela Pereira

Vision

Hildegard characterized her knowledge with the words *what I do not see I do not know*, and all the writings she has left us, be they prophetic, poetic, naturalistic, exegetic or hagiographic, are rooted in *vision*. She speaks of it in the singular, as in the prologue to the second book of her prophetic trilogy, *Liber vitae meritorum* (The Book of the Rewards of Life), 1158–1163, where she writes: *[...] true vision had shown me, a simple person, the true visions*. From Hildegard herself we learn that this vision was like seeing in the shadow or in the shimmering reflections on water. Shadow and reflection are both effects created by light, since vision originates from the *lux vivens* which, as testified by Pseudo-Dionysius the Areopagite, is blinding but also manifests itself in more attenuated forms that the human eye, and also the inner eye, can perceive *in the shadow of the living light.* The vision is the vehicle for messages whose origin lies beyond the consciousness of the person who received them; however, they were not personal messages concerning her spiritual life, but ones to be transmitted by her to the humanity of the period.

Hildegard finally understood that her task on earth was to communicate the messages she received through vision. But only after decades, from the time she was a little girl to the age of forty, at the beginning of which she was almost overcome by them: *I saw a splendor issuing from heaven that made my soul tremble in my body, but because I was only a little girl I was completely unable to speak of it.* Only later did she gradually come to understand them and accept them as a gift from above, in the monastic context in which she grew up and developed her inner life with the help of her wise teacher Jutta and later her "companion in the mysteries" (*symmistes*) Volmar. The little girl became a woman, performing daily the centuries-old bodily practices necessary to attain the ideal of virginal life, while embracing the symbols and ideas of the Bible and the patristic tradition: the rich heritage of knowledge she gloried in, that is wisdom. The orderly satisfaction of daily bodily needs in the sleep-wake cycle, diet, and care of herself and others, as well as of spiritual needs through prayer, song, meditation on the learned writings in books, and contemplation, made Hildegard a mature woman, ready to carry out her mission. Past the midpoint of her life (according to the medieval measurement of time we are familiar with from Dante) she had begun to write and, through skillful negotiating within the institution where she lived and, above all, in her dealings with the heads of the universal Church, she obtained recognition of her prophetic charisma and was allowed to continue with her writing, which at that point became a duty. And this is what she did in the following decades, building on the culture she had acquired and what new knowledge could reach her through the network of monastic relations, in that tumultuous era marked by major innovations. In the different domains of her writing there is unquestionably an evolution, which is quite evident if we compare the style and content of her first prophetic work, *Scivias* (Know the Ways, 1141–1151), with the third, the *Liber Divinorum Operum* (*Book of Divine Works*, 1163–1173), the definitive summa of Hildegard's thought. This development in the production of written and also musical works was witnessed and supported by the community of fellow nuns, of which Hildegard had become the *magistra* in 1136 upon Jutta's death, and which fifteen years later she was to lead in the founding of their new convent at Rupertsberg. Like Disibodenberg Abbey, where they had lived their life until then, their Rupertsberg home had a *scriptorium*, the writing room in Benedictine monasteries where the scribes (female at Rupertsberg) made copies of sacred books and volumes by ancient authors. However, the latter were not copied at Rupertsberg, where precedence was given to the works of Hildegard, founder and leader of the convent, in order to preserve and circulate them.

In this context, between 1160 and 1170, an important decision was taken to produce a manuscript of *Scivias* in which the text was accompanied and illustrated by, and interspersed and partially reworked with, miniatures of considerable visual impact. In these miniatures, elements of the Christian iconographic tradition were inserted in an unusual, and in many respects original, figurative context—just as the comments that follow the description of the visions in the text interpret the scriptural message using a language and style appropriate for its diffusion in a new time and milieu. In fact, in *Scivias* Hildegard remains faithful to the essence of tradition while offering an original interpretation of sacred history, the life of the Church and the vicissitudes of the human soul. She "translates" into words what the *vox de caelo*, the mysterious musical murmuring that accompanies the vision, reveals to her, making her a musical instrument, a trumpet (*tuba*) whose sound is comprehensible to the humanity of her day and reawakens it to the ways of salvation. This is the function of the text. But why the images? And why at that particular moment?

After lovingly contemplating and carefully studying the *Scivias* miniatures for years, making them readable in every detail, and testing her interpretive method with an innovative reconstruction of their relationship with the miniatures of the *Liber Divinorum Operum*, Sara Salvadori now offers us an answer to those questions. An answer that is utterly plausible on both a historic and hermeneutic level, since on the one hand, she points out the temporal coincidence with the last of Hildegard's preaching tours undertaken in 1160–1171, and on the other, stresses the significant interrelatedness of the overall vision that virtually embodies all the individual visions of the two (indeed three) prophetic works.

It should be mentioned that most of today's research tends to trace the origin of both illuminated manuscripts to Rupertsberg, albeit in different periods: the miniatures of the *Liber Divinorum Operum* conserved in Lucca, in fact, date to the 1220s, when Hildegard's canonization process was begun; however, according to some highly reliable studies they could also derive from sketches attributable to Hildegard herself, as has been ascertained in the case of the *Scivias* miniatures.

Incidentally, if we consider the two miniature cycles in relation to the cohesiveness of the vision, we can surmise the reason why the *Liber Vitae Meritorum* was not "translated" figuratively. There was simply no need, given that the work significantly expands and elaborates on the individual visions of the virtues in *Scivias* (III. 3–10) and thus is "implicit" in the building of salvation; and that the vision of cosmic man facing the four cardinal points is equivalent to the *anthropos* in the *Liber Divinorum Operum* (as well as the difficulty to represent this vision on paper, due to the movement. But the difficulty of creating "special effects" with the means available in the *scriptorium* does not seem to have stopped either Hildegard or the miniaturists, male or female, who executed her figurative project, as Sara Salvadori's work demonstrates).

The illuminated manuscript of *Scivias* is dated to 1170–1179. It certainly represents an advanced stage in the organization of the text, which in the Rupertsberg *scriptorium* must have gone through various editing stages, similar to the more widely documented phases of the *Liber Divinorum Operum.* Volmar's initial collecting of the transcriptions and his organizing them as a volume was followed by the scrupulous correction of the text, its division into chapters and their numbering, and the composition of titles for the single chapters in a separate fascicle. There still exists the prototype of the *Liber Divinorum Operum*, a manuscript now conserved in Ghent, but we do not have an equivalent for *Scivias.*

In a second stage, the text was laid out in two columns with the chapter numbers in the margins, while the chapter titles preceded of the three parts of the text itself. Most of the manuscripts produced at Rupertsberg were characterized by this format. Lastly, both of the illuminated manuscripts, although produced many years apart, bear witness to a third stage, or organization model, in which the titles of the chapters were inserted before each individual chapter as well as before each part of the text, and the space reserved for the miniatures within the text was carefully calculated and left blank. The miniatures were executed after the text had been written (possibly fascicle by fascicle).

The disappearance of the illuminated manuscript of *Scivias*, placed for safekeeping in the vault of the Girobank in Dresden in 1942 and never seen again, is an inestimable loss. However, this is compensated to some extent by the existence of two 1:1 copies of the original: a photographic facsimile, made in the early 20th century, and a handwritten one of the original produced in the Eibingen monastery between 1927 and 1931. Their combined use facilitates textual and iconological studies, but is of no great help to art historians and paleographers from a methodological standpoint.

In the two previous volumes, published respectively in 2019 and 2021, Sara Salvadori adopted an iconological approach, explaining in fine detail the composition of the miniatures in relation to the text, thus providing scholars with an internationally recognized innovative hermeneutic tool. In the course of the two projects and our collaboration over many years (my contribution, modest compared to the whole, consisted essentially in translating the Latin texts; however, it involved continuous discussion, which was most enlightening also with regard to interpretation), Sara shared her "discoveries" with me on more than one occasion. I was always astonished by them, and sometimes a little skeptical, basically due to the rigid boundaries of an ingrained academic approach that nevertheless slowly expanded and opened up to what the images communicate beyond their representation, as far as they correspond to the textual description of the visions.

Sara Salvadori's perceptive and thoroughly attentive gaze also "opens up" the images, bringing to light possibilities that cannot be grasped at first glance. This reminds me of a notion that often recurs, in all its shades of meaning, in *Scivias*, that of *acies*, the sharp edge of a blade, which in the metaphorical sense indicates a focused gaze, acute vision, a keen and lively eye, and in the metonymical sense, hosts—the term Hildegard uses to describe the ranks of angels, whose depiction is actually central in the visual hermeneutics proposed here.

The structure of the book is grounded on the Liberal Arts, which formed the late antique basis of *enkyklios paideia* (general education). In Christian culture, from Cassiodorus and Augustine onward, this provided the knowledge necessary to read the Holy Scriptures, and there is no doubt that it also constituted the educational framework, albeit limited, available to Hildegard.

Allegorical representations of the Liberal Arts surround that of philosophy in one of the most celebrated images from the illustrated monastic encyclopedia written by another 12th-century *magistra*, Herrad von Hohenburg, who was about a generation younger than Hildegard. She, too, was attentive to the spiritual and intellectual care of the nuns for whom she wrote, but she did not have Hildegard's prophetic voice or multifaceted creativity.

Thus, organizing the individual themes of the images or those inspired by them according to the schema of the Liberal Arts is more than an explicative device, since it places Hildegard's thought in the appropriate context and reveals its background. To a certain extent, this approach aligns with a tendency in current Hildegardian studies to reposition the "Sibyl of the Rhine" in her time, who for too long has been considered solely as a woman of undisputed and exceptional brilliance, but isolated from her context.

However, the most notable aspect of this book is the work on the symbols that innervate the *Scivias* miniatures, giving a vibrancy to the traditional images and the allegorical figurations with which they intertwine. In fact, motifs such as flowers, eyes, and clouds that allude to a mystery or are an invitation to go beyond what is seen, are interwoven with the illustrative and didactic aspects of those depictions, which correspond to the ekphrastic elements in the description of the visions. The presence of these motifs in the miniatures of *Scivias* makes each image symbolic as a whole, while as recurrent elements they establish subtle connections between the different images, similar to those between the texts. This makes Hildegard's writing a precious inlay of variations on some fundamental themes: the trinitarian structure of the divinity, in which the Holy Spirit is manifest as the female figure of Charity who gives life to creation; the close link between the Incarnation of the Word and the creation of dual humanity, man and woman, who represent, respectively, the divinity and the humanity of Christ; the centrality of Mary and her twofold relationship with Eve, whose sin she redeems and whose universal task she fulfills.

Symbolum, as defined at the beginning of the commentary to Pseudo-Dionysius' work *On the Celestial Hierarchy* by Hugh of Saint-Victor, an author coeval to Hildegard and with whom she was familiar, *is a composition of visible forms intended to reveal something that is invisible.* But the symbol, as the poet and Hildegardian scholar Kent T. Kraft, who died prematurely, wrote many years ago, *inevitably maintains what it represents in obscurity precisely while giving it form, because the visible image is, at best, a mantle that reveals only the contours of the unreachable*. Starting from these contours, Sara Salvadori reconstructs fragments of the mystery to which the symbols embedded in the *Scivias* miniatures allude, offering to the reader, and above all to their eye, the pieces of a wondrous puzzle, composed in Hildegard's time and recomposed in our own. Thus the words with which the prophet, poet and musician described her visionary experience in a letter written around 1175 take on a new meaning: *In this vision my soul ascends to the farthest reaches of the firmament*. The viewpoint in distant space that Hildegard reaches in the vision is mysteriously linked to the viewpoint in distant time from which Sara Salvadori contemplates her visions. Picturing the monks and nuns of Zwiefalten as they listen entranced to Hildegard as she explains how to recompose the fragments hidden in the miniatures and draws the motifs in the air for them, Sara writes: *those who have seen cannot but tell*, in the hope that their gaze can be ours *and guide us to the wonders of the vision that lie beyond the images.*

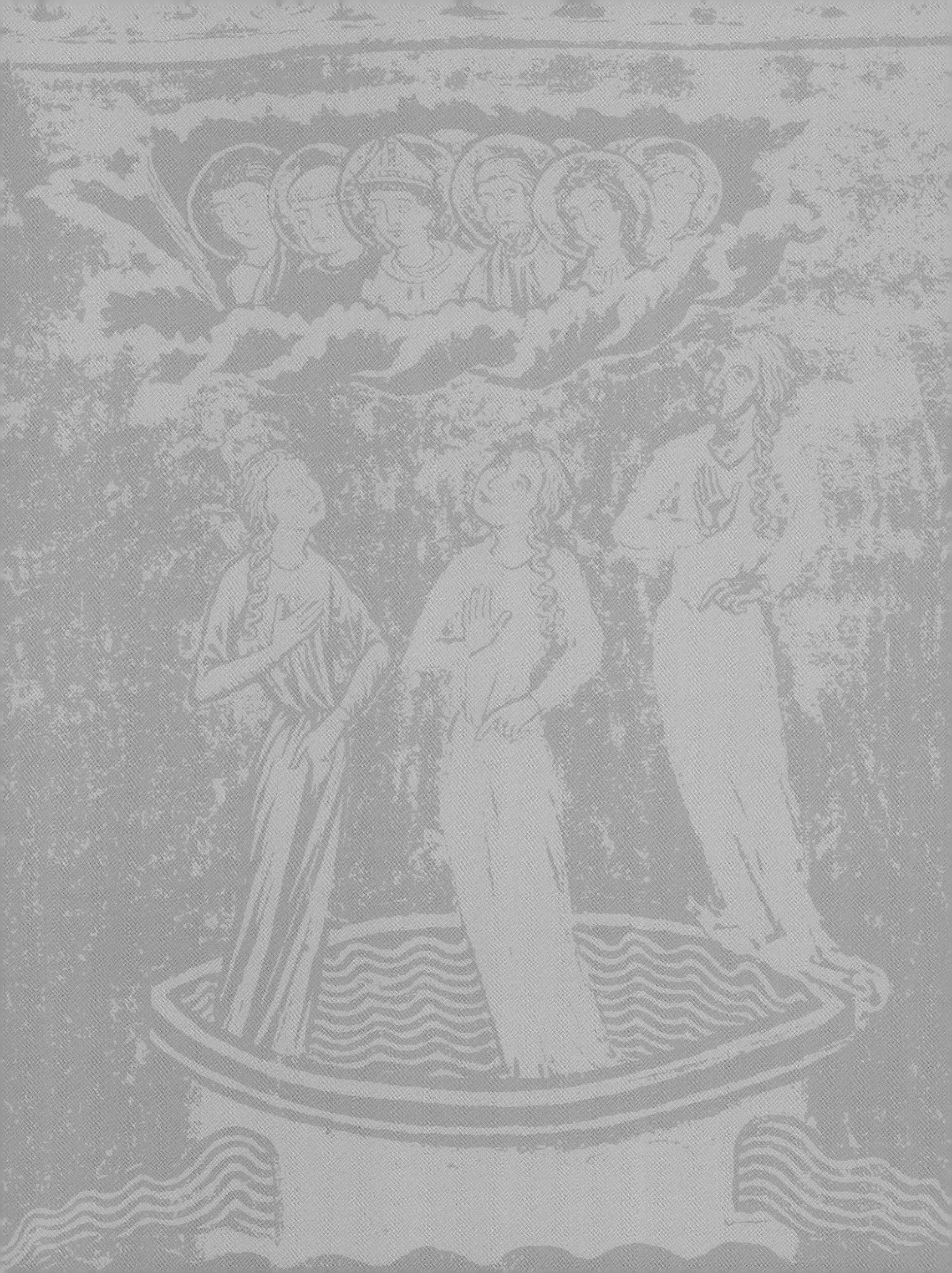

Sara Salvadori

The Fountain of Wisdom

[...] the living fountain is the Spirit of God, which he distributes unto all his works. They live because of him and have vitality through him, as the shadow of all things appears in water. And there is nothing that can clearly see this source of its life; rather, it can only sense what causes it to move. As water makes what is in it to flow, so too the soul is the living breath ever streaming in a human being, and it makes him to know, to think, to speak, and to work as if by streaming forth (*LDO* III.3.2 p. 388).

In 1170, at the age of seventy-two, Hildegard received another call from heaven. She was commanded to embark on her travels again, this time to Swabia, to the South, the place most in need of edification. It was her fourth and last preaching tour. She had already virtually written her entire oeuvre: three prophetic books, the *Symphonia*, the morality play, the book on the *subtilitates* (subtleties) of nature and healing, the unknown language and alphabet, the commentary on the rule of St Benedict, and much more. She had begun this work thirty years earlier, when a *flash of fire* descended on her, *filling her brain and kindling her heart and breast, like a flame that does not burn but warms, as the sun warms anything its rays touch*, which was followed by the command of the living light: *write and cry out.* Hildegard had crossed a threshold, she was carried forward by the gentle breeze of faith and touched by the blessing dew that heralds the dawn of a new day. The sun's delicate rays warmed her bones and the protective wings of wisdom enfolded her, enabling Hildegard to fly high and see the firmament from the heights of heaven.

The voice of the *living light,* which at the beginning of her journey had called her *ash of ash*, *rottenness of rottenness*, for some time had been addressing her with kind words: *how beautiful are your eyes.* No longer barren ground, mortal body, but fecund *viriditas*. Entrusting herself to God and responding to his call led her to embark on a journey of transformation that broadened her gaze and enabled her to rediscover her original integrity, to use her wings again to fly: those same wings that are given to every soul when it is infused in the nascent body and, as a *sphere of fire that touches the heart, reaches the brain and spreads through the limbs*, brings it to life.

In this new time, following the completion of her journey, knowledge was revealed in reflection, in water, in a mirror and in shadow, and the scriptures and words of wisdom could be understood. She beheld the beyond of God, through a meeting of gazes, *cor ad cor loquitur*, through other words, in a *different air.* Her face came alive, her lips were colored red, the stylus turned into a green *palm* dipped into the *blood of life.* The faces of Hildegard and Volmar, her companion in writing and in life, now shone like stars in the new sky of eternal blessedness. This was the moment of the marriage between male and female, of the meeting between God and humanity, his bride.

The world turned to Hildegard as a prophetess, adviser and teacher. Nourished by the inexhaustible Fountain of the divine her word spread, her letters and correspondence extended to the four corners of the earth, echoing the earlier exhortation: *Burst forth into a fountain of abundance, and overflow with mystical knowledge, until they who now think you contemptible because of Eve's transgression are stirred up by the flood of your irrigation.* This was a call to go forth and bear witness, to set out on another journey and address the public in the vast spaces of abbeys and cathedrals. The intimate vision was shared. The word left the silent space of the page and became incarnate, gained substance, rang out and reverberated in the space, where it was offered and listened to with that feeling of togetherness created by the Church. She returned to the dimension in which she herself had experienced this upon hearing the voice of the living light and the song of angelic praise, along with the lamentations of human beings and the raucous croaking of demons. What she saw and heard with her *inner eyes and ears* now entered the eyes and ears of her listeners, broadening their perception and their gaze.

When preaching to the public she addressed the burning issues of an age beset by struggles, divisions and violence, whereas in more personal and intimate exchanges, the wisdom of her visions and her wonderful poetry likely emerged. The word came alive and in the attempt to explain, to reveal, to make things understood, the hand began to move and to trace in the air the forms, the dimensions and the complex geography of the vision. There then arose the need to record it on the page. Like the psalmist who first traces the neumes in the air and then notes them down on paper, Hildegard decided to depict the images and bring together all the experiences she had lived. The moment of recapitulation became the time of her new and last creation, the symbolic writing of the Rupertsberg illuminated codex, which, as well as *Scivias,* contains the entire arc of her prophetic oeuvre.

The images were created to be viewed and contemplated attentively, enabling the symbolic layering of the sapiential codex to gradually emerge. Like *the Creator who first marked out each part with a compass and later painted each one with colors*, the image does not only represent the narrative dimension and the beauty of form. It pulses with life, to make the viewer hear the sound of the air as it brushes past bodies, to heed perfumes, sounds, the warmth of the sun, the terrifying blackness of fear, the violence of evil, the force of fire, movement, the solidity of stone, and the flow of water. And even the soundwaves of song and the ethereal music of Paradise and of angelic praise, the infinite beauty of the virtues with their silken robes, their flowers, their hands, and gossamer wings. All watched over by the unquestionable, reassuring, solid creative love of God, inscribed in the harmony of divine law.

A dialogue between visible and invisible, between what the outer eye and ear capture and what thrills, to their great wonder, the inner eye and ear: *the visible and temporal, but also the invisible and eternal.* This treasure is preserved through the creativity of the images and their being entrusted and transcribed to paper through the language of the arts of the *Trivium* and *Quadrivium*. A language that Hildegard had already drawn on years before in planning and organizing the text of the work, in which the symbolism of numbers marked the title, *Scivias*, with its seven letters representing the gifts of the spirit; referenced the Trinity through its tripartite division; and drew the overall map on the basis of the golden ratio. In the images, the numbers shine brilliantly in the forms of the circles and in the figures of the elements, strengthening their symbolic meaning. Arithmetic is combined with Geometry through triangles, squares, circles and spirals that describe the movement and forms of the divine and its encounter with humanity. The Music of the *Symphony of the Harmony of Celestial Revelations* is written in circular forms and in their proportional relationships. Lastly, Astronomy, the art of observing the wonders of the heavens, makes it possible to identify the orbits of the planets, whose seven circles combined with the nine circles of the Heavenly Hosts constitute the constructive matrix for the entire visual narrative. The contemplation of the skies allows humanity to perceive traces of its origin, stars deposited in the womb of mother Eve, and arouses in humans a nostalgia that is transformed into the desire to shine again as bright *sidera* in the celestial flowering.

The story of the visions is thus complete and its wondrous construction rendered to the full. The long journey now enables us to expand our gaze and allows the signs and pointers hinted at in the text and in certain figurative elements to emerge. In following them, the scene of a single great vision is reconstructed before the reader's eyes. All the images are gathered around the map of the Building, image of the altar with the chalice and bread of life, beneath the immense celestial vault of the firmament. The sky is filled with the angels' song and immersed in the divine light. Everything is inscribed in a single vast space, that of the *whole, round, and whirling* globe *in the heart of God.* A sphere in three spheres that surrounds and contains: the image of the Trinity.

Thus, the story of salvation unfolds in a multidimensional space where diachronic and synchronic time coincide. Everything lives and pulses in a single layered image. The story becomes the poetry of revelation contained in superimposed distant images, visible through the transparencies.

Finally, the song of the last vision reverberates with the hymn to Mary, the most resplendent jewel, of whom Christ was born as an offshoot from the Tree of Jesse. The richly interwoven branches and leaves in gold of the tree of life, stirred by the gentle breeze of the spirit, are partially hidden by the neutral background colors of the miniature. Bright blue flowers appear, like images of the just ones, amidst the branches, diffusing their perfume and accompanied by the songs of the symphony, in the new heaven and on the new earth.

These were perhaps the images that Hildegard illustrated on her last journey to Zwiefalten Abbey, where she had been invited by Abbot Wilhelm von Hirschau. Her heirs, well-versed in the arts of the *Quadrivium*, would have been able to grasp the beauty and wonder of the revelation when she showed them the designs of her work and explained how to recompose the images hidden in the fragments of the miniatures. Those who have seen cannot but tell. So it will come as no surprise that in the copy of the *Scivias* manuscript, known as the Salem Codex—named for the abbey that is about a day away on foot from Zwiefalten, and where it is thought to have been begun precisely when Hildegard was staying there—one sees that the text faithfully follows that of the original codex by Hildegard, but a decision was made to create ten completely new images. The Tree of Jesse is placed at the beginning of the work and in the sky of the genesis the moon and sun take the form of male and female faces. The design of the wheel, recalling the description of the wheel in the *Liber Divinorum Operum*, has been included without fear of possible misunderstandings, because everything is clearly a single great vision. Today, Hildegard's invaluable legacy is revealed before our eyes, just as it was, perhaps, in the Abbey nestled in the greenery of the Black Forest. So that the keen and receptive gaze of He who was then the last witness can be ours and guide us to the wonder of the vision beyond the images.

Note to the reader

The first part of the volume offers a poetic account of the journey into the sphere of creation held in the heart of God; the second, a description of the process of writing and composing the images hidden in the miniatures; the third, a detailed analysis of the use of numbers, forms and sounds, and the contemplation of the heavens, with observations gathered and arranged according to the disciplines of the *Quadrivium*.

Historians affirm that the text of *Scivias* was written between 1141 and 1151, while the illuminated images are probably coeval to the composition of the text of the *Liber Divinorum Operum*, dating to 1163–1173.

The images in the facsimile copy of *Scivias* illuminated at the beginning of the 20th century by the nuns of Eibingen Abbey, are taken from the Rupertsberg Codex Hs1, now lost, made under Hildegard's guidance. The images of the *Liber Divinorum Operum*, illuminated around the 1220s, are taken from the 1942 Codex held by the Biblioteca Statale di Lucca.

The two works are indicated with the initials *SC* for *Scivias* and *LDO* for the *Liber Divinorum Operum*. The images are indicated with a Roman numeral, which corresponds to the specific part of the work, while the number that follows indicates that of the vision; in the citations the third number refers to the chapter in question. For a complete vision of the images present in the two works and for guidance in interpreting the symbols, we refer the reader to the author's previous publications: for *Scivias*, *Hildegard von Bingen: A Journey into the Images*, Skira, Milan 2019, and for the *Liber Divinorum Operum*, *Hildegard von Bingen. In the Heart of God*, Skira, Milan 2021.

CHAPTER I

From the Heart of God to the Heart of Man

Journey into the Globe

In the breast of the aforementioned image there appears a wheel, wonderful to see, together with its signs and symbols. This wheel is nearly like that instrument that you saw twenty-eight years ago, signified in the figure of an egg *[...] though neither of these holds a complete likeness of the figure of the world in every detail, because it exists everywhere whole, round, and whirling. Rather, a globe that is whole and whirling better imitates the form of the world in its every part* (*LDO* I.2.2–3, pp. 54–55).

The winged figure of the charity of divine love stands out in the southern sky. Her arms are outstretched and the sphere of creation surrounding humanity appears in her heart. The voice of the living light reveals to Hildegard that *the firmament is like a well-turned bowl, and in the upper curve is positioned the sun* that *emits its brilliance, like wine poured into a bowl*. It is the *crater tornatilis* referred to in Song of Songs: *Your navel is a rounded goblet that never lacks blended wine. Your waist is a mound of wheat encircled by lilies* (7:2), meaning that the creation can be compared to the offering of bread and wine, flesh and blood of the Son of God, and the nuptial dowry given by Christ to his bride.

The momentous vision of *Caritas* in the *Liber Divinorum Operum*, came at the end of a path of knowledge that had begun *twenty-eight* years previously with the visions of *Scivias*, in which there appeared on the mountain at the center of the Earth, in the center of the firmament, the Building with the *pavement like white glass* that *shone with the most serene splendor of the Shining One seated on the throne*. In Revelation we also find the description of the Holy City that shone *with the glory of God and its brilliance was like that of a very precious jewel, like a jasper, clear as crystal* (21:11), which ultimately presents *the Lamb in the heart of the Father.*

The *servants* worship him while the *river* of the water of life flows in the Temple and the branches of the *Tree of Life* stir. Hildegard saw the passages of the Johannine book in the vision, which she depicted in the concluding images, even concealing fragments of the branches and flowers of the Tree of Life in the background of the last miniature.

The visions, which came one after the other during the time of her journey, are now seen to coincide with those of Revelation and, through the transparent veiling, sing the poetry of the eschatological story culminating in the face-to-face meeting with God. As we contemplate the images, we discern the cross and flowers that adorn the altar on whose green curtain is depicted the womb of Mary that holds the golden brilliance of the well-turned bowl. The numbers in the work act as a guide to the design of the cross and the triple wall of the celestial Jerusalem. It is the time of praising the Trinity, sound and life.

The journey has been completed. Hildegard has passed through the four elements of the sphere of the firmament and the nine skies of the sphere of the Heavenly Hosts, and finally entered the light of the sphere of the Trinity where Christ, *man of sapphire blue*, the pathway, has brought about a reversal of time and space. The three spheres are shown to be part of a single large sphere contained in the heart of God. Hildegard has made the entire journey, the light illuminates her completely and makes her shine, in a new sky, like the moon beside the sun.

Caritas

I am the supreme and fiery force, who sets all living sparks alight [...]
I am also the fiery life of the essence of divinity; I flame above the beauty of the fields, and I shine in the waters, and I burn in the sun, the moon, and the stars [...]
I also fulfill my function, since all living things are set ablaze from me; and I am uniform life in eternity, which neither begins nor ends. God is this life, self-moving and active, yet one life in three energies. Therefore, Eternity is called the Father, the Word is called the Son, and the breath connecting these two is called the Holy Spirit, just as God is signified in human beings, in whom are body, soul, and rationality (*LDO* I.1.2, pp. 33–35).

Hildegard is led out of the firmament and, from this perspective, sees *Caritas*, Divine Love, the winged figure of divine love, appear before her in the *southern sky*, place of purification, and the final stage of the human journey. The double face of the figure and the *circle colored gold* represent the benevolence of God's love and the gift of faith. They describe three intersecting circles.

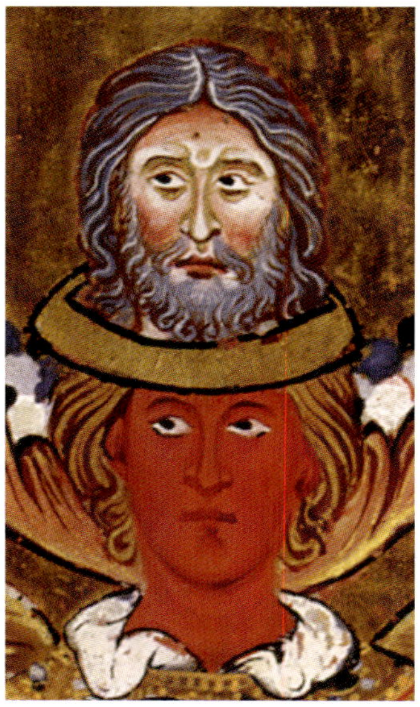

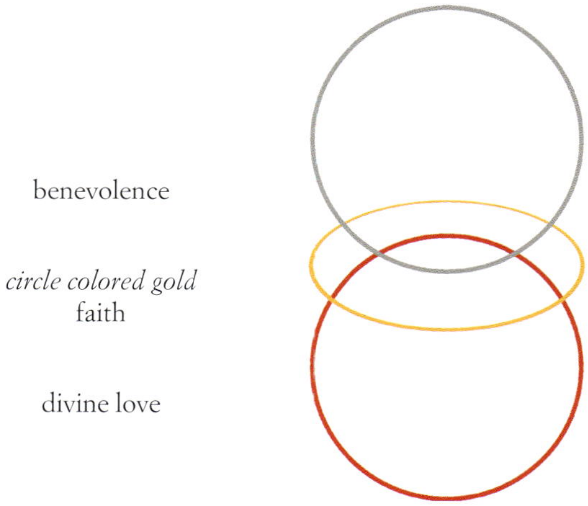

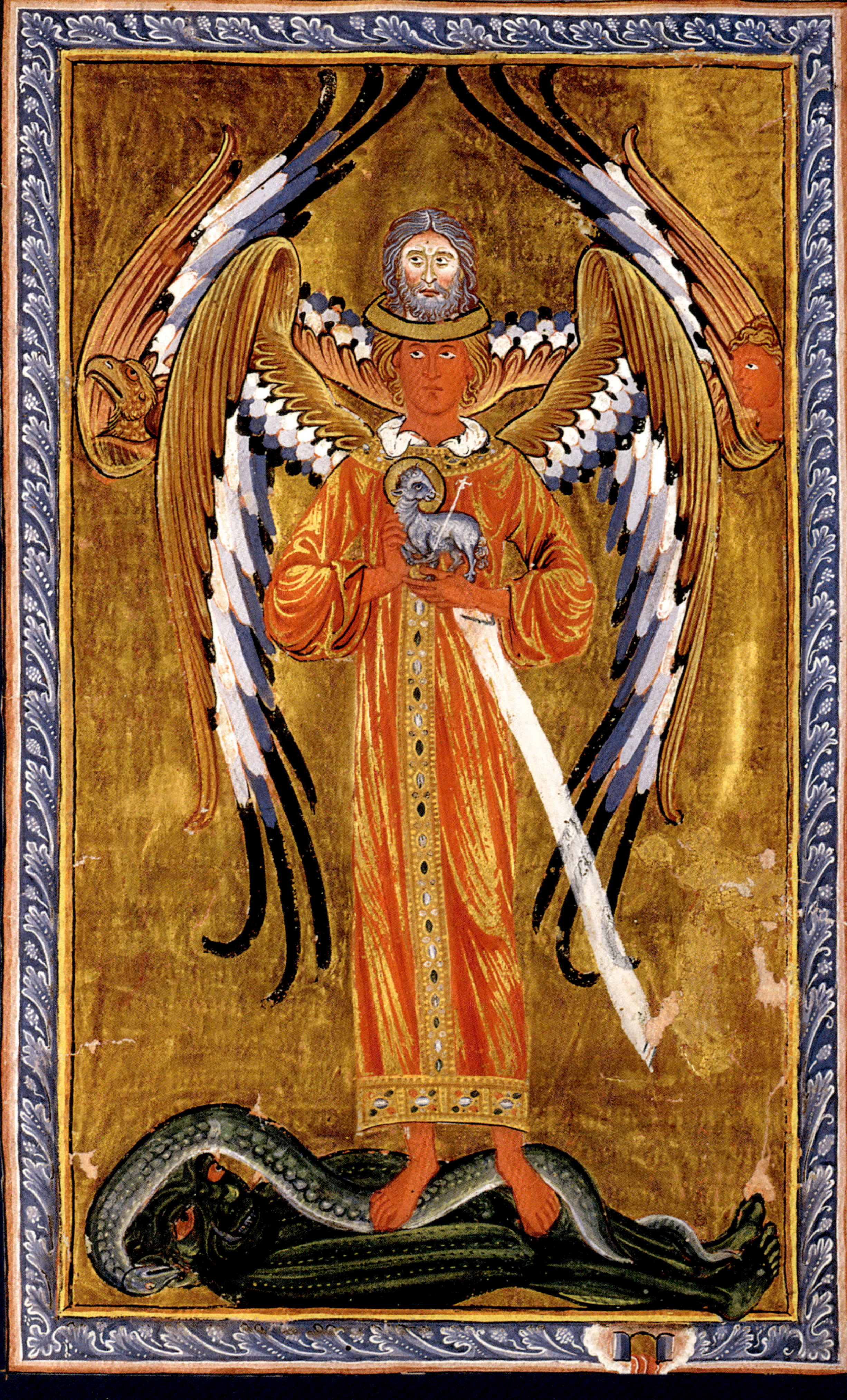

Globe

The form of the world exists, indissolubly whirling —the wonderful form too of human nature—so that it can neither be consumed by any old age nor increased by any novelty; but as it was first created by God, so it will endure to the end of the world (*LDO* I.2.2, p. 54).

The figure of the world [...] exists everywhere whole, round, and whirling (*LDO* I.2.3, p. 55).

"And God saw that it was good," commending it because, [...] through this breathing sphere of light his work was full, elegant, and prepared for service (*LDO* II.1.35, p. 316).

Something that appeared as a ball of fire, completely without human features, embedded itself in the heart of that body and reached its brain, pouring into all its limbs (*SC* I.4.D, p. 109).

In *Charity*'s breast there is a *whole, round and whirling* globe, a sphere. Hildegard sees it hovering in space: it is the image of divine eternity, of its power and its essence, which surrounds and comprises everything. The *breathing sphere of light*, God, generates the *sphere of creation* and through the soul, the *sphere of fire*, instils life in the body of the nascent human creature.

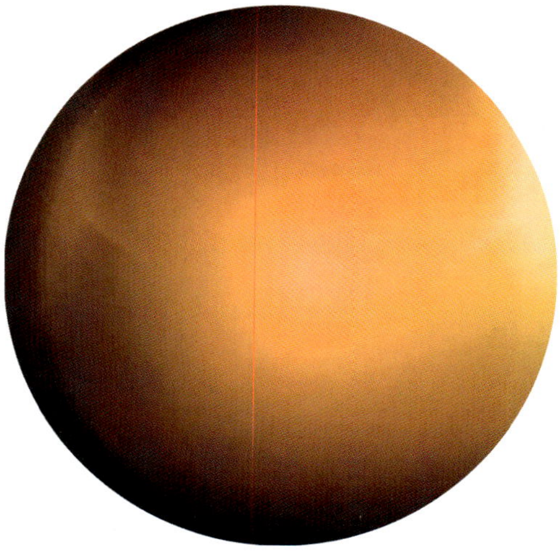

globe
sphere

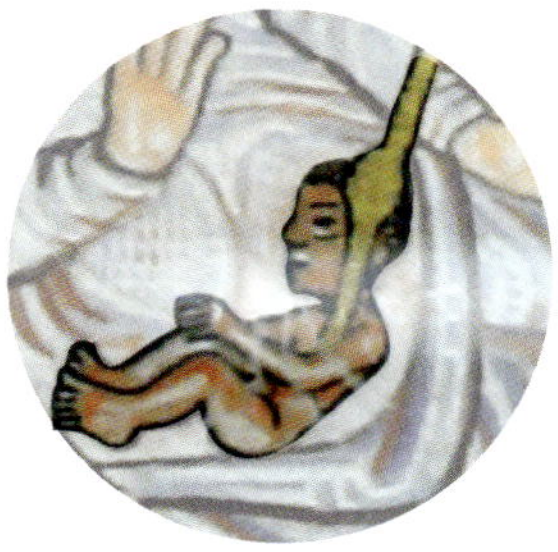

sphere of fire
soul

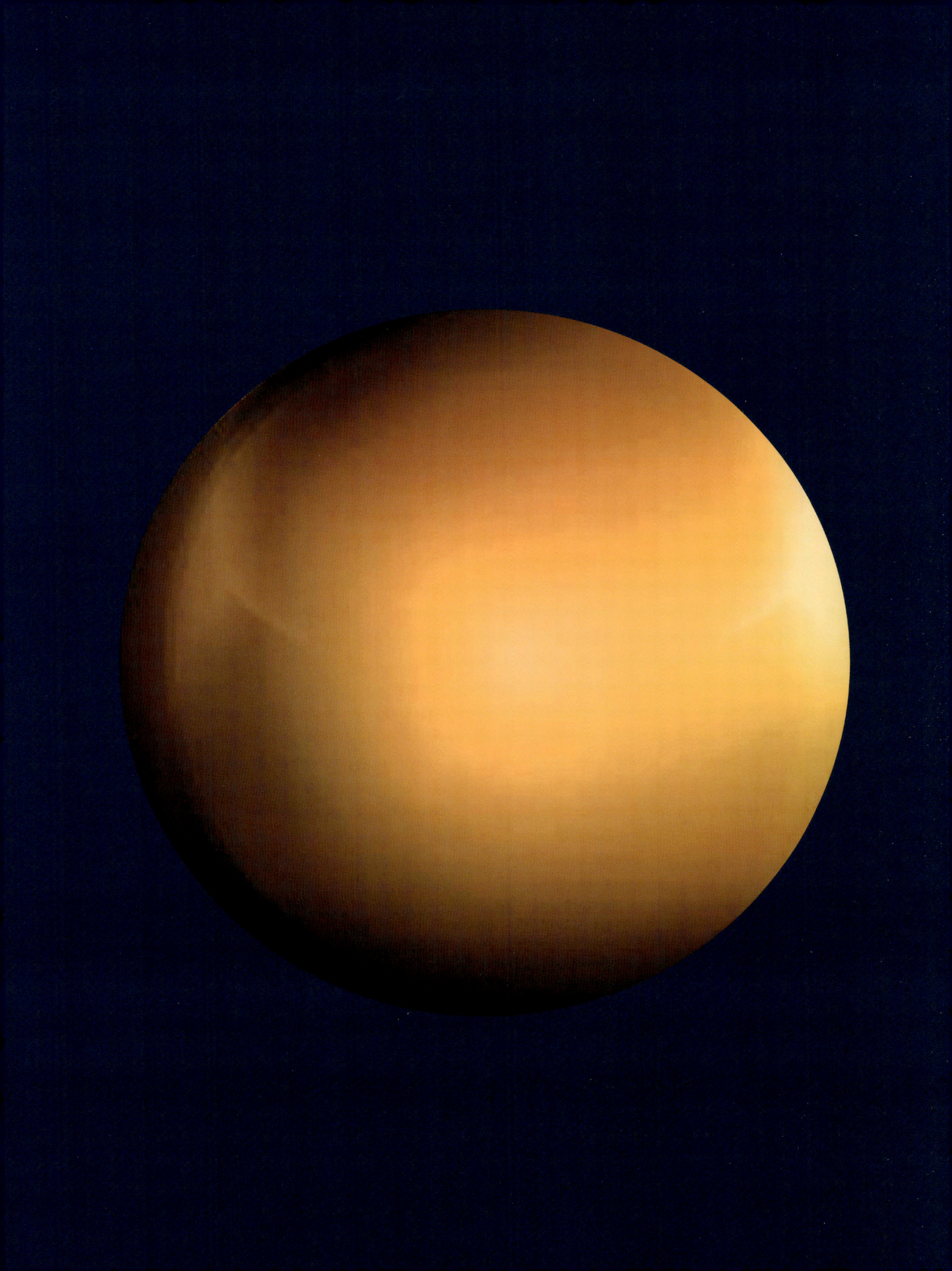

Wheel

And so Love is in the wheel of eternity outside of time, just as heat is in fire (*LDO* I.1.13, p. 42).

But now, the circumference and correct proportion of these elements is shown only in a wheel (*LDO* I.2.3, p. 55).

In the roundedness of the human head is shown the roundedness of the firmament, and in the right and equal dimensions of the head are shown the right and equal dimensions of the firmament (*LDO* I.4.16, p. 141).

For the top of the head signifies the beginning of the soul's operation (*LDO* I.4.15, p. 140).

The divine roundness of the globe cannot be expressed or understood through its perfect shape. To make it knowable, the vision reveals to Hildegard its two-dimensional form, visible in the circle of the wheel and in the inner circles of the elements described in their correct proportions. The roundness of the human creature's head is a mirror image of the globe. The circle defines the section of a sphere. Thus, the wheel with its inner circles is the image of a sphere in three spheres.

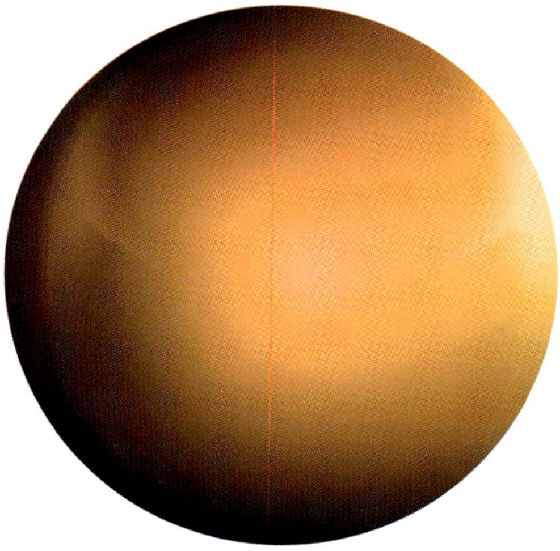

globe
sphere

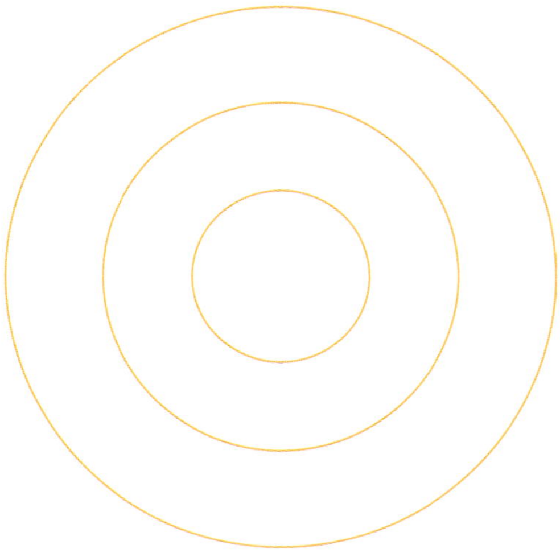

wheel
circle

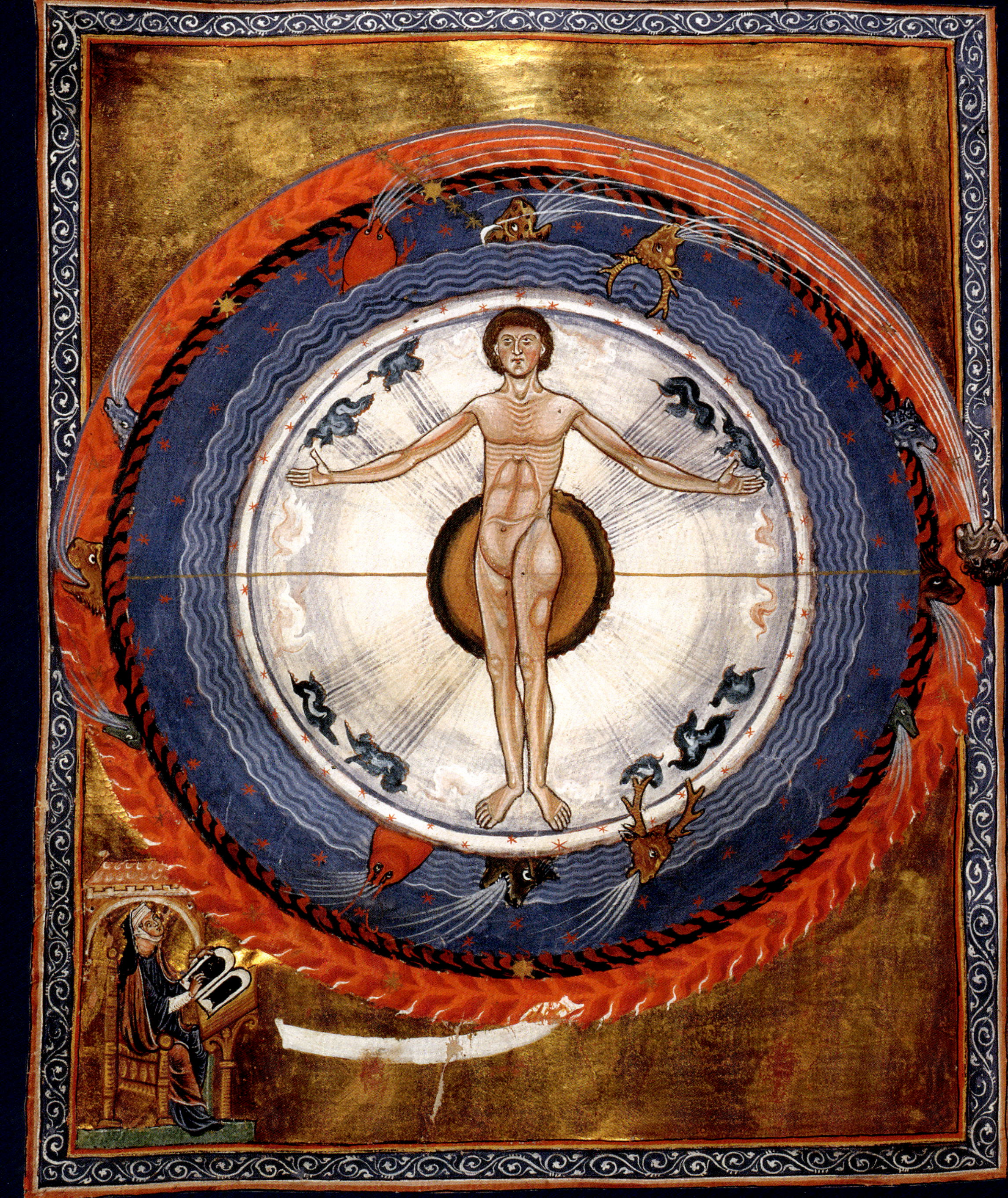

Egg

I saw a vast instrument, round and shadowed in the shape of an egg, narrow at the top, wide in the middle, and narrow again at the bottom (*SC* I.3.D, p. 94).

But when the instrument described above was laid out in your earlier visions in the shape of an egg, this was to show that only the division of the elements was signified in that likeness (*LDO* I.2.3, p. 55).

For I am a living breath [Spirit], which God placed in dry mud [. . .] When my tabernacle saw that it could turn its eyes into all the ways, it turned its attention toward the North (*SC* I.4.1, p. 109).

The vision of the wheel, Hildegard writes, was similar to the vision she had twenty-eight years previously of the *round* instrumentum *that cast a shadow similar to an egg*. On the journey along the ways, which leads from darkness to light, God makes himself known gradually, first in the shadow, in the generative form of the egg in which the elements are distinguished, and then in the light, in the perfection of the circle of the wheel and its proportions. The soul is also an *instrumentum*, a mirror image of the firmament. The figure of the circle projected onto the plane describes an ellipse (see p. 204).

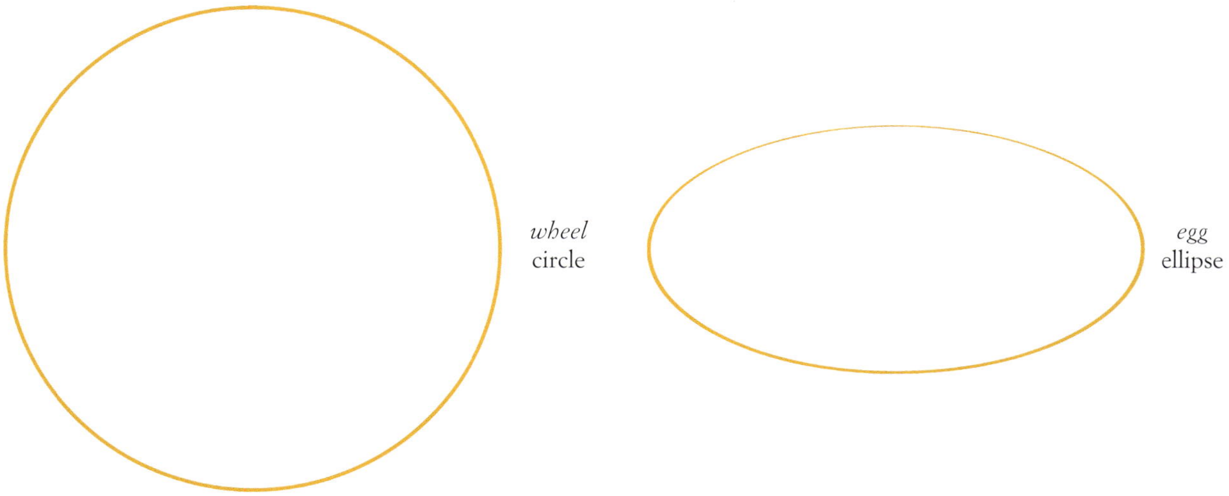

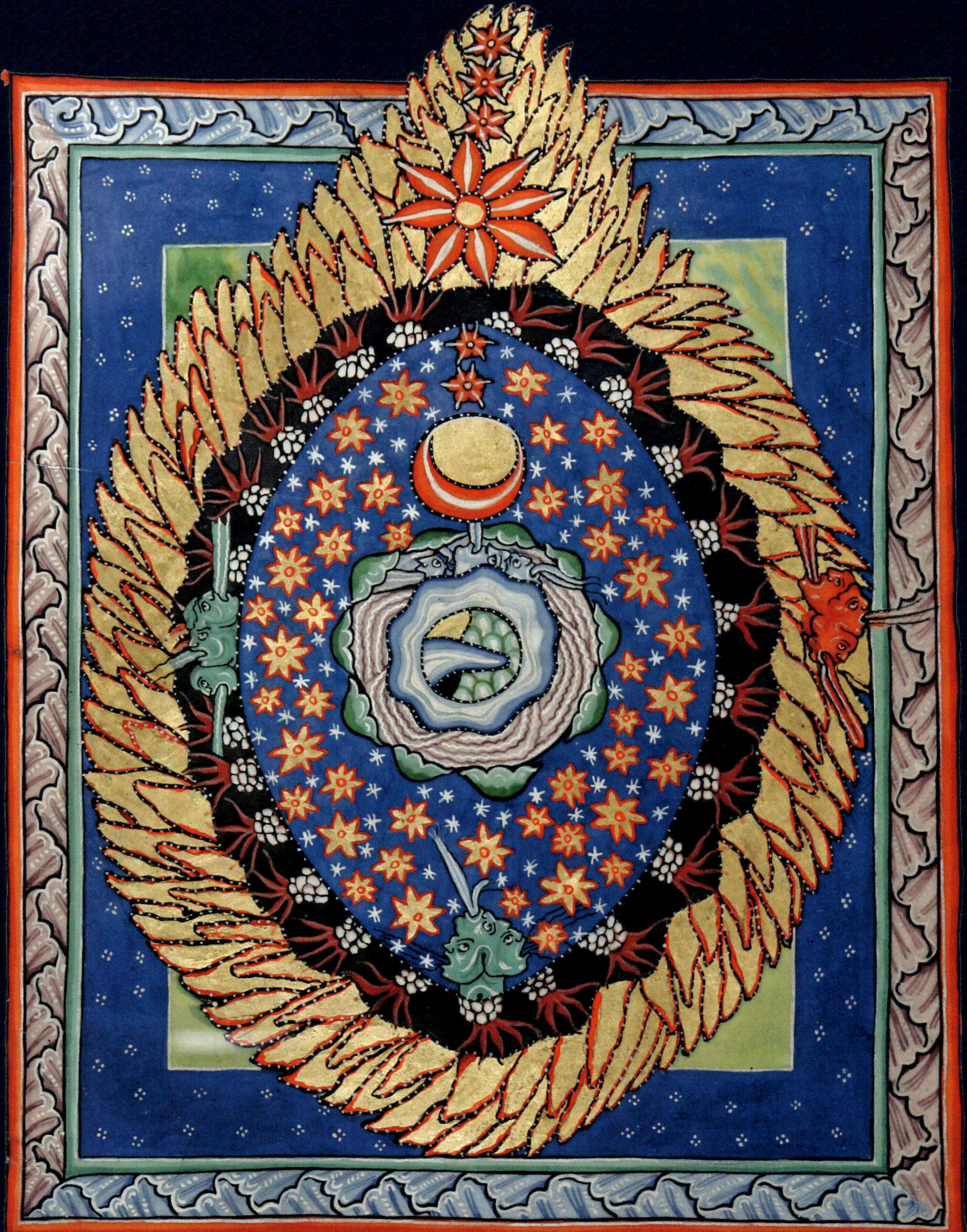

Earth

And the soul exists with the body like the atmosphere with the earth and the honeycomb amid the honey (*LDO* I.4.80, p. 204).

And in the midst of these elements was a globe of heart of great magnitude, which these elements had so surrounded (*SC* I.3.D, p. 93).

And I saw between the North and the East a great mountain, which to the North had great darkness and to the East had great light, but in such a way that the light could not reach the darkness, nor the darkness the light (*SC* I.3.D, p. 100).

And where are you, O mother Zion? Woe is me [Soul] that I so unluckily drew back from you [...]
And when I had said these things, I went away by a narrow path and hid myself from sight of the North in a small cave, bitterly weeping for the loss of my mother [...]
And behold! A most sweet fragrance touched my nostrils, like a gentle breath exhaled by my mother. Oh, what groans and tears I poured forth then, when I felt the presence of that small consolation! And in my joy I uttered such cries and shed such tears that the very mountain in whose cave I had hidden myself was shaken by it (*SC* I.4.1, pp. 110–111).

In the middle of the egg is the *earth*, image of humanity, placed at the center of creation, like a *honeycomb amid the honey*. In the middle of the earth is the mountain, image of God's presence, which separates the light from the darkness. The mountain is the place where the soul finds physical and spiritual refuge, when, after losing the way, it keeps a prayer vigil. This is when it is touched by the perfume of mother Zion, which enables the soul to remember its origin, dispel the darkness and choose the way of light.

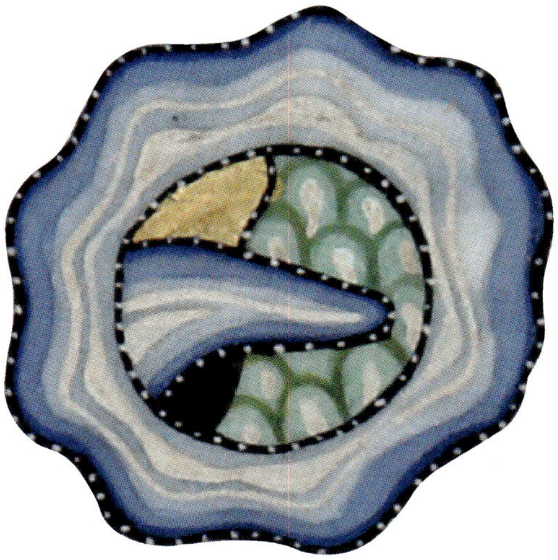

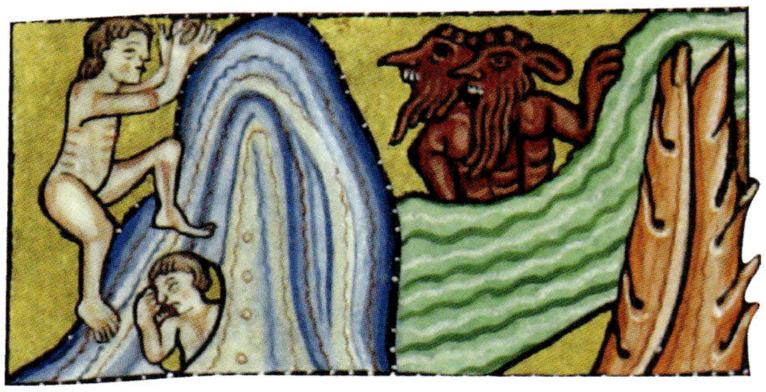

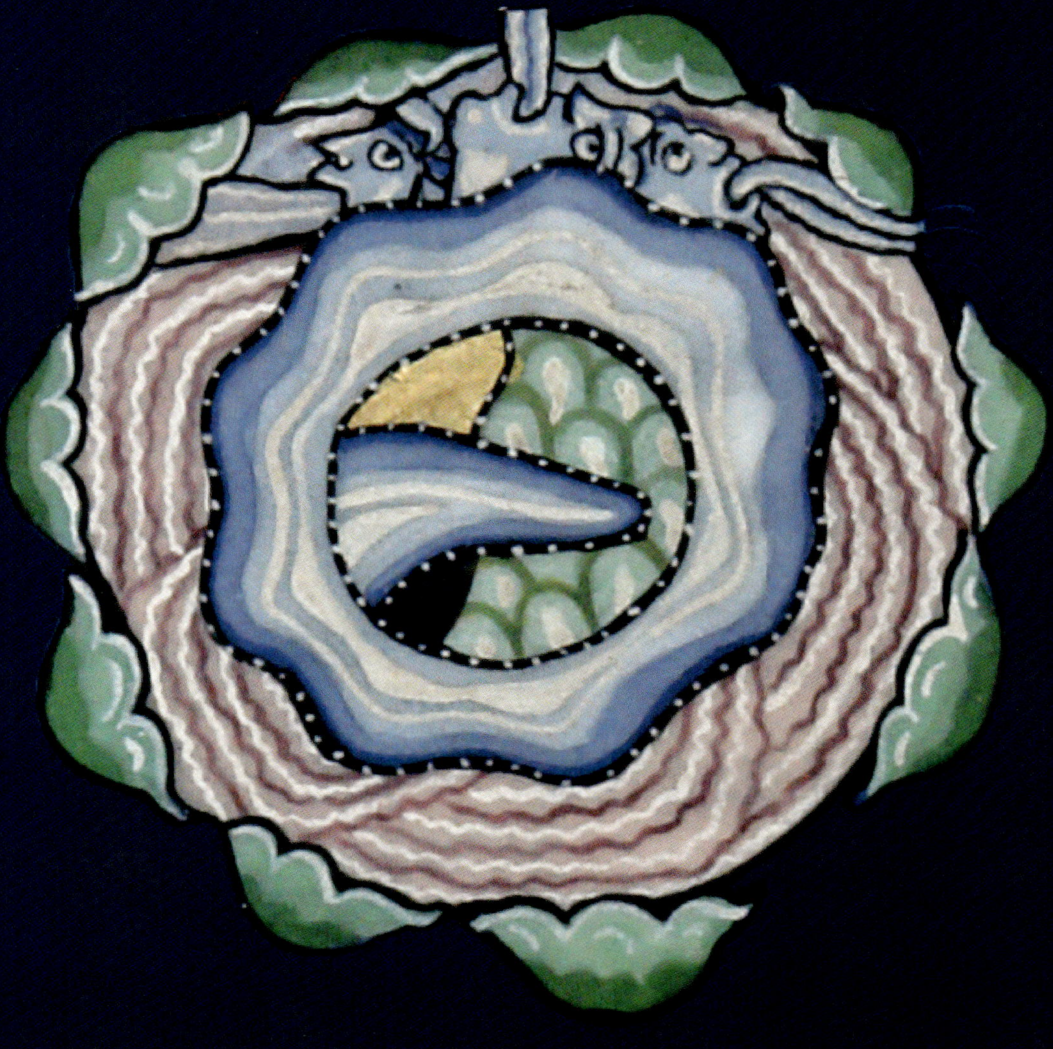

Mountain

I saw a great mountain the color of iron, and enthroned on it One of such great glory that it blinded my sight (*SC* I.1.D, p. 67).

Before him, at the foot of the mountain, stood an image full of eyes on all sides, in which, because of those eyes, I could discern no human form (*SC* I.1.D, p. 67).

Also, I perceived in this mountain many little windows, in which appeared human heads, some of subdued colors and some white (*SC* I.1.D, p. 67).

For in the most high and profound and perspicuous science of God the aims of human acts cannot be concealed or hidden. Most often they display both lukewarmness and purity (*SC* I.1.5, p. 69).

But I [Soul] came secretly out of the cave in which I had hidden and tried to go up to such a height that my enemies would be unable to find me (*SC* I.4.1, p. 111).

The *mountain*, at the center of the earth, is revealed at the beginning of the journey in all its immense height, an image of the strength and stability of the kingdom of God, who scrutinizes the souls of men through the windows in the mountain, similar to the cave in which the soul found refuge. Like the soul, humans are called upon to choose between the two ways. The virtue of the Fear of God, a blue figure composed solely of eyes and placed in front of the mountain, exhorts them not to sink into tedium, but to turn their gaze toward the light, and live diligently in love.

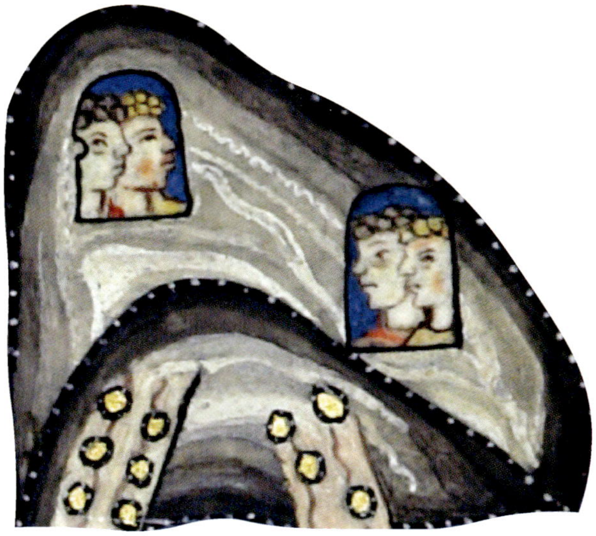

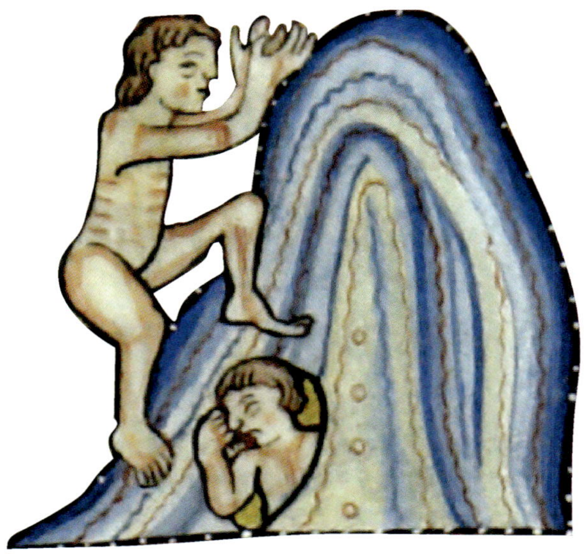

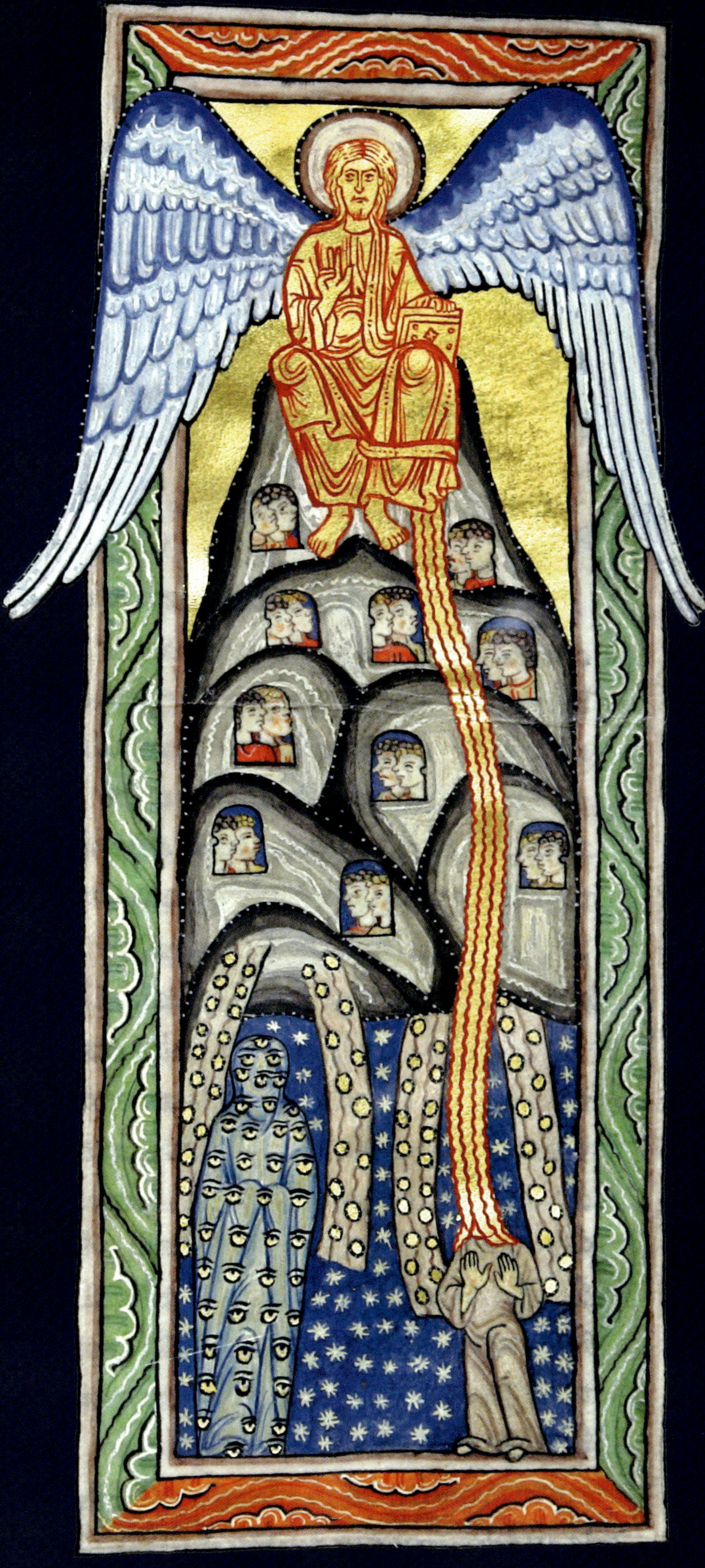

Stone, Throne, Circle

I looked toward the East. And there I saw a single block of stone (lapidem integrum)*, immeasurably broad and high and the color of iron, with a white cloud above it; and above the cloud a royal throne, round in shape, on which One was sitting, living and shining [...]*
And from this Shining One seated upon the throne extended a great circle colored gold like the dawn, whose width I could not take in; it circled about from the East to the North and to the West and to the South, and back toward the East to the Shining One, and had no end.
And that circle [...] extended everywhere, from the heights of Heaven to the depth of the abyss, so that I could see no end to it (*SC* III.1.D, p. 309).

At the midpoint of the journey the revelation of the cross offers access to a new life and allows our hearts to see again the *whole, round and whirling* globe that appeared at the beginning, in the *whole block of stone* of the Fear of God, in the *round throne* of faith, on which the Shining One is seated, and in the *whirling circle colored gold* of the power of God that emanates from him—the same circle that joined the two faces of *Charity.* Everything is a trinitarian image. One sphere in three spheres.

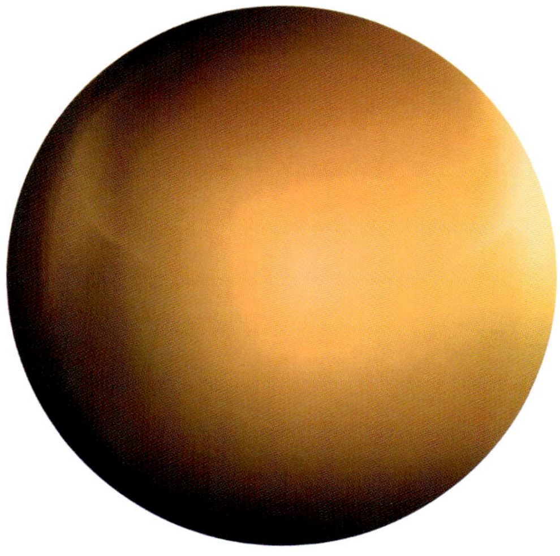

whirling

round

whole

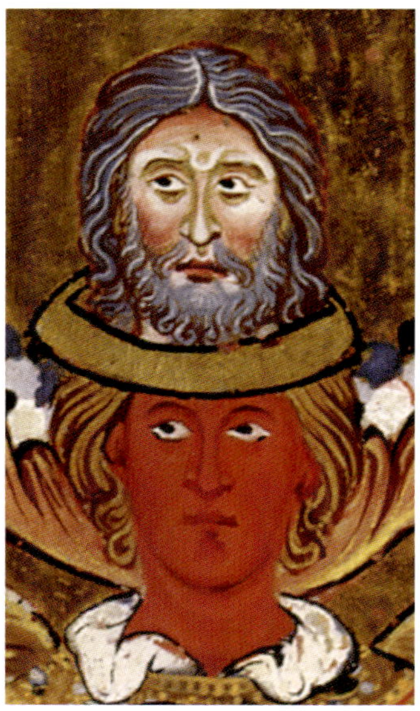

circle
colored gold
faith

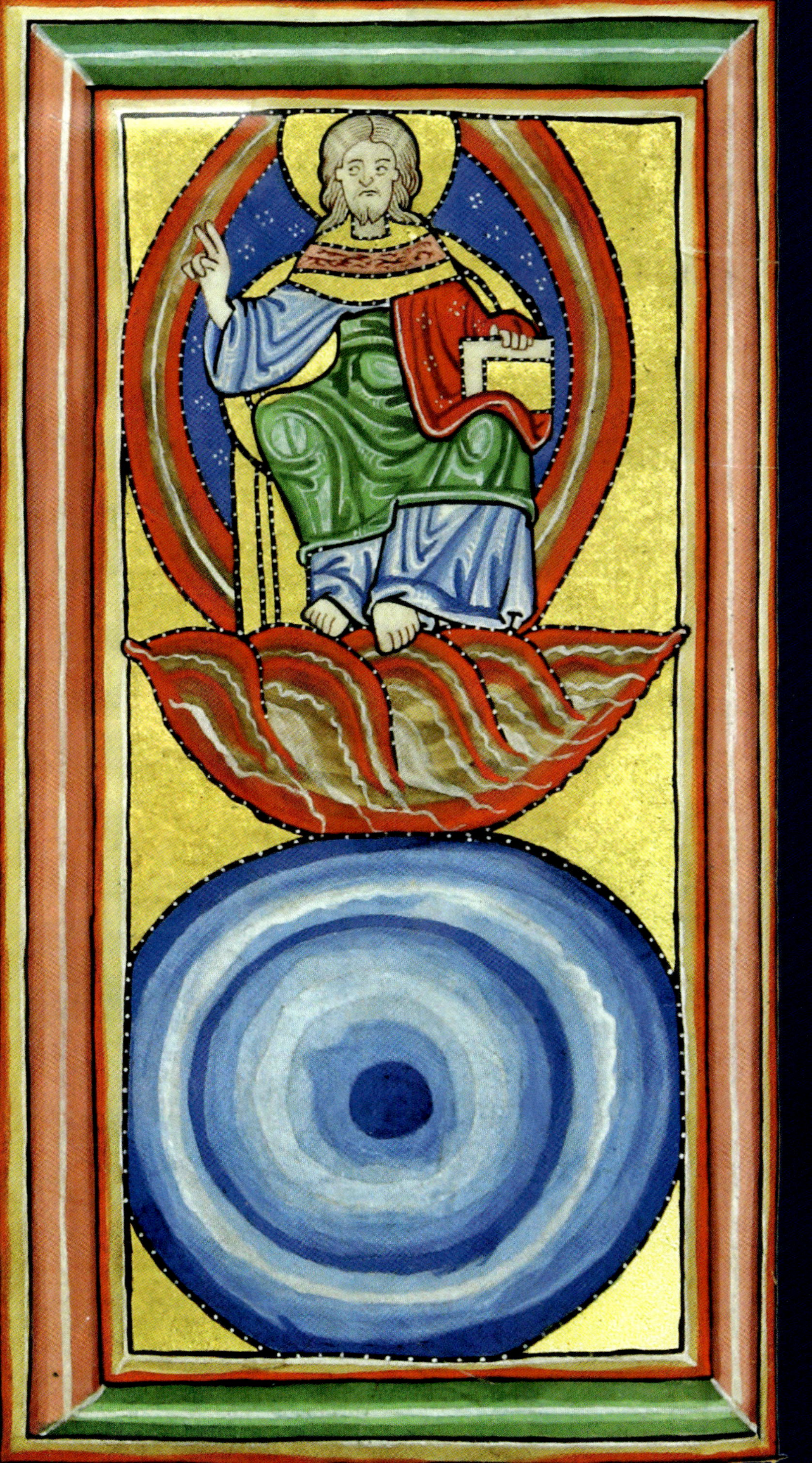

Building

Then I saw, within the circumference of the circle, which extends from the One seated on the throne, a great mountain, joined at its root to that immense block of stone above which are the cloud and the throne with its Occupant; [. . .] And on that mountain stood a four-sided building [. . .] (*SC* III.2.D, p. 326).

The *circle colored gold* emanated by the Shining One forms the outline of the sphere, generated by the heart of God. It embraces the whole firmament, from the depths of the abyss to the highest heaven, and surrounds the *Building* positioned on the mountain, at the base of the blue *rock* of the Fear of God on which the Shining One stands out, as in the opening image.
The geography of the vision is now complete, revealing that it coincides with the three circles of the two faces of *Charity* and the *circle colored gold* of faith, telling us that all creation is in God's image.

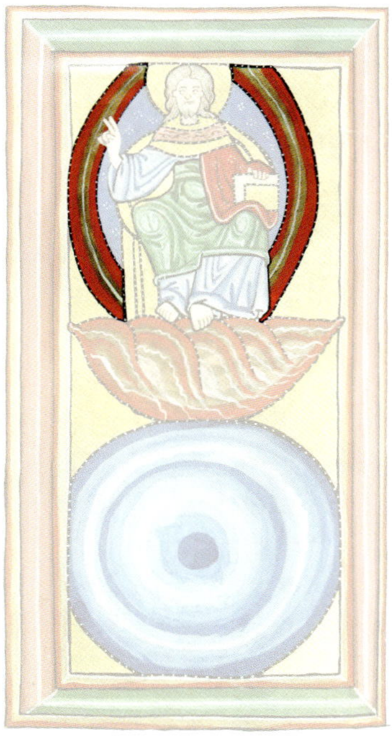

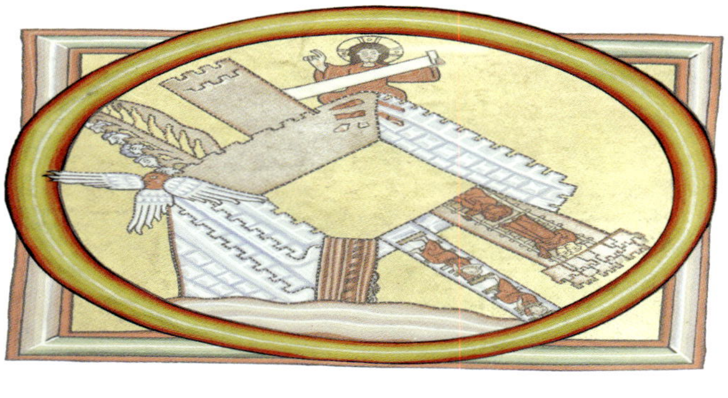

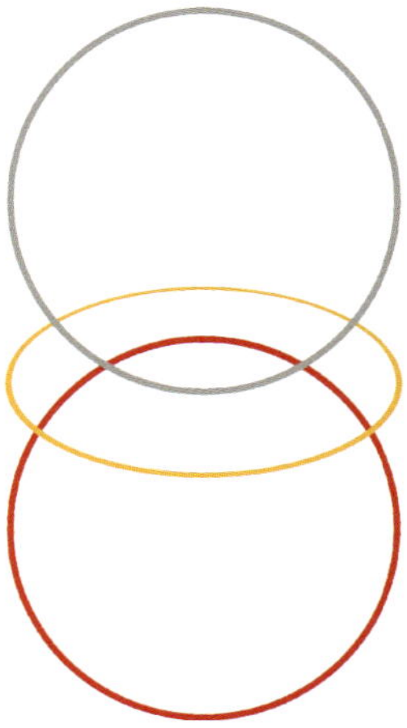

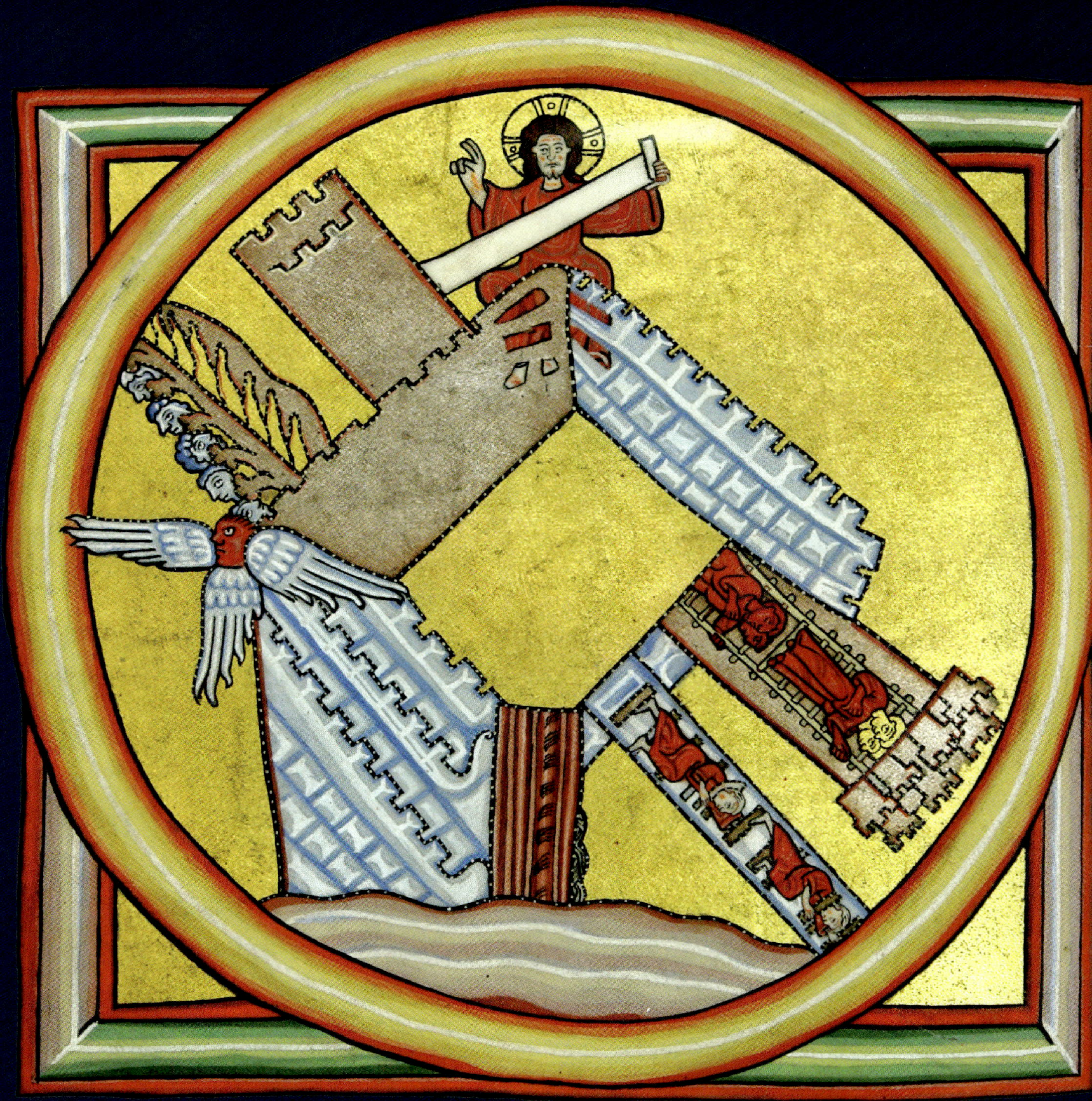

Crater Tornatilis

God placed the firmament as the footstool of his throne, and it has the form of a circling circle in likeness to God's power, which has neither beginning nor end, for no one can discern where a revolving wheel begins and ends (*LDO*, I.4,11, p. 137).

And so the upper and lower part of the firmament is rounded like a well-turned bowl, and in the upper curve is positioned the sun, which passes through both the upper and the lower firmament and emits its brilliance like wine poured from a bowl (*LDO* I.4.22, pp. 147–148).

Speak of the revelation of the bread, which is the Son of God, Who is life in the fire of love; Who raises up everyone dead in soul and body, forgives all repented sins in His serene clarity (*SC* III.1.D, p. 310).

After we have reached the center of the sphere of light, held in the heart of God, the vision reveals that the firmament corresponds to the gift of a new life, offered by the reality of bread and wine. In the mystery and miracle of shadow, the chalice, *crater tornatilis* of the Song of Songs, becomes visible, on the altar table: the golden quadrangle of the Building (see pp. 102–103).

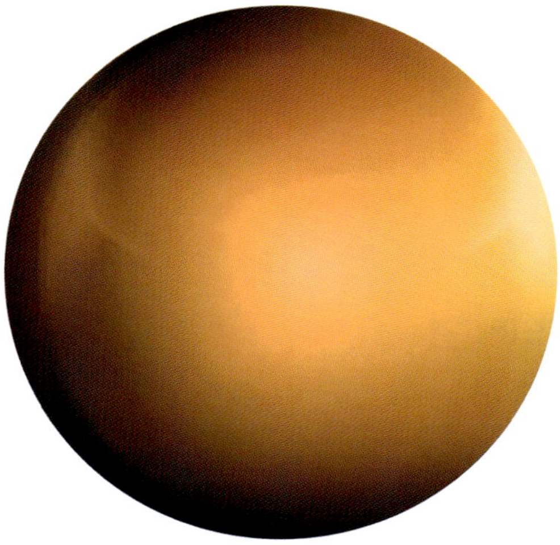

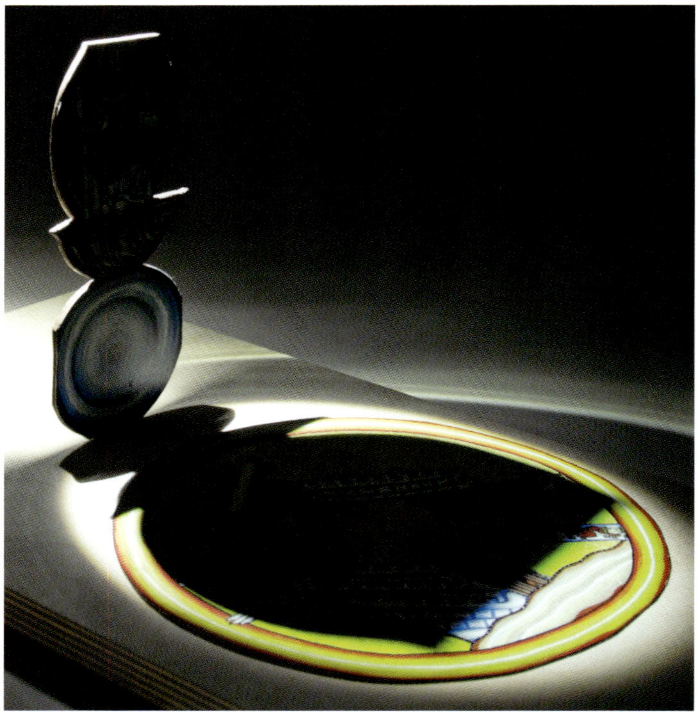

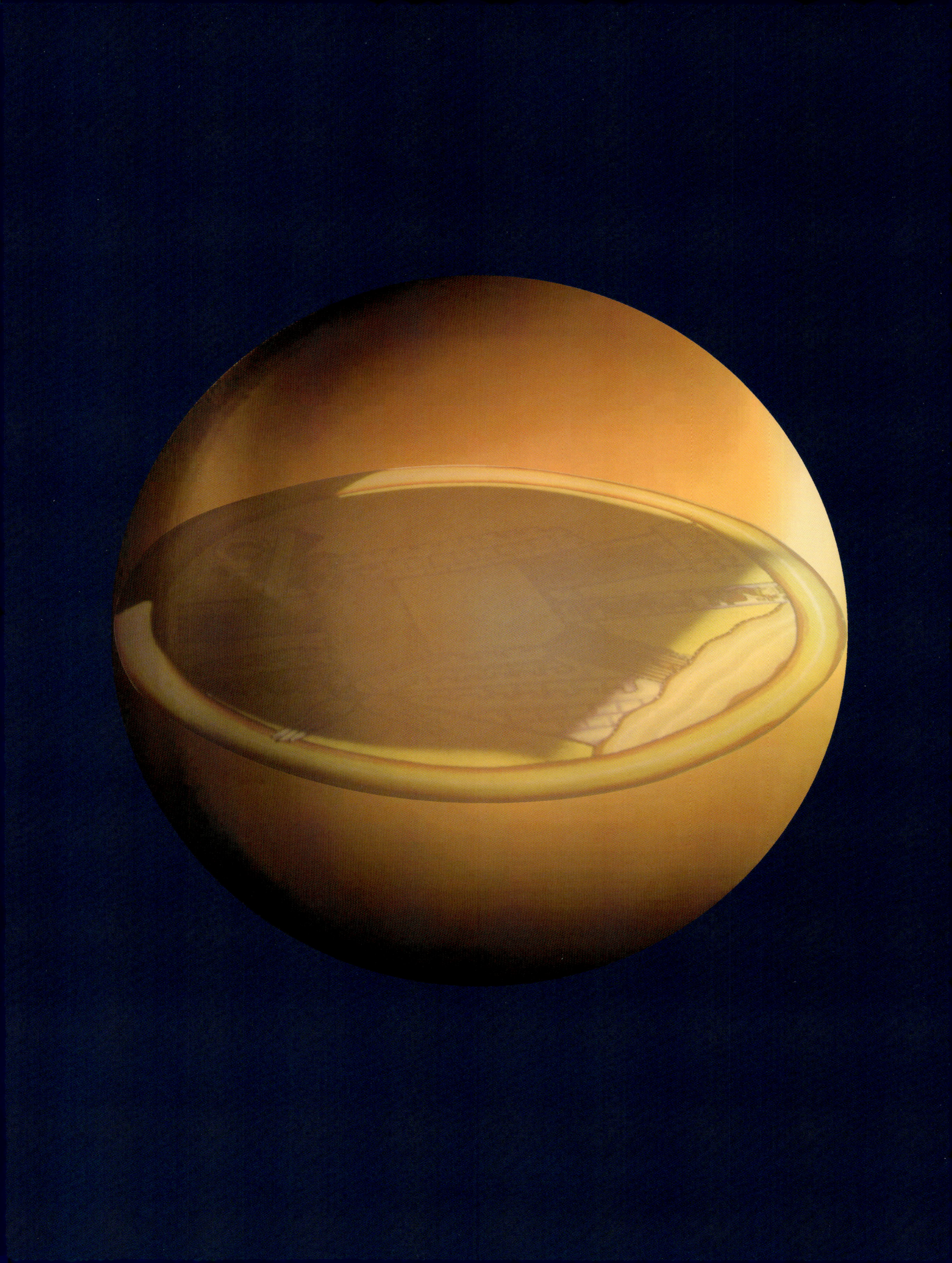

Know the Ways

And there faith draws and joins to itself all the virtues, like wine poured into a vessel to be given to humans to drink (*LDO* I.2.19 p. 68).

[…] the goodness of the Father builds good works on faith. Gathering multitudes of the faithful from the four corners of the earth, he draws them to celestial things (*SC* III.2.3, p. 326).

The path along the ways, depicted in the images, unfolds around the altar, inside the Building, above the mountain, in the center of the sphere, and in the heart of *Charity*. It is the story of humanity's meeting with God told chronologically and in the simultaneity of the vision of eternal time. The superimposition of the images reveals new images through the transparencies, allowing the poetry of the revelation to emerge (see pp. 107 and 131).

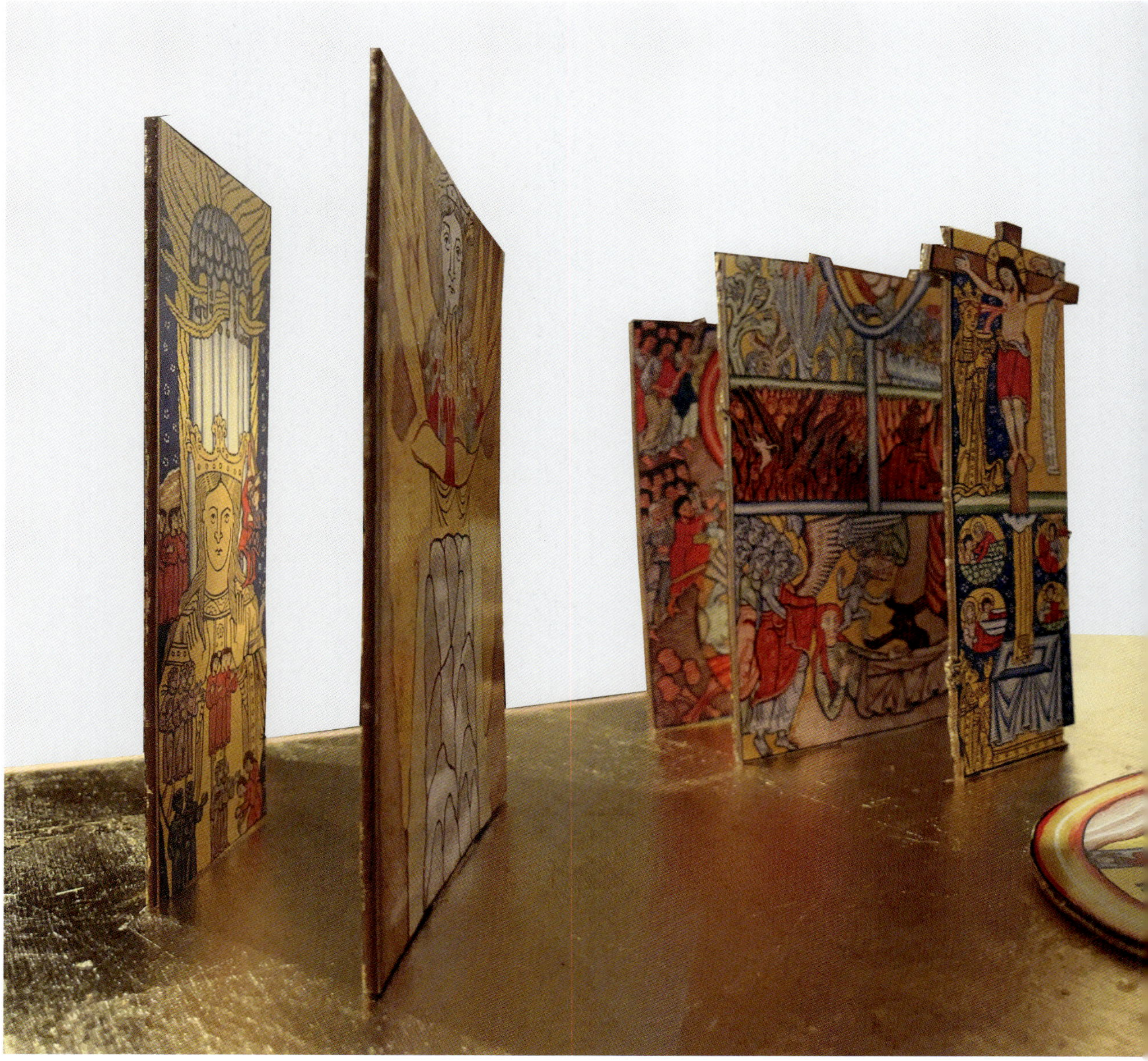

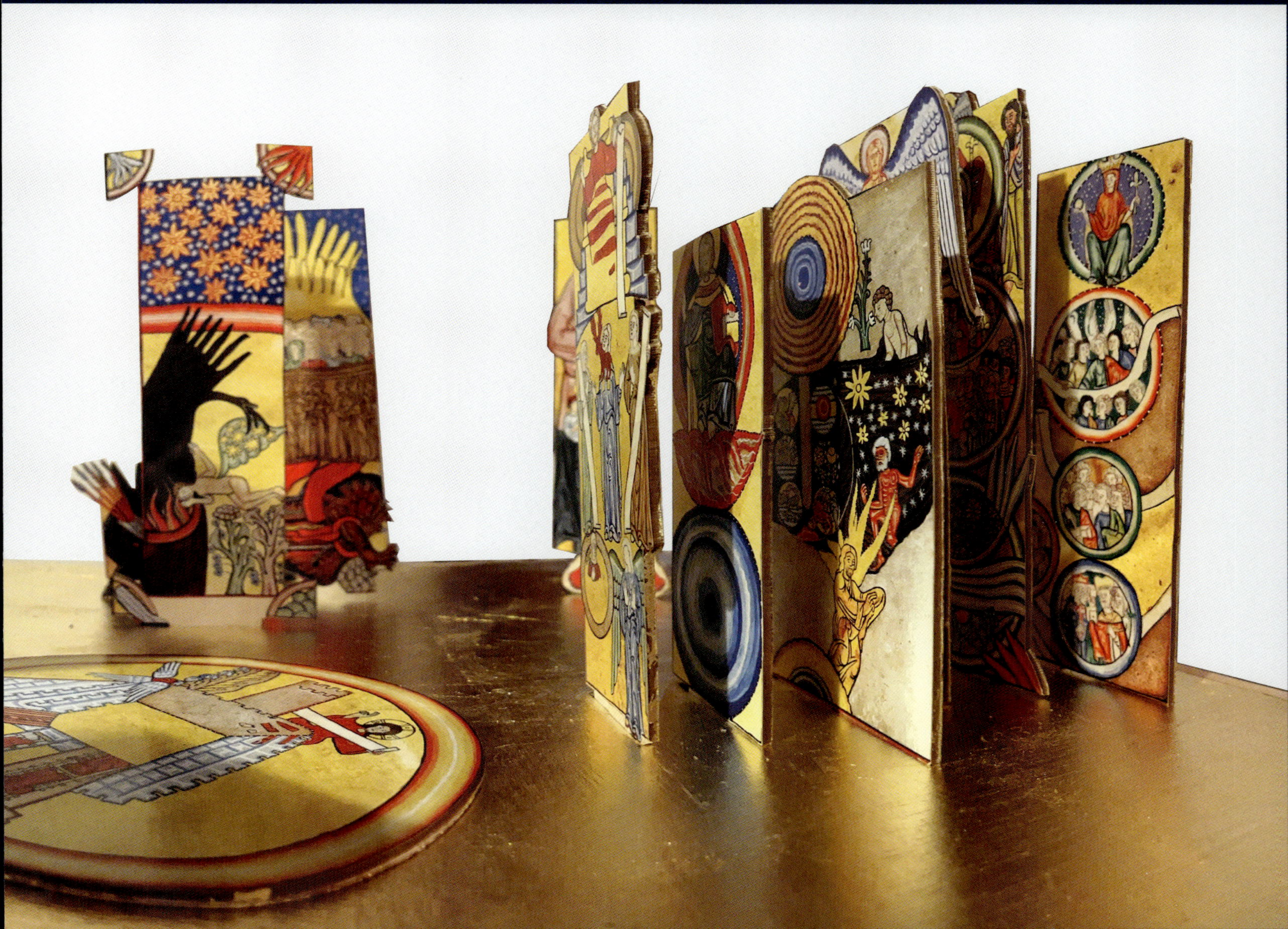

Nuptial Dowry

For when the sun, which is My Son, stands forth in the flesh, the light of the holy Gospel shines (*SC* III.4.10, p. 361).

That when blood flowed from the wounded side of My Son, at once salvation of souls came into being (*SC* II.6.1, p. 238).

Indeed, God sealed all the beauty of the works of his potential in the first angel, and adorned him with the stars and the beauty of viridity and every kind of sparkling gem like the starry sky, and called him, "Lucifer," for this angel bore light from him who alone is eternal (*LDO*, I.4.12, p. 373).

Then God caused another life, which he contained within a body, to arise, and this is humankind. To them he gave the place and the glory of the lost angel, to complete in the praise of God what the latter had refused to do (*LDO* I.1.9, p. 40).

The circle of light, adored by the angels, is the bread of life. It contains the essence of the story of salvation, from the star of the first angel to the new humanity. The flesh and blood of Christ, fruit of the mystical winepress, are the nuptial dowry for his bride, gathered beneath the cross by the Church. The light of the *sun shining from the heart of God to illuminate the world* radiates from the cup (see pp. 132 and 135).

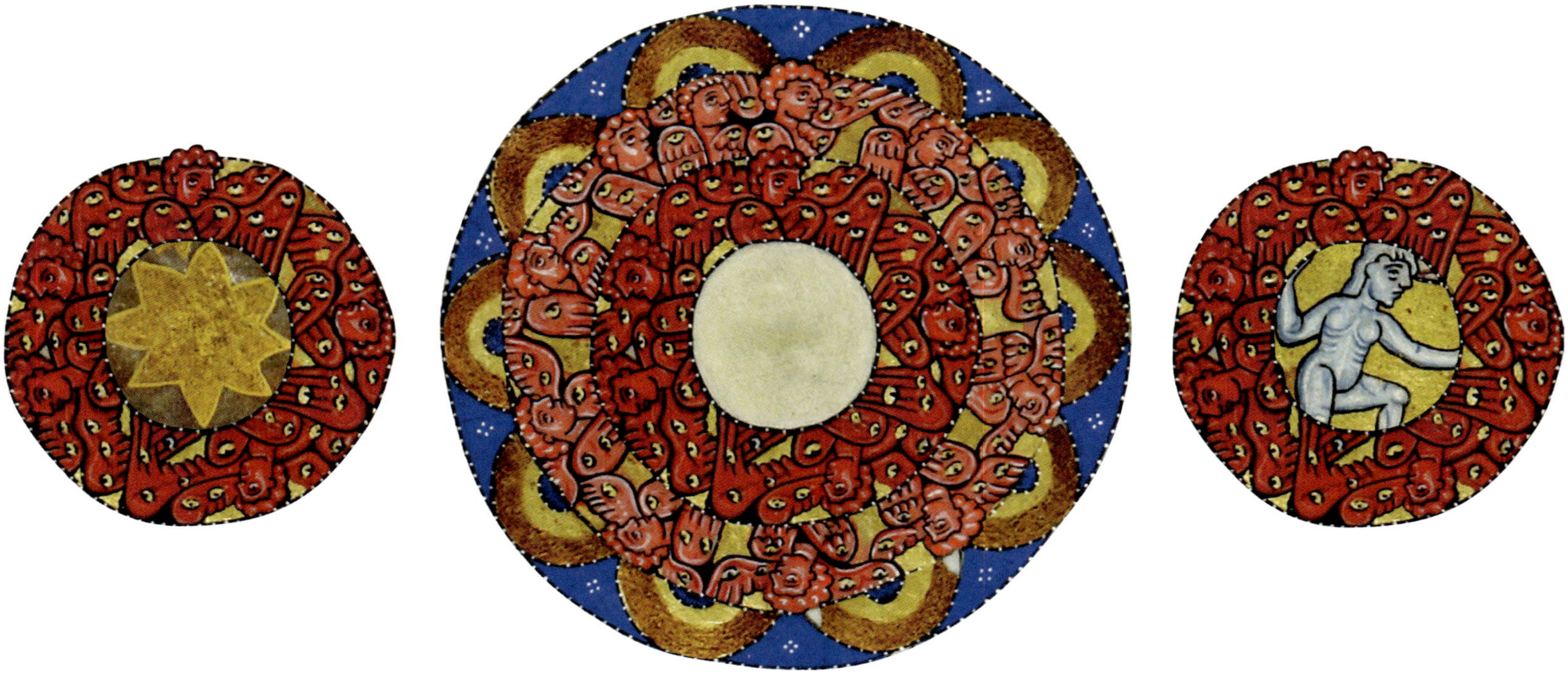

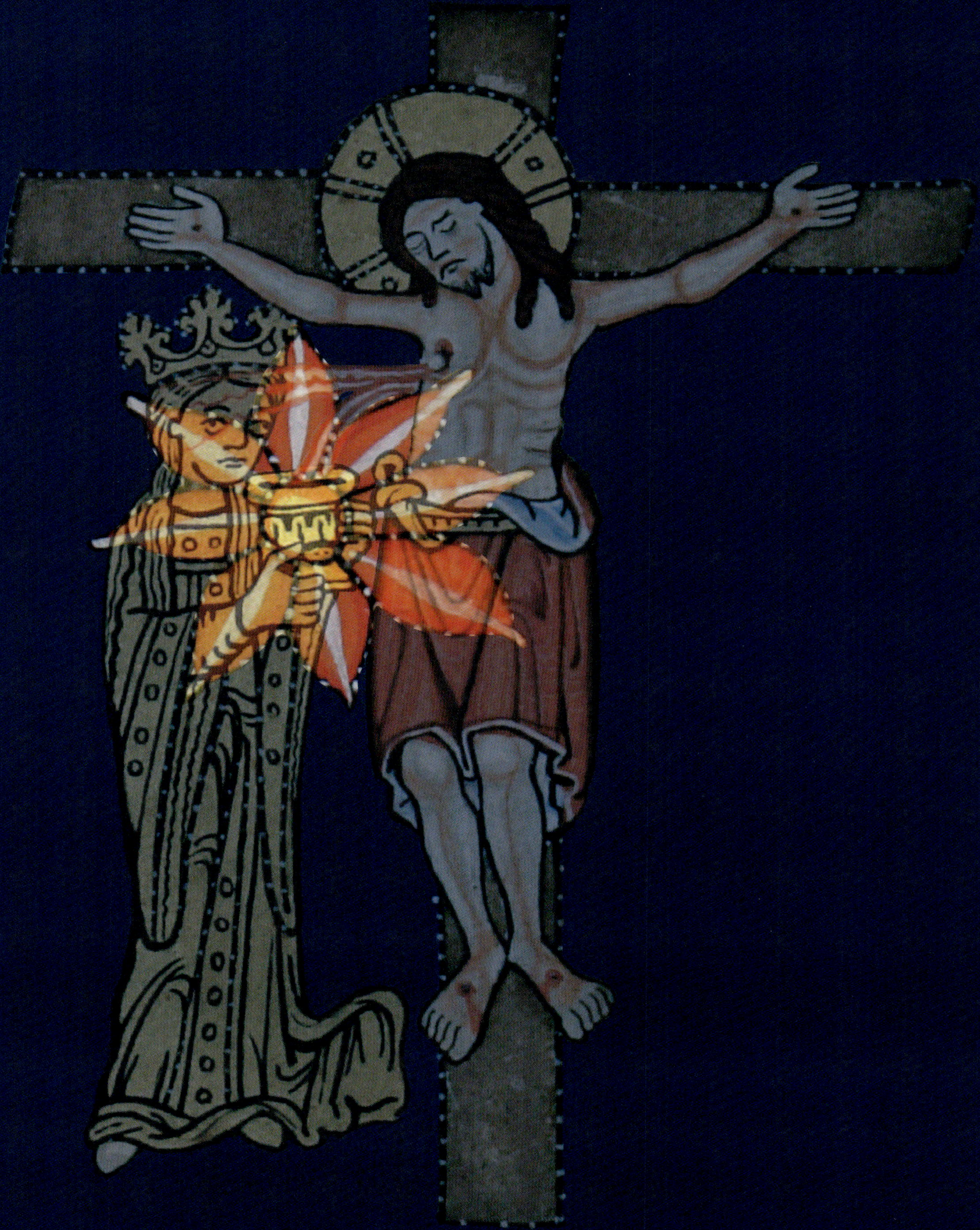

Soul

O human, regard what you were when you were just a lump in your mother's womb! You were mindless and powerless to bring yourself to life; but then you were given spirit and motion and sense, so that you might live and move and come to fruitful deeds (*SC* III.10.1, p. 473).

"O daughter, run, because you were given wings to fly by the powerful giver, who no one is capable of resisting. And so fly fast beyond all of these adversities" (*SC* I.4,2, p. 66).

When Adam refused the flower of obedience to the Word out of fear, he was banished from the Garden of Eden and descended to earth. He sank into darkness, and humanity's journey in the world began. The same journey awaits the soul, contained in embryonic form in the seeds of the Science of God and which, called upon to enter the world, descends into the body of the nascent child. It is then that the soul becomes self-forgetful and, united with the body, passes through the mystical winepress in its wandering through the world. The journey ends when it rediscovers its wings, the sign of its original divine dimension. Thus, each new creature retraces the entire history of humanity (see pp. 142–143).

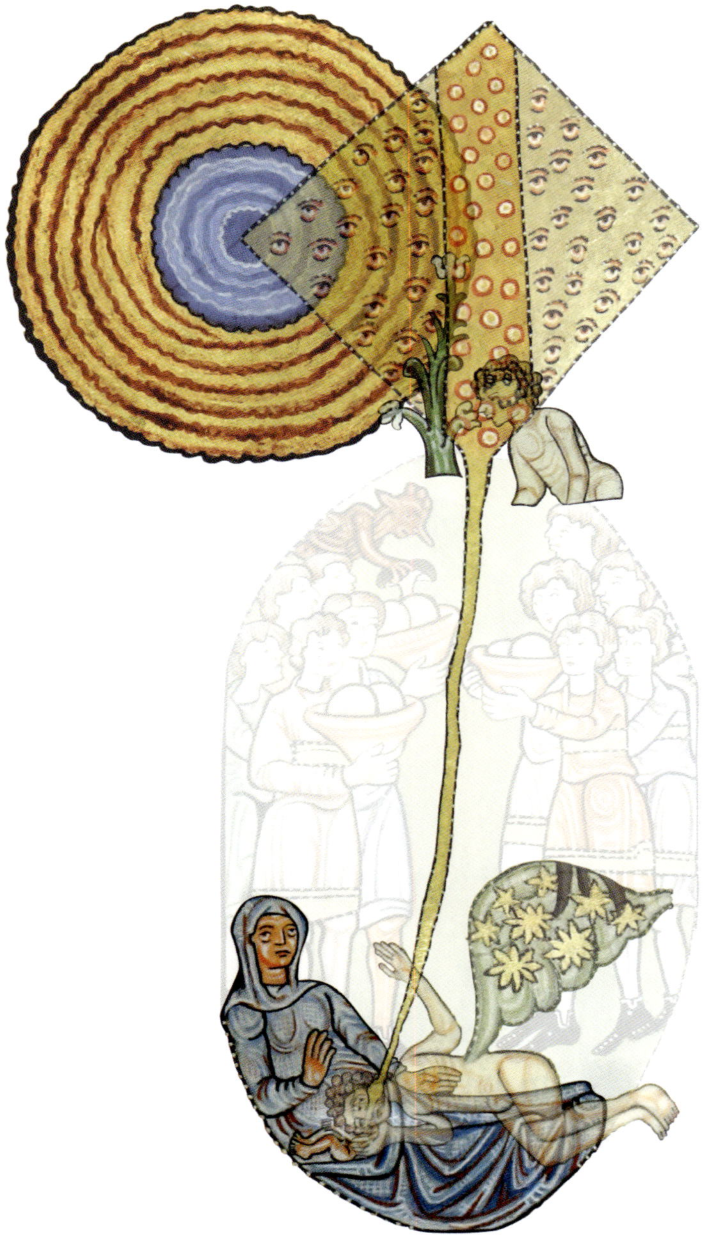

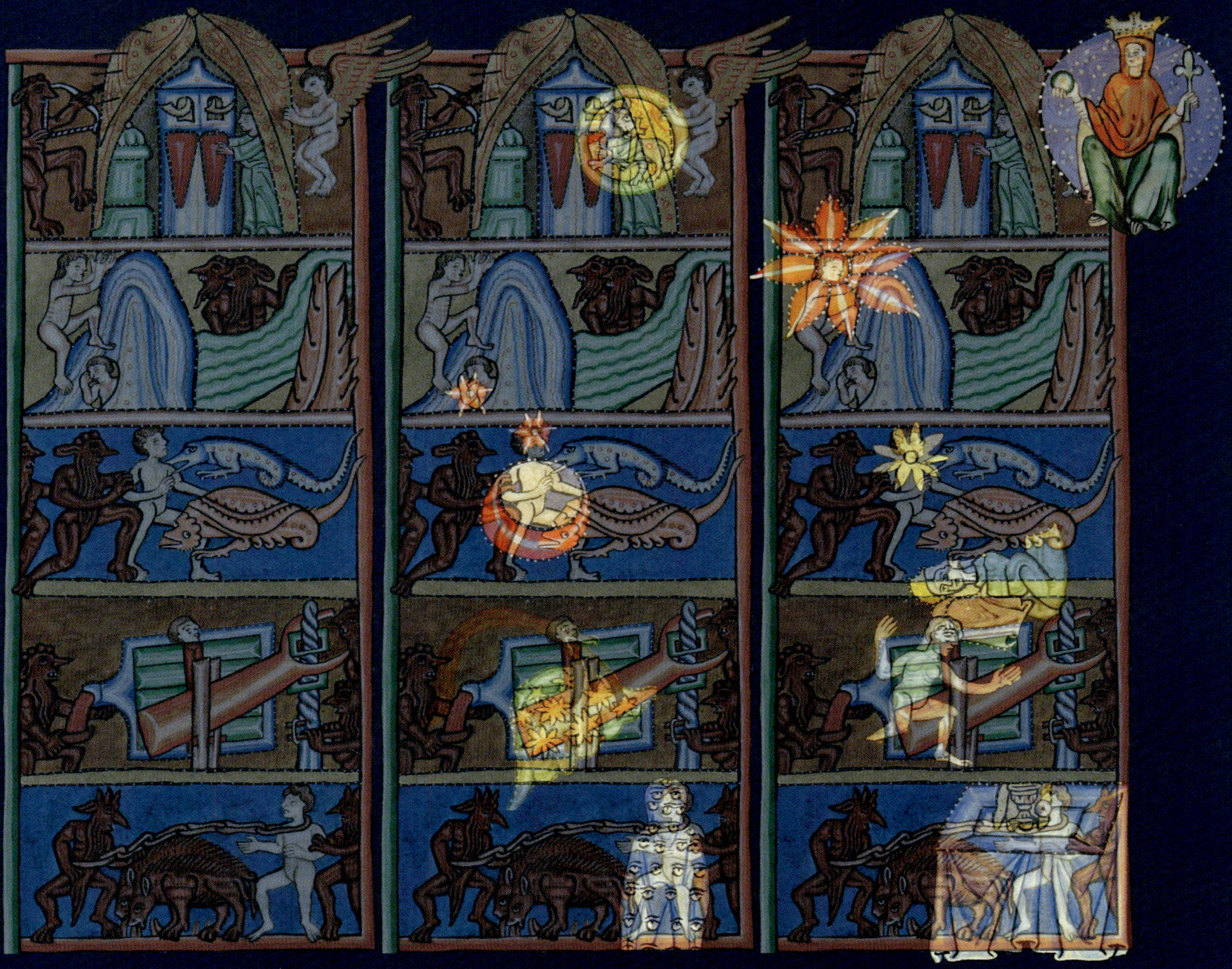

Symphonia

The bride signifies the holy and adorned soul that has been joined to Christ in the dowry of his blood and looks to him as a bride to her bridegroom (*LDO* I.4.87, p. 210).

For, as the air encloses and sustains everything under the heavens [...] a sweet and delightful song [...] sings with joy of the wonders of the elect who dwell in the heavenly city (*SC* III.13.10, p. 532).

And from the waist down to the place that denotes the male he glowed like the dawn, and there a harp was lying with its strings across his body (*SC*, III.11.D, p. 492).

The way of *virginitas*, the rediscovery of one's integrity through the divine calling, marks the last stage of the journey. After having traversed the body of the world, the space and time of repentance and forgiveness, the heavenly city resting in God's lap is revealed. This is the time of the *symphonia*, of the marriage between the Church and her bridegroom, when the images of the harp and the city become one (see p. 139).

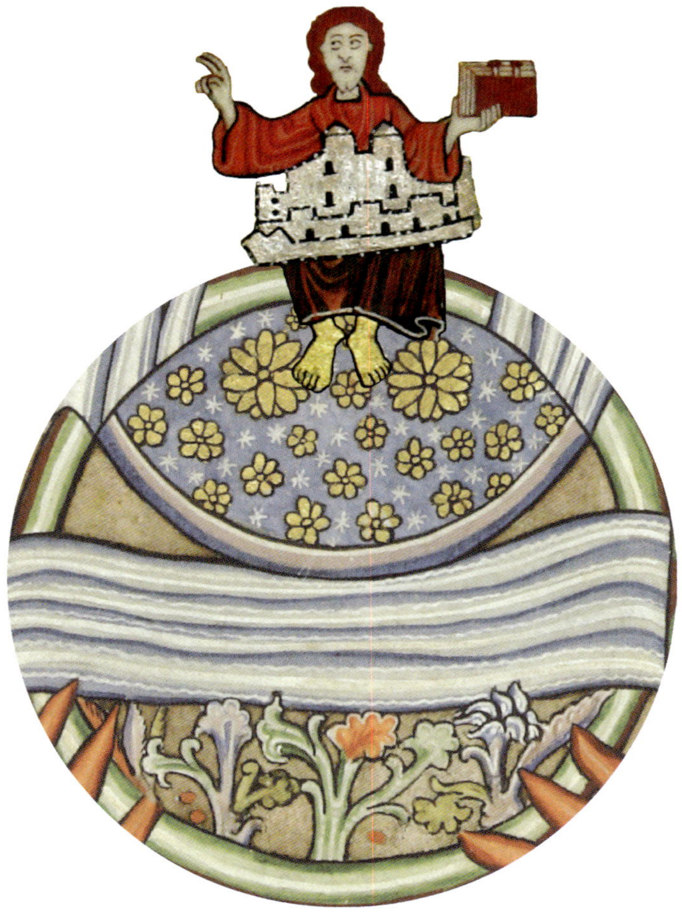

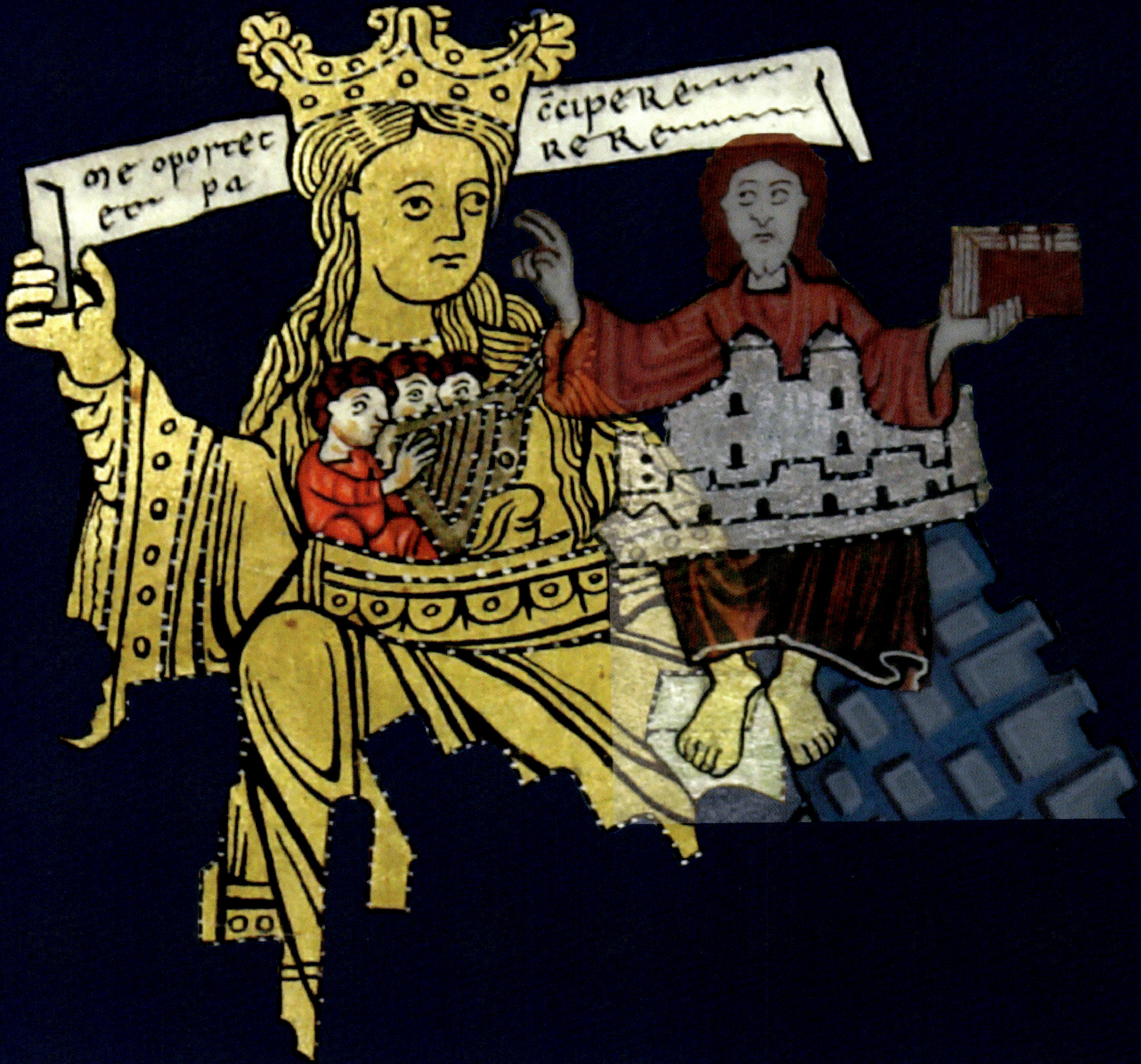
me oportet
et pa
ccipere
rere

O quam mirabilis est
prescientia divini pectoris,
que prescivit omnem creaturam.
Nam cum Deus inspexit
faciem hominis quem formavit,
omnia opera sua
in eadem forma hominis
integra aspexit.
O quam mirabilis est inspiratio,
que hominem sic suscitavit.

How wondrous is the prescience
of the heart of God,
which foretold every creature.
For when God looked on the face
of man whom he formed,
he saw all his works complete
in that same human form.
Oh, how wondrous is the holy breath
that brought man to life.

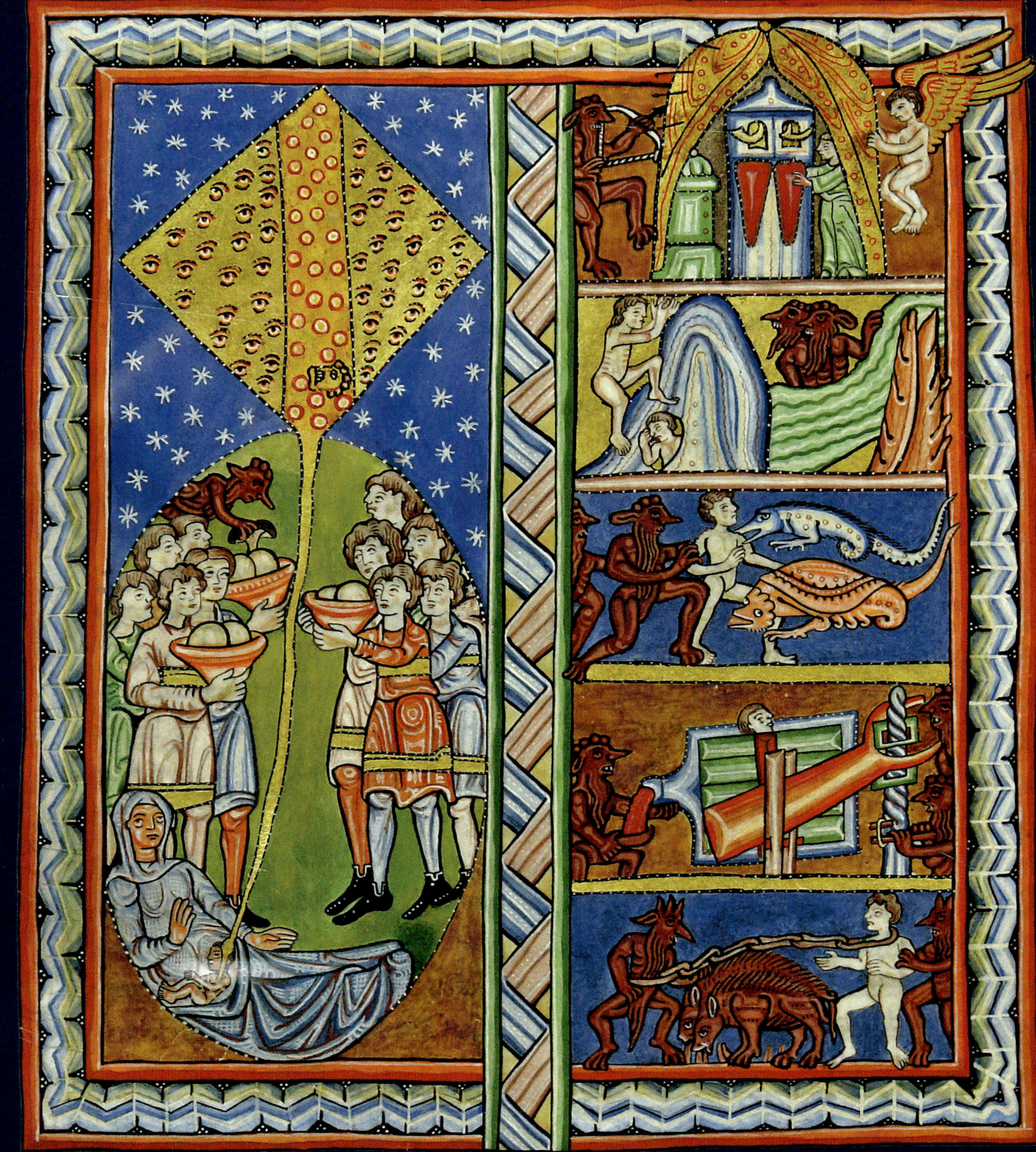

Eyes

For the eyes, which behold very many things, reveal the stars of the firmament, shining everywhere. The white of the eyes signifies the purity of the ether, and their clarity its splendor; while the pupil signifies the stars that are in the ether. Moreover, the eyes' moisture demonstrates the moisture that wets the ether from the waters below so that it is not harmed by the fire above. This also means that because the soul is stationed in true repentance between conscience and circumspection, by God's grace it drives its vessel to repentance (*LDO* I.4.31, p. 160).

When for love of God you free your body from earthly affairs, you will grow as a beautiful flower, blossoming and never withering in the heavenly Jerusalem with the Son of God (*SC* II.5.31, p. 219).

The Science of God radiates to the depths and extends its *keen vision to the four corners of the earth*, where it scrutinizes and knows human hearts. In the triangular shapes that make up the square form *filled with eyes*, is concealed the design of the flowered cross, made up of circles and blossoms, visible in the recomposition using a mirror (see pp. 146–149). It is the image of those who, by choice and through their constancy, have passed through the darkness, who adorn the precious altar cloth, and will shine in the eternal sky.

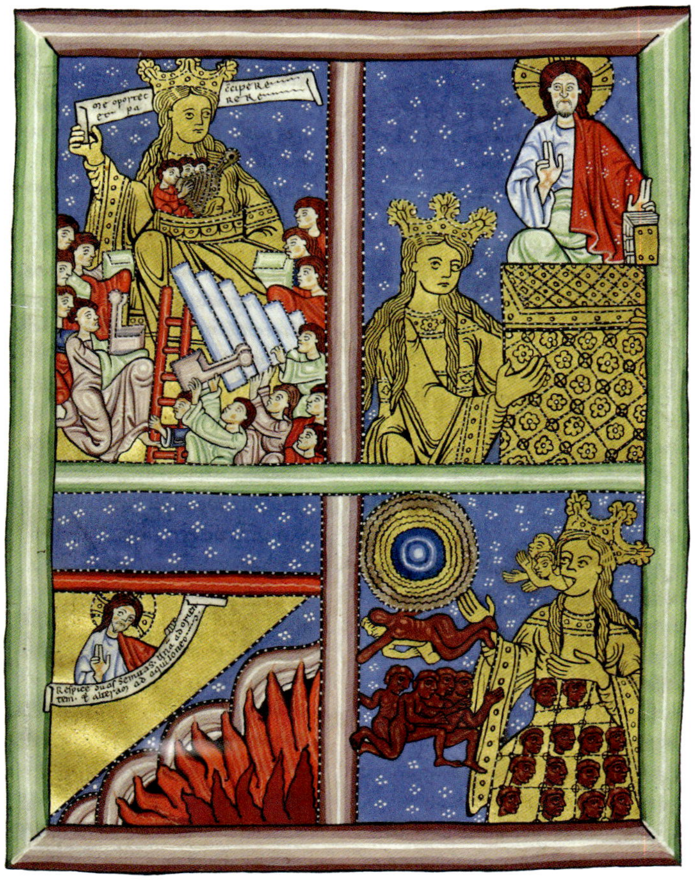

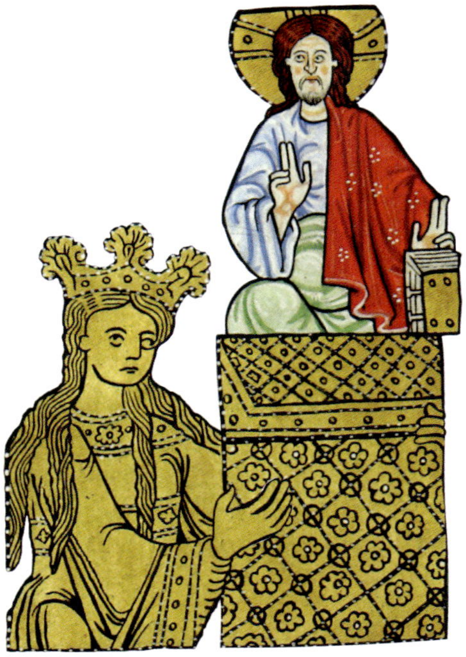

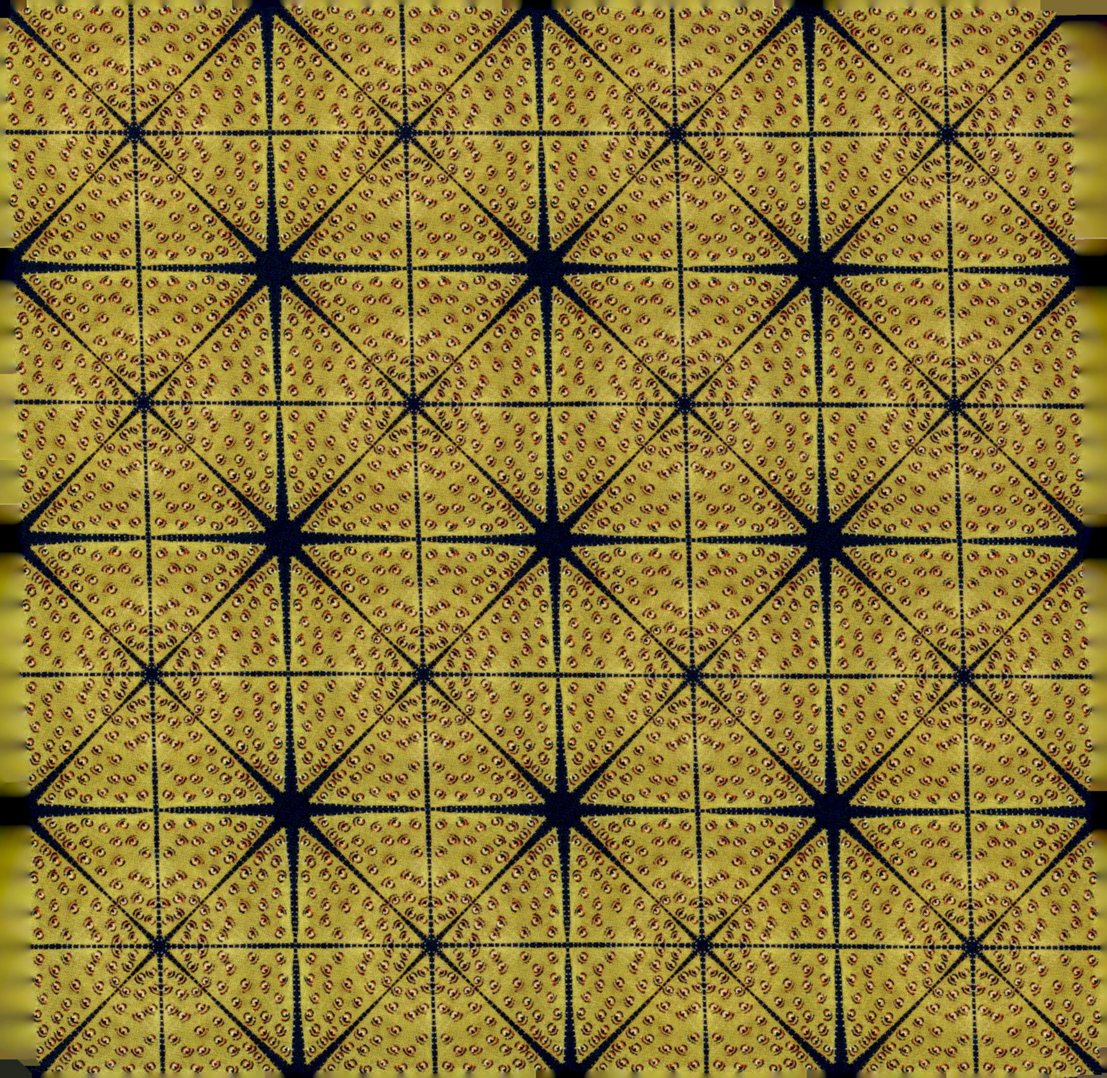

If a necessity arises a monk who is firmly rooted and competent for it may be a messenger and priest, prophet and counselor of the Church. He is not to be kept away from these offices, as long as his sight is clear (*SC* II,5,17, p. 211).

Likewise, the priest's robe is decorated with quadrilobate flowers that appear in the recomposed triangles (see pp. 146–149). The revealed design elicits wonder and reverberates with sung prayers that open with the awestruck invocation "O," whose perfect roundness is reminiscent of the perfection of the circle of the divine wheel.

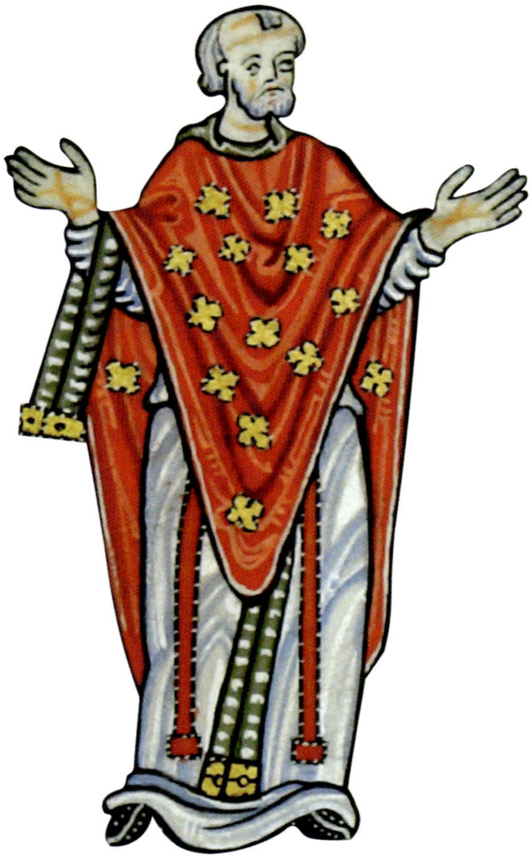

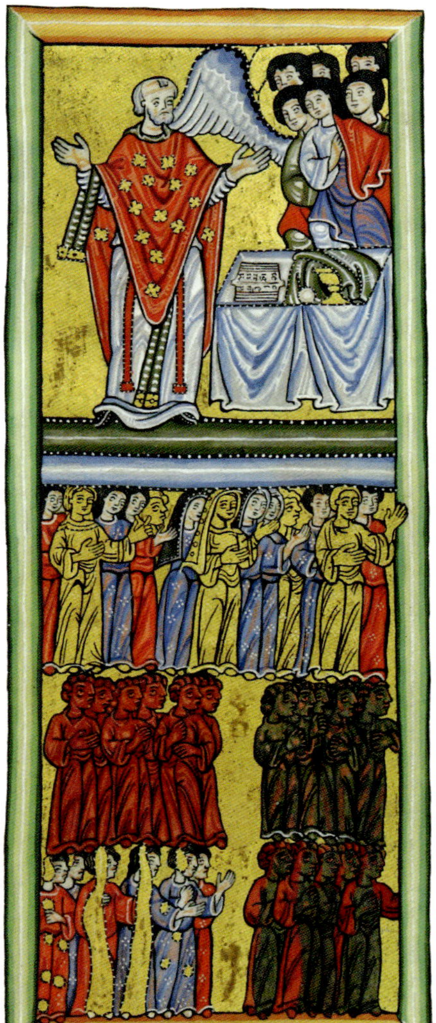

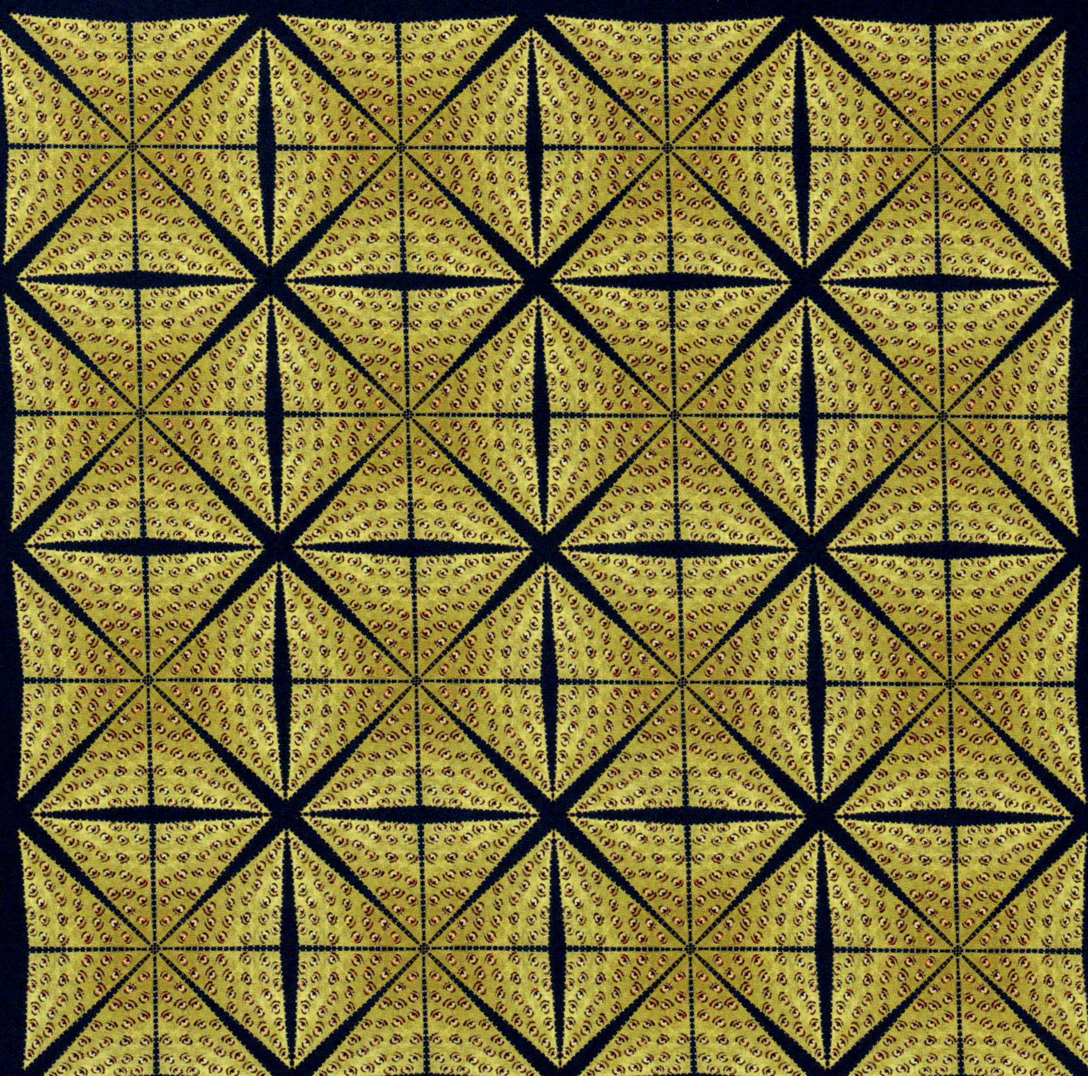

Gazes

Because fear of the Lord, with its sharp contemplative sight, penetrates the secrets of Heaven; for fear is the beginning of a just intention, and when that flowers into sanctity by good works, it joins with blessed faith and reaches God in full perfection (*SC* III.2.2, p. 326).

Indeed, how would one recognize that he alone is eternal, if the angels did not offer such contemplation? (*LDO* I.4.11 p.137).

In the eagle are signified those spiritual people who, with the heart's every devotion and in contemplation, gaze often upon God as do the angels (*LDO* I.1.5, p. 37).

The blue virtue of the Fear of God invites us to lift up our eyes and look beyond the confines of everyday life marked by tedium, fear and egoistic pride. This is when humanity enters the vital dimension of angelic praise and the teaching of virtue. These expand its gaze and transform it into circles, waves that spread and correspond, in which hearts beat in unison in the symphony of the adoration of the light.

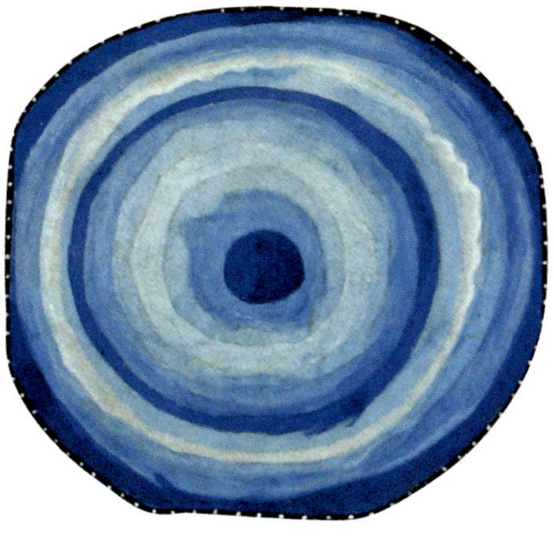

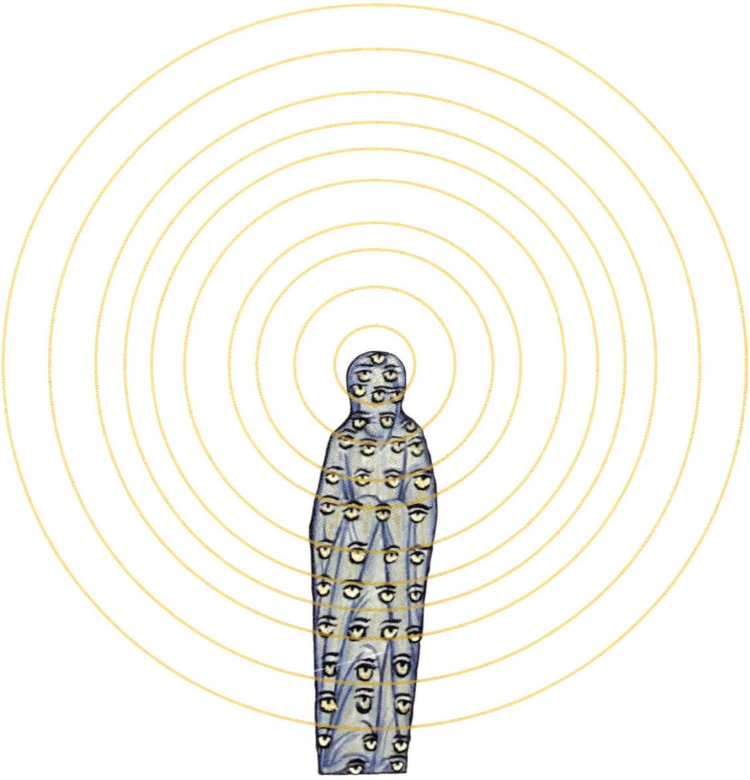

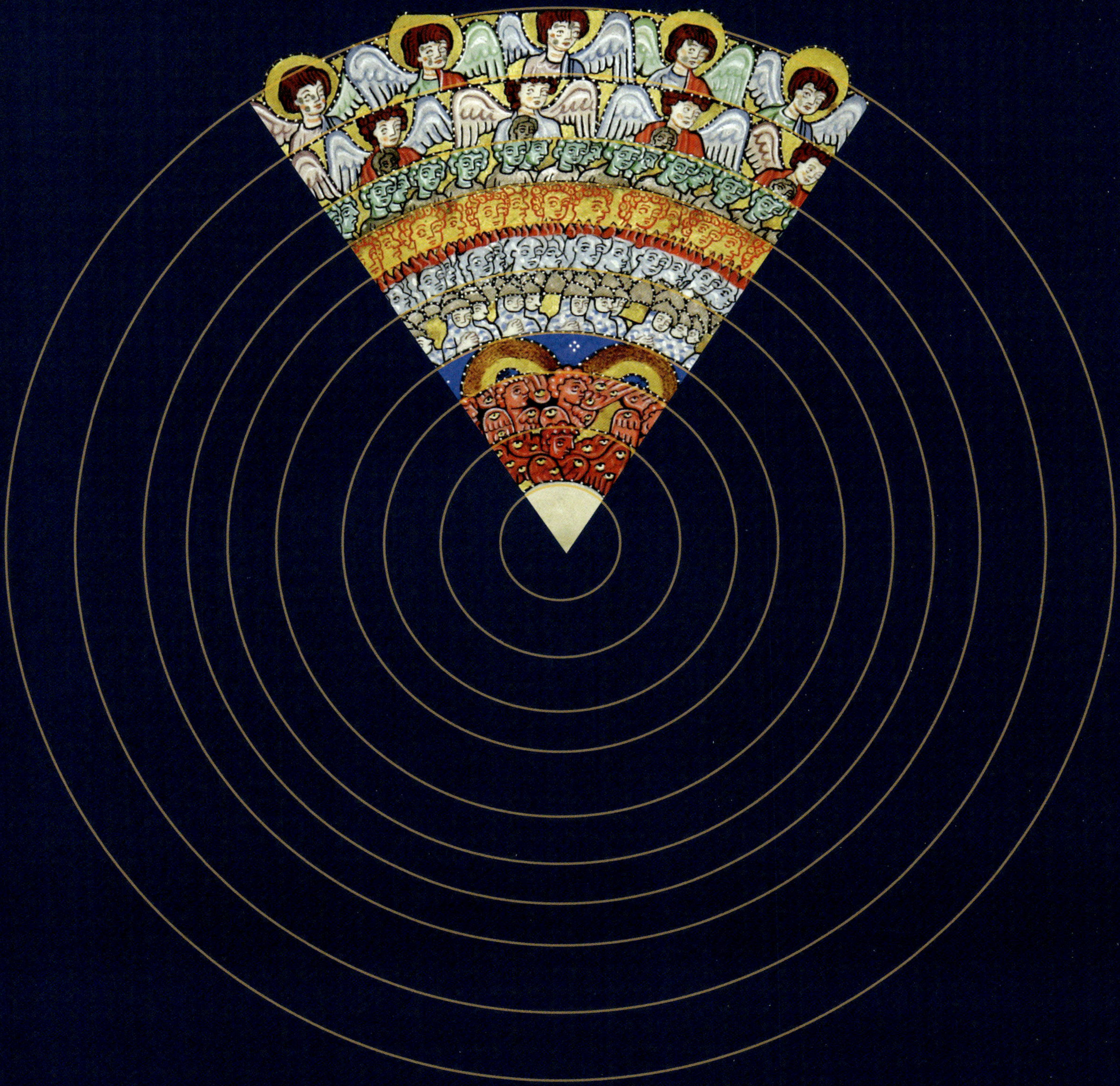

Eye of God

The living eye is light, but blindness is darkness (*LDO* I.4.12 p.138).

Thus God sees all things, and nothing is hidden from His divine sight; He knows and observes all things, and so He can deal rightly with each and every case (*SC* III.4.21, p. 368).

If you knock at the door, I will open to you. You are given a spirit of profound knowledge, and so have in yourself all that you need. And, this being so, My eyes will search you closely and remember what they find (*SC* III.10.3, p. 474).

The praising and praying gaze is thus receptive to the vision of the celestial vault of the firmament. The egg lying on its side is the shape of the eye as the image of God who is all-seeing and omniscient. In the iris is the splendid crown of the angels with, in the center, the white of divine light with touches of the *silvery white* light of the Father, which encloses the *splendid gold color* of the spirit, and the *sapphire blue* of the Christ man. The circle of light is like the oculus in a temple vault, through which the light enters and the gaze can embrace infinity (Salvadori 2019, pp. 134–135).

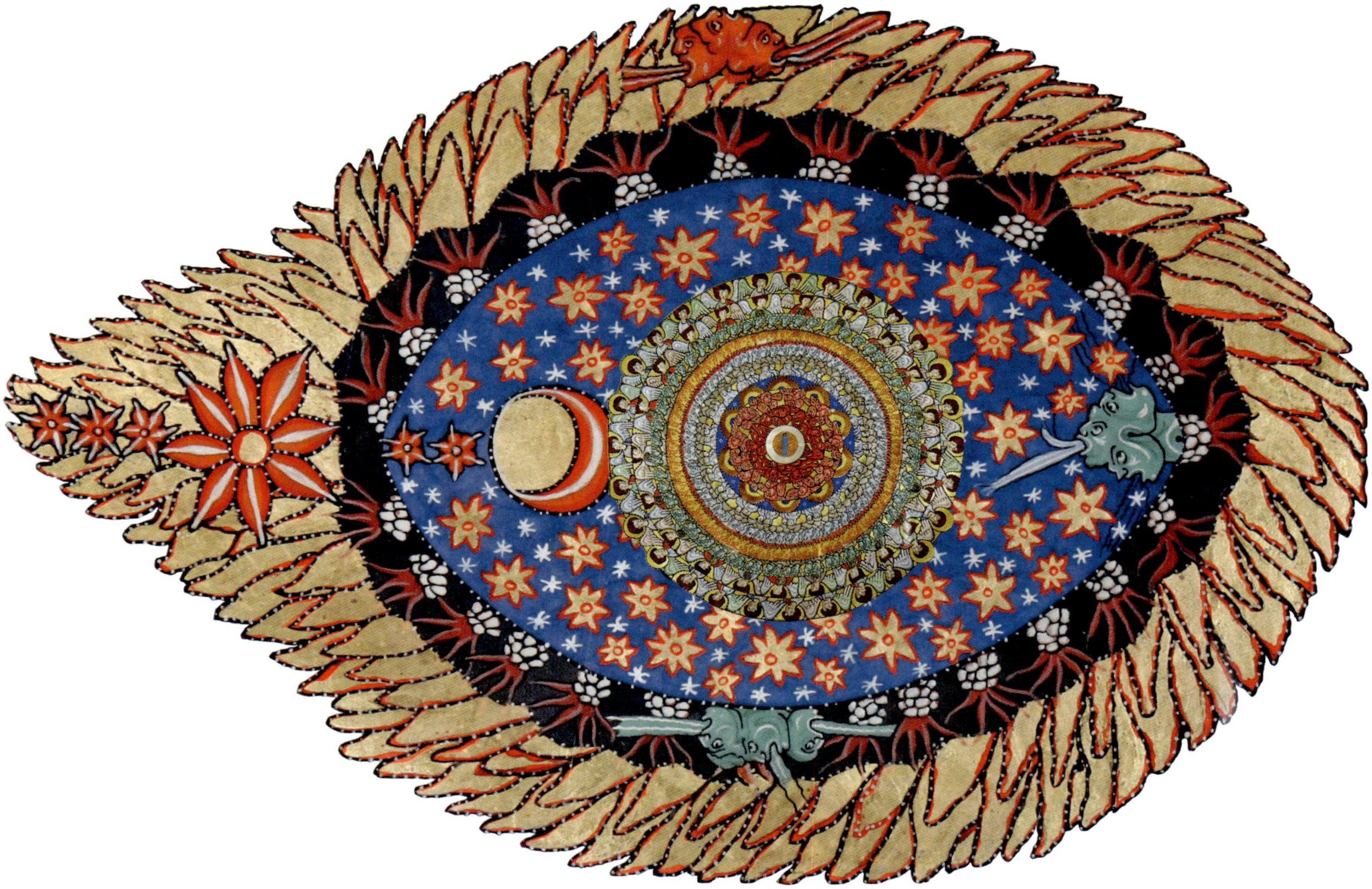

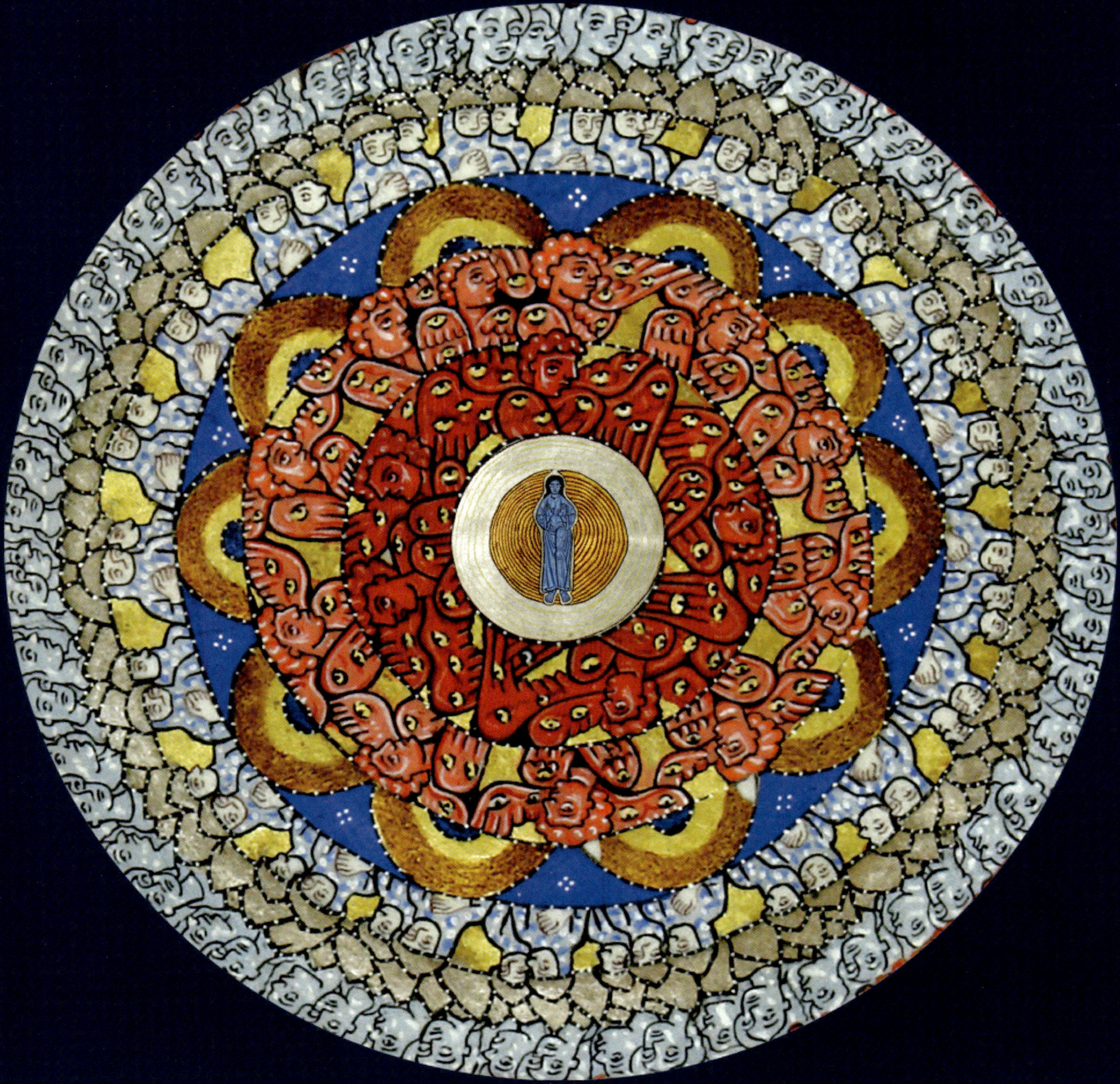

O splendidissima gemma et serenum decus solis,
qui tibi infusus est fons saliens de corde Patris,
qui est unicum Verbum suum
per quod creavit mundi primam materiam
quam Eva turbavit;
hoc Verbum effabricavit tibi Pater hominem,
et ob hoc es tu illa lucida materia
per quam hoc ipsum Verbum expiravit omnes virtutes,
ut eduxit in prima materia omnes creaturas.
O tu suavissima virga frondens de stirpe Iesse,
o quam magna virtus est
quod divinitas in pulcherrimam filiam aspexit,
sicut aquila in solem oculum suum ponit,
cum supernus Pater claritatem Virginis attendit
ubi Verbum suum in ipsa incarnari voluit.
Nam in mystico mysterio Dei illustrata
mente virginis mirabiliter clarus flos
ex ipsa Virgine exivit.

O splendid jewel,
serenely infused with the Sun! The Sun is in you
as a fount from the heart of the Father;
It is His sole Word,
by Whom He created the world,
the primary matter,
which Eve threw into disorder.
He formed the Word in you as a human being,
and therefore you are the jewel that shines most brightly,
through whom the Word breathed out
the whole of the virtues, As once from
primary matter He made all creatures.
O sweet green branch that flowers
from the stem of Jesse!
O glorious thing, that God on His fairest daughter
looked as the eagle looks on the face of the sun!
The Most High Father sought for a Virgin's candor,
and willed that His Word should take in her His body.
For the Virgin's mind was by His mystery illumined,
and from her virginity sprang
the glorious Flower.

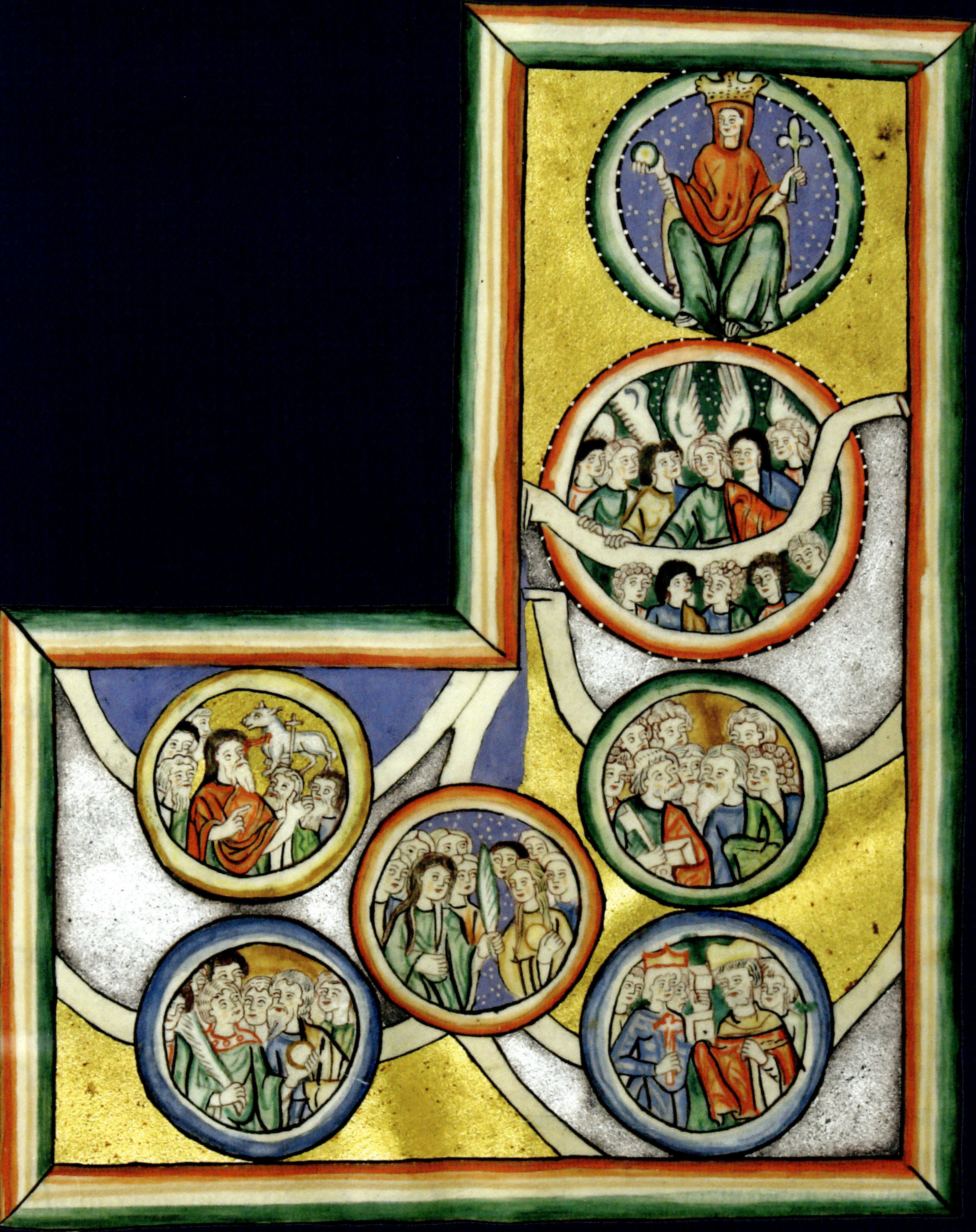

Leafy Branches

Therefore, O virginal Origin, You arise, grow, spread out and produce a great branch with many shoots from which to build the heavenly Jerusalem, beginning not in a man's semen but in a mystical breath (*SC* II.6.24, p. 252).

In the *lucent air* of Paradise the choirs of the blessed exult with joy. Music and dance are echoed in the movement of the gentle breeze of the spirit that wafts through the splendid, golden weave of the colors of the carpet of leaves and branches of the Tree of Jesse. Invisible to external eyes, it can be discerned by contemplating the backgrounds of the image of the symphony—the last vision—and recomposed by following the invaluable clues hidden in the colors of the frames and in the singular form of the miniature itself (see pp. 150–151).

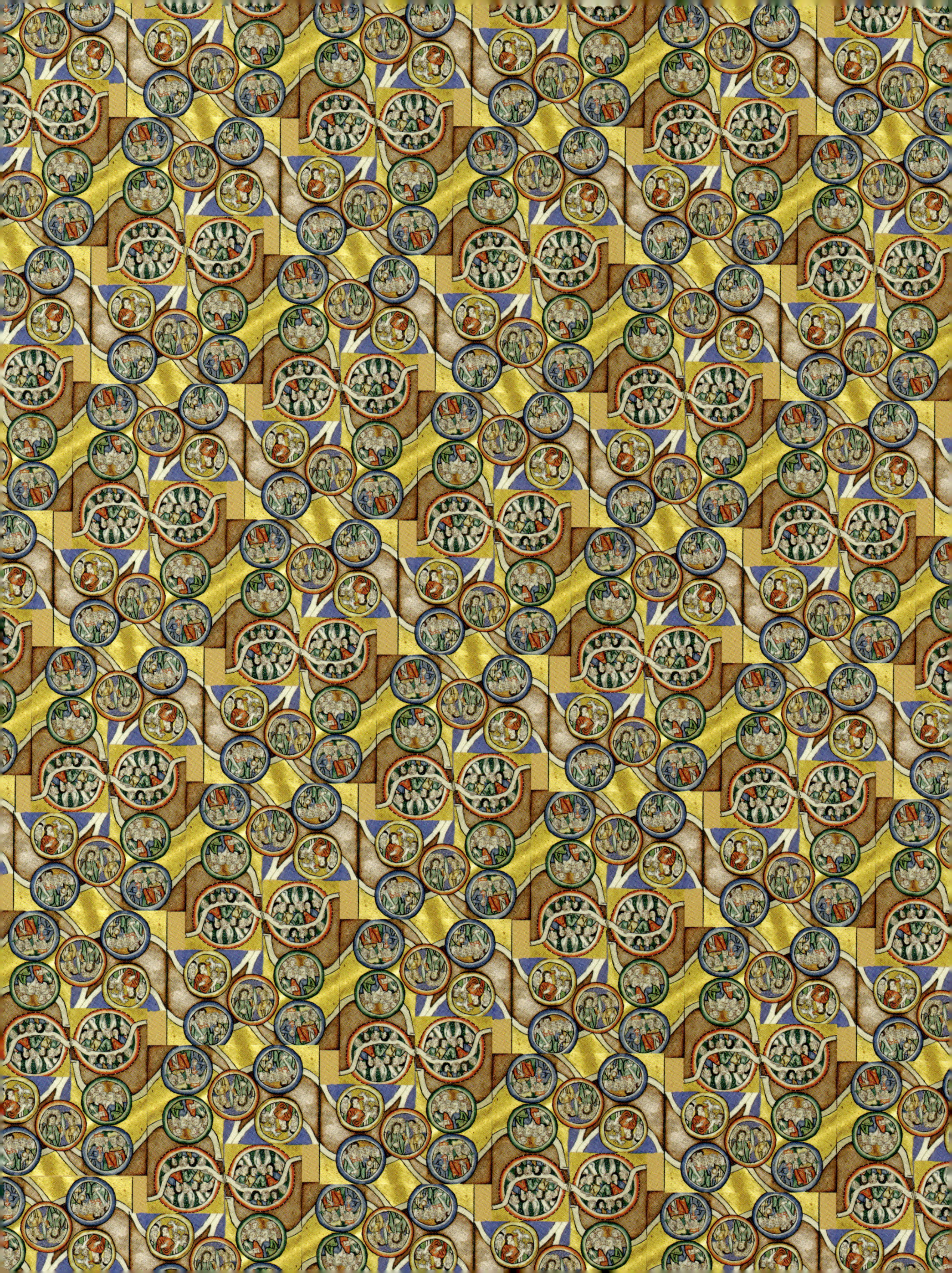

Flowers

When a person works according to the soul's desire, he becomes a flourishing garden on which the Lord feasts his eyes (*LDO* I.4.82, p. 206).

But now I shall speak of my beloved children, who receive me with open senses [...] O my flowers, who when they feel my presence rejoice in me, and I in them [...] When they feel my touch, they hasten to me like the hart to the water-brook (*SC* III.8.8, p. 432).

But Paradise is the place of delight, which blooms with the freshness of flowers and grass and the charms of spices, full of fine odors and dowered with the joy of blessed souls, giving invigorating moisture to the dry ground, it supplies strong force to the earth, as the soul gives strength to the body (*SC* I.2.28, p. 86).

The carpet of leaves and branches of the Tree of Life is studded with brilliant blue flowers with four petals. They represent the blessed who adorn the sky of Paradise like blossoming stars. The flowers grow out of the fragments of color inserted in the background of the image: a subtle chromatic pointer that enables the figure to be recomposed in a few steps (see pp. 152–153).

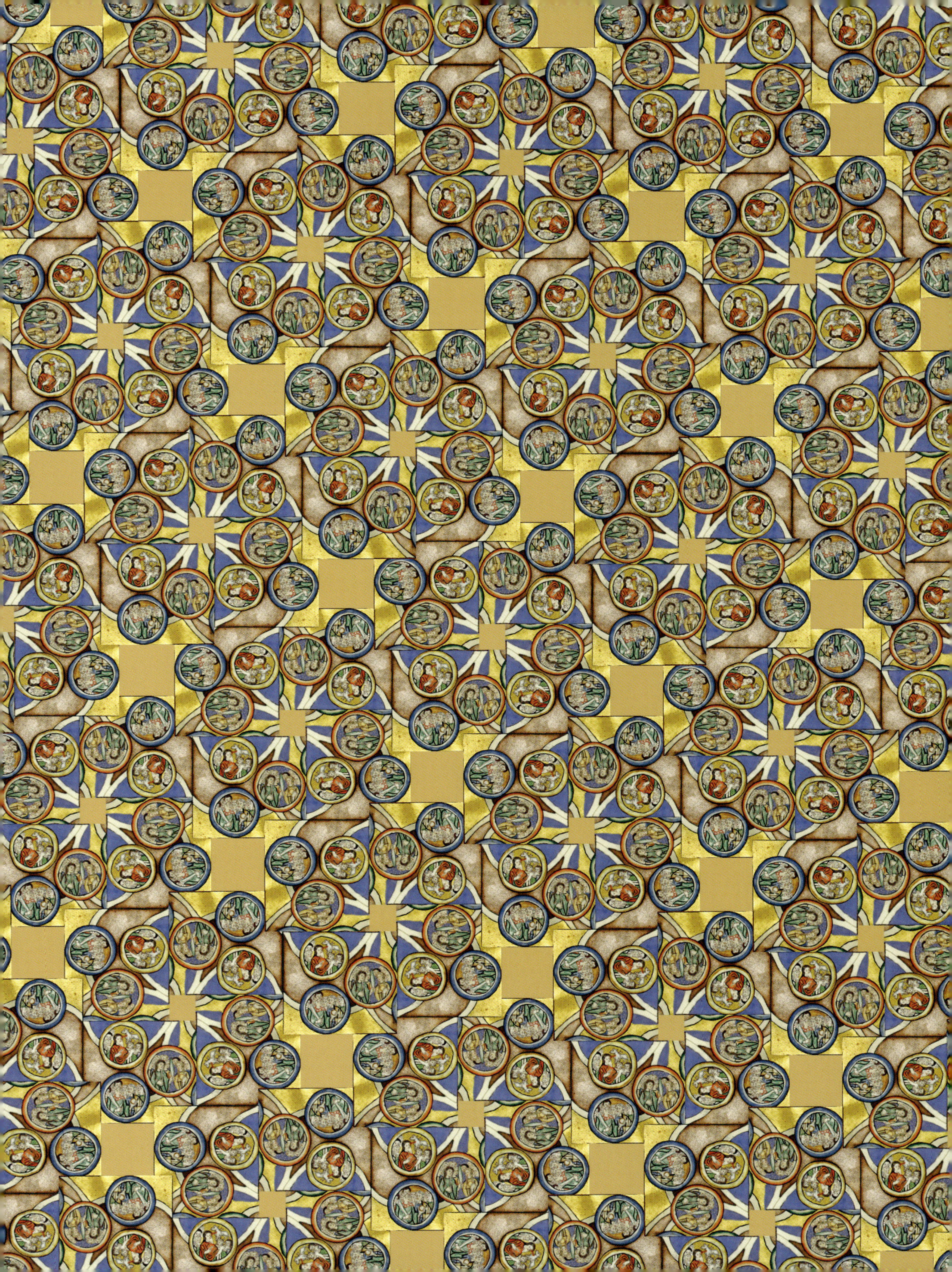

Viriditas

So too the one part towards the east bestows upon the middle zone a good sap and useful viridity, as too a person's sight, when directed as to the origin of brightness, supplies to that person [...] health in both body and soul (*LDO* II.1.3, p. 268).

For as water's moisture exists in the viridity of a tree, so the Son of God existed always in the Father until the predestined season of his humanity, when he became the food of life for all spiritual people (*LDO* II.1.19, p. 291).

At the moment of prayer, following the invocation of the Spirit, *viriditas* descends with a *fiery flash* on the Eucharistic offering. The *palest of curtains* has been opened and the warmth of the Father pervades the circle of the offering, *like the sun brightens anything its rays touch* (see p. 199). The power of the mystery cannot be expressed in words and in the image it is once again concealed in the fragments which, recomposed and multiplied, offer a complete vision of the chalice and a new design, in green and interwoven like a knot, representing the union between the divine and human dimension. The wonder of discovery and the beauty of the composition are a hymn to the vital force of the spirit (see pp. 154–155).

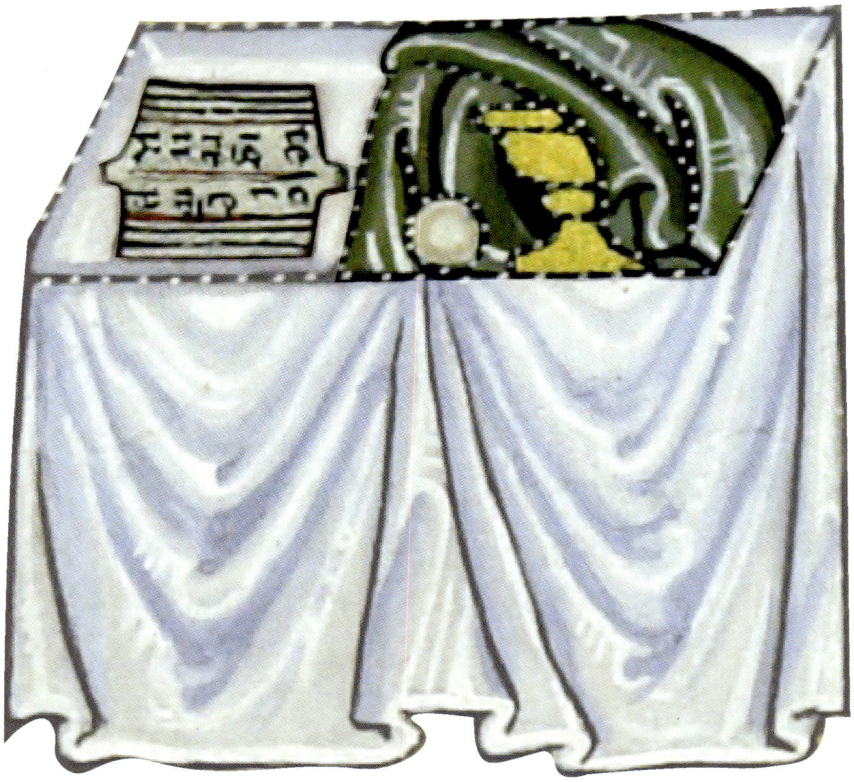

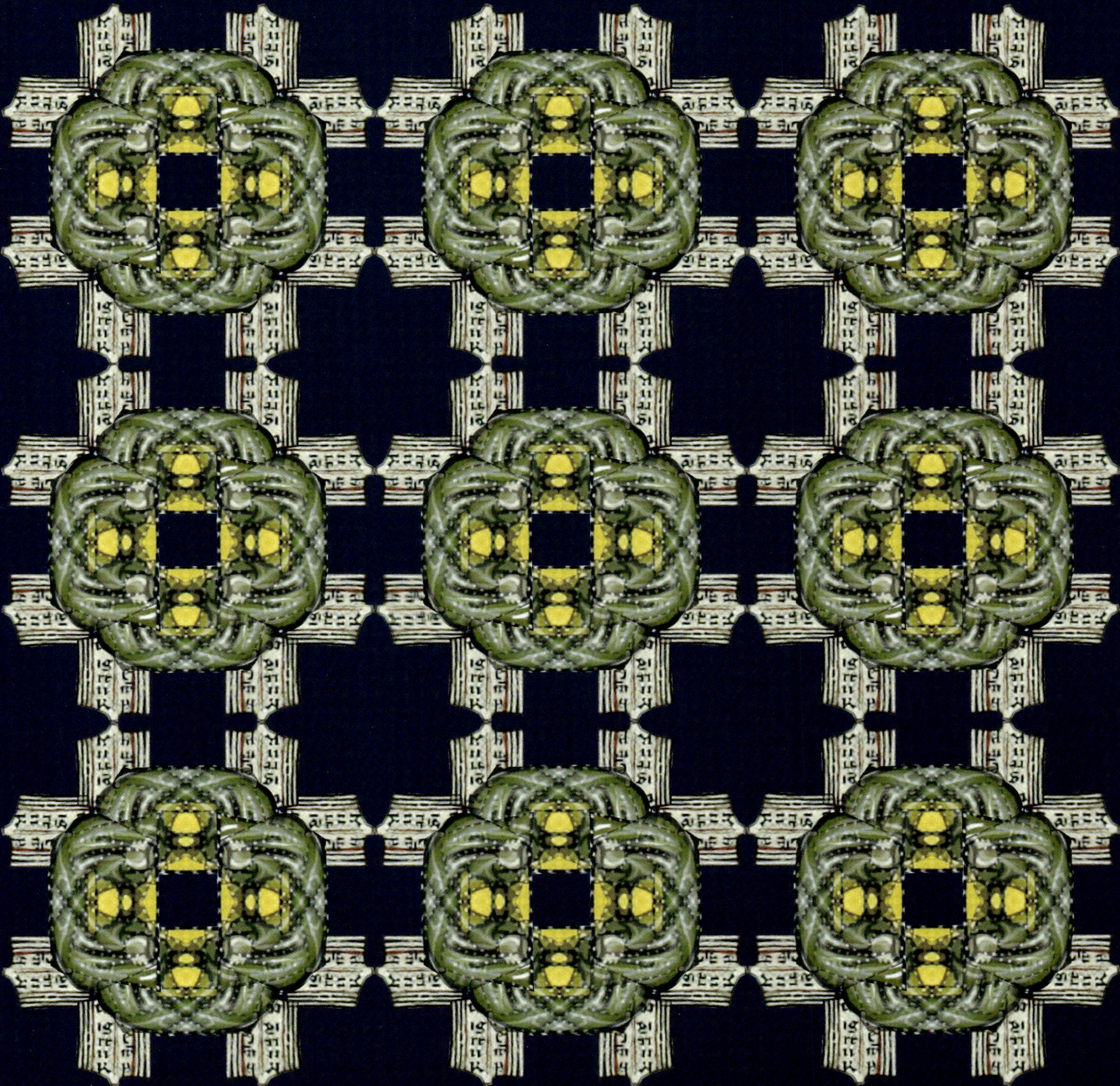

Living Stones

[My beloved children] are to me, indeed, the finest cut stones (*SC* III.8.8, p. 432).

For this you see all the virtues of God descending and ascending, laden down with stones and going with keen zeal to their work. [...] lucent virtues [...] they offer to God the heavenly works people have done with rejoicing, that the body of Christ may be perfected as quickly as possible in His faithful members (*SC* III.8.13, p. 436).

Praise reverberates in every stone of the architecture of the work. In the title *Scivias* is concealed the flowered cross of the seven gifts of the Spirit, in the splendid style of the *carmina figurata* by Rabano Mauro. The twenty-six visions are arranged in the form of a Greek cross, axis of conjunction between heaven and earth (see pp. 173–175).

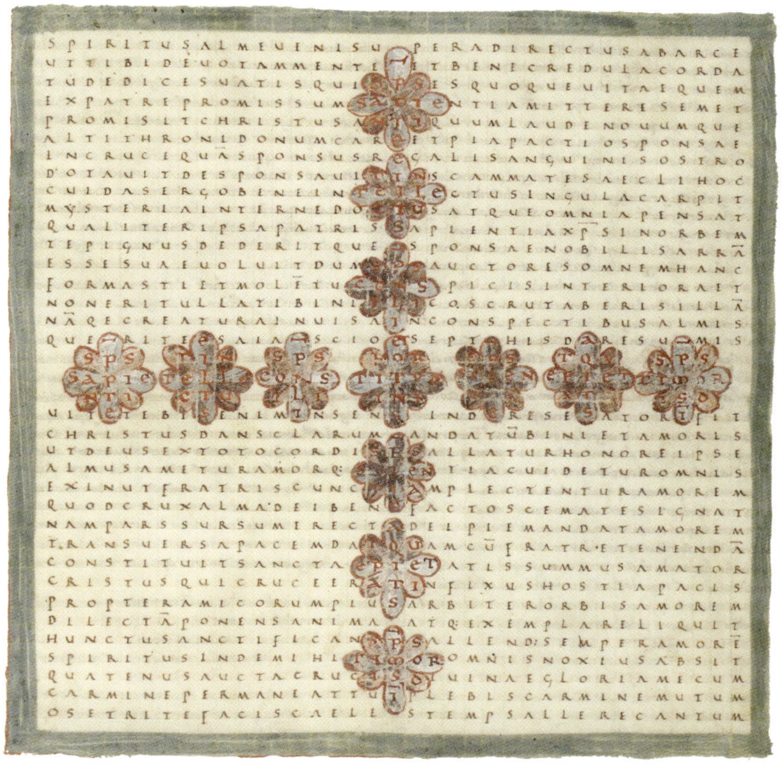

S C I V I A S

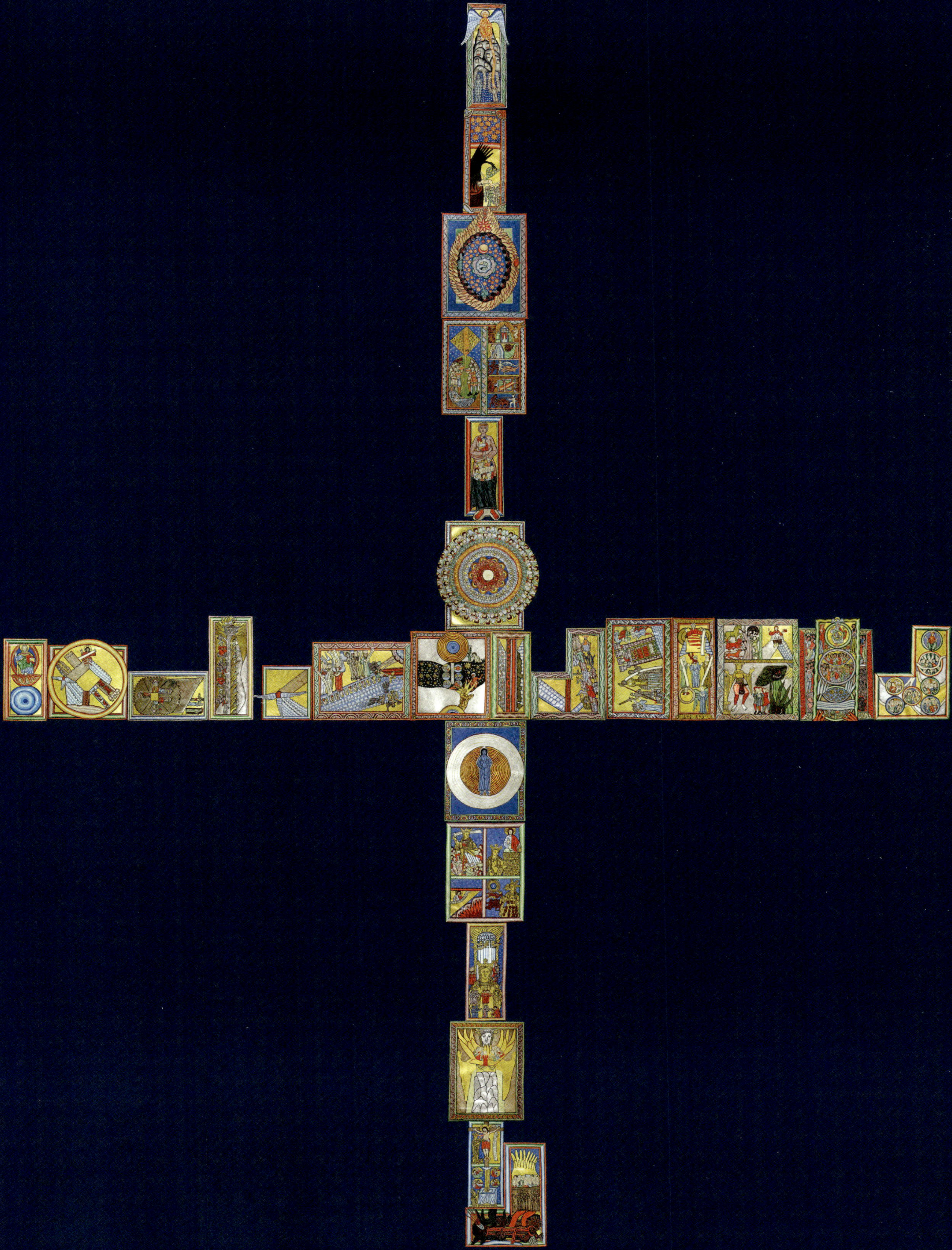

Heavenly City

"And he carried me away in the Spirit to a mountain great and high, and showed me the Holy City, Jerusalem, coming down out of heaven from God." (Rev 21, 10–11)
The Holy Spirit lifts the human spirit upward to the mountain of heavenly desires, that it may clearly see the works to be done in the Spirit, the great works of God (*SC* III.10.31, p. 488).

For you, O streets of Jerusalem, will then shine with the purest gold which is the blood of the saints (*SC* III.11.16, p. 498).

The numbers of the chapters, living stones of the cathedral, create, through a complex numerical dance, the geometric form of the triple wall, image of the celestial city. A prayer path is revealed by the numbers, whose arrangement and sum disclose the reference number of the four psalms with which humanity entrusts itself to God, embarking on the journey and worshipping him (see pp. 168–172).

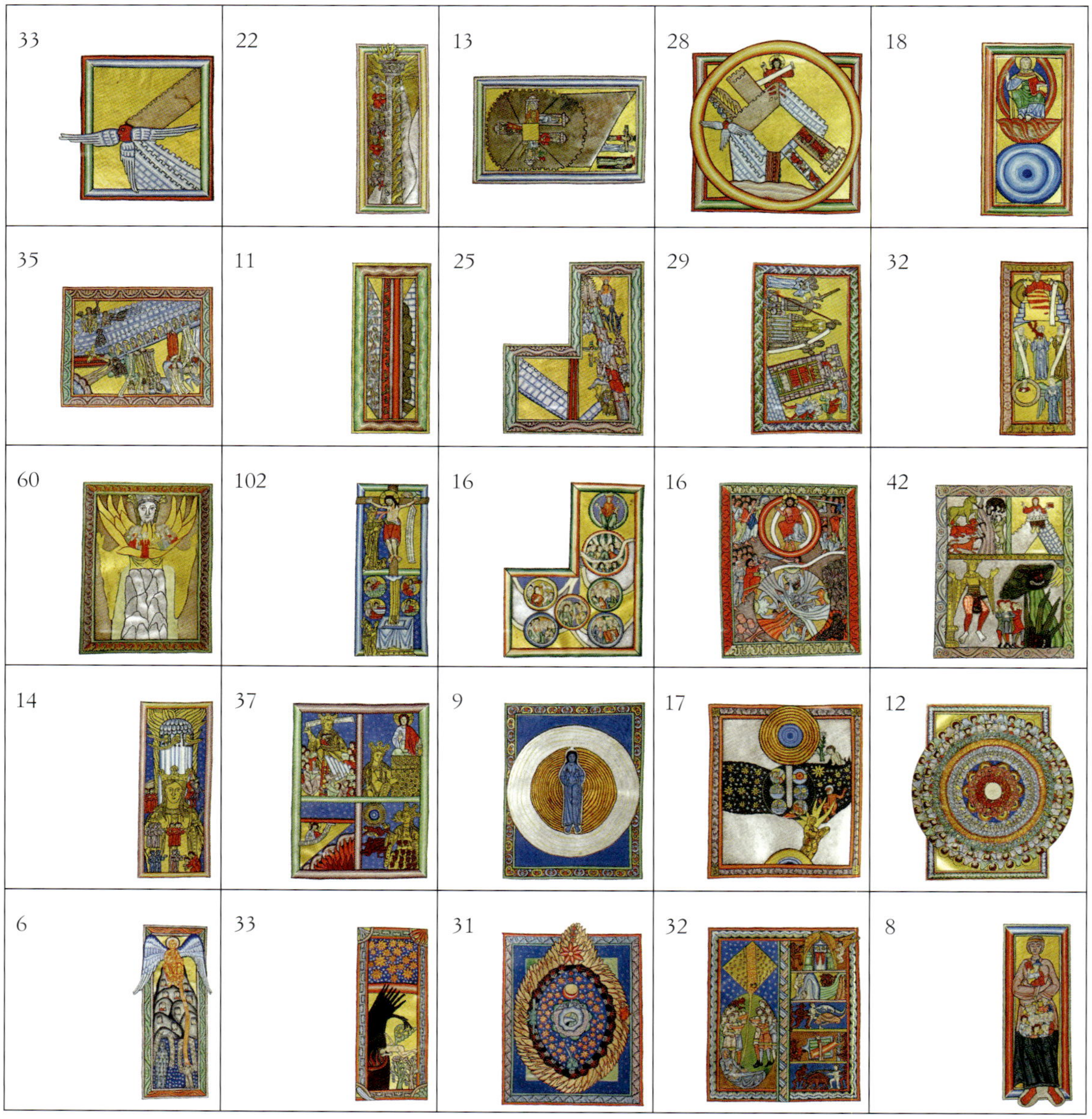

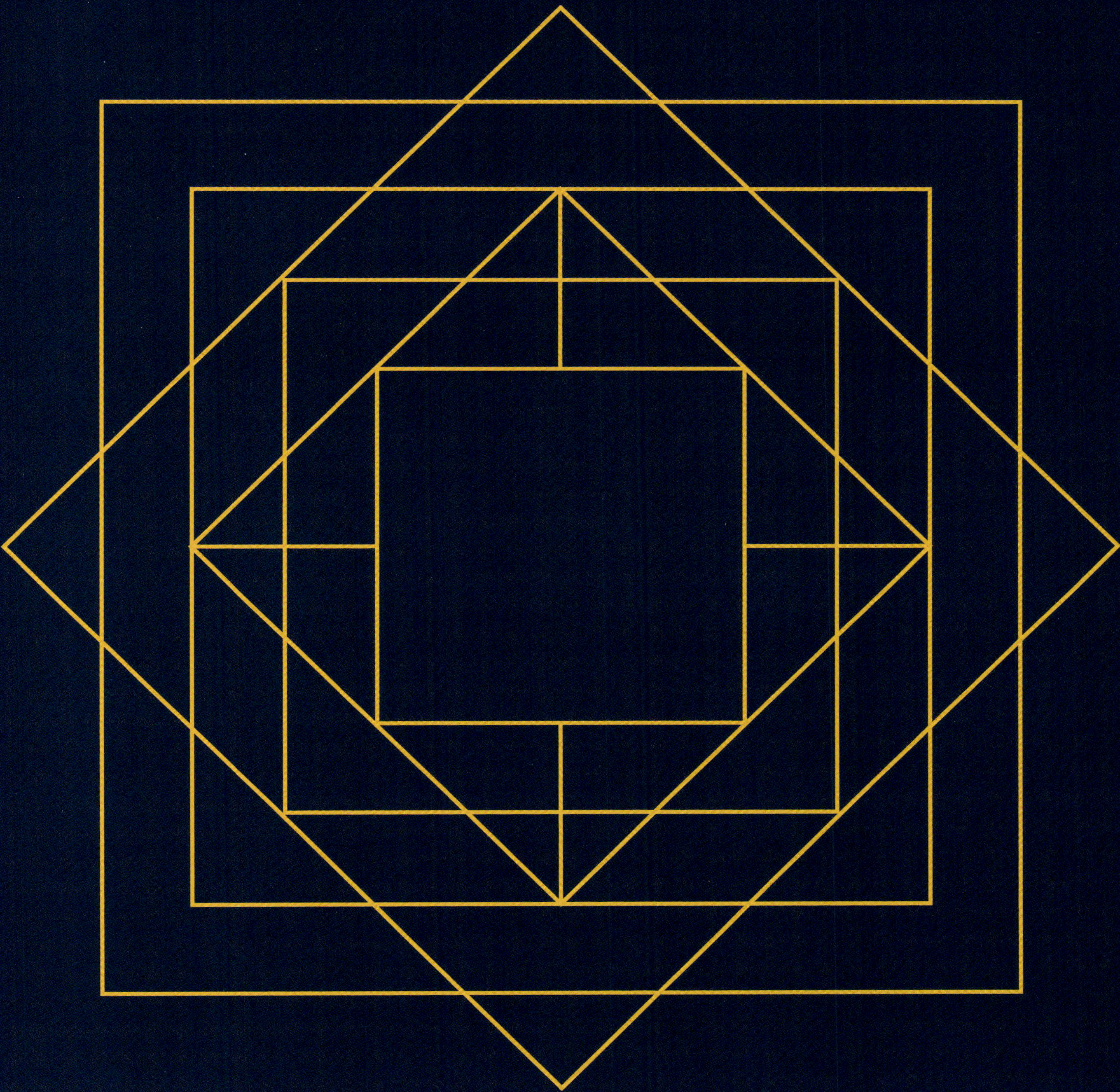

Laus Trinitati
quae sonus et vita
ac creatrix omnium in vita ipsorum est.
Et quae laus angelicae turbae
et mirus splendor arcanorum,
quae hominibus ignota sunt, est,
et quae in omnibus vita est.

Praise to the Trinity—the sound and life
and creativity of all within their life,
the praise of the angelic host
and wondrous, brilliant splendor hid,
unknown to human minds, it is,
and life within all things.

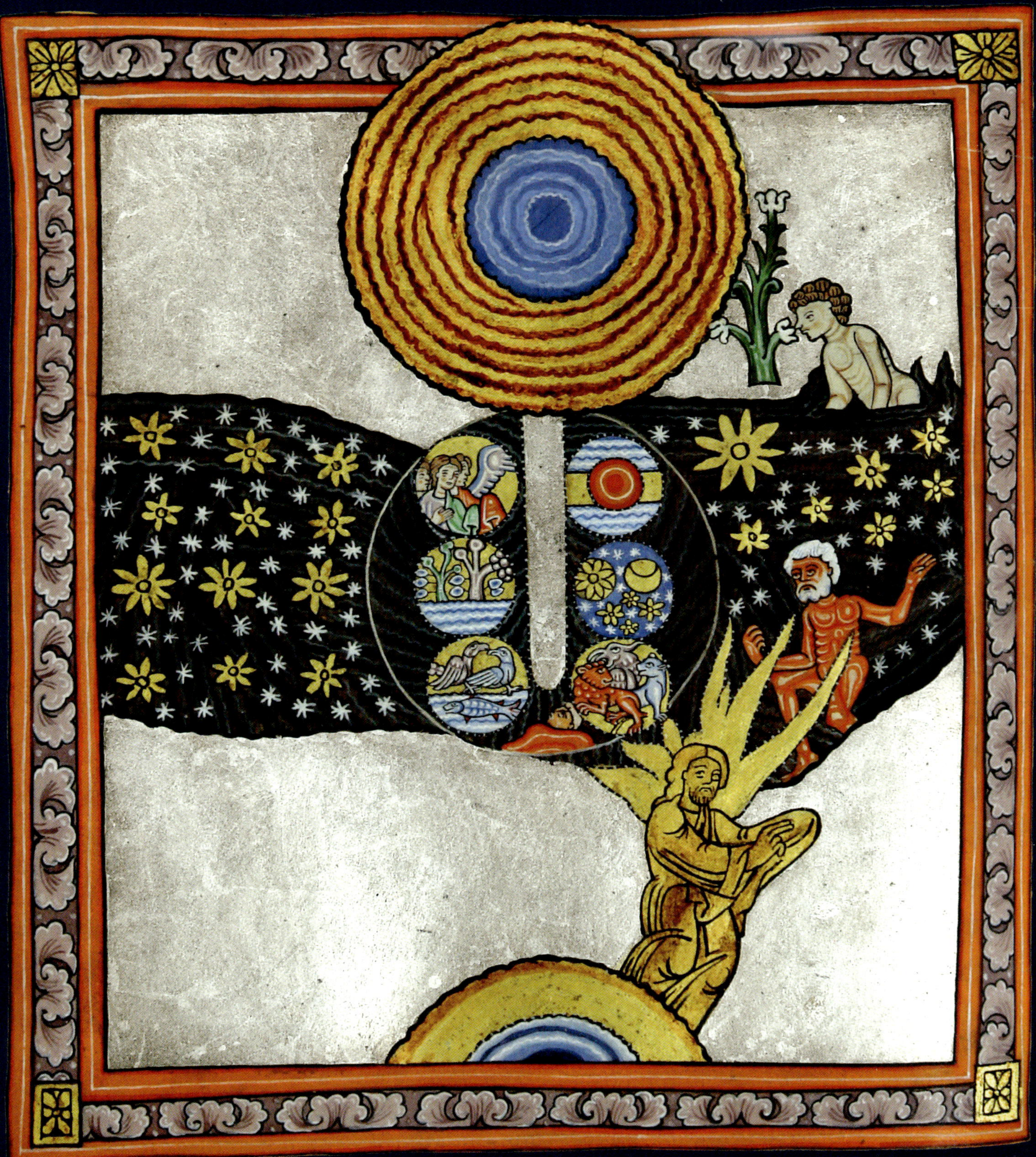

Sound

I am also rationality, possessing the breath of the resounding Word through which every created thing was made (*LDO* I.1.2, p. 34).

But both in the intellect and in the will reason stands forth as the loud sound of the soul, which makes known every work of God or Man. For sound carries words on high, as the wind lifts the eagle so that it can fly. Thus the soul utters the sound of reason in the hearing and the understanding of humanity, that its powers may be understood and its every work brought to perfection (*SC* I.4.23, pp. 122–123).

In the heart of *Charity* the *resounding word* of God expands in concentric soundwaves, giving life to creation, the *globe of dark air*. In the six days of the time of the genesis he instilled harmonious sound and life in every human being. The symphonic soul, *symphonialis est anima*, vibrates in unison with the energy of fire from which it originated. On the journey, blessedness descends on the soul when, imitating the virtues, it moves in accord with the body and with the other souls, achieving concord through shared togetherness, through the harmony of the symphony of hearts as one (see pp. 210–212).

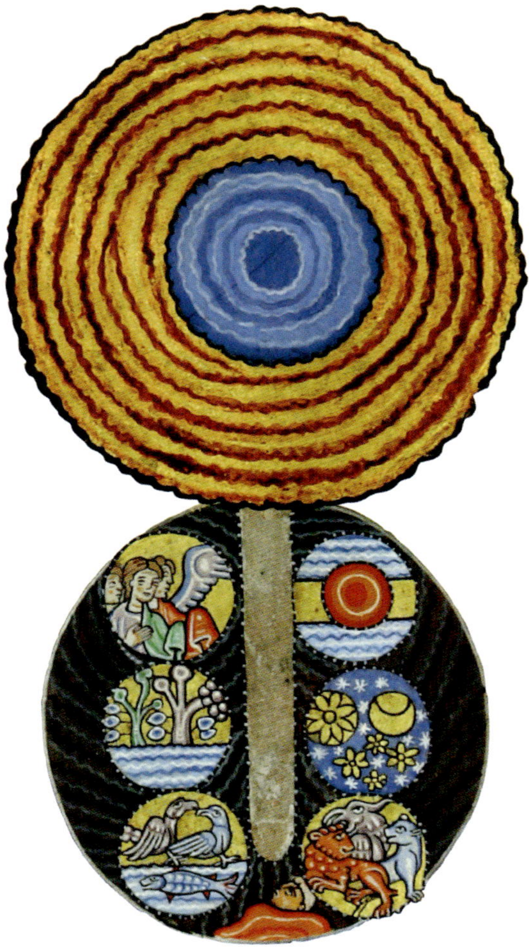

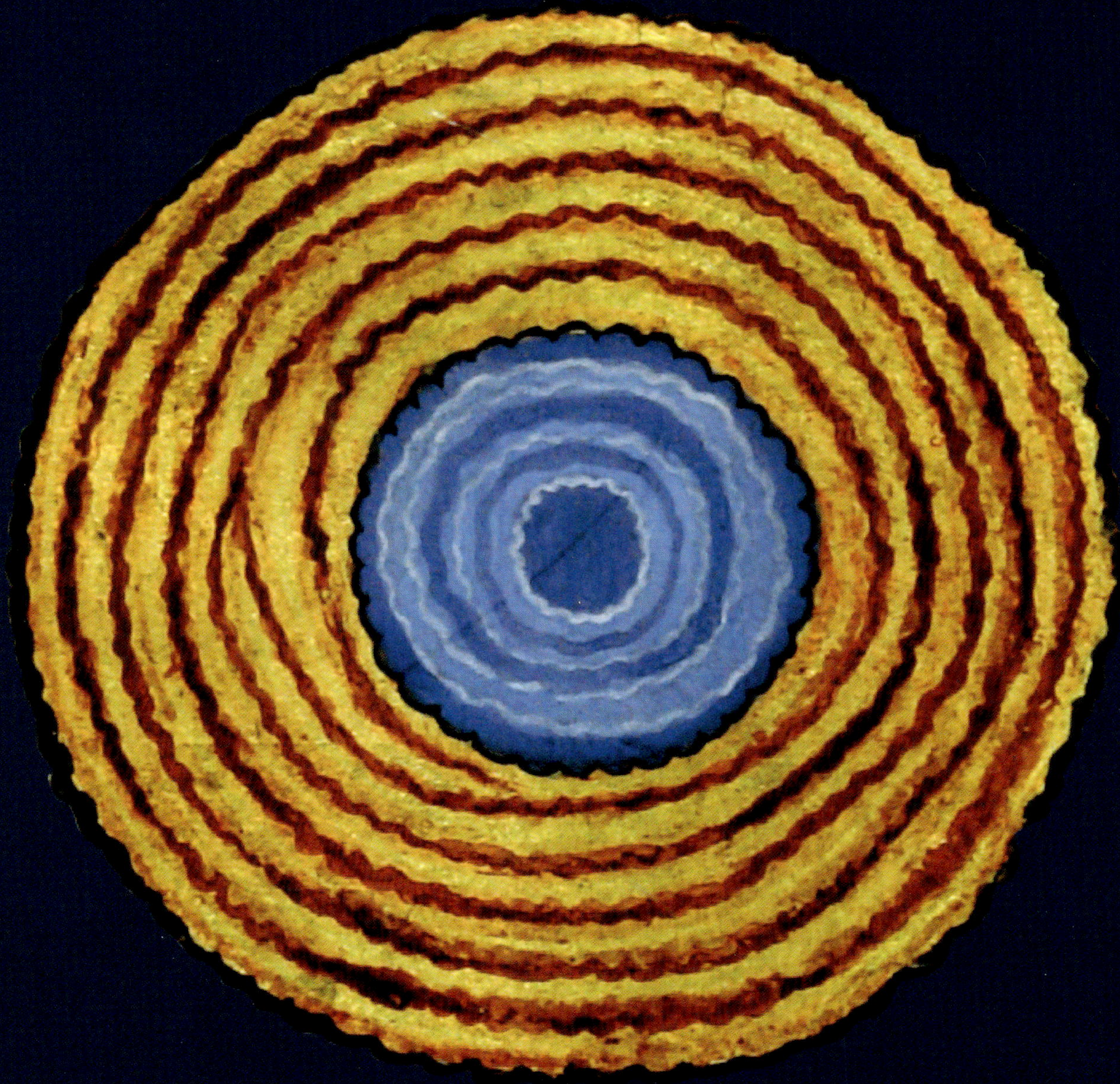

Way

O my dearest children, who are rising like the dawn, and who must burn in charity like the sun; run and make haste, dearest ones, in the way of truth, which is the light of the world, Jesus Christ, the Son of God (*SC* III.8.8, p. 433).

But one who does strong works of salvation, running in the way of truth, obtains the upwelling fountain of glory, by which he prepares himself most precious riches on earth and in Heaven (*SC* I.1.6, p. 69).

Indeed, the soul, which is a breath from God, possesses a rushing course, as too wisdom encircled the compass of heaven with a rushing course. Thus, with the seven gifts of the Holy Spirit and the five senses, a person begins and perfects all his works through the soul, as too the seventh month ripens all the earth's fruits (*LDO* I.4.98, p. 231).

And so, from these sighs and tears the viridity of repentance surges up within that person (*LDO* I.4.32, p. 162).

The sun in the egg marks the east, destination of humanity's journey. In the vision of the *Liber Divinorum Operum*, the body of the world is lying on its side, just like the egg, and the east and the wings of the figure are on the left of the image. This is the time of repentance, of awaiting forgiveness, which leads to the last stage on the *via della virginitas*, of following the divine calling that leads to the *globe of reddish fire* of the Spirit. At the end of the journey in Purgatory the figure will be seen with wings, and the fire above it, like the egg with the sun above. And just as the egg on its side was the image of an eye, the winged figure on its side, as can be seen in the vision, is the shape of an eyeball, meaning that an inner vision, illuminated by the white light of the east, is necessary for the gift of *viriditas* (viridity) to fecundate the human soul and meet God's gaze.

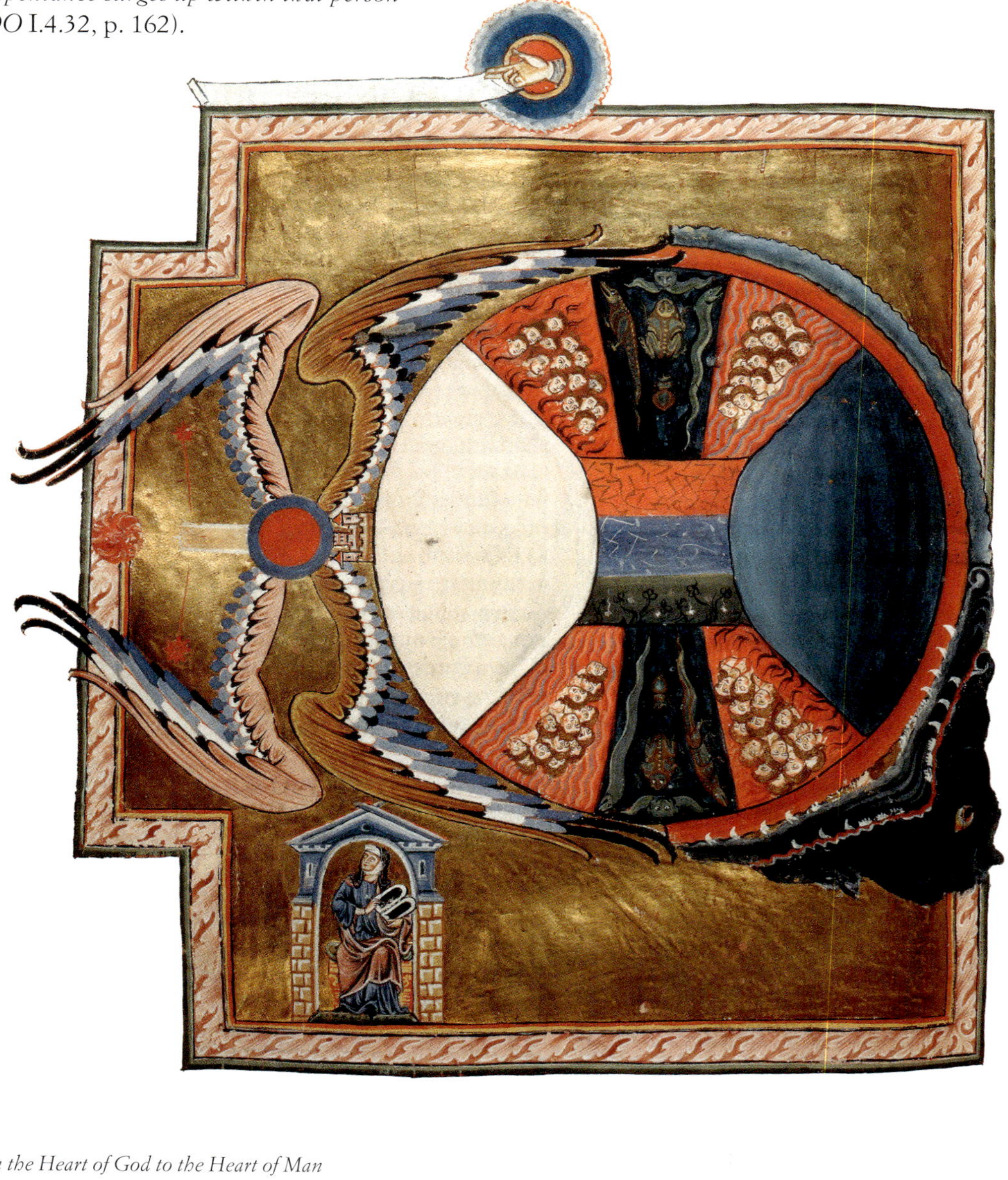

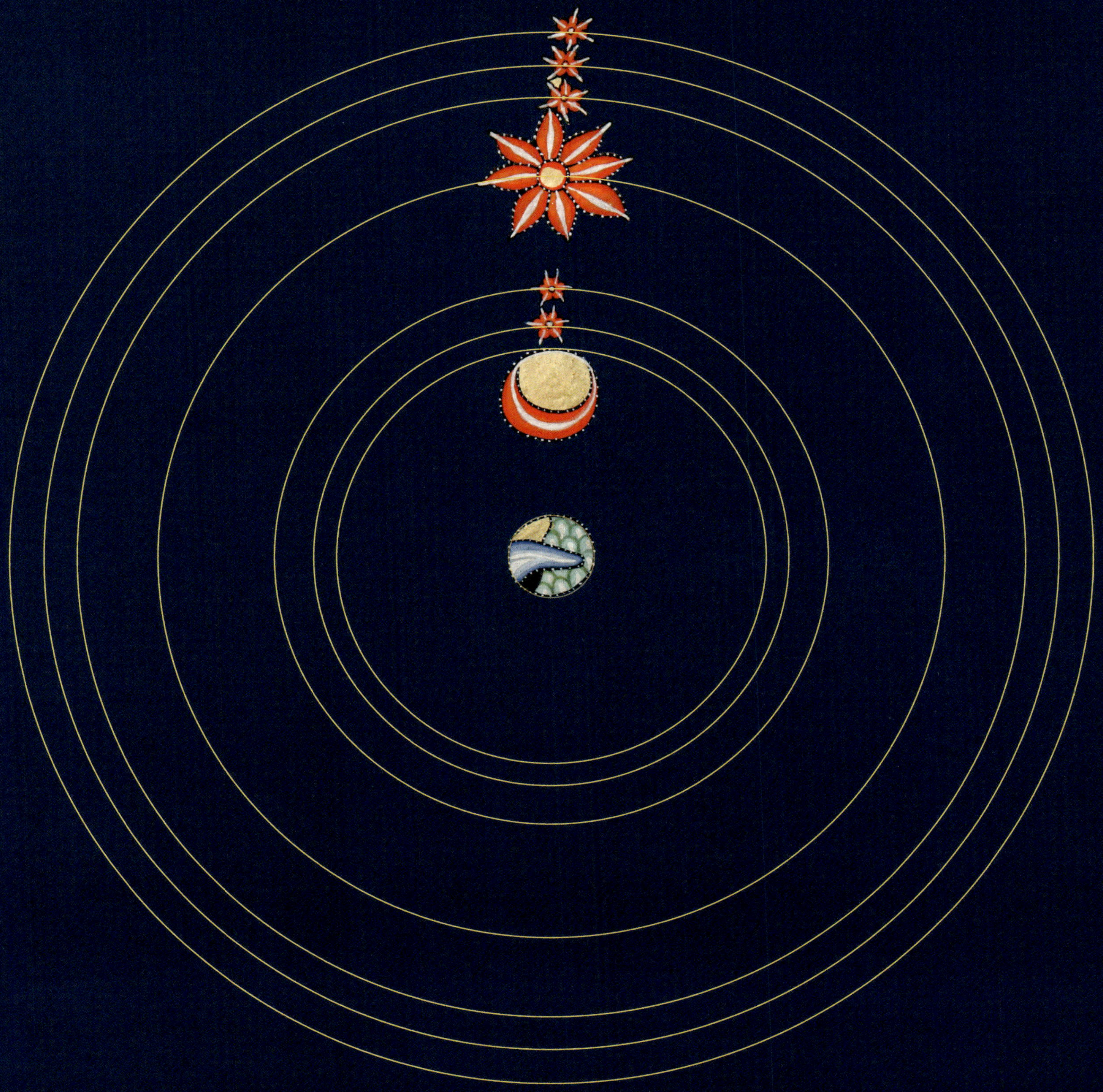

Celestial Vault

Therefore, God also called the firmament heaven, because it excels all things and tells ever of his glory. When a person looks upon it, he cannot fully comprehend what it is, because neither can a person perfectly comprehend God, whom he nevertheless sees in faith. But a person will not see heaven, which is God's abode, unless he is first made wholly spiritual, for it surpasses his sense perception and knowledge (*LDO* II.1.24, p. 297).

Accordingly, the soul, which, sent by God, descends into the body invisibly and secretly, causes a person to recognize God through faith, to look up to heaven and do heavenly deeds (*LDO* I.4.49, p. 176).

From the center of the sphere, humanity begins its journey through the four elements of the firmament: the *earth* from which man was made, the *water* of benediction, encircled from the *white skin* of innocence, the *air* of faith, the black *fire* of darkness and the *fire* of divine light.

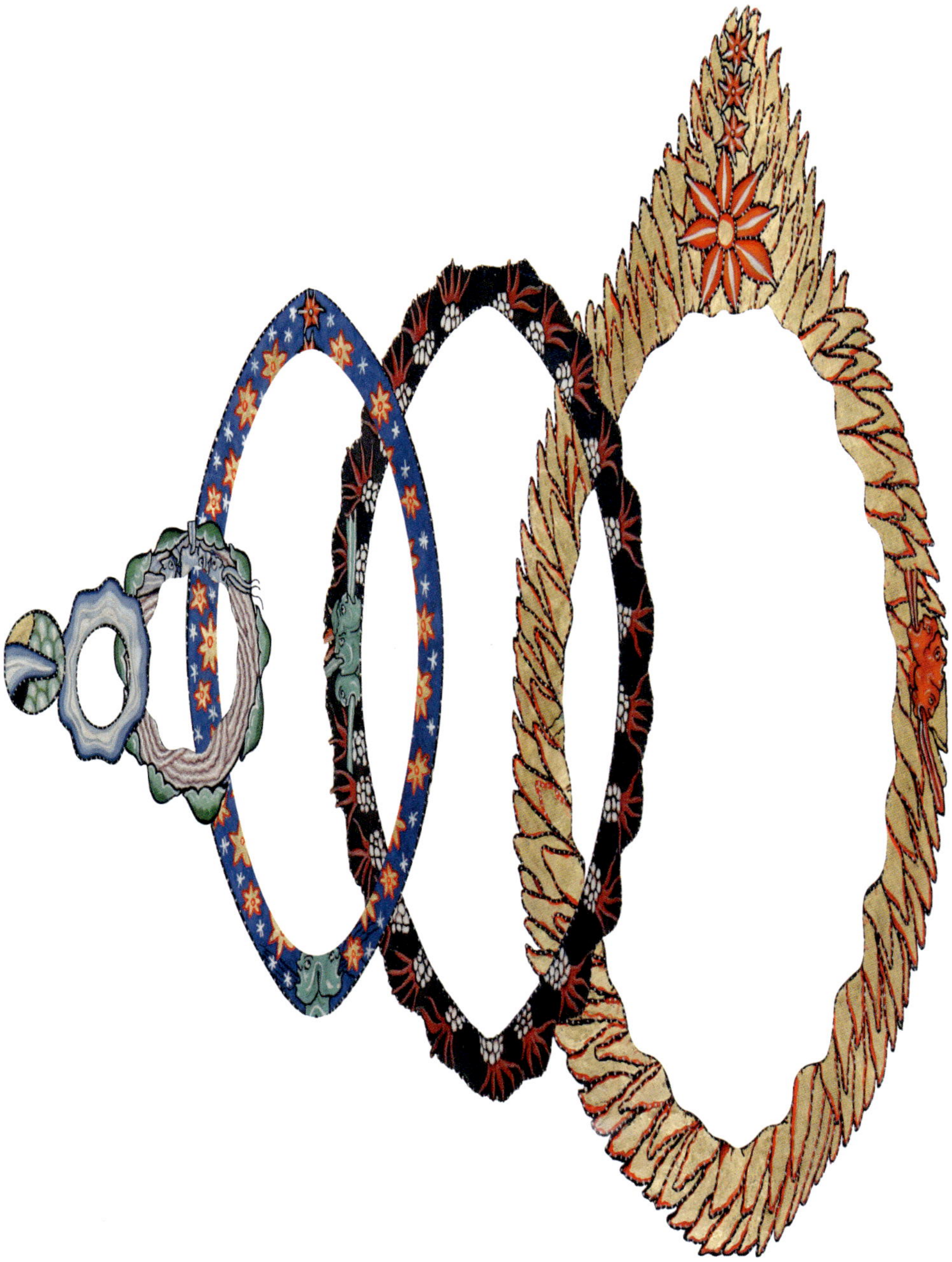

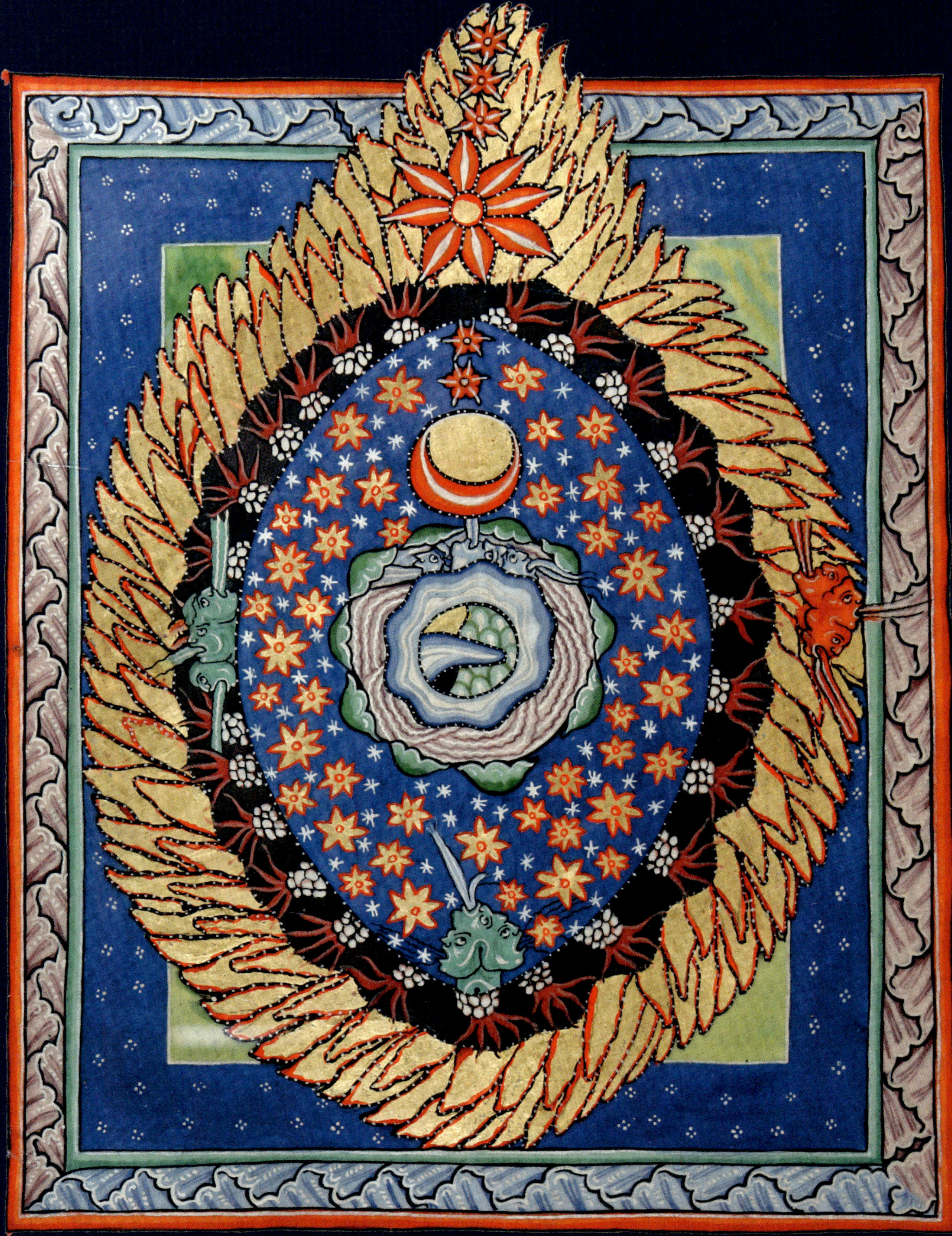

Light

God indeed, who made everything just described, is the unique Life from which all life breathes as a ray from the sun. He is that Fire from which every fire that provides for happiness is kindled, as sparks come forth from fire. How would it be fitting if nothing alive hewed to this Life, and this Fire neither warmed nor illumined anything? And how would it seem for no life nor any brilliance to come forth from the Godhead, which was Life before the ages? What good would it be if Light kindled by Fire gave light to nothing, since fire does not hide its light, nor does the sun bury its rays? For God is that Life through which the angels' multitude was kindled, like a spark coming forth from fire. So it would be unseemly for that Life not to shine brilliantly—and that brilliance is unfailing, for no death can exist within it (*LDO* II.1.14, p. 282).

After passing through the fire of the firmament, humanity continues its journey into the sphere and crosses the nine Heavenly Hosts—*angels, archangels, virtues, authorities, principalities, dominions, thrones, seraphim, cherubim*—until it reaches the center of the divine light.

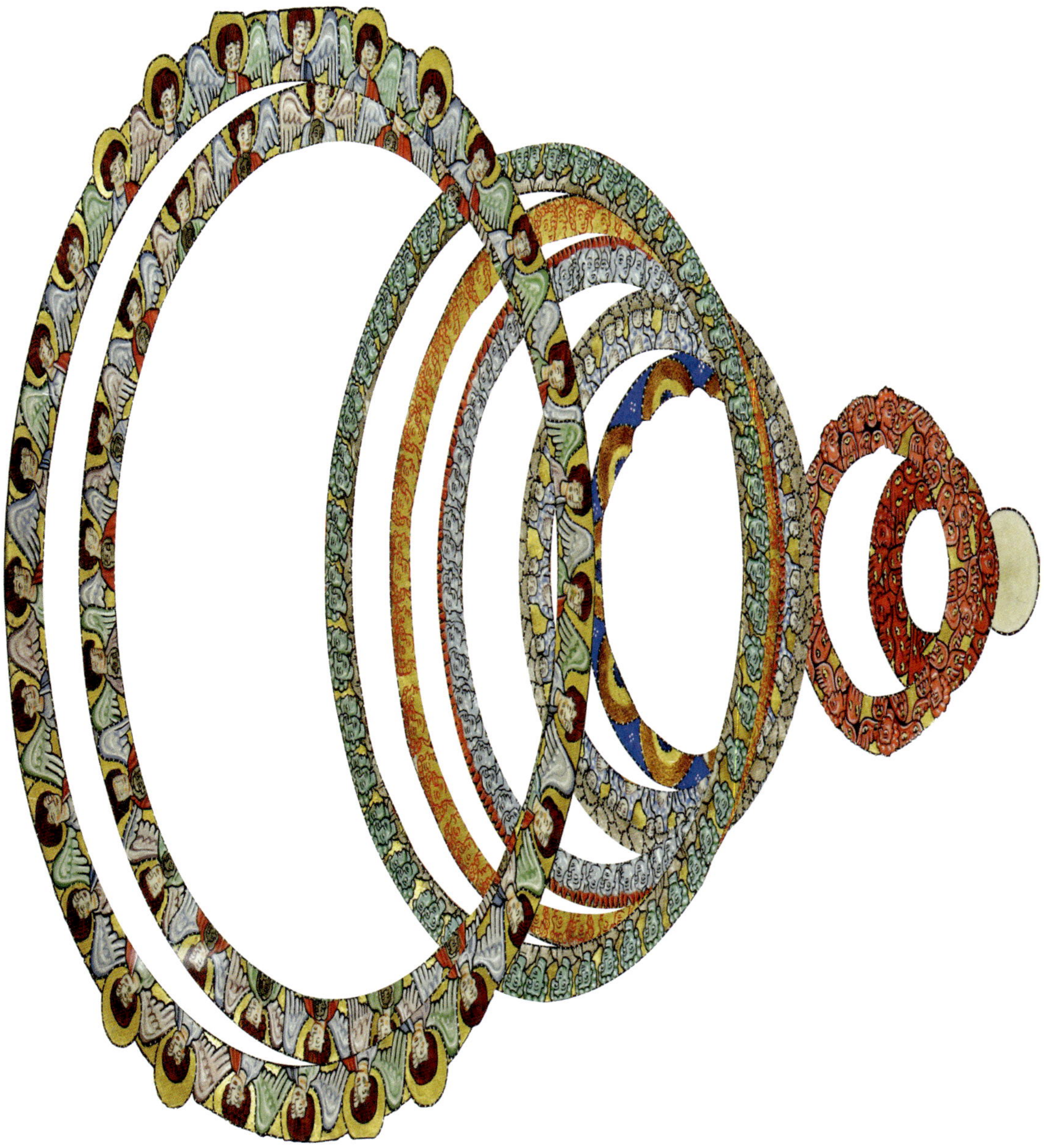

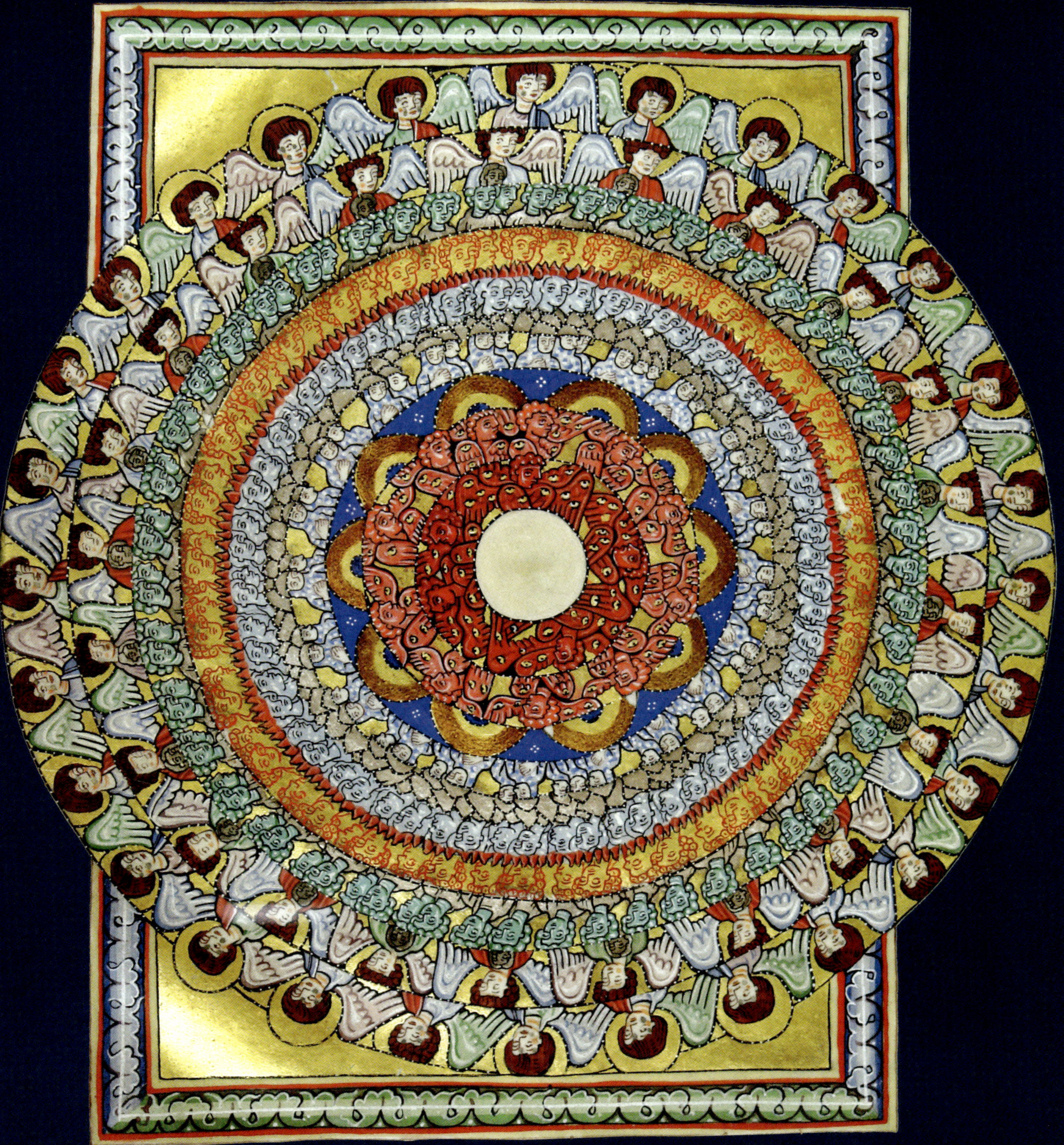

Door

My Son, Who cleaves to Me in brightest warmth of love as the comb to the honey (*SC* II.3.26, p. 179).

He came from the heart of the Father and the womb of a virgin (*SC* III.4.8, p. 360).

The Word [...] shone forth within time as a Flower, visible as a human being and offering good understanding to all humans by His words (*SC* III.8.15, p. 438).

After entering the light, humanity meets the three persons of the Trinity: the silvery white *Father*, the *Spirit,* the color of reddish fire, and the *Son*, man of sapphire blue; they are the door connecting the visible and invisible worlds.

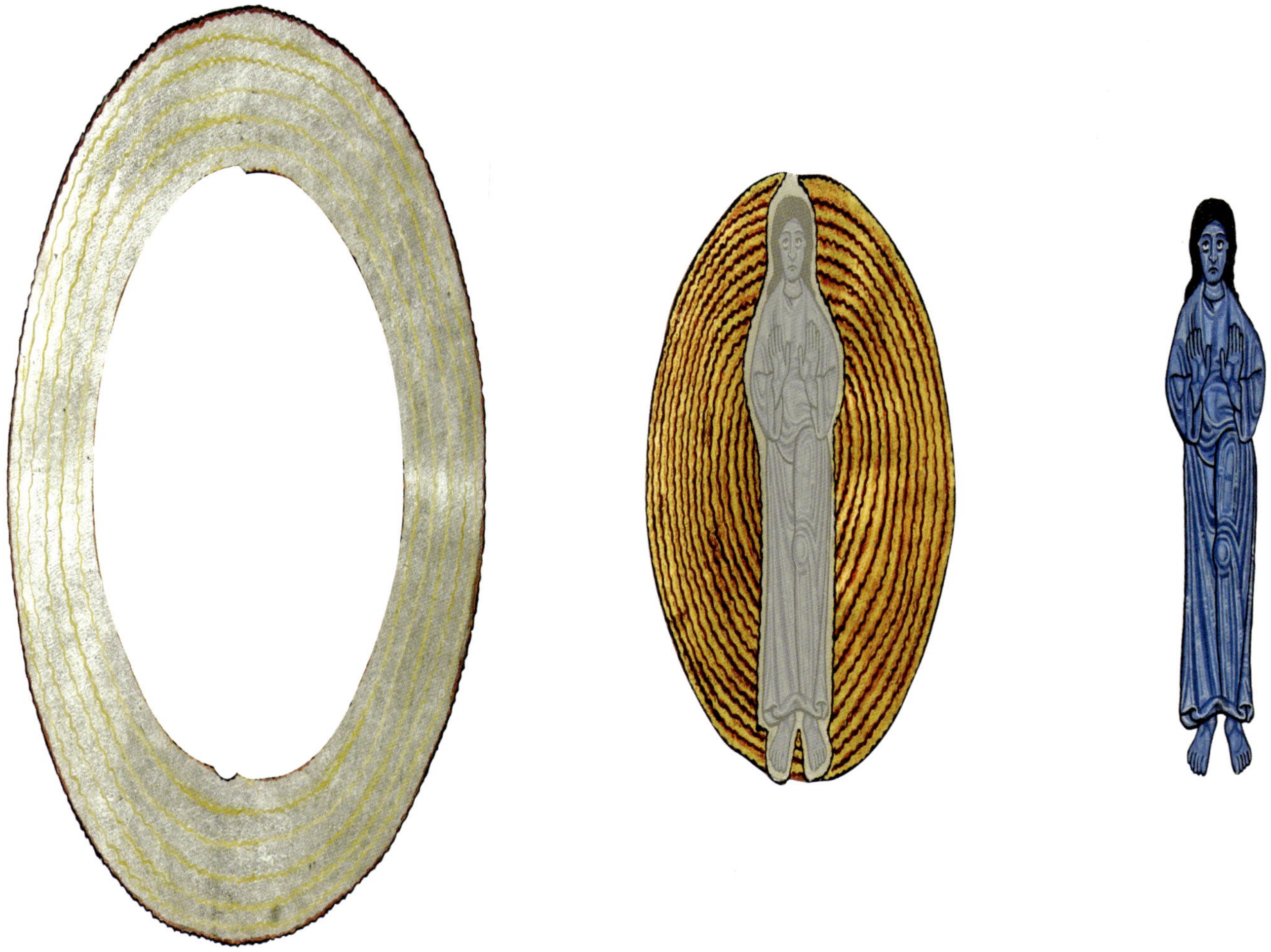

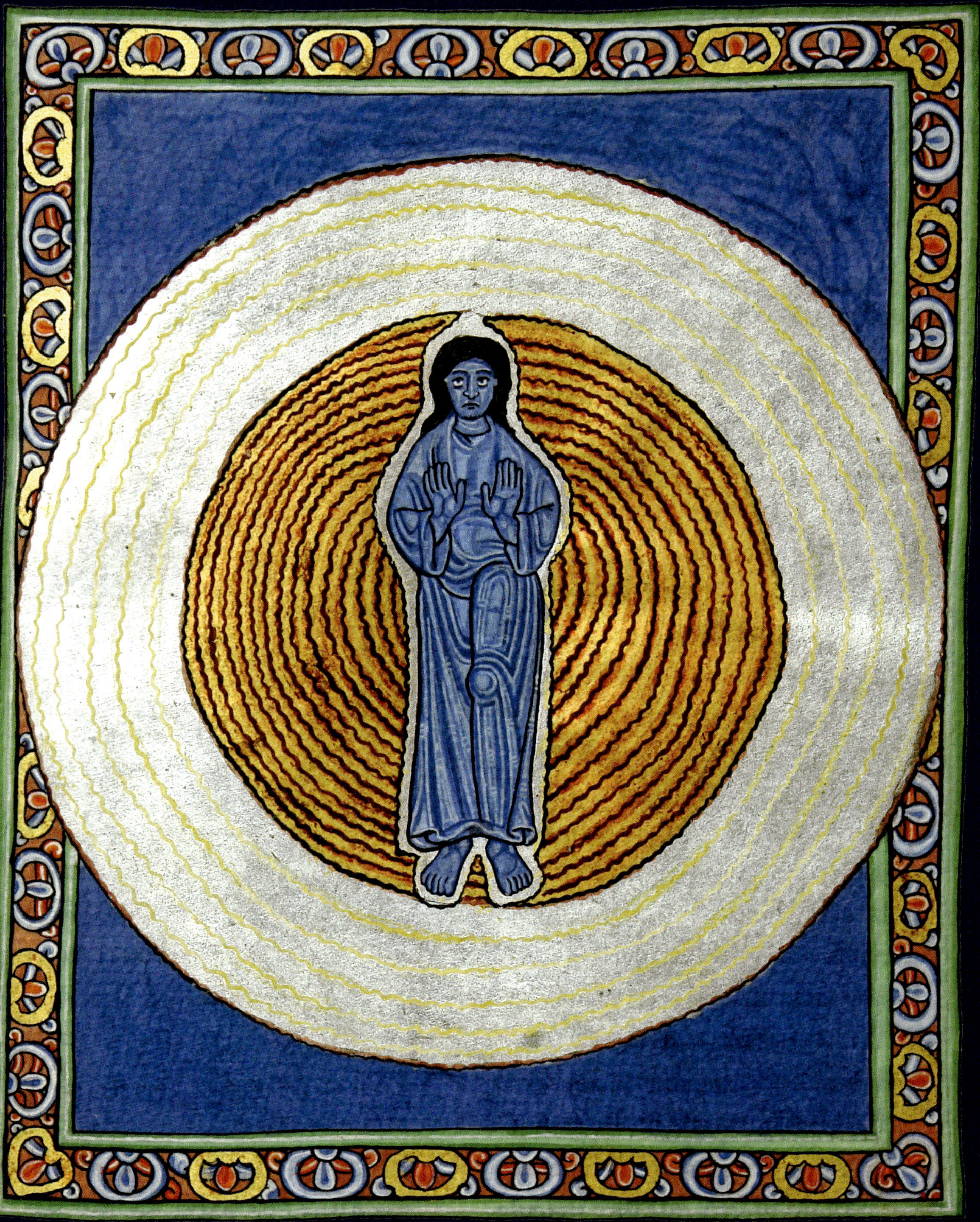

From Heaven to Earth, from Earth to Heaven

Thus Man was lifted up above the heavens because through the Son of God, God appeared in Man and Man in God (*SC* I.2.32, p. 89).

Christ, Son of God and Son of Man, is the door of light that opens up a pathway through time and space that connects heaven and earth, historical time and eternal time.

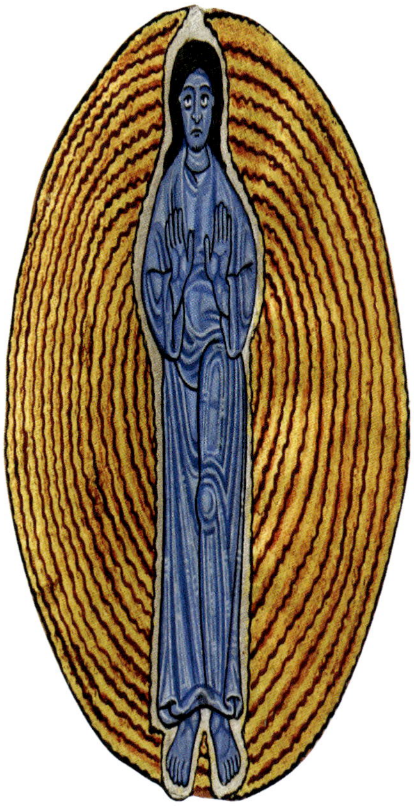

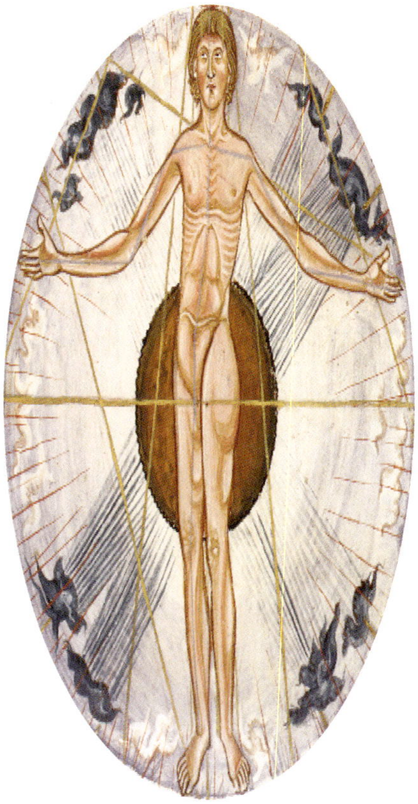

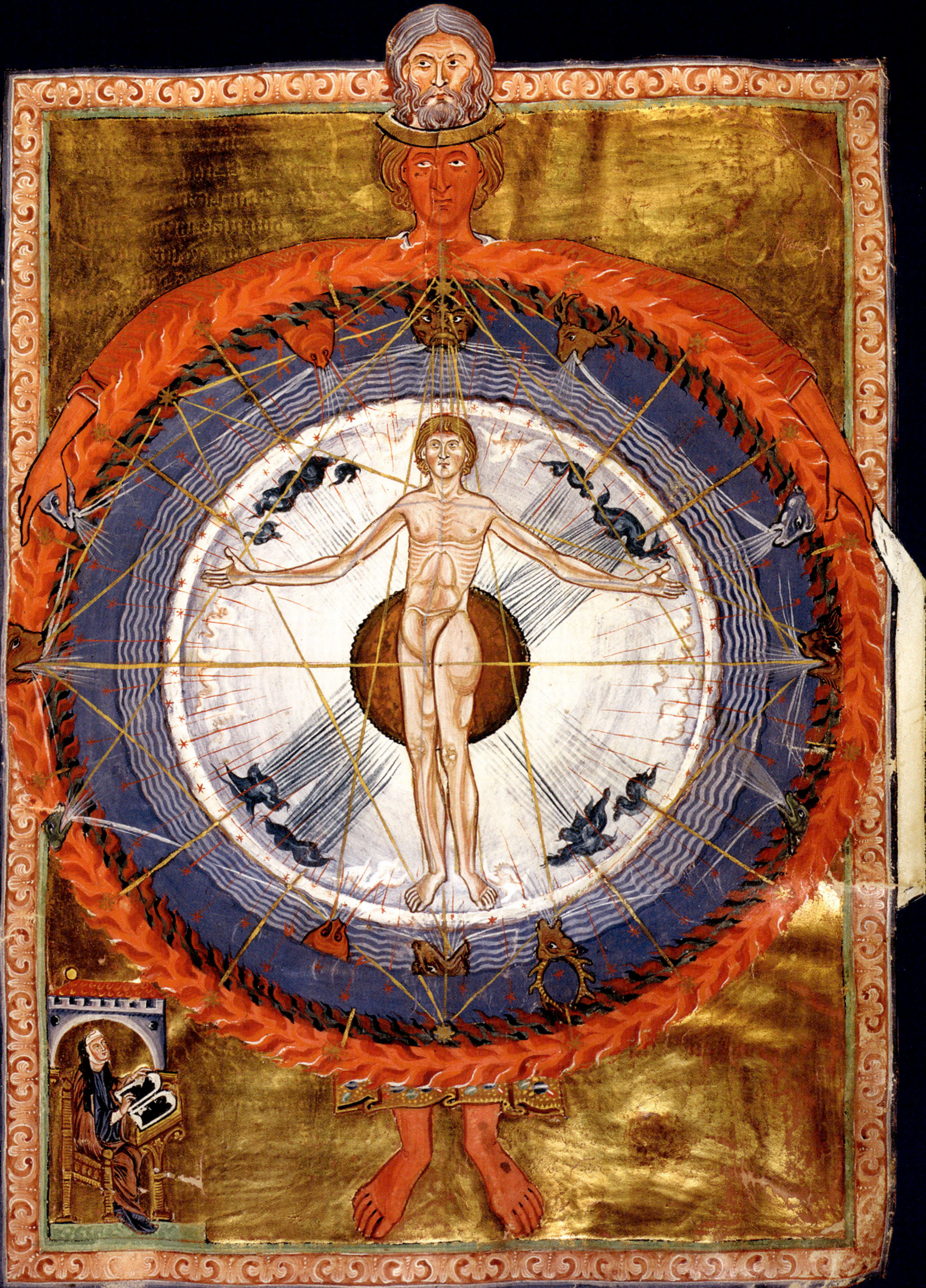

Journey Through Space and Time

God himself is that living fire through which souls breathe—God who was before the beginning and exists too as the beginning and entire course of time (*LDO* III.5.2, p. 418).

In the "time machine" journey each of the three spheres—the firmament, the Heavenly Hosts, the Trinity—is shown as it surrounds and is surrounded by the others. Everything is part of a single space, a sphere, in which moving through time evokes the mystery of the trinitarian dance. Every soul is called upon to experience this journey in the flow of life, until it perceives that the time and space of eternity, image of blessedness, exist in every moment (see p. 218).

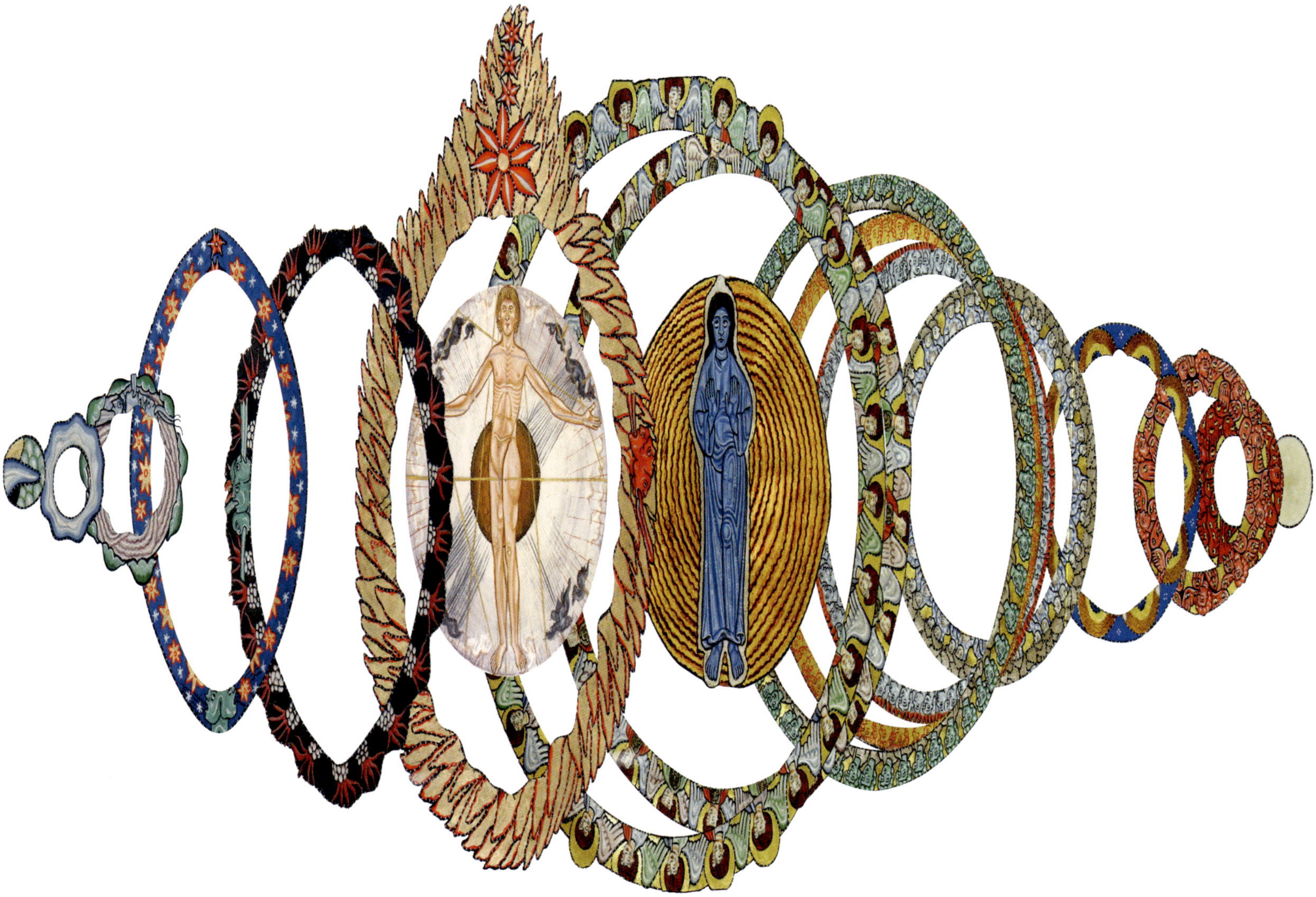

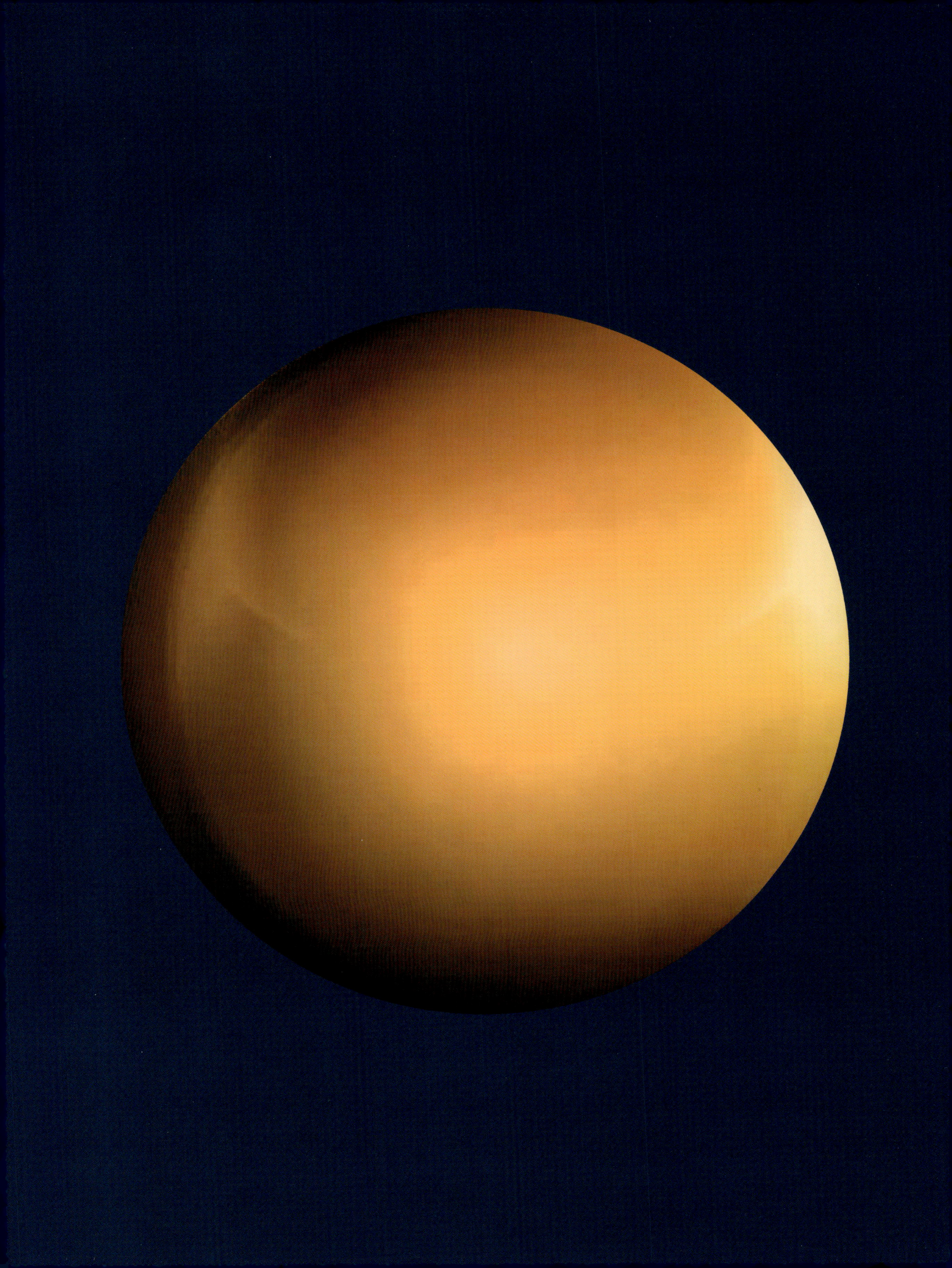

Hildegard

And so the Word was incarnate, and the whole world then wondered—and to this miracle the prophets' tongues swiftly crossed the world when they affirmed that to the lands he would come to earth, the most splendid among the sons of men (*LDO*, III.2,9, p. 891).

[Man] finds that it is not enough to have faith in God, and so builds virtues that rise higher; and so he grows, like a flourishing palm tree, from virtue to virtue, and by these virtues his righteous faith is exalted and adorned as bulwarks do a city (*SC* III.2.26, p. 338).

O lovely faces who look on the face of God and build in the dawn (*SC* III.13.7, p. 528).

Hildegard was the first to make this journey, while experiencing life and visions. As she starts out along the ways she depicts herself in her study, writing with a stylus on three tablets of green wax; at the end, her face corresponds with that of the Virgin in the central circle of the *Symphonia*, her lips are colored red, and the stylus becomes a green quill, which she dips into the red blood of life in the chalice.

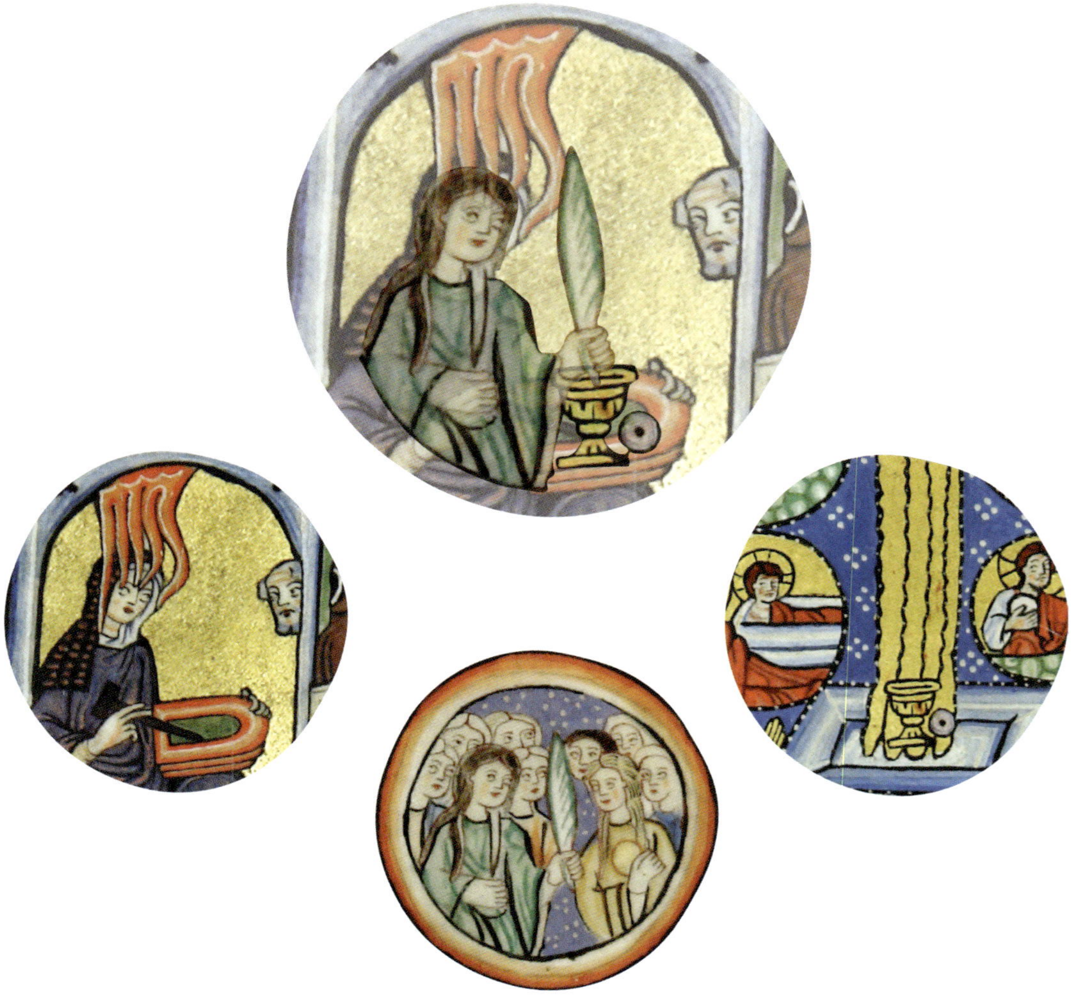

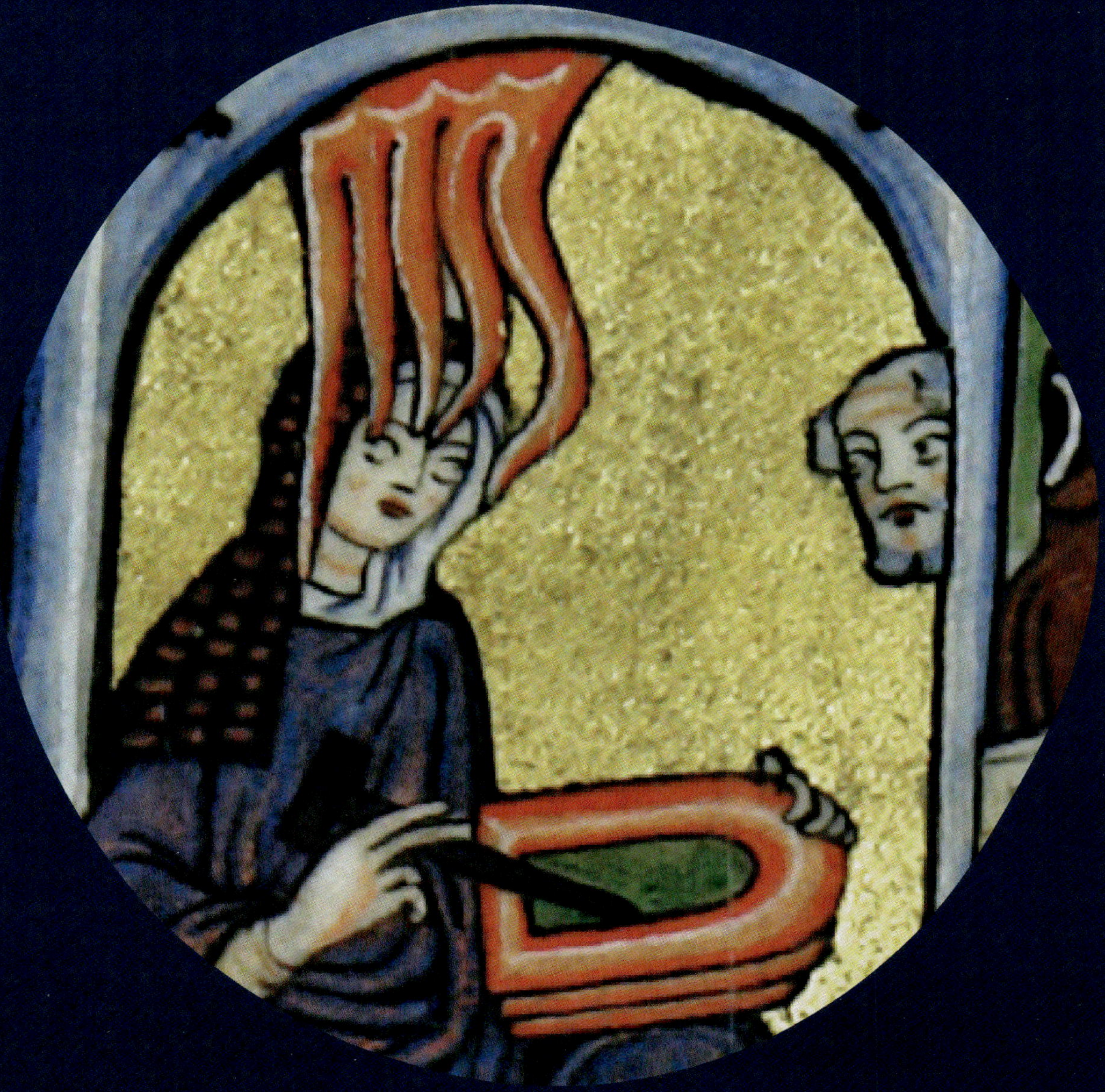

The Sun and the Moon

And, as you see, when all these things are over the elements *will shine out with the greatest brightness and beauty [...]. And* fire, *without its raging heat, will blaze like the dawn,* air *without density will be completely limpid;* water *without its power to flood or drown will stand transparent and calm, and* earth *without shakiness or roughness will be firm and level. And so all these will be transformed into great calm and beauty.*
And the sun and moon and stars *will* sparkle *in the firmament like precious stones set in gold, with great glory and brilliance; and they will no longer restlessly revolve in orbit so as to distinguish day from night. For the world will have ended and they will have become immutable; and from that time on there will be no darkness, and day will be perpetual* (*SC* III.12.15–16, p. 520).

Indeed, man and woman are thus commingled, as one work exists through another—for man would not be called man without woman, nor would woman be called woman without man [...] And man signifies the divinity, while woman the humanity of the Son of God (*LDO* I.4.100, p. 238).

At the end of the journey Hildegard's soul is touched by wisdom and is revealed in the mirror. The green column of the study corresponds to the green column of the tabernacle of the soul. Now Hildegard can take flight. It is the time of flowering, joy, integration, and marriage. The faces of Hildegard and Volmar shine in the light of the sun and moon in the quietude of Paradise, surrounded by song. We are invited to journey like her and to wish to shine again like *sidera*, spheres of light, stars of Paradise.

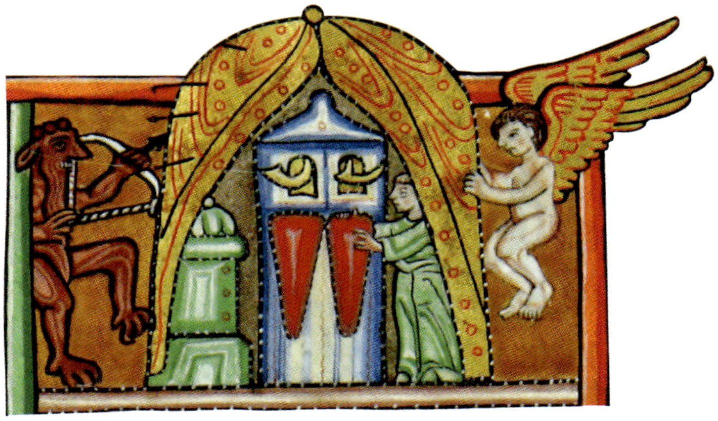

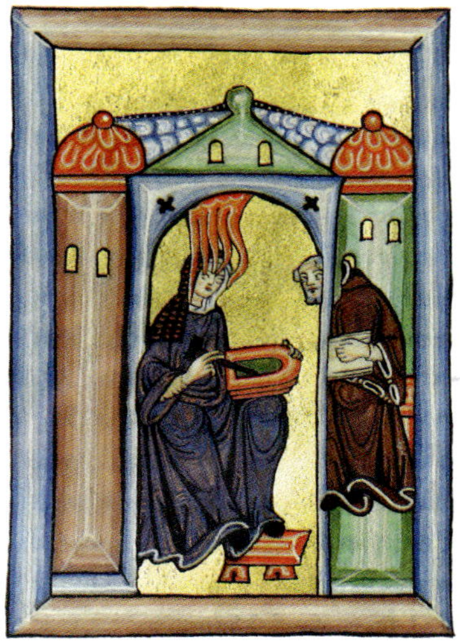

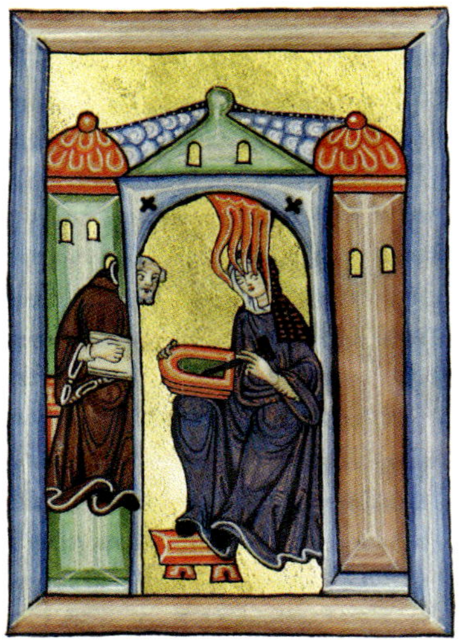

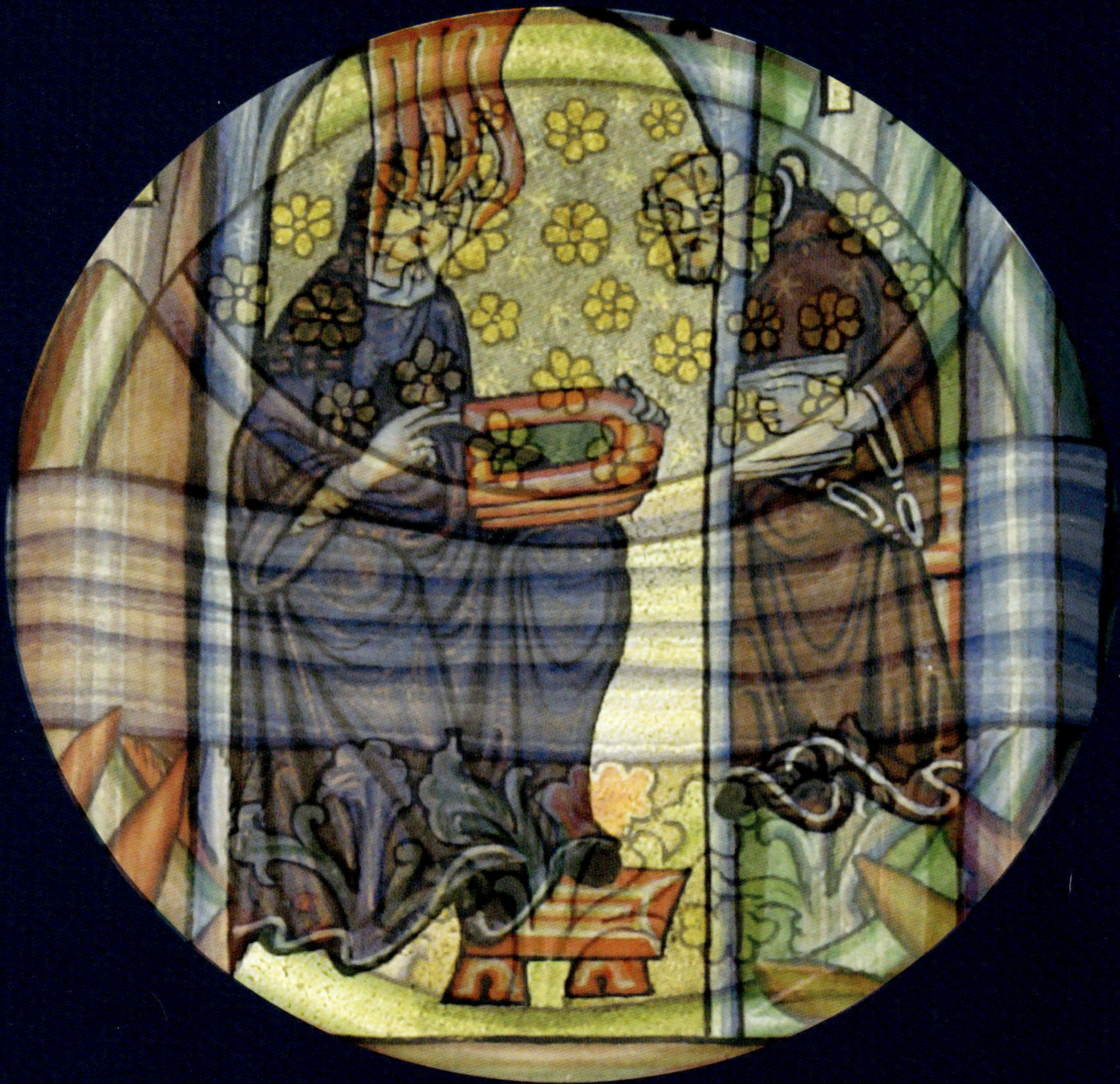

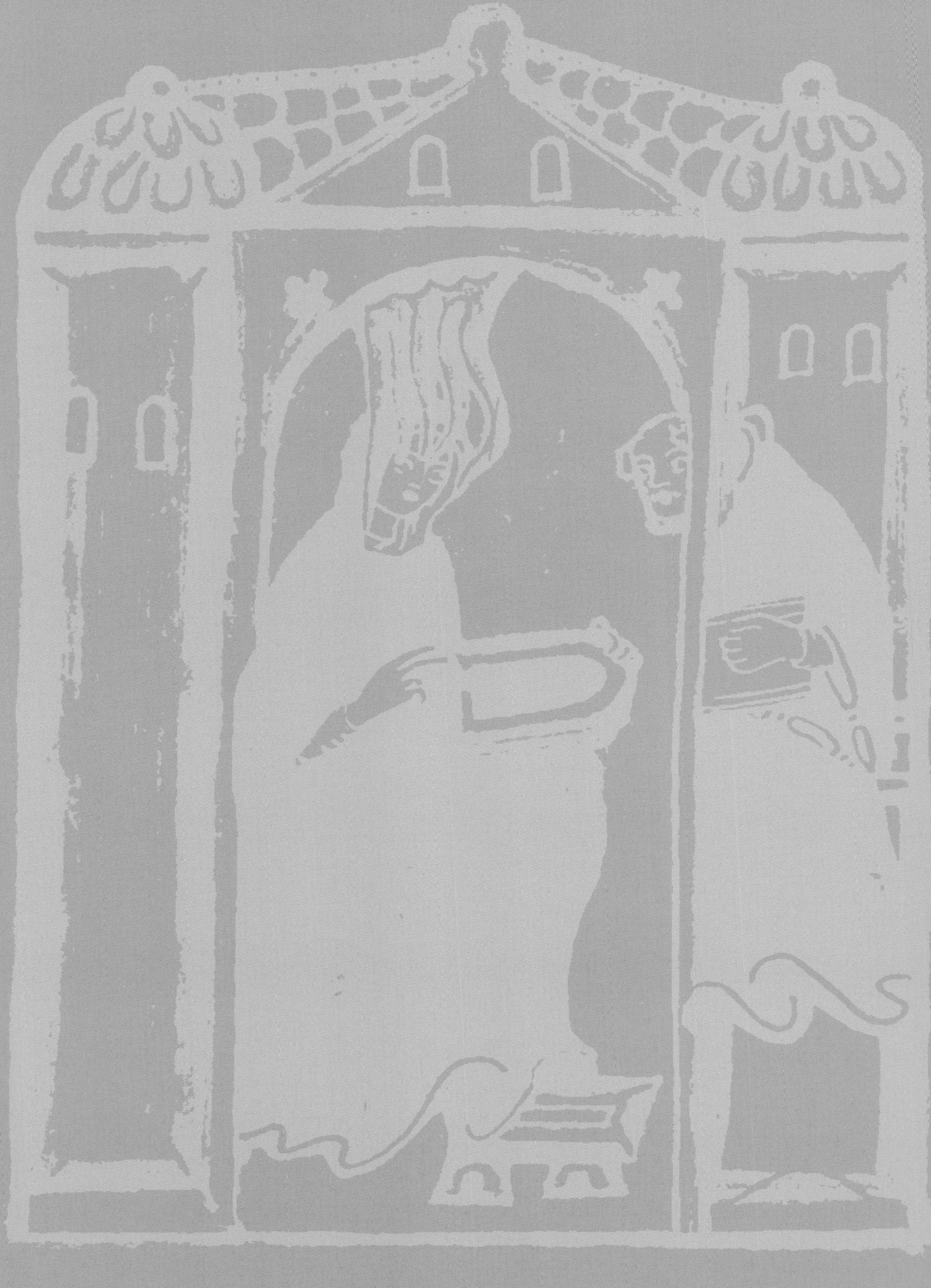

CHAPTER II

Writing Through the Images

God did not immediately illumine the firmament or the earth; rather, he did as one does who is planning out certain forms, for first one marks out each part with one's compass, and then afterwards paints each one with colors (*LDO* II.1.17, p. 288).

In embracing the vision *with the wings of faith, vigilant eyes*, and *the keen ear of inner intelligence*, one perceives the *ardent love visible in the mirror* of God. In doing so, Hildegard was filled with a fervent desire to record *the words she had heard and to transcribe them*, following the divine command: *write by the will of him who knows, sees and disposes all things in the secret of his mysteries.*

The way to do this was to draw on the language of God himself, creator, who *skillfully makes forms out of bronze* and reveals *that what was above reflects the splendor of what was below and what was below, reflects what was above*. In the heart of God there appears the sphere of creation, represented by the sphere of fire of the soul. Within it, in shadow, is the divine chalice, image of the mystery of the incarnation of the Son of God made man. Within the sphere Hildegard disposes the single vision, imitating the creator who, like an architect, with *a compass marks out an as yet unfashioned form*, and she arranges all the images, like God who has the power *to ordain each thing as He wills*. She seals this with the musical harmony of the Heavenly Hosts and the light emanated by the stars, which become the constructive matrix of the entire opus.

The grid axes form a sapiential pentagram in which the narrative of the human journey can be read as a musical score. At the same time, all the images can be superimposed on the organizing grid.

The transparency reveals new images, created by the correspondence of elements of different ones. The poetry that springs forth possesses a remarkable force that touches both mind and heart and works on the body, illuminating its desire to act. To this are added the designs deriving from the recomposition and enlargement of the fragments hidden in the eyes of the Science of God, in the backdrop and on the green curtains placed on the altar. Here, again, Hildegard imitates God who, like an artist, *decorates with elegance* and *paints with many colors.* Thus, she creates the subtly interwoven patterns of quadrilobate flowers and circles, the exquisite carpet of branches and flowers—a fragrant foretaste of the vision of Paradise— that adorn the altar; the weave of white, gold and green of the fecundity of the Word and of the bread of life. The images leap off the manuscript page, and it is as if we could see the plasticity of reality, hear the harmonious sounds of creation, smell the perfume of life, appreciate and savour the beauty of wisdom, and directly witness the power of revelation.

The Vision in the Shadow

For just as a ray of light reveals the particular shape of a created thing through its shadow, so God's pure foreknowledge looked upon the form of every created thing before it was embodied (*LDO* I.1.6, p. 38).

God is light and *all things God wished to make were foreshadowed in him before they came to be*. Thus, the Creation and the Creator are bound like shadow to light, *but as a shadow in a mirror would not exist without the physical form it reflects, so neither can the firmament's ornaments enact anything on their own, but only through the heavenly mysteries*.

The human, conceived, willed and created by God, feels an attraction to the light that generated him, but which he cannot see directly: *For as long as a person waxes and wanes like the moon—as long as he is mortal—he shall not see God, except insofar as he reveals himself to humans*.

In the boundless charity of his love, God offers to all humanity the possibility of knowing him and he reveals himself in the shadow, *like a painter shows people invisible things through the images he depicts*. God reveals himself *in the shadow of his mysteries, the shadow of creation, the shadow of miracles, and the shadow of prophecy*, even offering up his Son, so that humanity might *through true faith perceive in the visible what is invisible*, and arrive, illuminated, at the time of fulfillment. The long journey toward revelation is the time of *faith*, of trusting one's inner vision that discerns in the invisible, in the nebulous forms of shadows, what is not visible, just as it discerns the immensity of the divine presence in the simplicity of bread and wine: *with its knowledge, which is the inner eye, it sees what is hidden to the outer eye and does not doubt it, but believes it with absolute certainty*.

Hildegard gathered all this from the divine voice of the living light and, faithful to the revelation she depicted, like God, the images using the language of light and shadow. The chalice, the altar, and the prophecy are thus revealed in the shadows of the forms in the miniatures, showing that the whole journey within the sphere revolves around the altar and the chalice of the new life.

The Chalice

O human, I give you His body and blood in the oblation of bread and wine, so that by true faith you may perceive by that which is visible that which is invisible (*SC* I.6.19, p. 248).

The light that illuminates the figure of the Shining One, Almighty God, projects a shadow in the form of a chalice, image of the Son. In the details, we note that: the shadow of the *circle colored gold*, image of the power of God, defines the Holy Communion chalice (Salvadori 2019, p. 174); the shadow of the *blue rock*, image of the Fear of God, defines the vessel's octagonal base, symbolizing the square of the earth that is connected to the circle of the divine sphere; the circle surrounding *the Building that welcomes the faithful to guide them to heaven* defines the shape of the Host, sign of humanity destined to unite in a single body, the body of Christ, the body of the world.

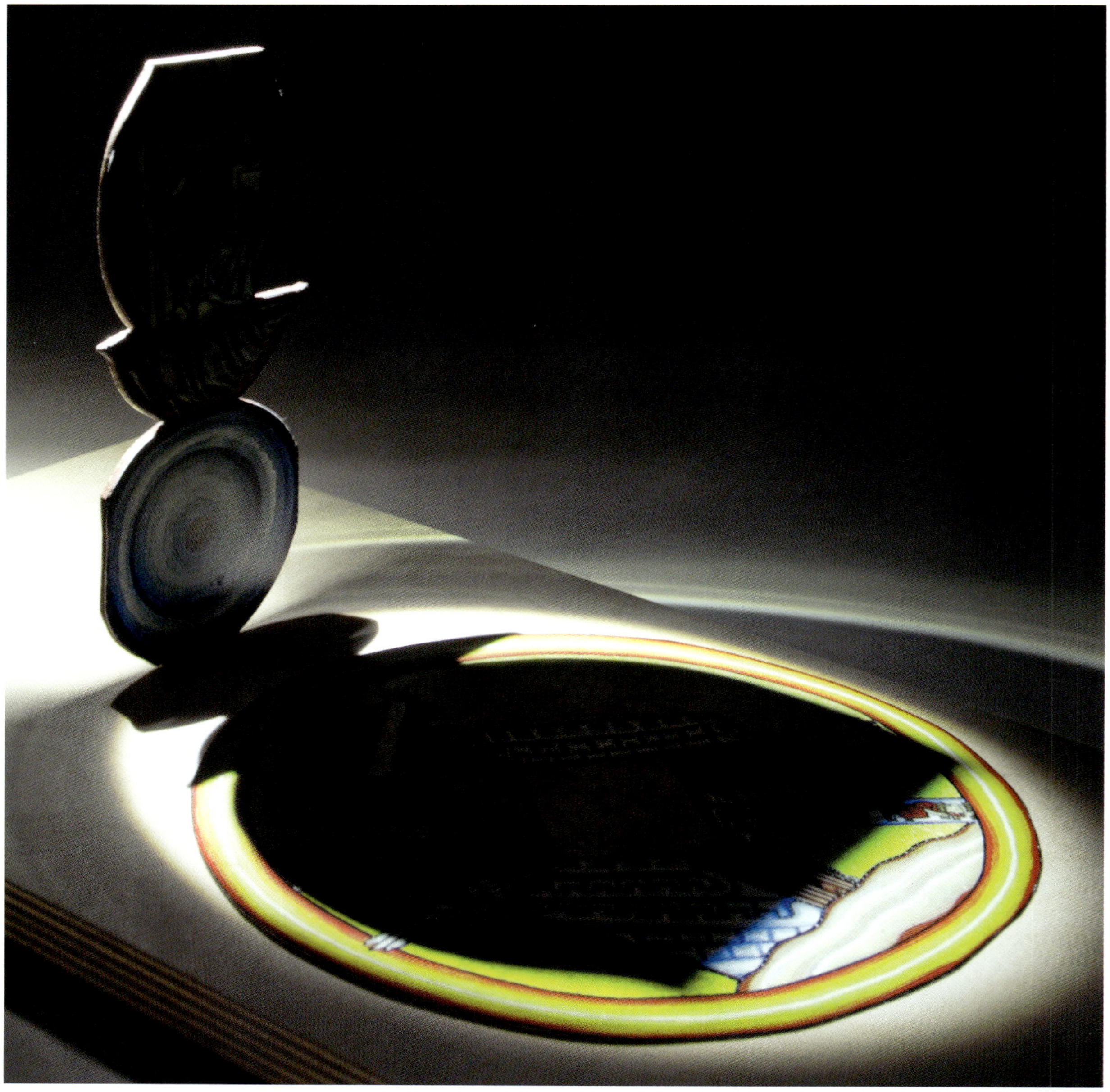

The Altar

[...] the science of God [...] extends its all-piercing gaze [...] to the four corners of the earth. There this knowledge most clearly foresees those who will be rejected as well as those who will be gathered in (*SC* I.4.9, p. 116).

[...] the goodness of the Father builds good works on faith. Gathering multitudes of the faithful from the four corners of the earth, he draws them to celestial things (*SC* III.2.3, p. 326).

From the square of the Science of God descends a golden ray of life that infuses the soul into the body of the infant in the womb of the woman, whose attire is reminiscent of the altar cloth, signifying that the human body is the building and temple of God. At the same time, the eyes of the Science of God scrutinize the hearts of humans and decide who can enter the square of the Building and approach the altar of God, to rediscover their own life. The indissoluble link between the two images is represented by the shadow of the heavenly square that coincides perfectly with the square of the building, and we read: *the white glass pavement of the Building shines with a most serene splendor.*

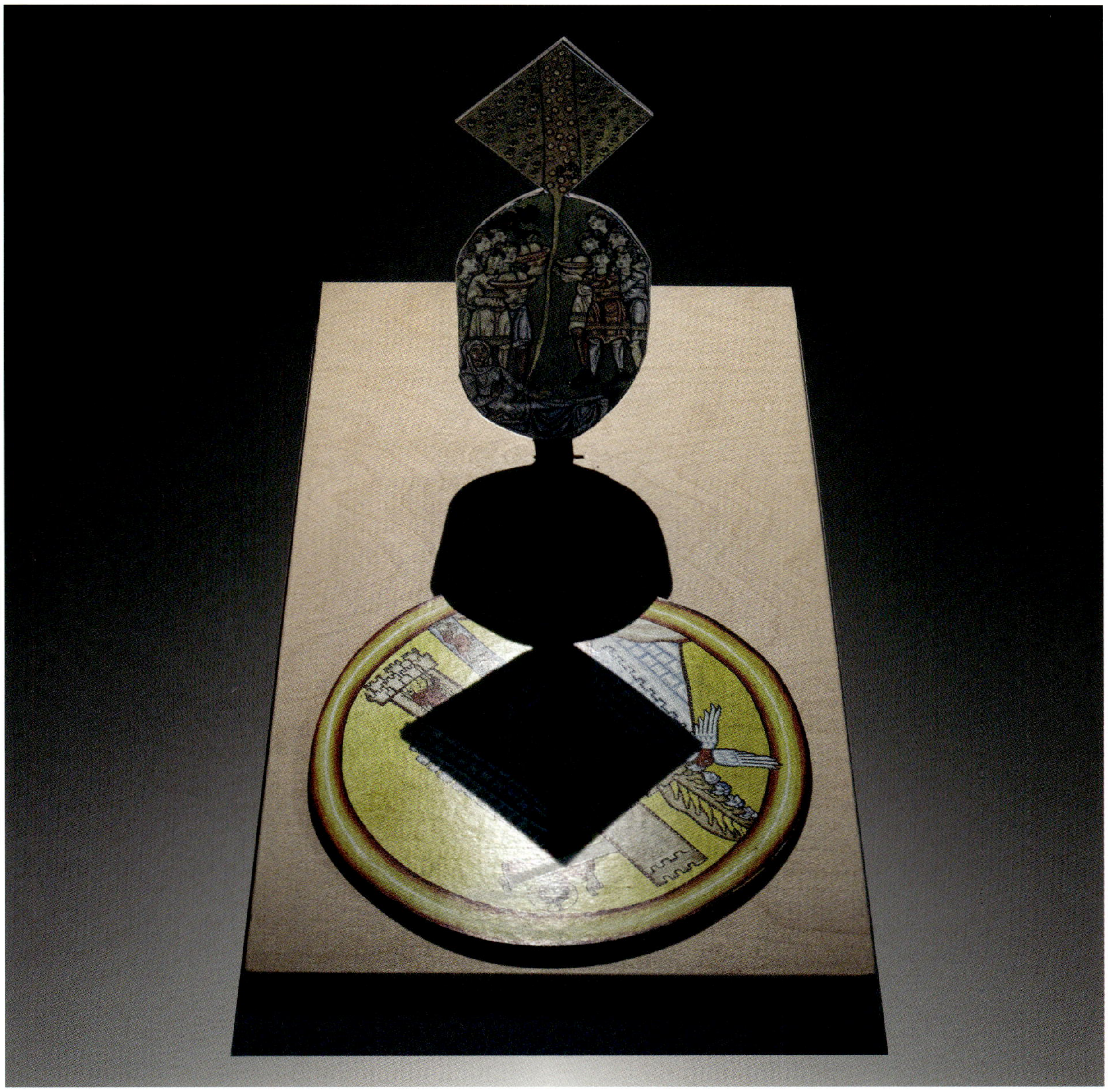

Prophecy

O eminent men, who traversed the hidden ways, and looked with the eyes of the spirit, and in lucent shadows announced the Living Light that would bud from the stem which blossomed alone from the Light that rooted within it (*SC* III.13.3, p. 526).

The four great prophets are seated on the branches of the Column of the Word (III.4), with their shadows falling across the wall of the Building (III.6) until they coincide with the faces of the people of Israel as they journey, depicted in the arches of the wall. The Column is surmounted by the dove of the Spirit, whose shadow lengthens until it coincides with the figure of the virtue of God's Grace on the Column of the Savior (III.8), located on the opposite side of the Building. The *splendor of the Son shining in the heart of the Father* is now openly revealed in the most splendid of virtues, the grace, *fullness, and strength of God*, who guides humanity.

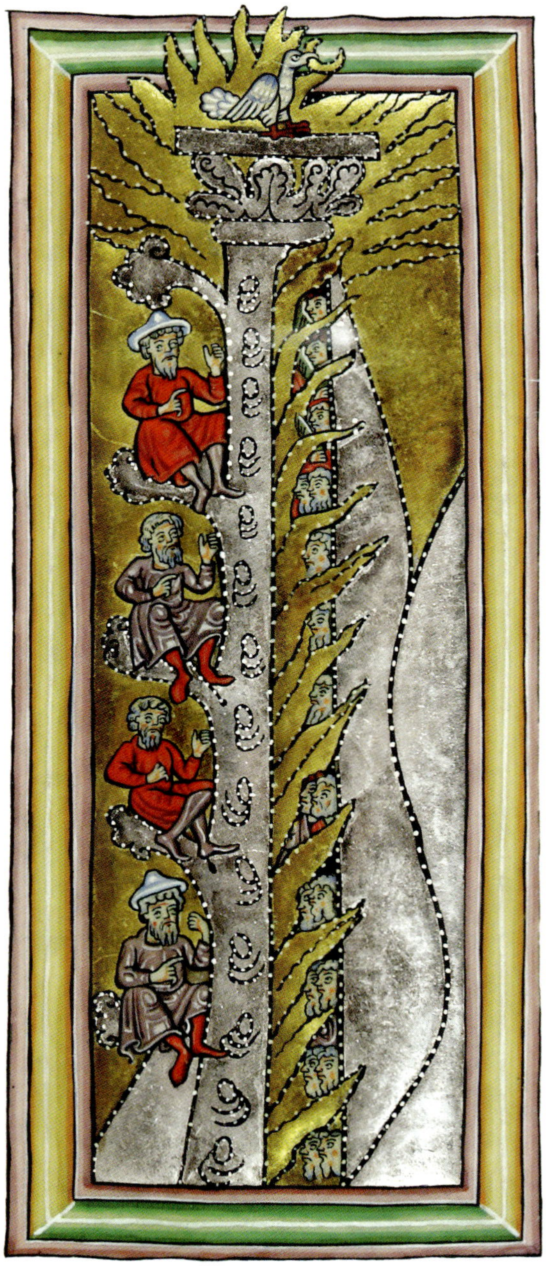

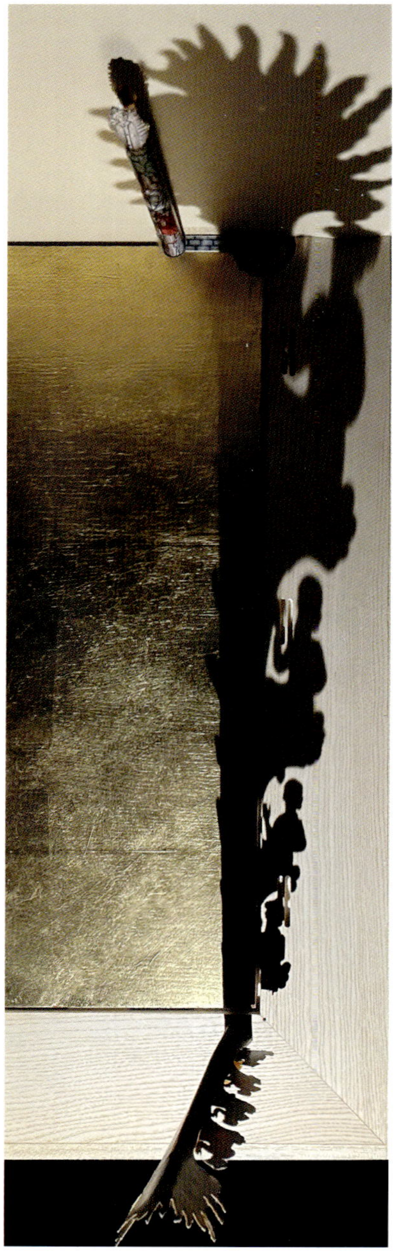

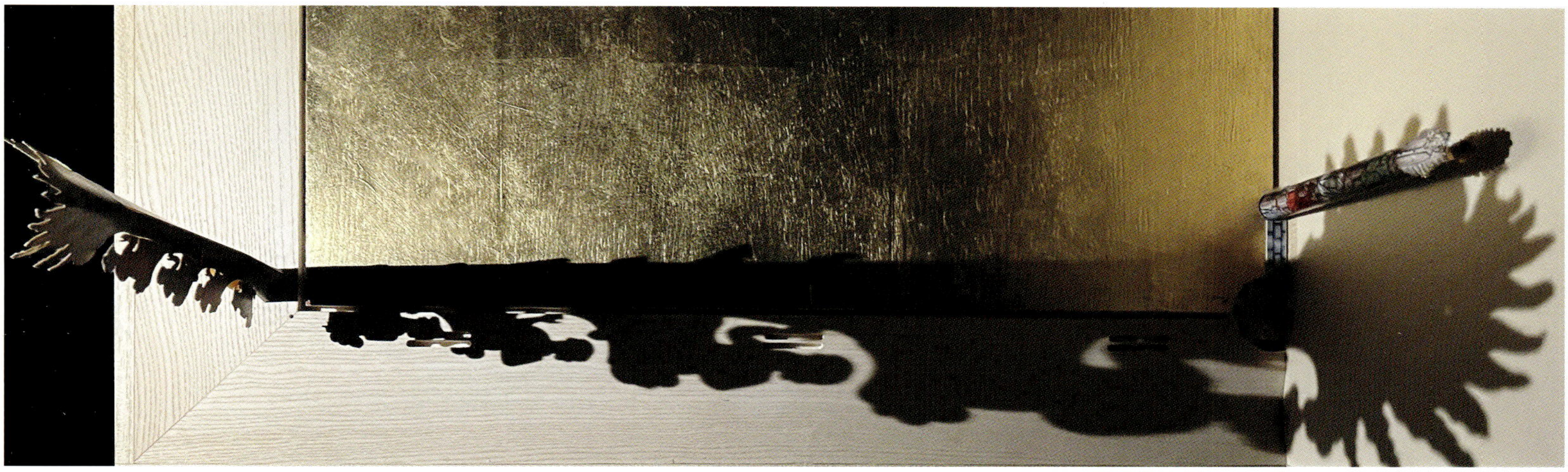

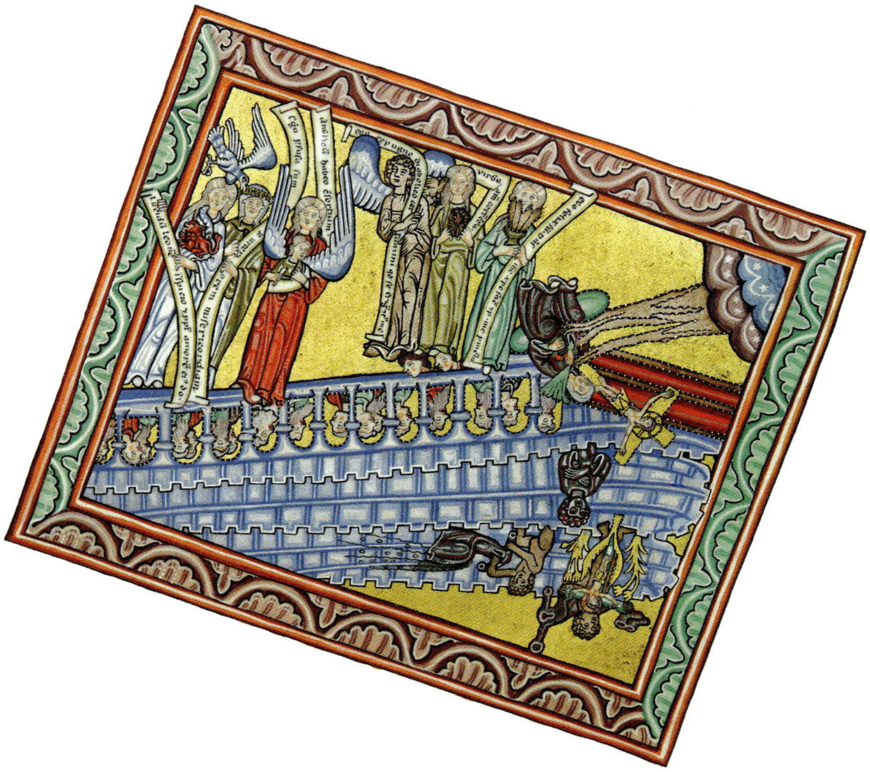

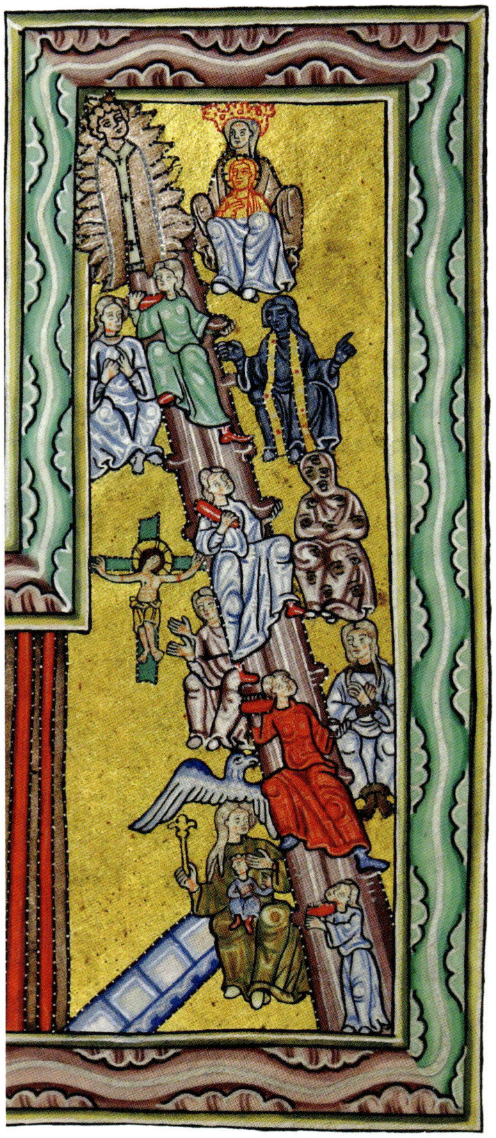

The Unified Space of the Vision

[...] the firmament of Heaven contains the lower regions and touches the higher (*SC* I.4.16, p. 120).

Hildegard's prophetic work follows the layered style of Sacred Scripture, requiring different interpretive tools: *grammar*, which allows us to understand the figures and their symbolic meaning; *rhetoric*, which enables us to broaden our gaze and to associate similar figures depicted in different images; *dialectic*, which identifies the signs that connect the images and enables us to reconstruct the single space of vision in the *sphere of light*.

The celestial vault, composed of images of the firmament, the Heavenly Hosts, and the Trinity, is visible within the sphere. In the center, beneath the vault, is the Building surrounded by the gold-colored circle that marks the circumference of the sphere, while the map of the Building delineates the sacred space, image of the altar. The light of the chalice is projected onto this sacred space, which is surrounded by all the images of the visions, positioned vertically. The journey of humanity thus takes place within the sphere and revolves around the mystery of the incarnation and resurrection of the Son.

The weave of words and images contains cleverly hidden clues for an accurate reconstruction of the complete scene of the vision. These can be found in the descriptions of geographical spaces, such as the *north*, indicated in the visions depicting darkness; in expressions like *it was in the same place; where earlier I had seen... now I see; what I said before*, etc., which reveal the coexistence of several images in the same space; and also in the descriptions of different figures placed near the same element, as in the case of the Synagogue and the Church, both located in front of the altar.

The superimposition of several images in the same place enables us to perceive the chronological vision of the story and the synchronic vision of eternity simultaneously, and thus the path of transformation harbored in the oneness of the divine embrace.

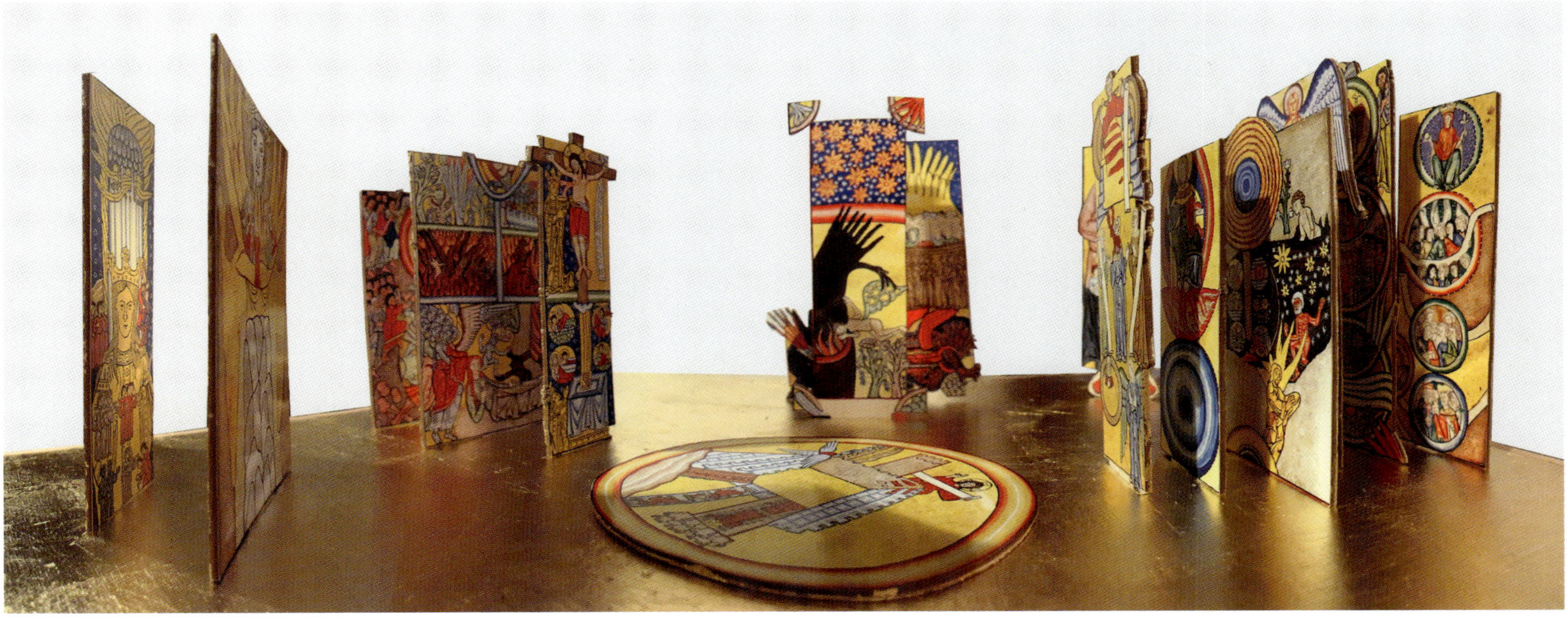

Before and Now

We can begin to reconstruct the single vision following the identification of the first three pointers described below:

Therefore, you see on the summit of the eastern corner of the building, where the shining part and the stone part of the wall came together, seven white marble steps, which rose like an arch up to the great stone on which the Shining One sat on the throne (*SC* III.10.D, p. 473).

In the east corner of the Building, where the Father was visible (III.1a), the Son now appears (III.10).

But this shadowed pillar is standing in the same place in the building, where I previously had seen in the celestial mysteries of God, a great four-sided radiance of brilliant luminosity. This radiance, which signifies the secrets of the supernal Creator, was revealed to me in the greatest mystery (*SC* III.8.D, p. 435).

The Column of the Savior (III.8) is shown in the place where the square filled with eyes of the Science of God (I.4) previously appeared.

I saw the image of a woman [...] of great size like the tower of a city [...] She stands next to the altar that is before the eyes of God [...] she is the Synagogue, which is the mother of the Incarnation of the Son of God (*SC* I.5 D-1, pp. 133–134).

After this I saw the image of a woman as large as a great city [...] she stood balanced on her womb in front of the altar that stands before the eyes of God [...] And thus the Church is the virginal mother of all Christians (*SC* II.3 D and II.3.12, pp. 169–173).

The figures of the Synagogue (I.5) and the Church (II.5) are both in front of the altar. In the Building, their position corresponds to that of the two towers: the Tower of the Law (III.3a), image of the obedience of the Jewish people, and the Tower of the Church (III.9).

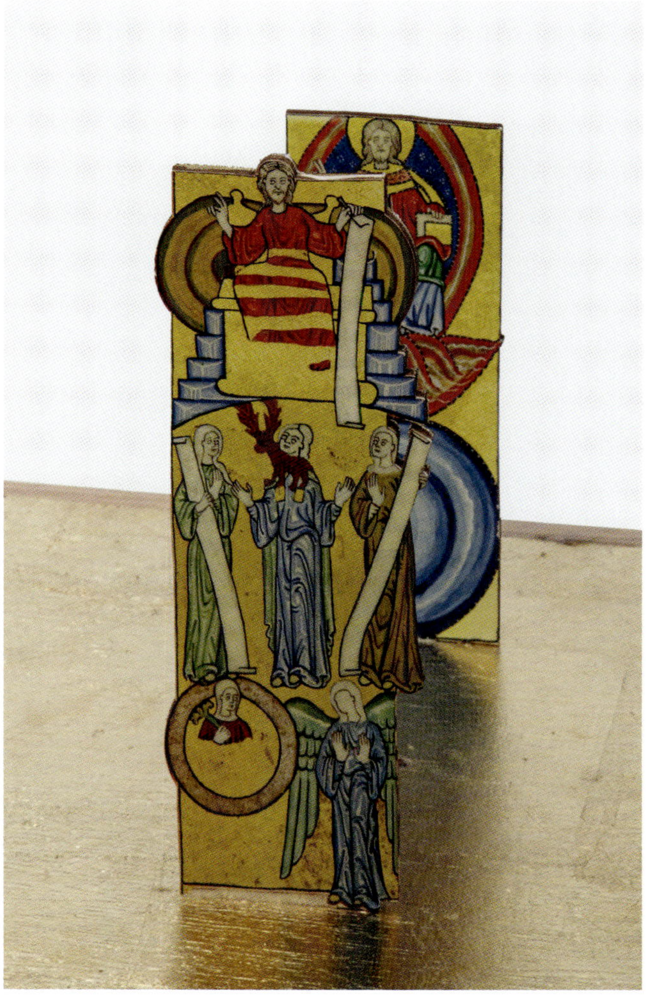

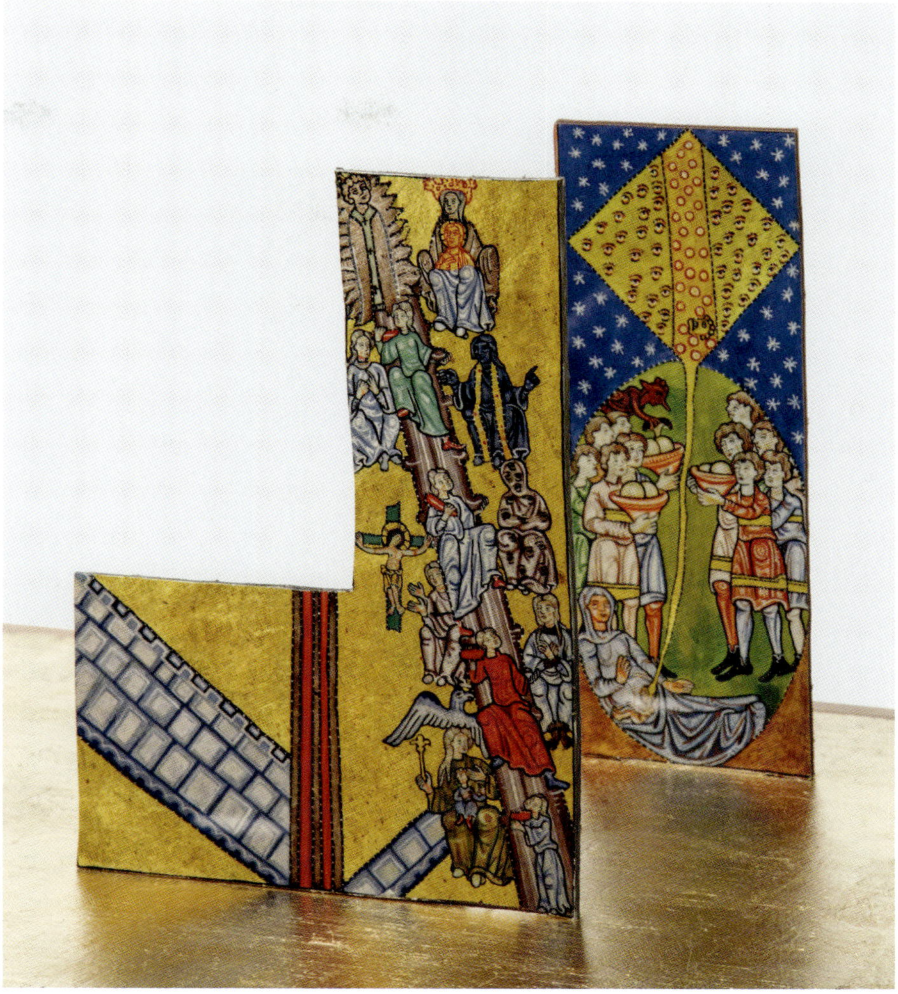

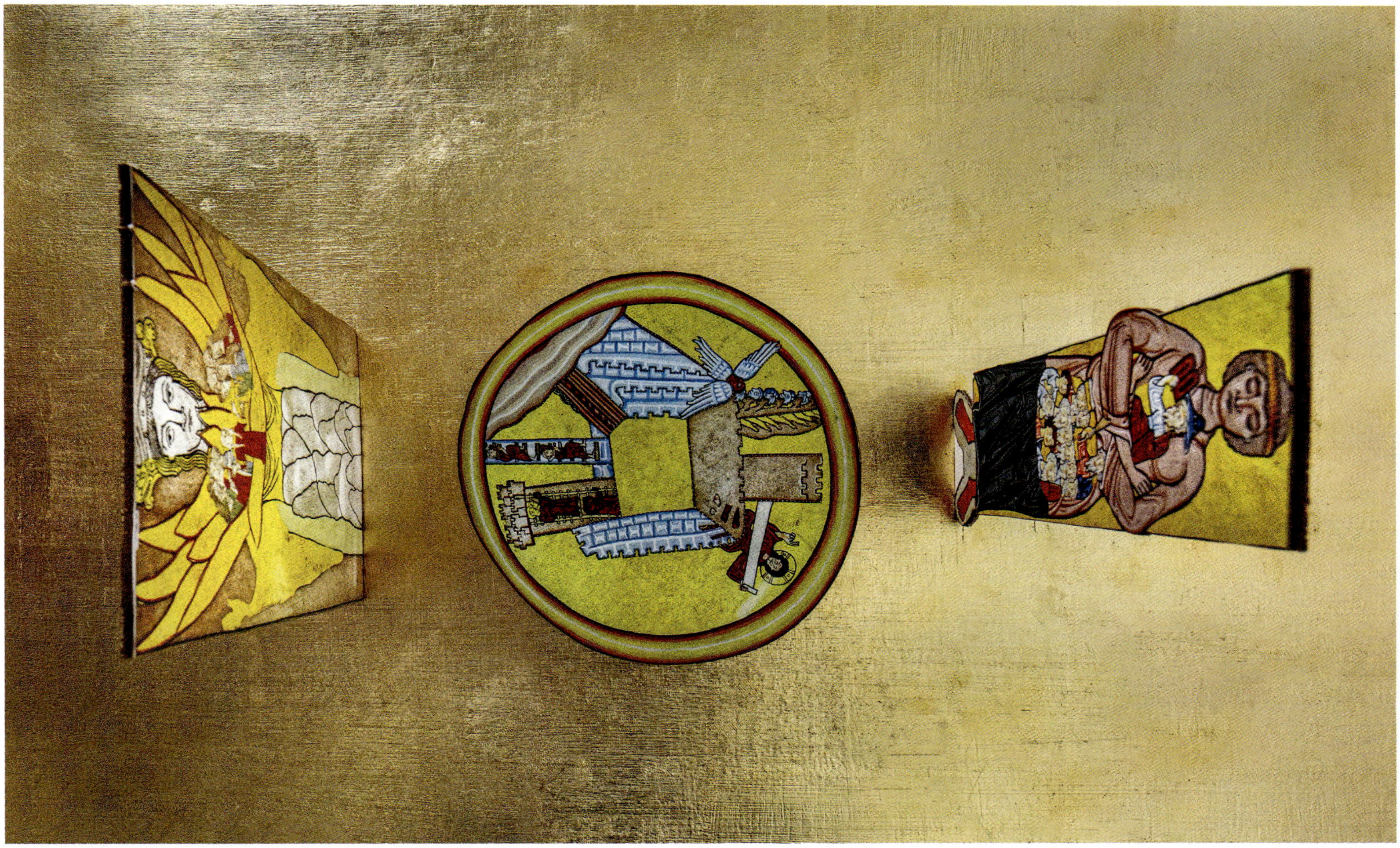

The Golden Square

The golden square inside the building marks the center of the sphere. Superimposed on the vertical axis are: the square filled with eyes of the Science of God; the square of the Building; the square of the altar, and the square of the tabernacle of the soul.

The Science of God

I saw a most serene splendor, flaming, as it were, with many eyes, with four corners pointing toward the four parts of the world (*SC* I.4.D, p. 109).

Square Building

And on that mountain stood a four-sided building, formed in the likeness of a four-walled city (*SC* III.2.D, p. 325).

The Altar

And he called that holy place the house and temple of God, which is the name of the city of the heavenly Jerusalem, the living temple of the Living God (*SC* III.5.21, p. 380).

The Tabernacle of the Soul

And I came to a tabernacle, whose interior was all of the strongest steel (*SC* I.4.3, p. 112).

The Unified Vision

Opposite, the complete reconstruction of the unified vision with the images of the individual visions arranged around the map of the Building, where east lies at the top of the miniature.

At the three corners of the map, we find images representing:

– to the east, Almighty God and the birth of the Son (above);

– to the west, death, resurrection and the time of judgment (below);

– to the north, darkness and the victory over evil (left).

On the two opposite sides:

– north/east, the Synagogue and the beginning of the alliance between God and the people of Israel (left);

– south/west, the coming of the Son of God and the building of the Church his bride (right).

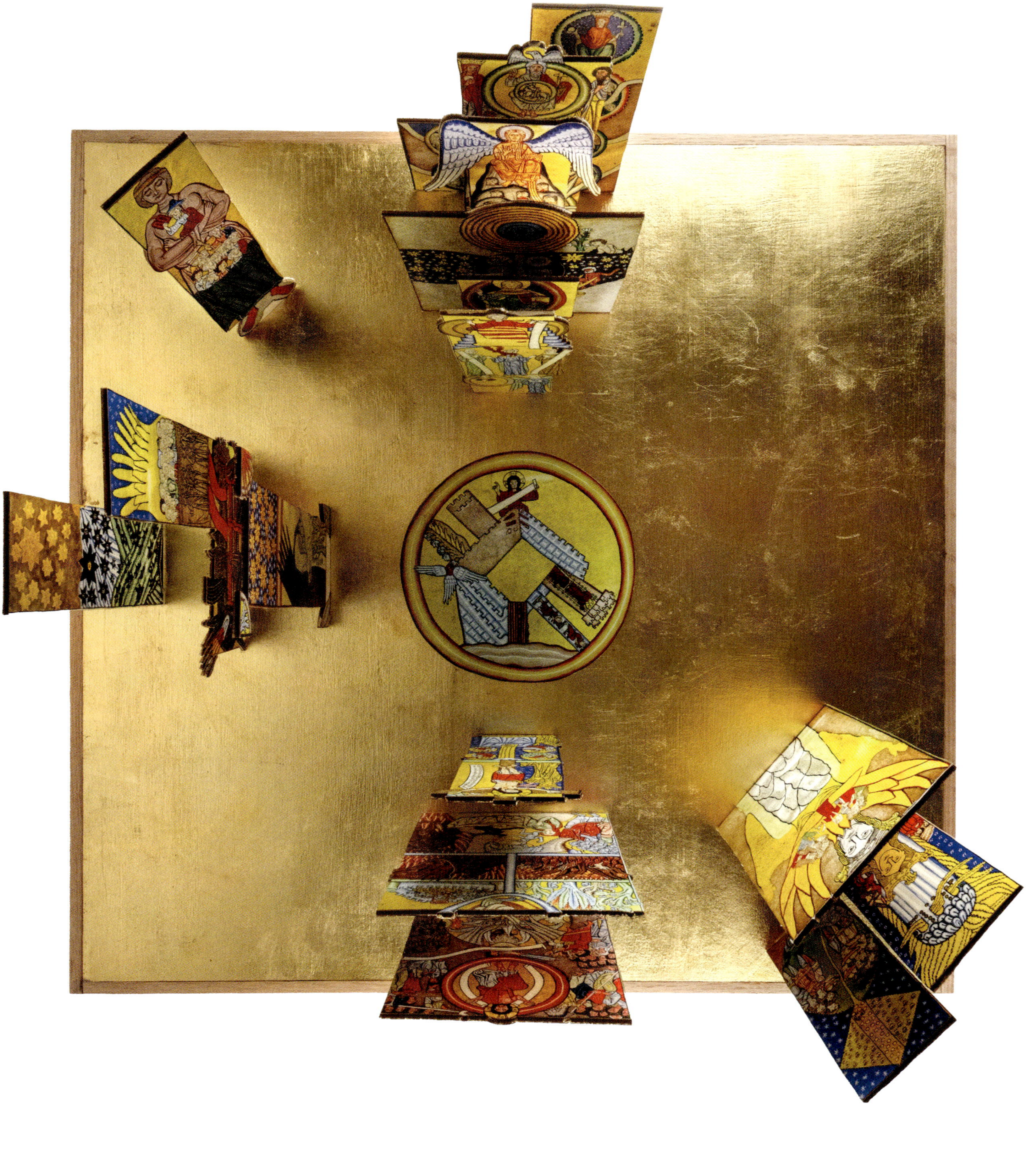

The Time of History and the Time of Eternity

A globe of sparkling flame […] His ineffable Only-Begotten, the sun of justice (*SC* I.3.4, p. 94).

A flame in it the color of air […] the Infinite Word (*SC* II.2.3, p. 151).

[…] the One who sat enthroned upon that mountain (*SC.* I.1.4, p. 67).

At the cardinal points of the map there are groups of images that occupy the same space. This creates sequences and clearly shows the non-uniformity of the measurements and the misalignment of the silhouettes of the different images. It also shows the correspondence between the same figurative elements present in diverse miniatures, like the circle that marks the center of the blue flame of the Trinity, of the sun of the firmament, and the throne of the Shining One, or the features of the faces of the Son and the Father.

These observations have led to a realignment of the images, following the guiding figurative elements and through constructive syllogism (see pp. 116–120).

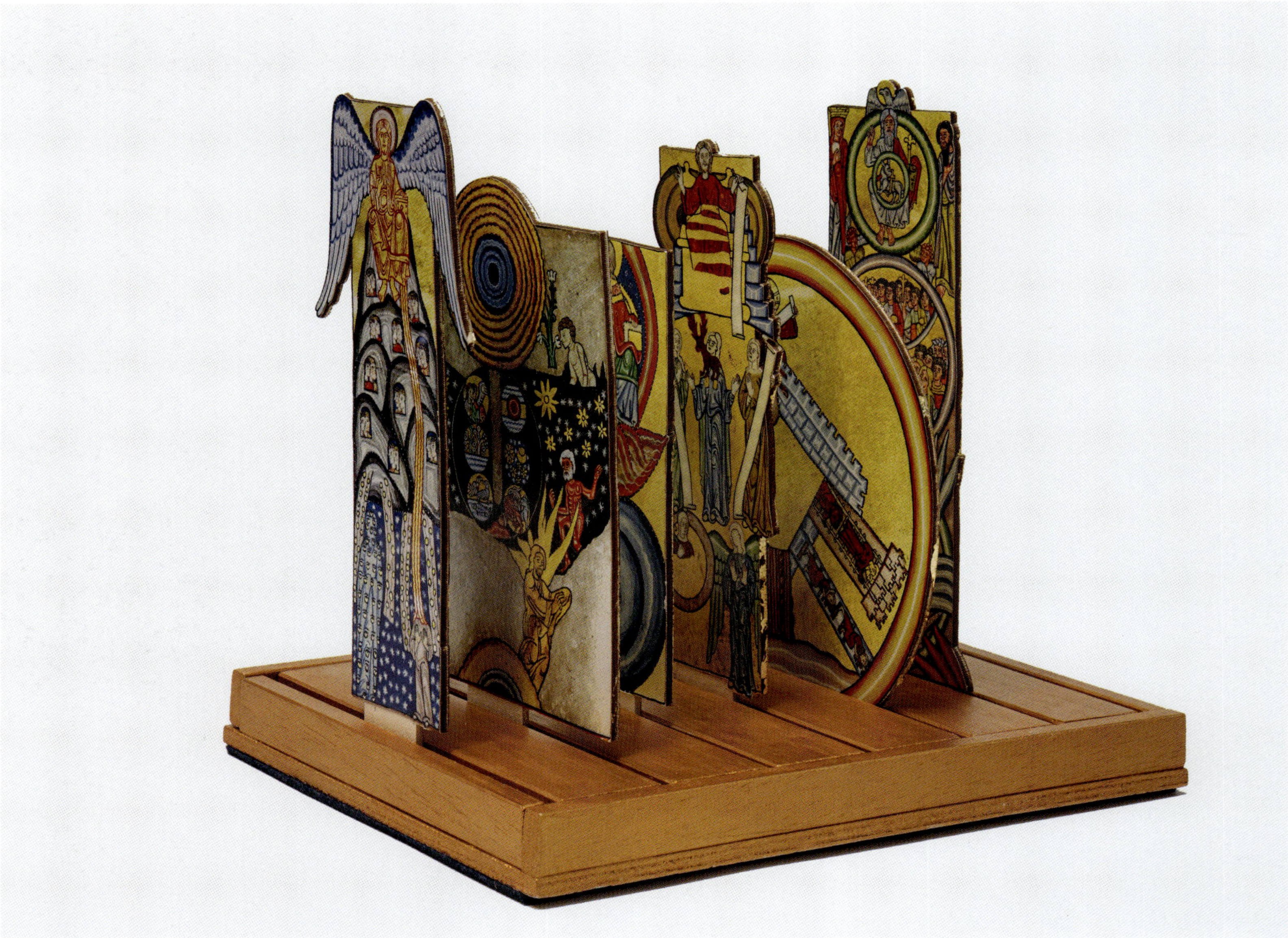

And One is sitting on that throne [...] the Living God (*SC* III.1.3, p. 311).

And on these steps a chair was placed, on which sat a man of youthful appearance [...] the Son of Man, Who reigns as One God in all justice with the Father (*SC* III.10.17, p. 482).

The placement of the images on transparent supports has shown the perfect coincidence of the size and form of the previously identified circle and of the minute details of the faces. This alignment has created a new positioning of the images with respect to the plane and has revealed the presence of parallel axes, superimposed vertically, which form an actual sapiential pentagram (see p. 124). When read horizontally and synchronically, the images describe humanity's journey and the eschatological stages of the story, such as the representation of God in the sun of justice, in the winged figure, in the flame and in the revelation of the Son, culminating in the representation of the Trinity in the form of the dove, the Father and the Lamb.

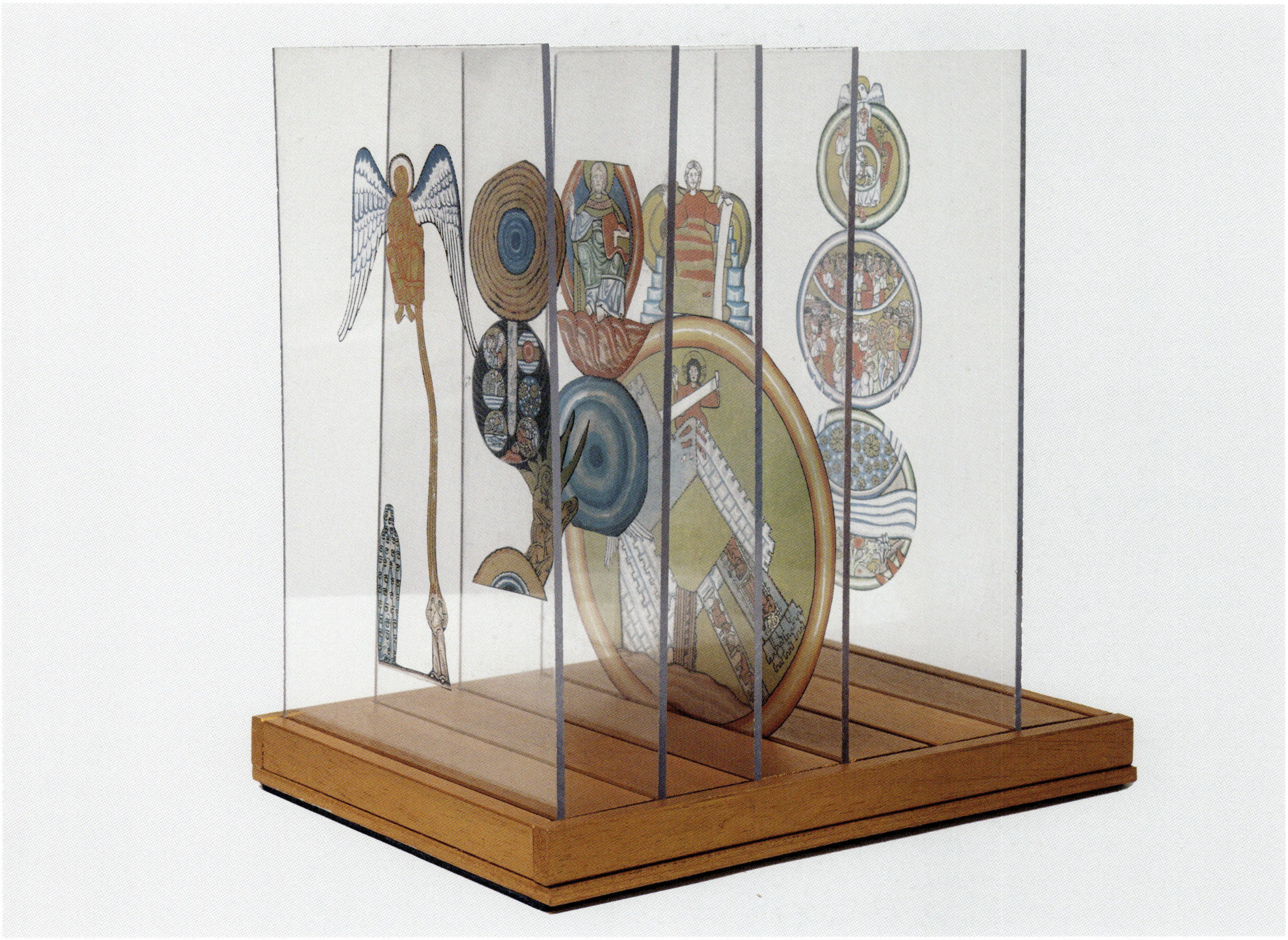

Divine Order

For from the virtue of true Divine Love, in whose knowledge the circumference of the world exists, proceeds her elegant plan of order, shining above all things and containing and constraining all things (*LDO* I.2.46, p. 103).

God, the Creator, begins his work by ordaining *all things like a man who silently plans out all that he wills.* The Creator, who is pure rationality, has given the *human the capacity to think, so that before carrying out his works he might ordain them in his heart, which contains the wonders of God.* Hildegard, together with her collaborators, draws on this capacity to ordain and shape the story written in images of her visions, so that they might be the harmonious mirror of the beauty of creation and of the final meeting between humanity and its creator.

Thus the *harmony of the symphony of celestial revelations* is the chosen matrix for the construction of the work. *To humans God has given the ability to think, to the angels he has offered the gift of divine science and their voices ring out ceaselessly to praise and honor him.* This is why the concentric soundwaves of the Heavenly Hosts and the harmony of the planetary orbits inspire the creation of the constructive matrix, on which all the images are planned and designed. The creatural sound of the beginning, and its harmony, underlie all of the design, through which it sings the poetry of the revelation.

Horizontal and vertical axes drawn on the edge of the circles of the angelic hosts create the rhythmic and orderly cadence of the sapiential pentagram, on which the images are aligned through the constructive syllogism, and each axis corresponds to a symbolic plane.

The space of vision is defined as follows: on the vertical axis are represented its breadth and layering, *from the depths of the abyss to above the stars*, marking the human journey of transformation from birth to re-entry into the divine light; on the horizontal axis, the eschatological stages of the human story. The individual details can be seen simultaneously, as they coincide through the transparencies (synchronic vision), or arranged along the lines as if on a pentagram, enabling a narrative reading of events (chronological vision).

Hildegard utilizes the constructive matrix to seal the work with the dimension of sound, song and music, the quintessence of harmony; to describe the immense space of the vision that would not fit into the manuscript page; and to conceal the revelation but make it accessible to those who answer the call to immerse themselves in the sapiential dimension of a different gaze.

Constructive Syllogism

The technique of constructive syllogism—which Hildegard also used in the *Liber Divinorum Operum* (Salvadori 2021) and in the glossary of the *Unknown Language*, where seven hymns in praise of God are hidden—connects figurative elements from different images: element A connects to B and B connects to C in such a way that A and C can be united. The alignment of the center of the Heavenly Hosts and the egg marks the beginning of the syllogism and at the same time defines the central axis of the sapiential pentagram (see p. 124) indicated by the continuous gold line.

The thirty-five miniatures of *Scivias* are thus linked in a unique sequence and identify the other lines of the sapiential pentagram. The figure below illustrates the first five steps of the constructive syllogism by way of example: the center of light of the Heavenly Hosts (I.6) coincides with the center of the egg (I.3); the center of the sun in the egg (I.3), with the center of the flame of the Trinity (II.1); the center of the flame, with the center of the body of the Shining One (III.1a); the face of the Shining One, with the face of Christ the Judge (III.12a); the halo of Christ the Judge, with the circle of the Lamb in the Father's lap (III.12b).

In this first example we already find important confirmation of the validity of the constructive process: the Trinity in the last miniature, represented by the dove of the Spirit above and by the Lamb in the Father's lap, is actually in a higher position than the circles of the celestial hosts and of all the other figures.

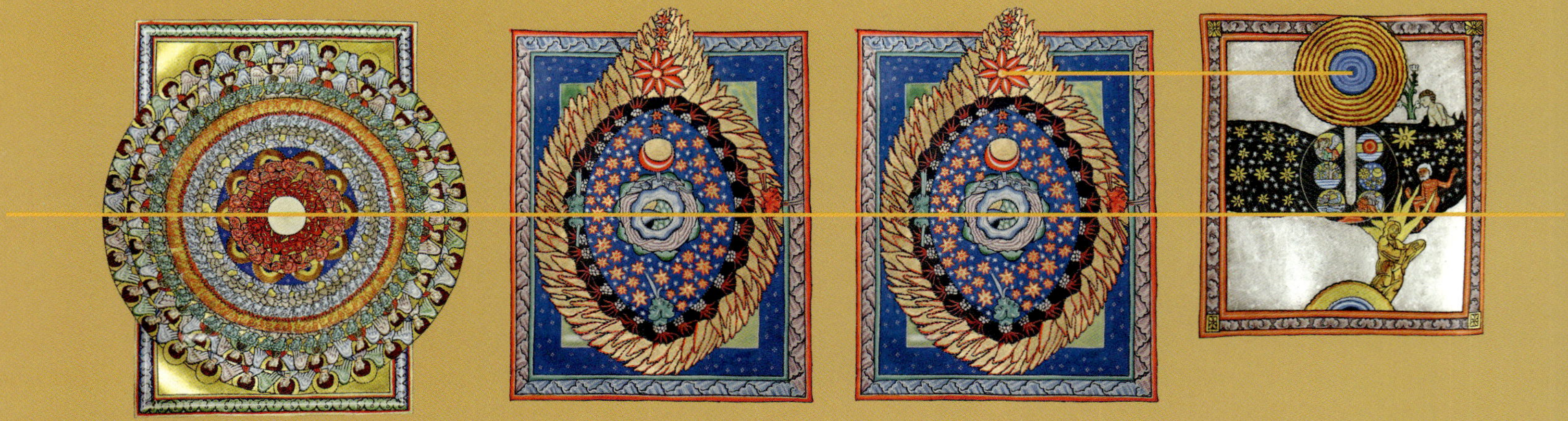

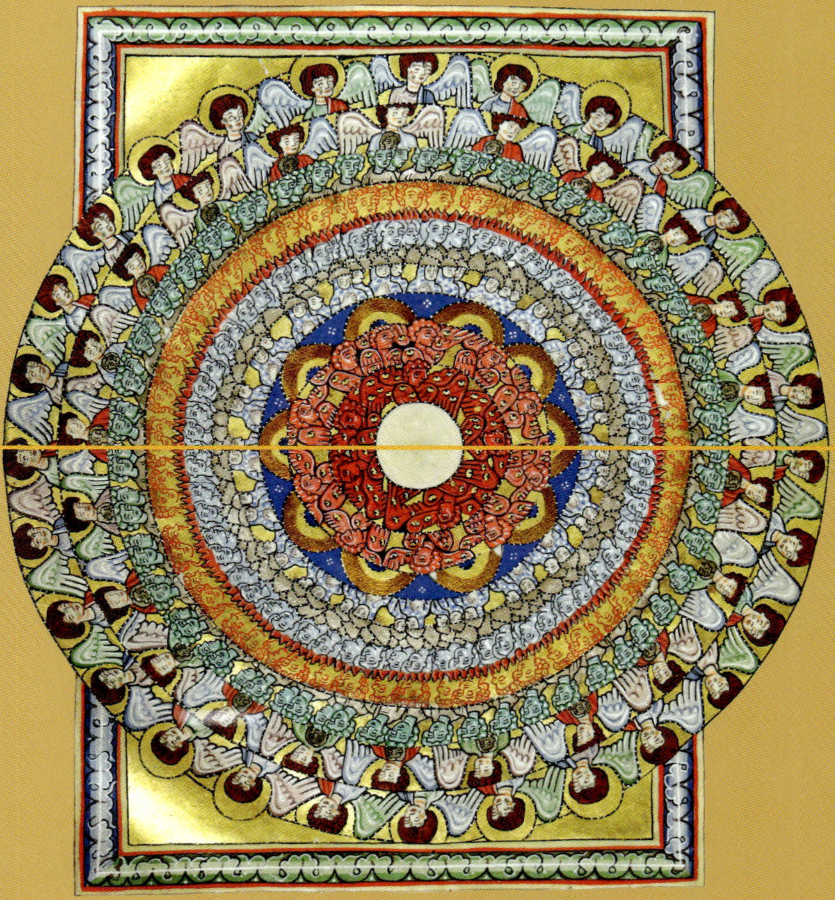
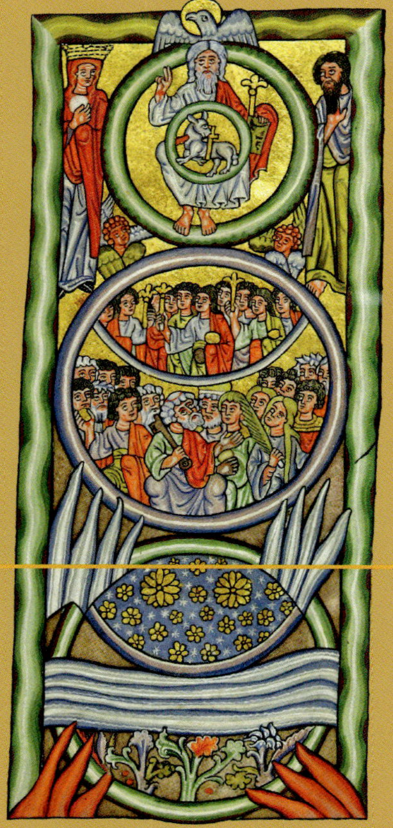
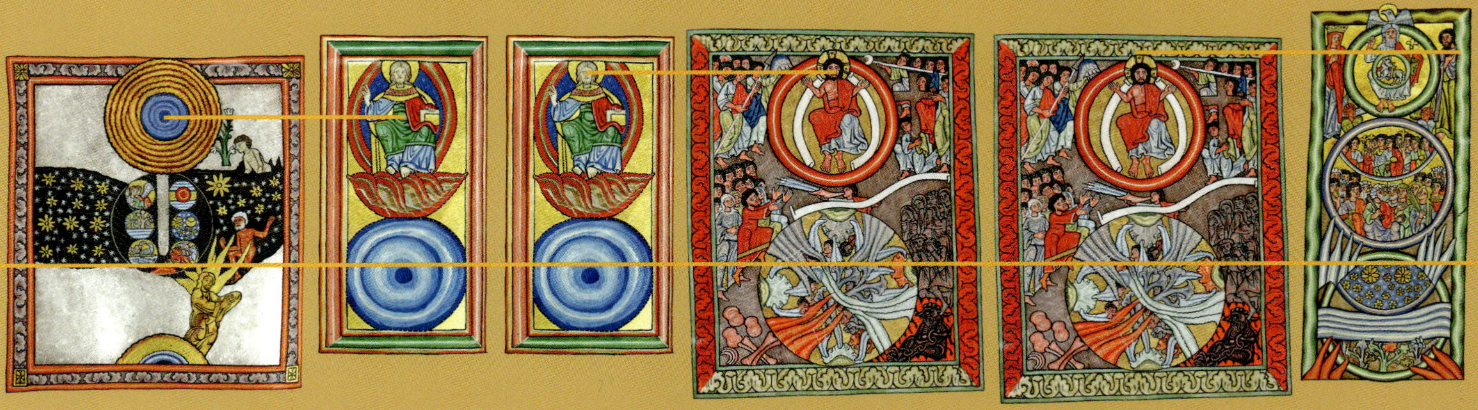

Alignment

For when humankind is perfected in the full number as God established them, they will arrive at that land that for earthly humans is called "the land of living," and then they will have fellowship with the Lamb in the heavens (*LDO* II.1.43, p. 333).

The alignment of the images through the constructive syllogism has been completed (see opposite page). The gold line marks the central axis and divides the two great spaces: the darkness below and the spirit above; the beginning of man's journey at the bottom and the manifestation of the celestial and divine dimension at the top. The unfolding narrative of the images can be read along the lines of the sapiential pentagram (see p. 124), or in the poetry revealed by reading the superimposed images rendered legible through transparency (see pp. 132–143).

The images of Judgment and Paradise (III.12a and b) exemplify this: the reading of the pentagram images highlights the transition from the face of Christ to the Lamb; the reading of the superimposed images reveals the perfect coincidence of Christ's halo with the inner circle of the Lamb, and that Christ's red circle completes the semicircle of Paradise, signifying that the time of revelation is fulfilled, as described in chapter five of Revelation.

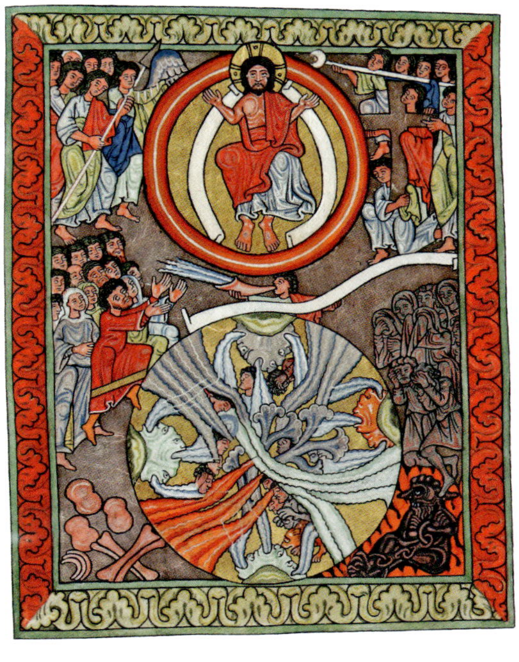
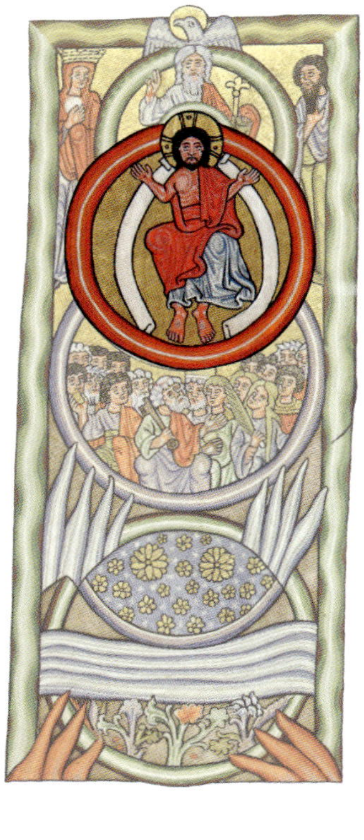
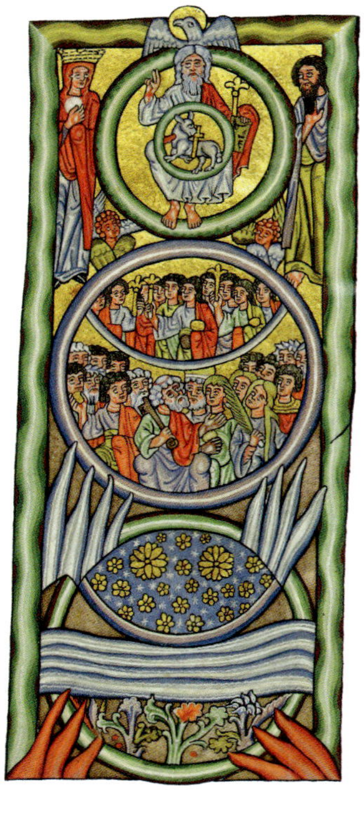

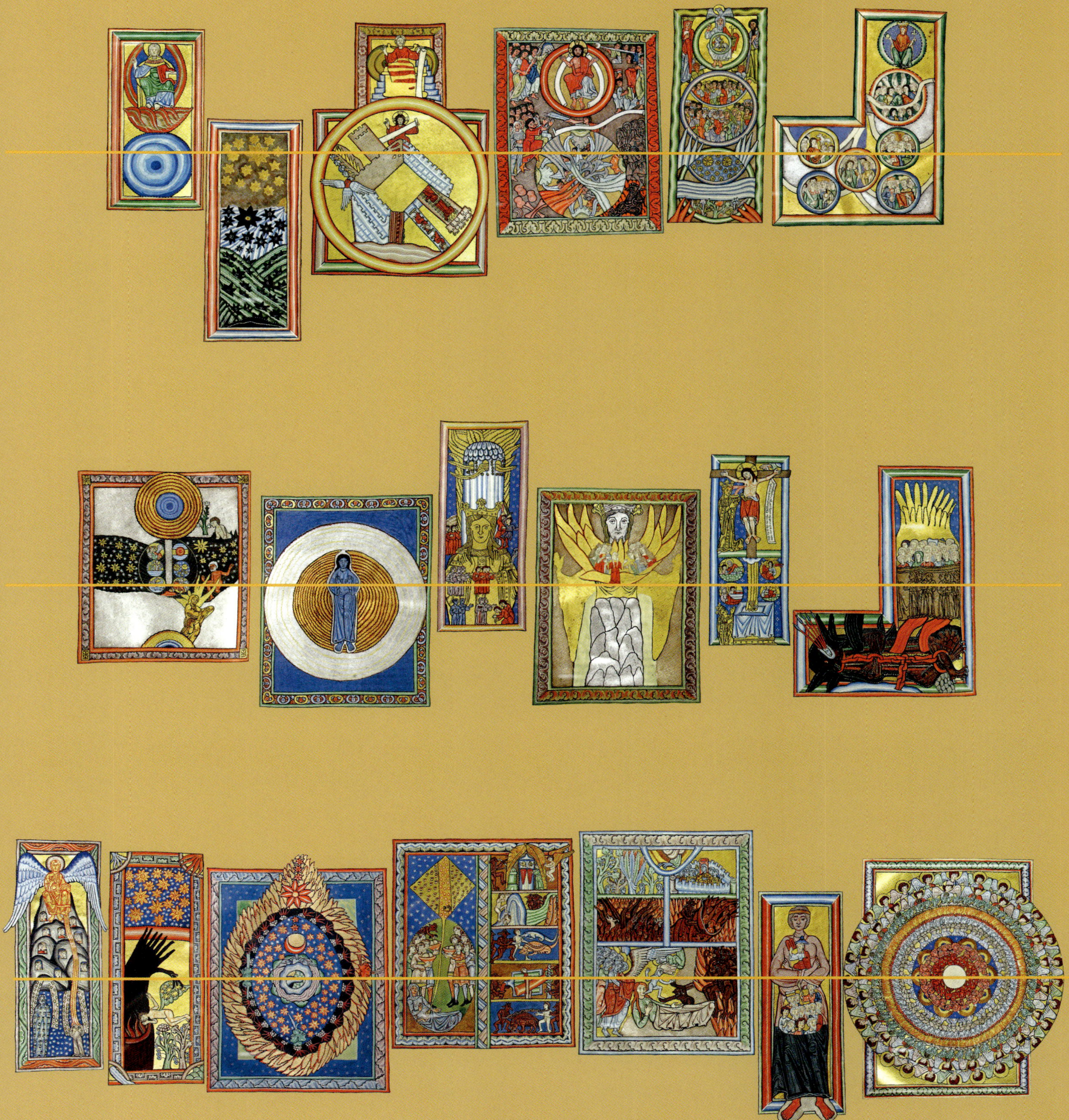

Beyond the Space of the Page

You see the tower as immense and round, all made of a single white stone. [...] It has three windows in its summit from which shine so much brilliance that even the roof of the tower, which is constructed like a cone, shows very clearly in its light; for the ineffable Trinity is manifested in the outpouring of the gifts of the power of the Holy Spirit (*SC* II.4.2–3, p. 190).

[...] the splendid brilliance with which the divine power had clothed them was extinguished in Lucifer himself and all the followers of his malice; [...] and [they] were precipitated by their pride into the abyss of eternal death, which is their doom [...] in the darkness of the North, which is to say in Hell (*SC* III.1.14–15, pp. 318–319).

The single vision encompasses a vast space *from the depths of the abyss to above the stars.* The extreme points are marked by the darkness in the Fall of the First Angel (III.1b), below, and by the golden flames of the Holy Spirit in Confirmation (II.4), above. The space of the vision is infinitely larger than the page of the codex.

The size of the page is approximately thirty-eight centimeters, exceeding the twenty-four centimeters of the largest miniature, that of the Heavenly Hosts (I.6). Hildegard chose to assign the individual visions to the manuscript page, in large format and centered on the folio, to offer the reader a cognitive and contemplative experience. On the other hand, she assigned the single vision to an imaginary, plastic, three-dimensional space beyond the page, to enable an immersive experience. A choice which, aside from technical solutions, sends the message that only a path of listening, elaboration, and edification can lead to the majesty of revelation.

Trinity

Sun/Christ

Moon/Church

Earth/Humanity

Darkness

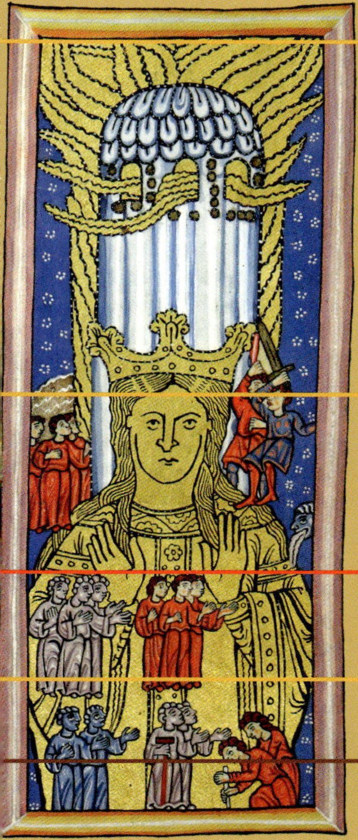

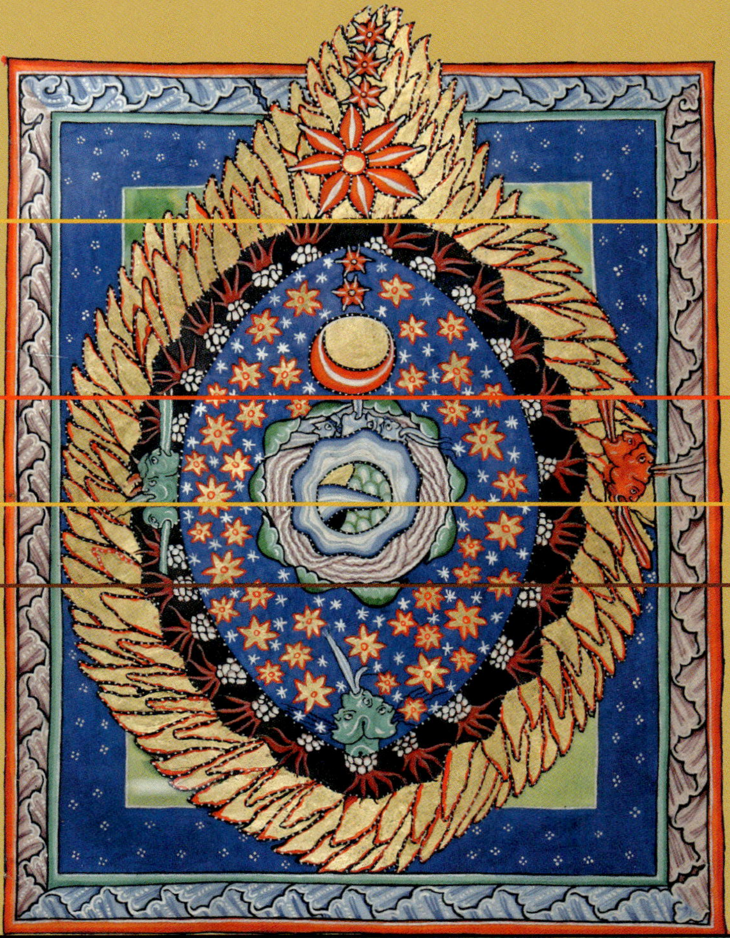

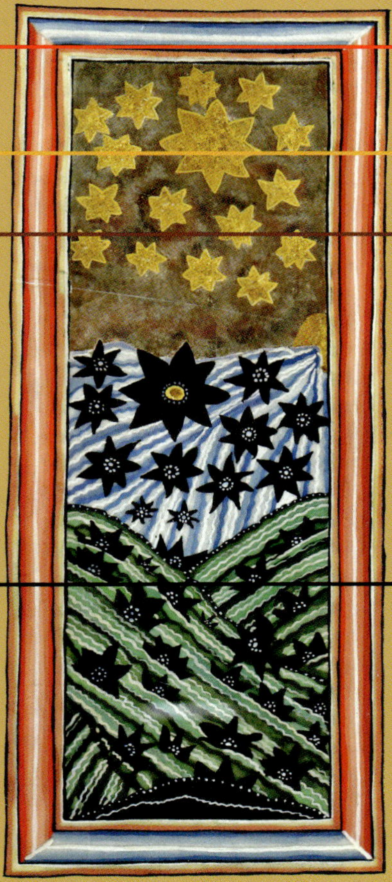

Constructive Matrix

And all these armies were singing with marvellous voices all kinds of music about the wonders that God works in blessed souls, and by this God was magnificently glorified (*SC* I.6.D, p. 139).

The circles of angelic praise and planetary orbits, signs and symbols of the sound and creatural light of God, define the constructive matrix of the work. They are overlapping and form a rose of fourteen concentric circles, a multiple of seven, symbolizing the protective invocation of the Holy Spirit. The circle of the star at the top, image of the Trinity, embraces all of creation and delimits the ultimate space reserved for the human, who at the End Times will complete the circles of the Heavenly Hosts, taking the place of the fallen angel.

The square grid of the constructive matrix is delineated by lines tangential to the circles, both on the horizontal and vertical axes, which are framed by the black line of darkness at the bottom and the yellow line of Spirit at the top of the space. They have a harmonious rhythm because the diameters of the circles are all multiples of the diameter of the central circle of light, adored by the angels, which thus becomes the reference unit of measurement for the construction. The total space is sixteen times this measurement and a symbol of blessedness.

The entire design of the miniatures, image of creation and the human journey, is therefore created in relation to the measure of God's light (see table below) and based on the constructive matrix. This is exemplified by the miniature of the *Protestificatio* (Declaration), an image of Hildegard's tabernacle of the soul, which is half as high and one-third as wide as the grid, and thus fits into it six times (see image below). The number six is the symbol of the sixth day of the Creation, when humanity was created, and in fact marks the beginning of the human journey along the ways—the theme of the work—to which Hildegard herself bears witness.

	Measurements	Heavenly Hosts	Planets
14	10		star
13	9.5		star
12	9	angels	star
11	8	archangels	
10	7.5		sun
9	7	virtues	
8	6	authorities	
7	5.5	principalities	
6	5		star
5	4.5	dominions	star
4	4		moon
3	3.5	thrones	
2	3	seraphim	
1	2	cherubim	
0	1	light	

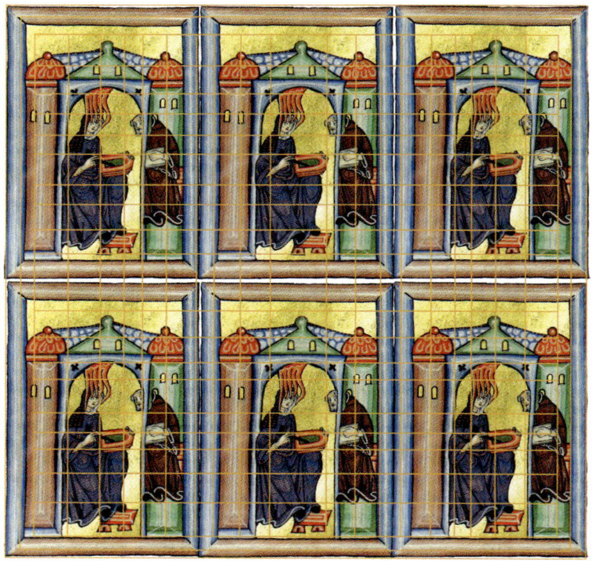

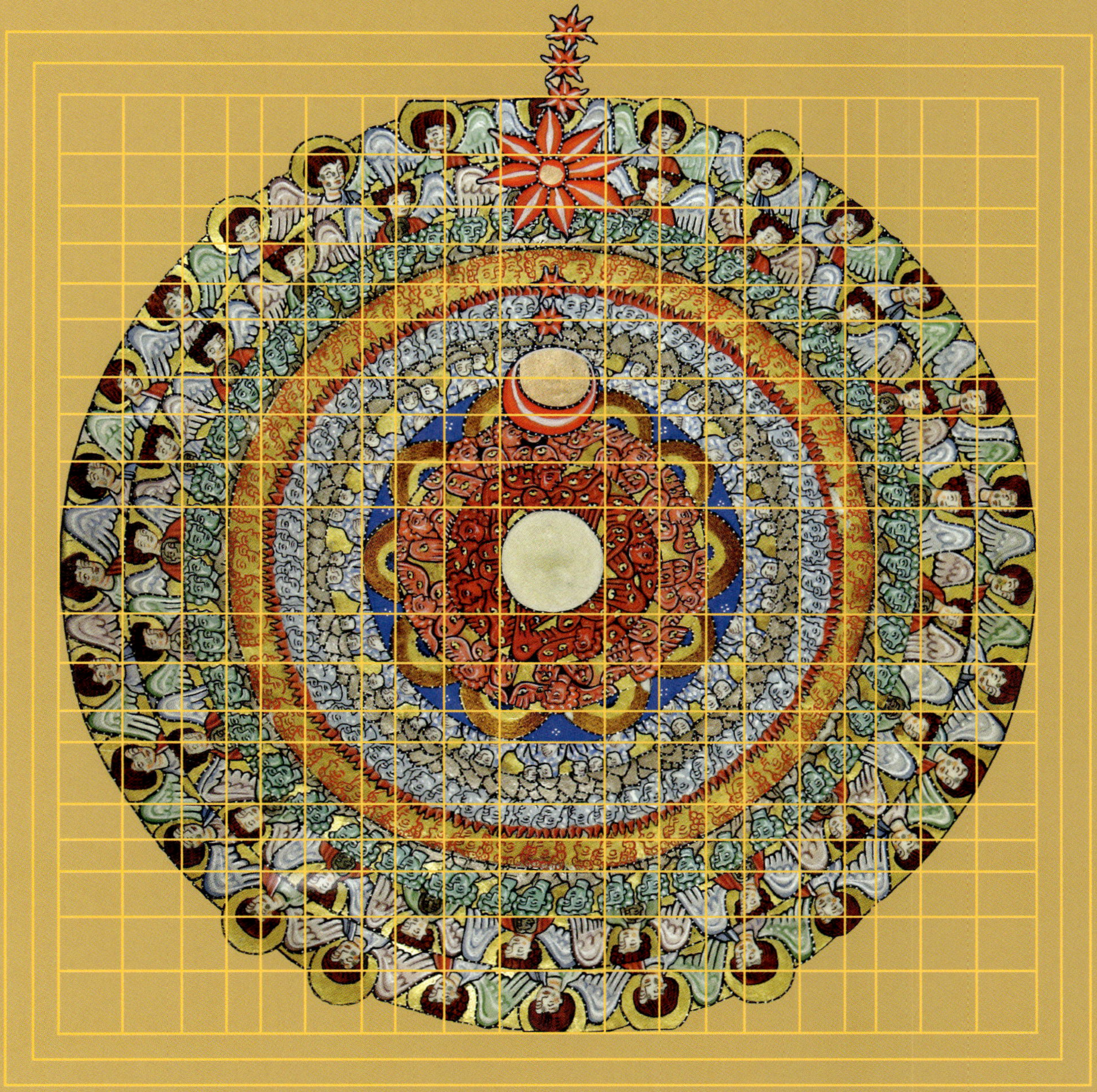

Sapiential Pentagram

The story of humanity's journey of salvation unfolds on symbolic planes, indicated by the lines of the pentagram. The spaces, marked by the stars of the firmament, guide the reading, and certain chosen details, on the symbolic axis, make the construction immediately understandable as well as revealing the wondrous poetry of Hildegard.

Three Stars/Trinity

The dove of the Spirit, the Father and the Lamb.

The flames of the Spirit and the three windows.

And in this light appears a dove [...] in the brilliance of the light of the Son of God, burns the Holy spirit (*SC* III.4.14, p. 363).

Globe of Fire/Sun/Christ

The Shining One seated on the throne of faith.

The Flame the color of air, the Word.

For the Son of God existed according to divinity like a root in the Father's heart and the force of divinity (*LDO* II.1.19, p. 291).

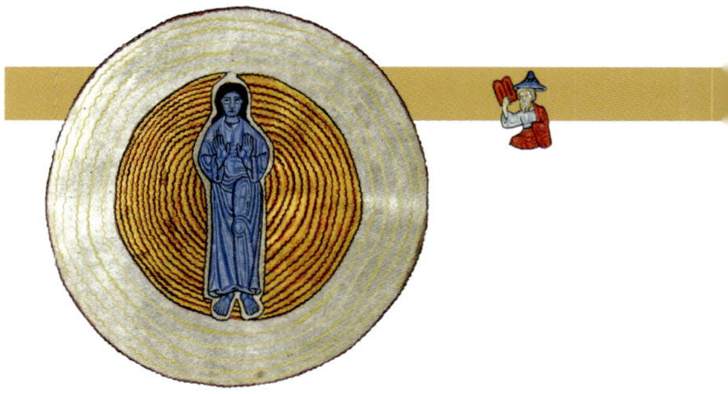

Incandescent Globe/Moon/Church

The bridegroom of the Church is born as if in the womb of the Father.

Abraham, first among the prophets of the Church.

And since Abraham trusted faithfully in God in all things, so he is called the father of those who will be the heirs of the Kingdom of Heaven (*LDO* I.1.17, pp. 44–45).

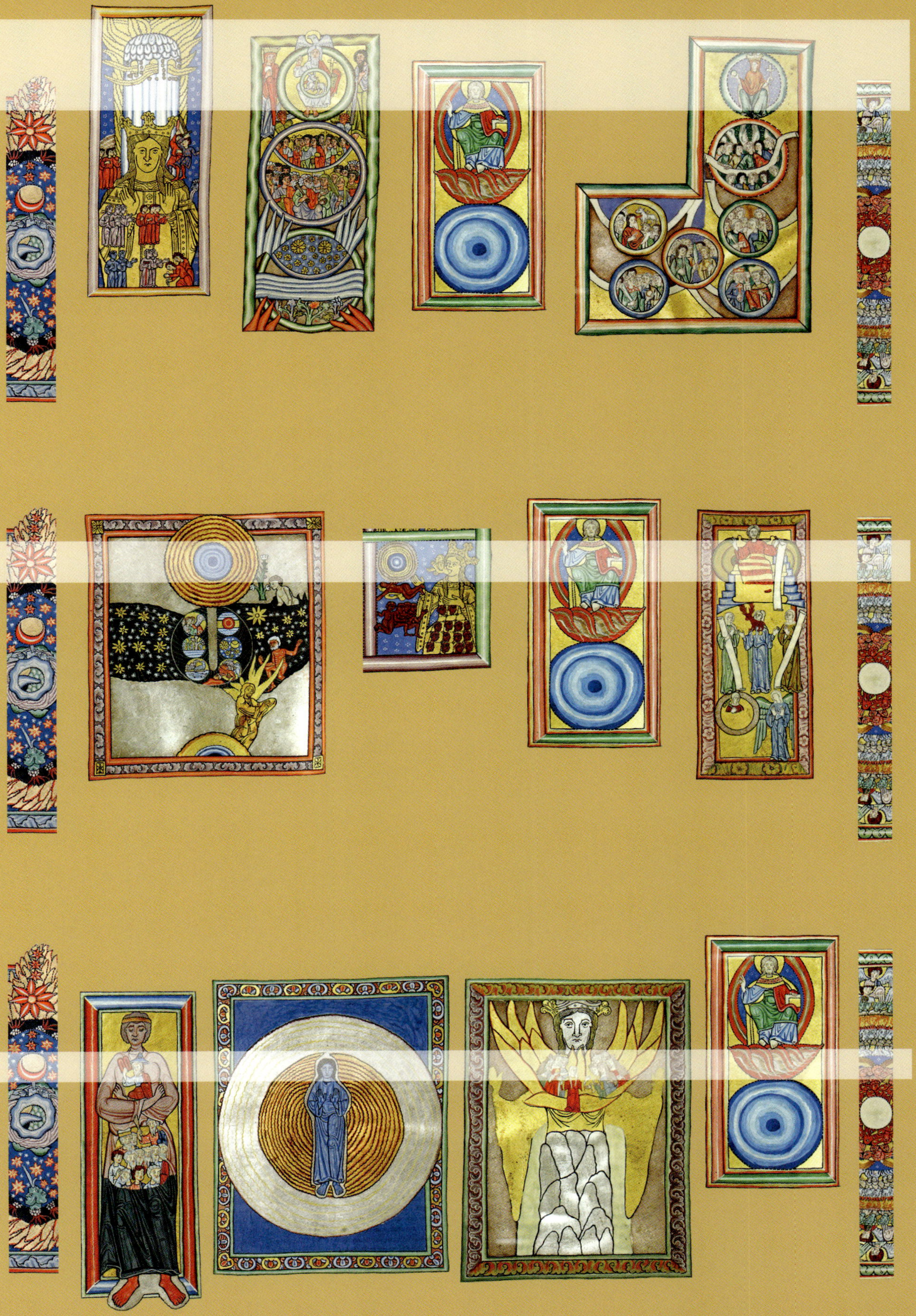

Above the Earth

The wind of the watery air, the baptism.

The exit of the soul at the end of the earthly journey when it takes off the garment of the body and dons anew the celestial garment of the spirit.

And so they resume the dress of true faith, which they received in baptism and threw away in error when they scorned the true God (*SC* III.9.19, p. 460).

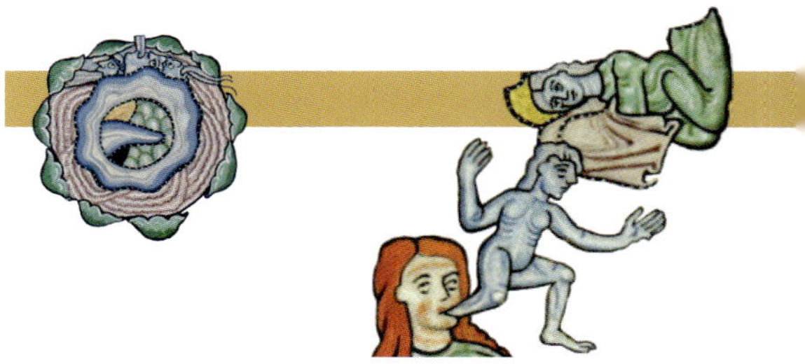

Sandy Globe/Earth/Humanity

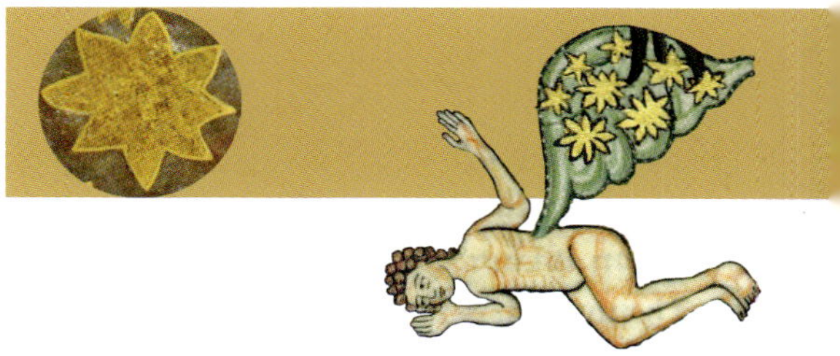

The star of the first angel.

The multitude of stars of humanity that will take the fallen angel's place at the End Times.

Then you will be converted to us as you gaze upon the Day that the dawn's shoot—Mary, the Star of the Sea—has revealed to us (*LDO* III.5.455).

Below the Earth

The birth of Eve, last act of the genesis.

The Eucharistic offering, beginning of the new life.

Praise, therefore, praise God, ye blessed hearts, for the miracles God has wrought in the frail earthly reflection of the beauty of the Most High; as He Himself foreshadowed when He first made Woman from the rib of the man He had created (*SC* III.13.16, p. 536).

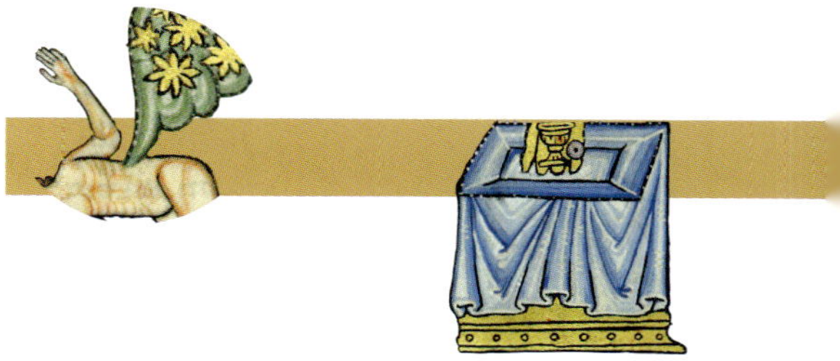

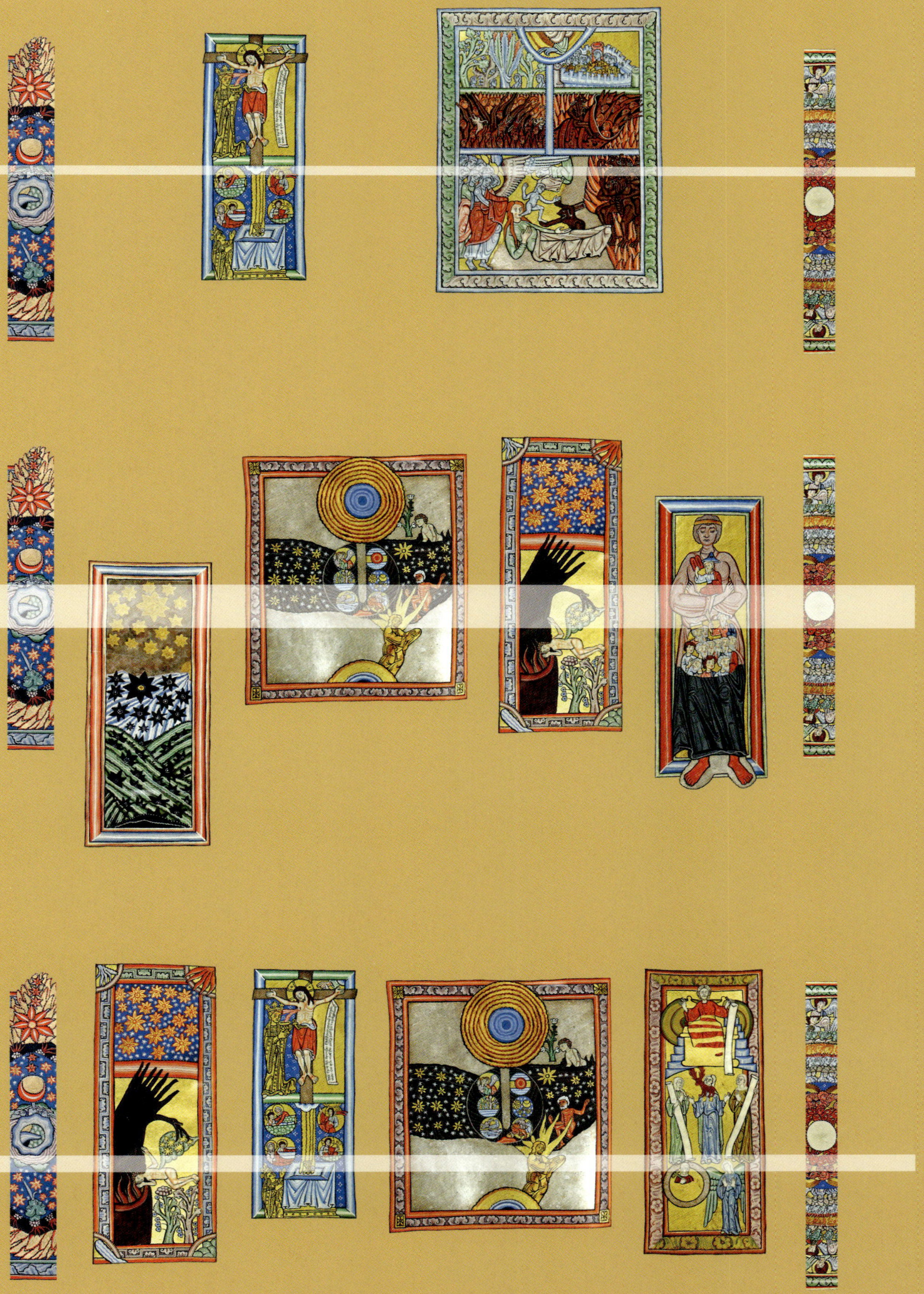

The Light of Hope on the Abyss of Hell

Lucifer plunges into the darkness and his splendor returns to God.

On that very spot, on the edge of the abyss, rises the auroral light of Mary, in whose womb the flower of Christ will be born.

But when they are extinguished, you see the light that was taken from them immediately return to Him Who sits on the throne. That is to say, when the Devil, because of his pride and obstinacy, lost his exceeding brilliance, that brilliance returned to God the Father to be kept in His secret heart; for the glory of that splendor was not allowed to go for nothing, but God kept it as a light for another of His creations (*SC* III.1.16, pp. 319–320).

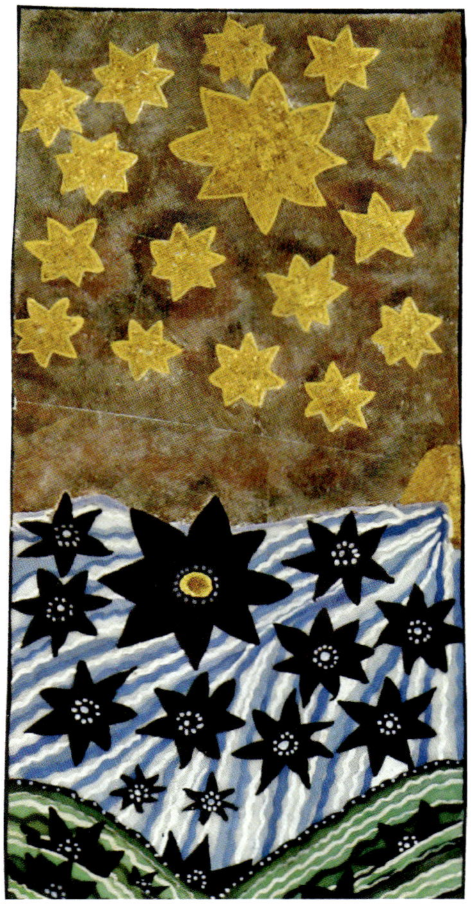

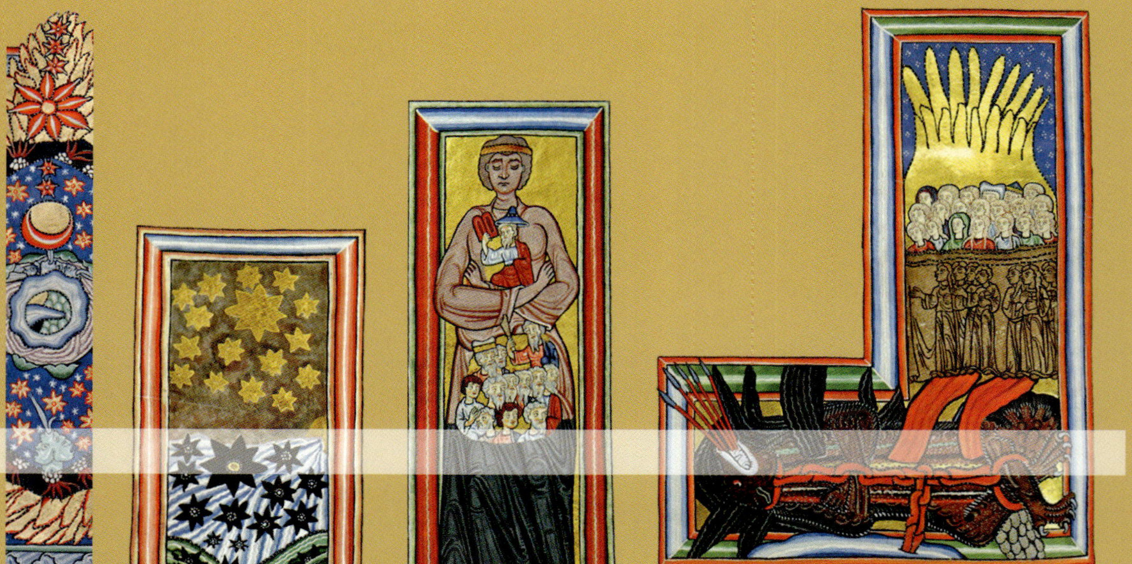

And in the earth too appears a fulgor like the aurora, into which the flame is miraculously absorbed, without being separated from the blazing fire. This is to say that God set a great splendor of light in the place where he would bring forth His Word [...] He gave that profitable fruit and brought Him forth as a great fountain, so that every faithful throat could drink, and never more be dry (*SC* II.1.11, p. 154).

For in this transmutation to dispel the darkness, light will not be needed; and the sun will not move and by its motion bring times of darkness. For then the day will arise without end (*SC* III.12.16, p. 521).

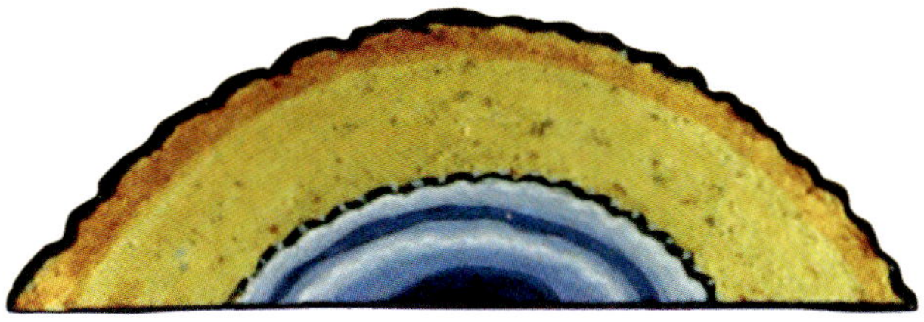

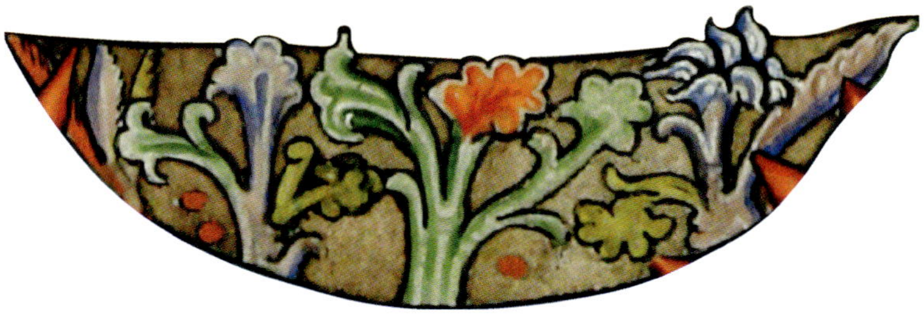

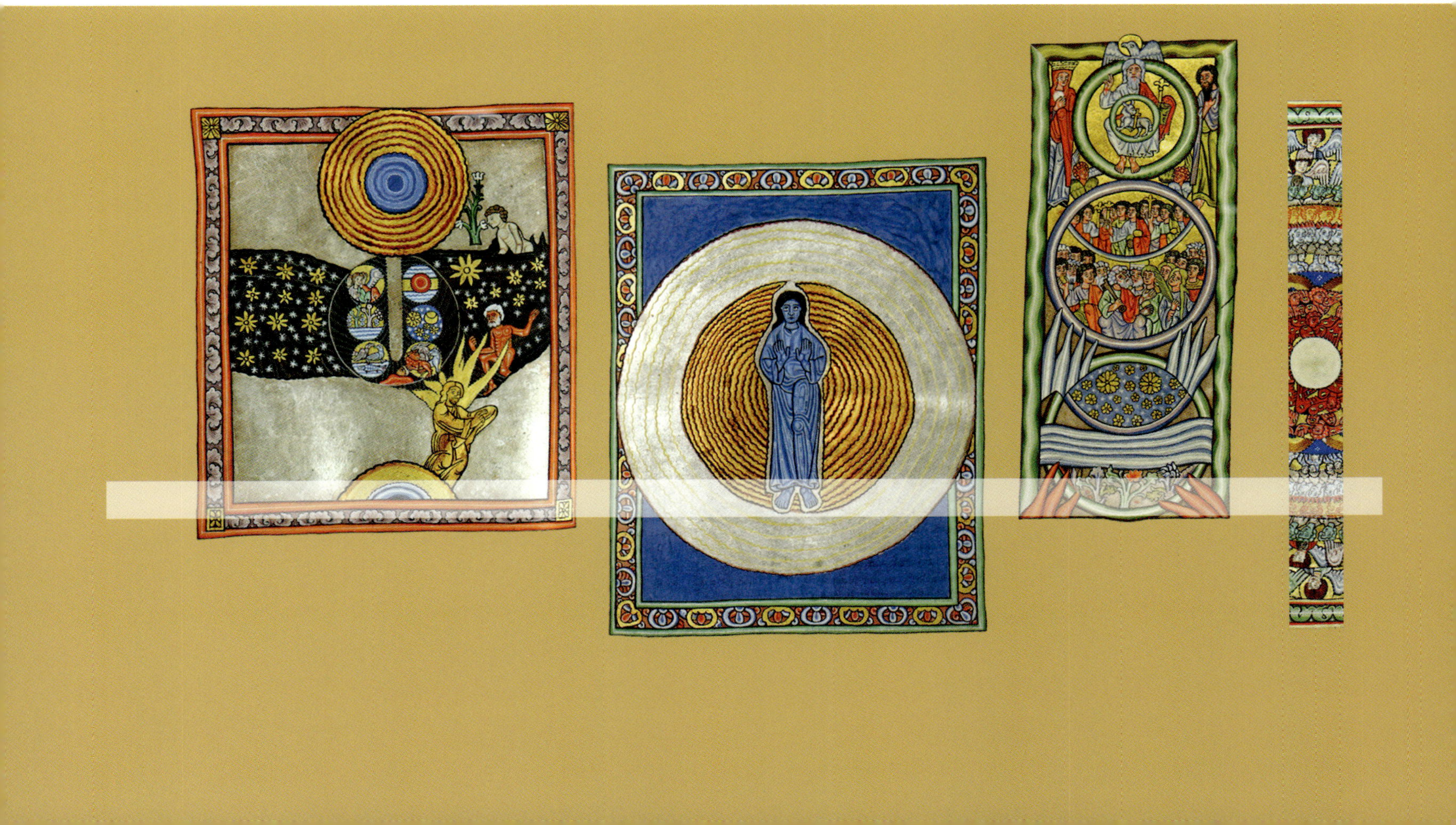

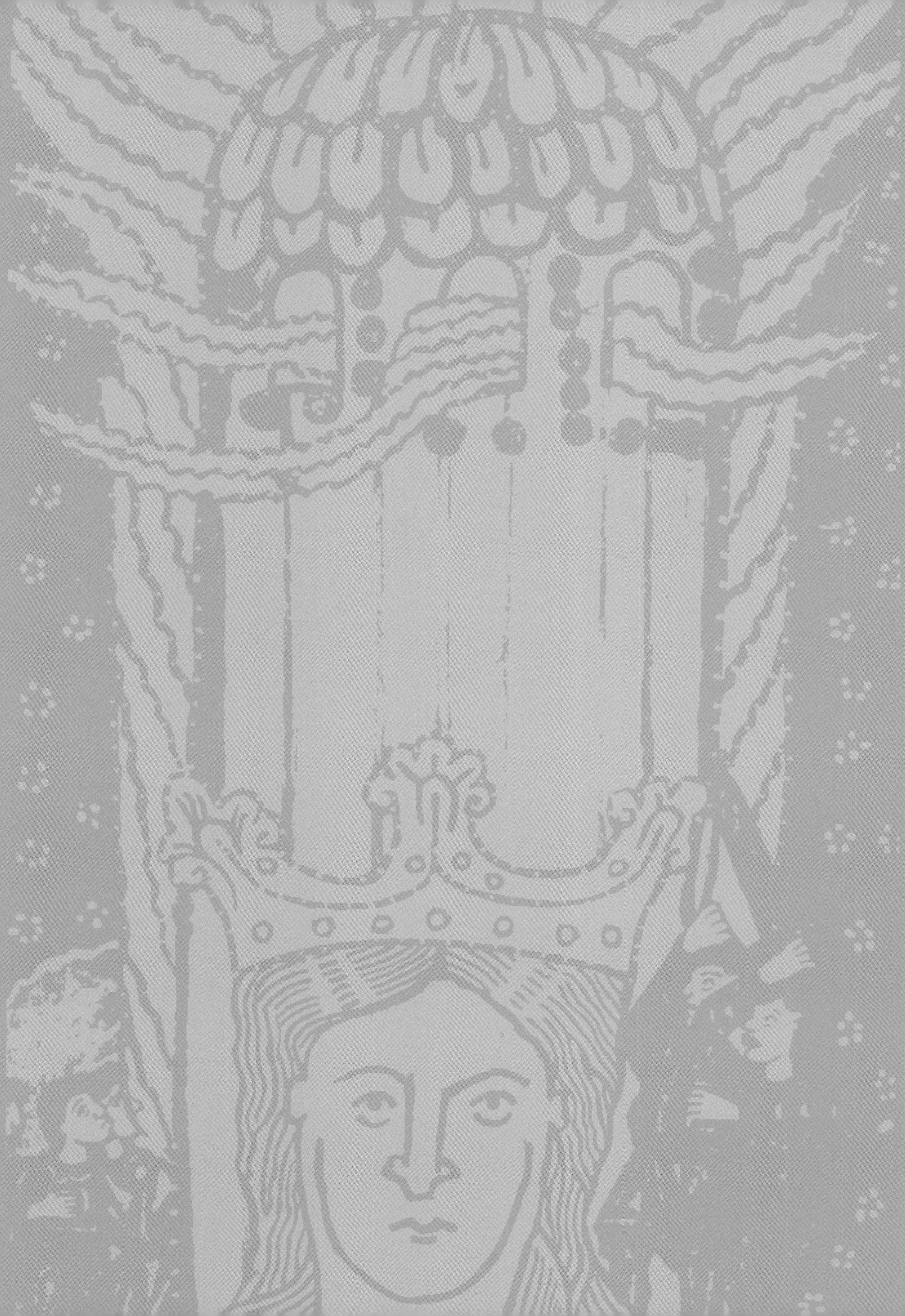

The Poetry of Revelation

The magnificence of Divine Love [...] shows symbolically that through her, he is recognized in faith who is not seen visibly with the visible eyes (*LDO* I.1.3, p. 36).

The voice of the living light commands Hildegard thus: *write what you see and listen to reveal the hidden secrets*, which speak of the *royal revelation of the mystery of the Son of God Incarnate.* Like the water of the spring *it must not be kept hidden, but made visible, until all those who thirst may drink from it; thus the Son of God is neither inaccessible to, nor hidden from, his chosen ones, but visible.*

But neither words nor images are enough. The magnificence of divine love can only be revealed by finding wonder, awe, and hidden signs, in what is known but unseen. Indeed, as *with draught animals a plow turns over the earth in which seed is sown that will bear great fruit to feed humans, so too the people of the law kept the written letter of God's precepts; but they were not satisfied by their fruit, because they did not know what was hidden within the letter. But through the seeds of his words the Son of God revealed to those who believe that, filled up with his flesh and blood, they can have life; and this, once hidden within the divine secrets, he disclosed through himself.*

In designing the layout of the miniatures with her collaborators, Hildegard placed the images on the axes of the constructive matrix in such a way that through transparency the light would reveal new images created by the superimposition of known ones. This creates a poetic dynamism that unites separate elements and reveals the mystery in a few signs: what was visible to the outer eye sings to the heart through the eyes of the soul, to which all is now revealed.

This happens *when a person sometimes consents to the soul in its desires,* [and] *he burns completely in the love of God. Thus flying from day to day in the mirth of eternal happiness, he delights in reflective faith and in the wisdom of the Holy Scriptures, by whose sweetness he is invisibly nourished and strengthened, like a fish that, strengthened by the air and by the water's flow, lives for a long time in water without food.*

Prophecy

[...] the profound and rich wisdom of the principal doctors, who through the fire of the Holy Spirit made known what was obscure in the Law and the prophets, and showed their fruition in the Gospels. Thus they made these things fruitful to the understanding; they touched on the outward content of the Scriptures in the work of the Father's goodness, and sweetly ruminated on their mystical significance (*SC* III.4.6, pp. 359–360).

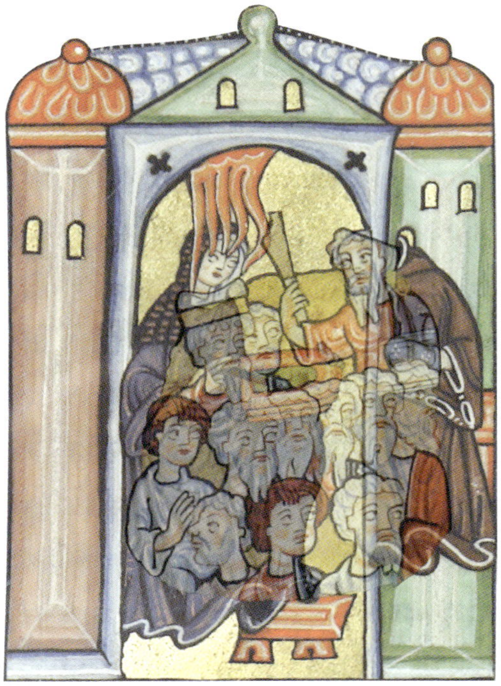

The gifts of prophecy
the coincidence of the faces of Abraham and Volmar is a testimony of obedience; the face of John in Hildegard's lap, a testimony of faithfulness.

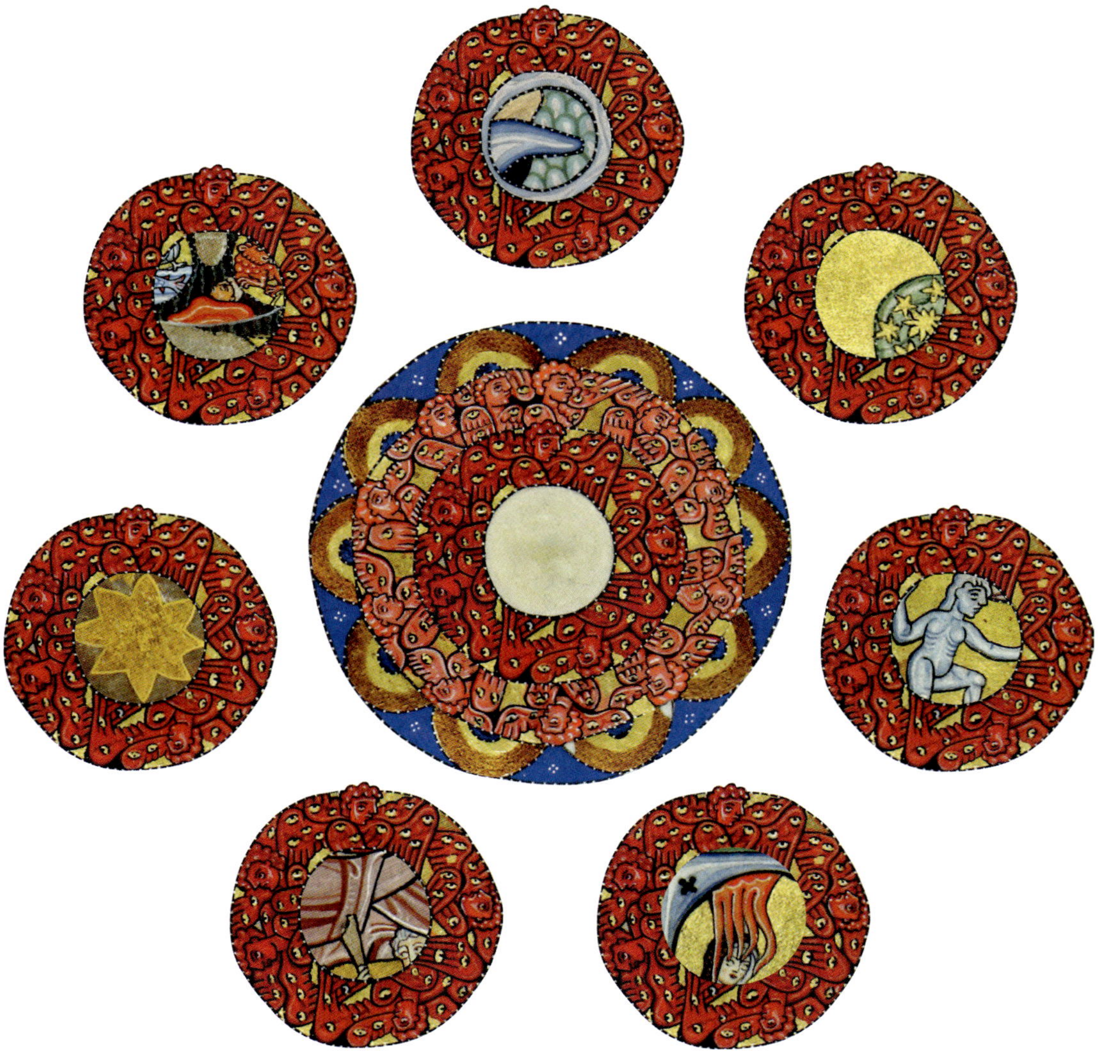

Prophecy in the story
(above) on either side, Adam born from mud and the green cloud of Eve with the stars; and in the middle, the mountain of faith separating the light from the darkness; (center) the fall of the first Angel at the beginning of the story and the fulfillment with humanity; (below) from the first prophet Abraham to the "Sybil of the Rhine".

Flower of Life

But I, Who am the Beginning and the End, again say to you, O human, that My noble Son is the flower of roses and lilies of the valley (*SC* II.6.34, p. 259).

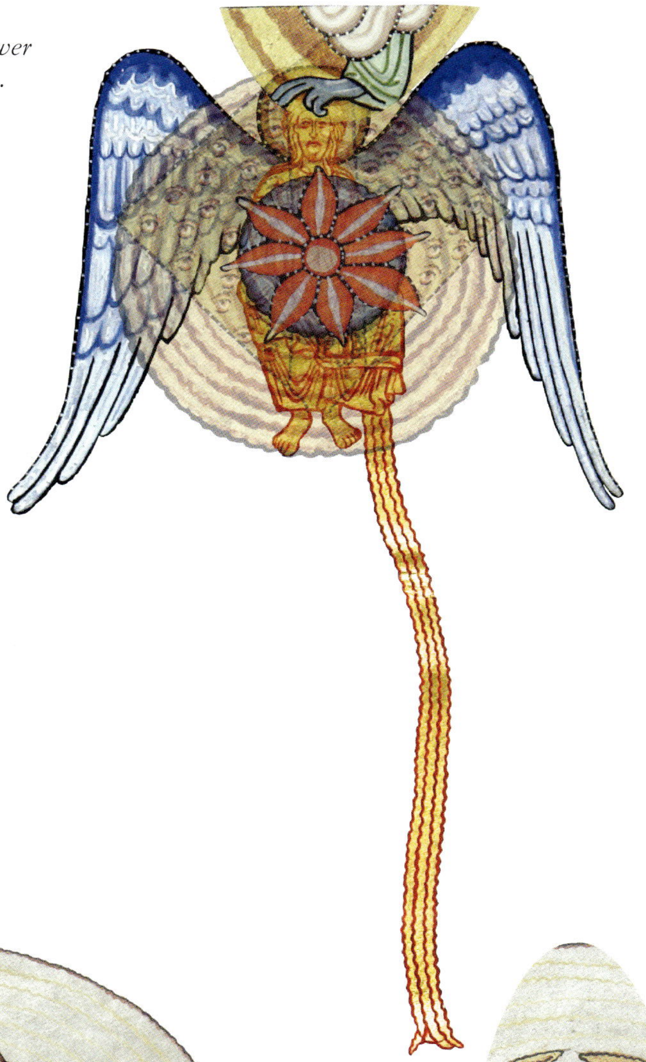

The Son of God sent by the Father
appears as a flame the color of air; seated on the mountain with wings; and as the sun of justice.

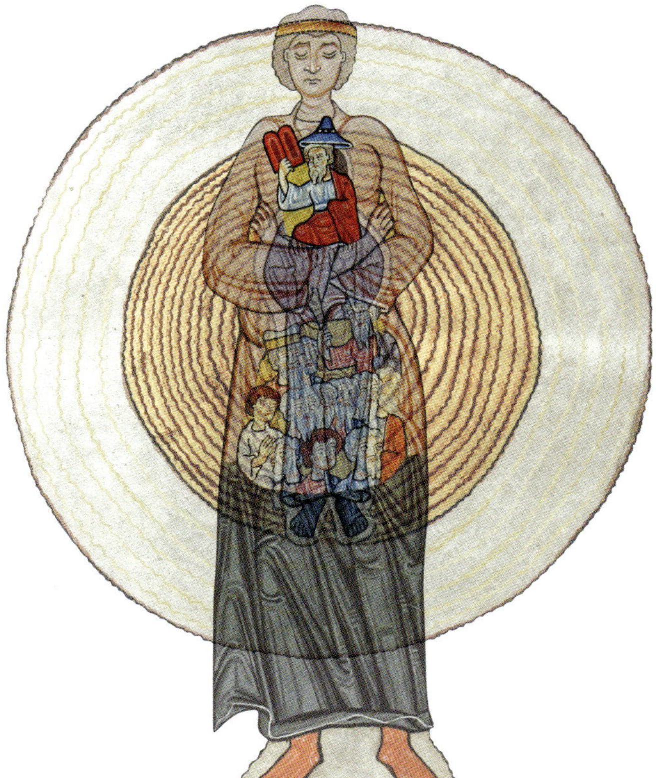

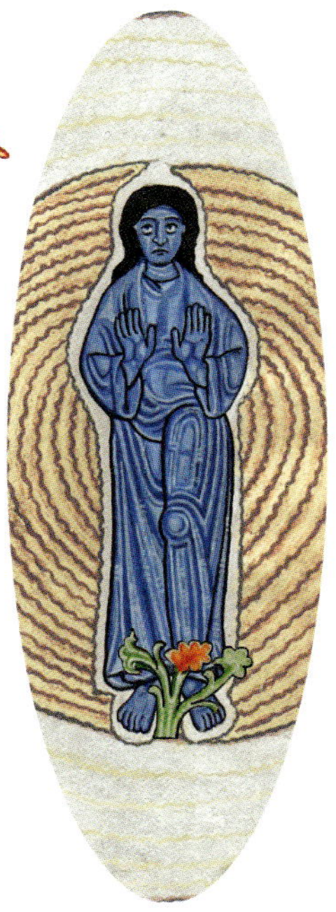

From the ancient to the new alliance
(left) in the white of the Father, the gold colored circle crowns the Synagogue, prefiguration of the incarnation of the Son: the blue hat of the prophet Abraham completes the figure of Christ, last of the prophets, who has appeared as an offshoot of the Tree of Jesse (right).

Fountain of Life

Just as water floods the whole earth, so the soul permeates the whole body (*LDO* I.1.2, p. 35).

The waters of Paradise
envelop Adam as he plunges into the darkness; the descent of the soul into the body; the altar with the new life.

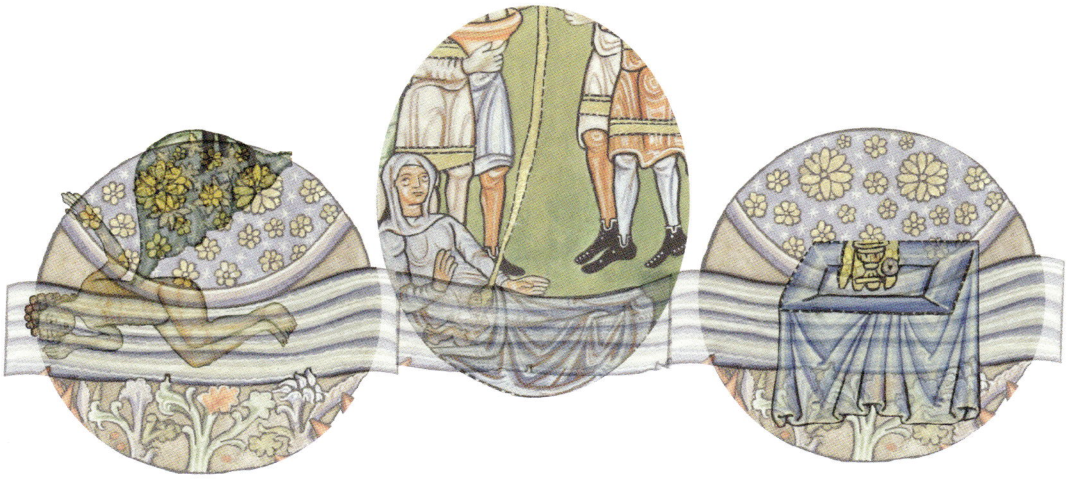

The journey of water
flows from the waters of the genesis to the star of John who baptizes Christ, the baptism of the Church; the wind that gives the water for the baptism and irrigates the cloud beneath the cross from which *viriditas* descends on the Eucharistic offering, and the waters of Paradise in the altar.

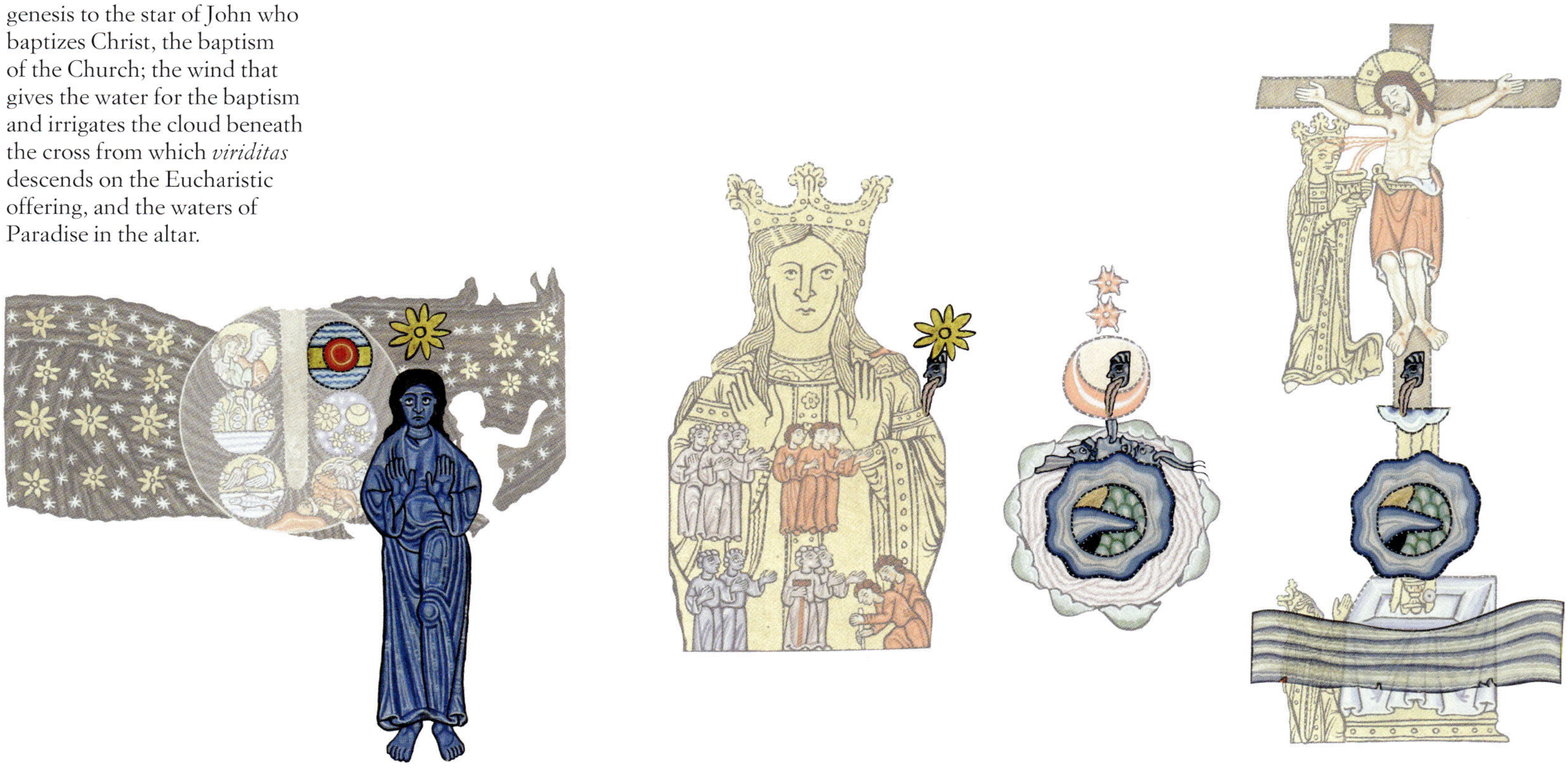

The Chalice

And so the Bridegroom of souls is the cluster of grapes of Cyprus, Whose fruit will not fail. How? A blind man who has come in through the door asks for his sight. How? The person who did not have the vision of faith attains to faith and enters by the squeezing of the winepress into the dew of the blood of Christ (*SC* II.6.29, p. 256).

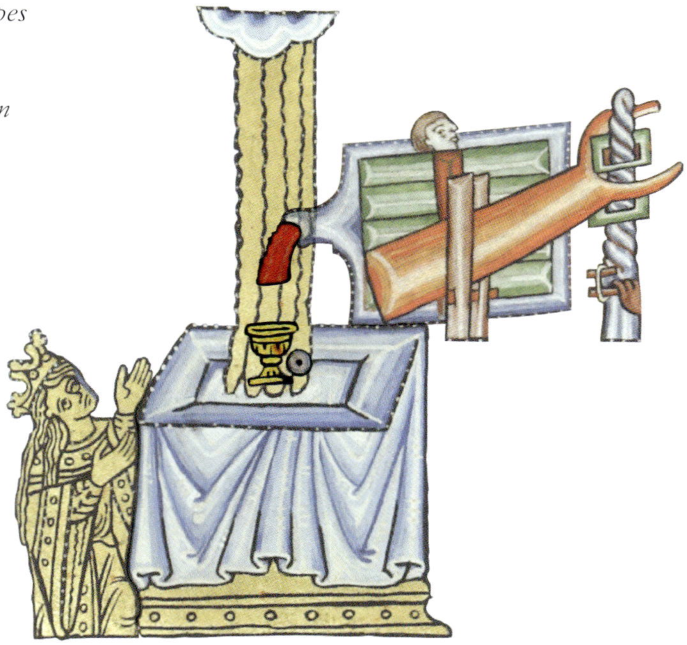

The blood of life descends into the chalice from the soul squeezed in the winepress, image of the mystical winepress of Christ.

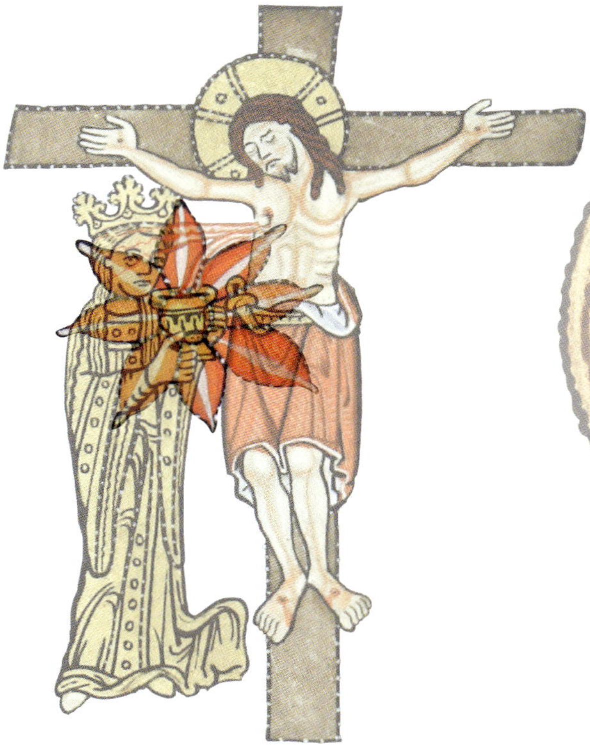

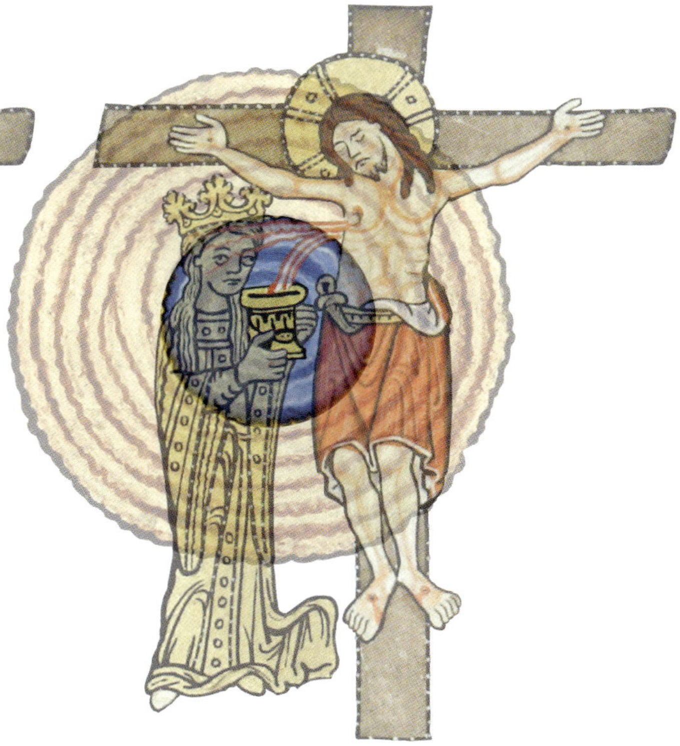

The bride and the nuptial dowry are gathered in the chalice, whence shine forth the rays of the sun of justice and flames the color of air of the Word that has become *flesh and blood*.

The Nuptial Dowry

[...] by the will of the Heavenly Father, she was joined with Him in happy betrothal and nobly dowered with His body and blood (*SC* II.6.D, p. 237).

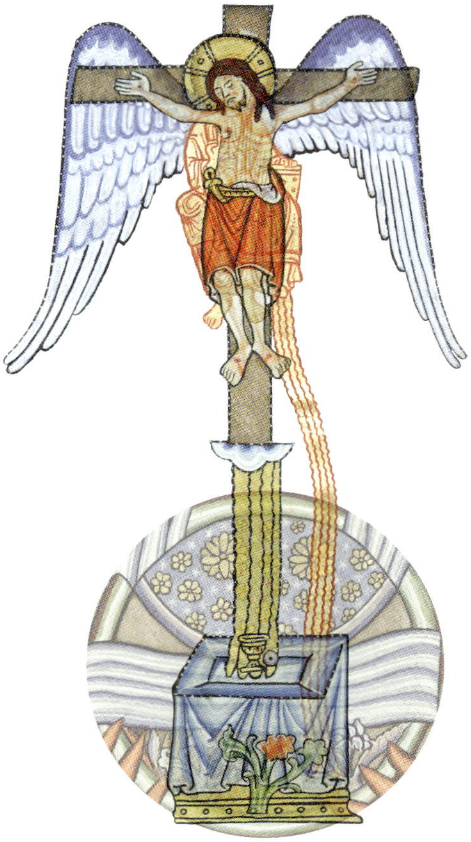

The gift of Christ
who is born as a flower, dies on the cross, rises again with the wings of blessedness, and gives us the new life.

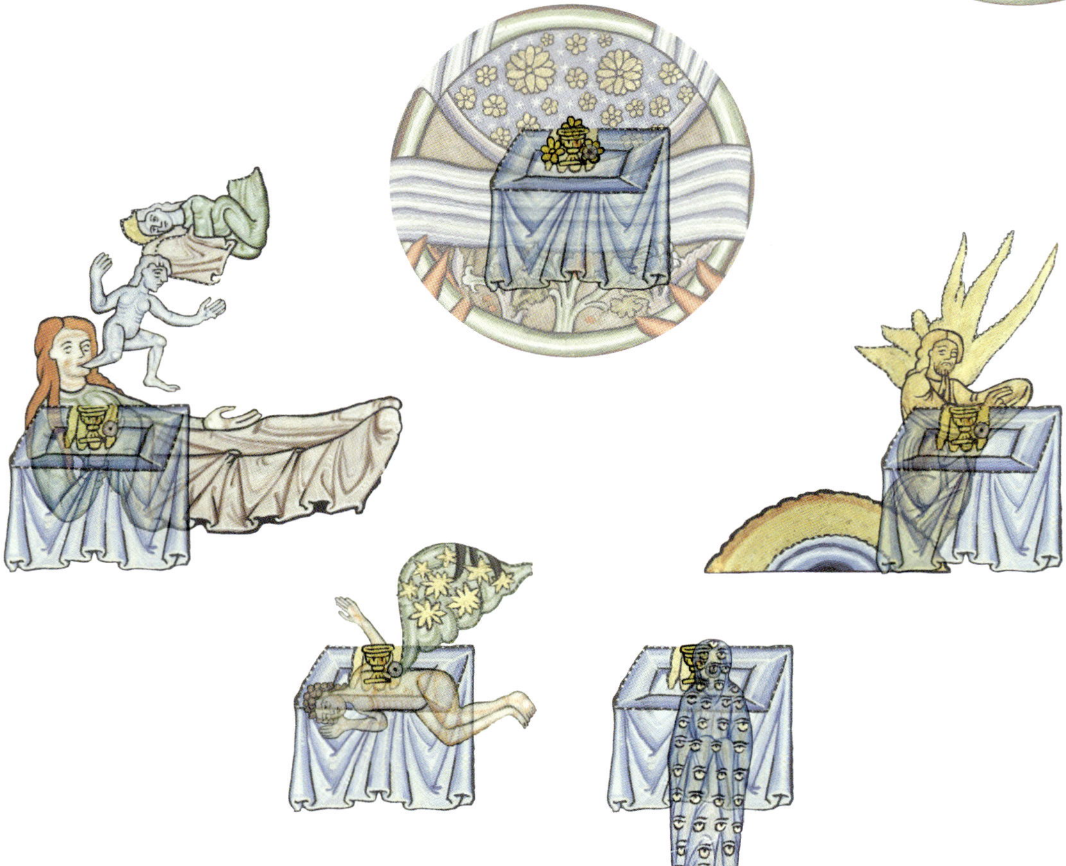

The nuptial dowry
(from below) the Eucharistic offering, coincides with the birth of Eve as a cloud. It is food for the virtue of the Fear of God; it is held in the hand of the Soul while it exhales the spirit, and by Christ, beneath the humeral veil; and it blossoms in the three stars in the sky of Paradise.

The Fall

My Heavenly Father foresaw that in the latter days He would conquer the ancient seducer [...] through Me his Son, incarnate of the Virgin (*SC* II.5.44, p. 227).

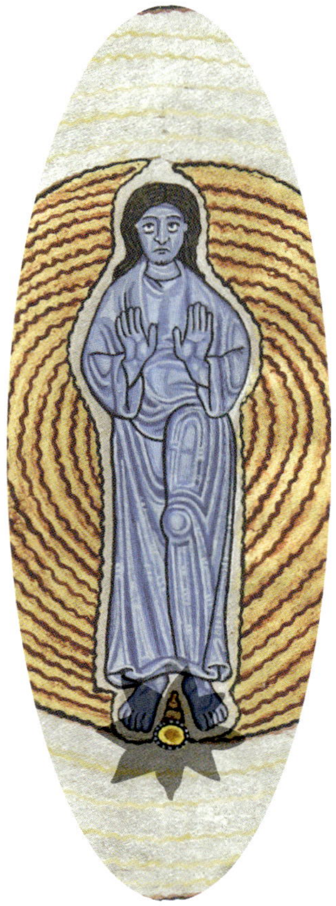

Christ conquers death
and crushes beneath his feet the star of the first angel, while the star of John the Baptist shines on his head (see p. 134).

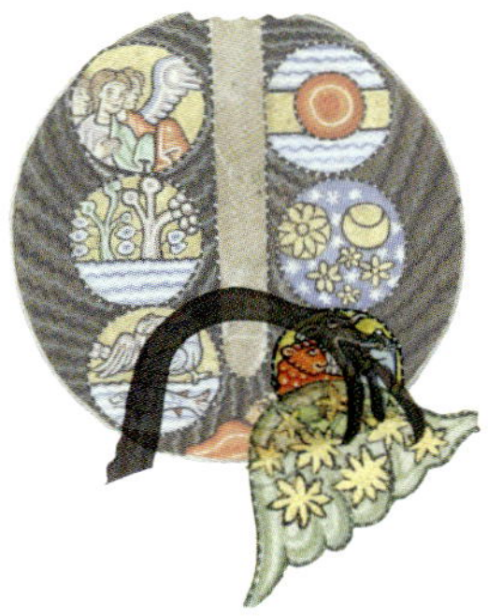

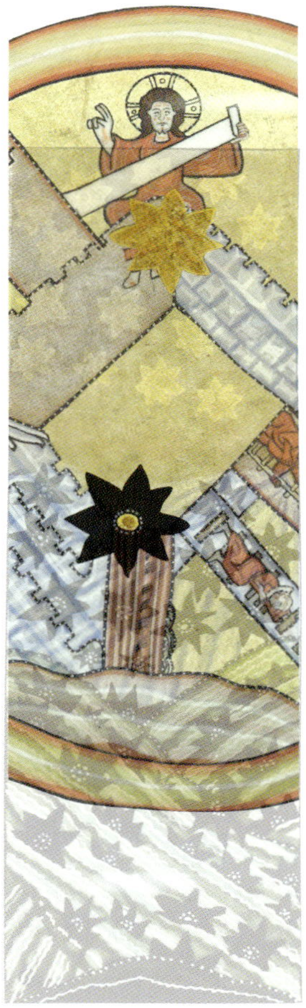

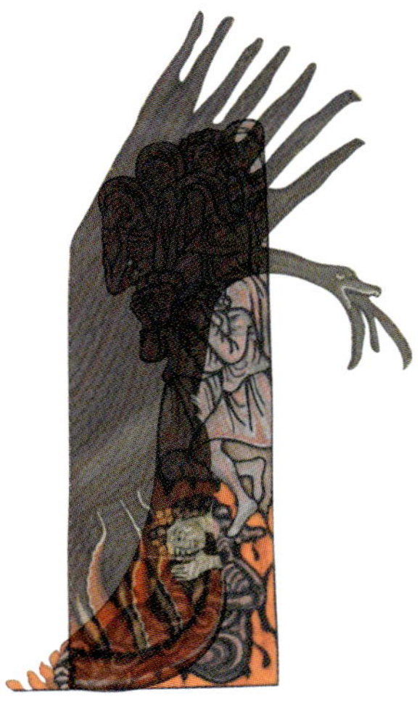

The birth of darkness
marked by the coincidence of the reptiles in the genesis with the serpent of temptation; by the last splendor of Lucifer that is extinguished on the top of the column of the Trinity; and by the condemned of the judgment who enter the darkness of the image of the fall of the progenitors.

Cornerstone

"As the hart pants after the water-brook, so my soul pants after You, O God (Psalm 41:2)" (*SC* III.10.11, p. 481).

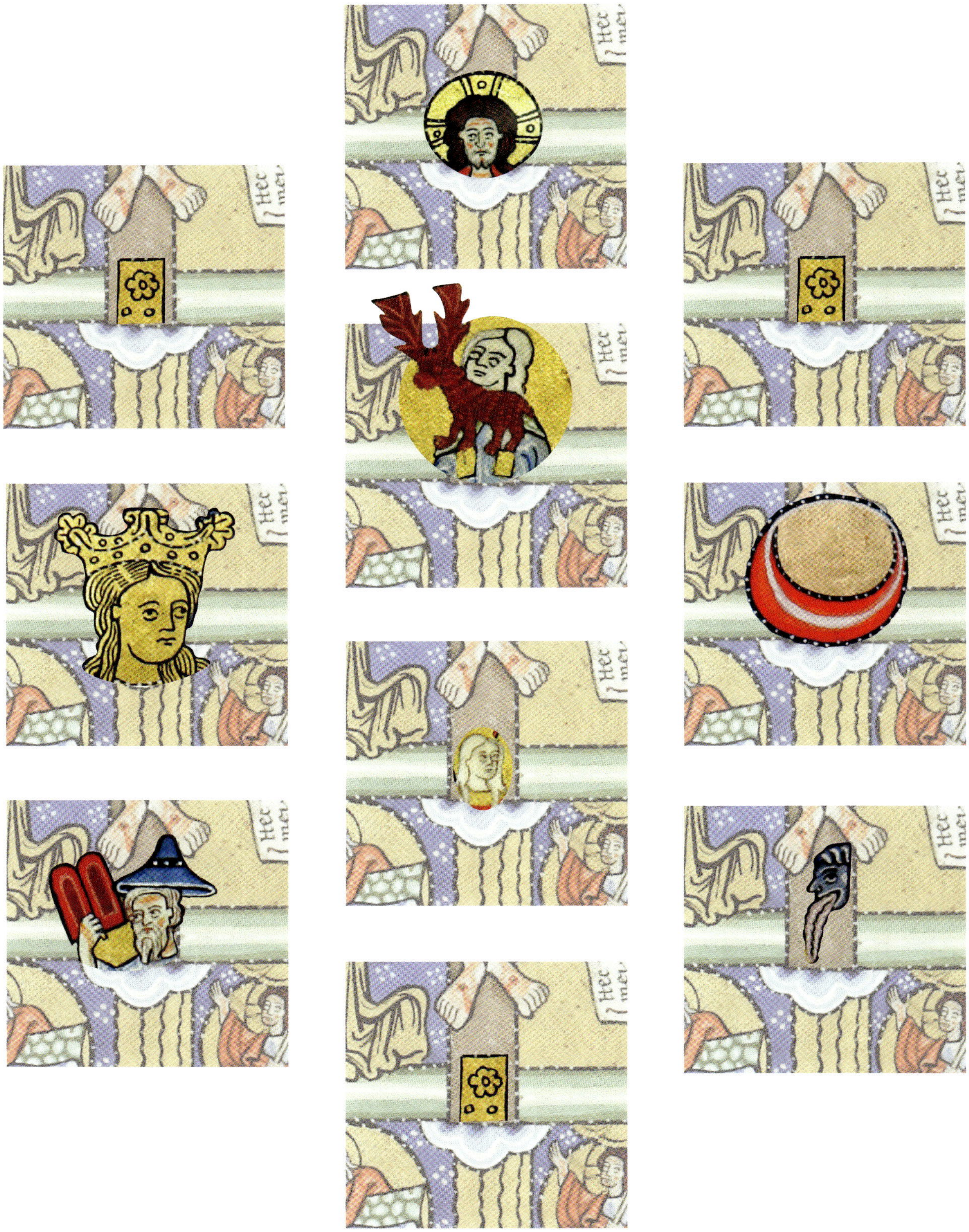

Christ as cornerstone coincides with (from the bottom): Abraham; the face of *virginitas*; the water of baptism; the face of the Church as bride; the moon; the virtue of Constancy with the stag, image of the divine and human aspects of the Son of God; and the face of Christ as the cornerstone of the Building of salvation.

The Bride and the Bridegroom

O dearest seeds, O flowers sweeter and more exquisite than any perfumes, whose soft fragility rises like the dawn to betrothal with My Son, loving Him dearly with chaste love; she is His bride and He is her Bridegroom (*SC* II.3.23, p. 178).

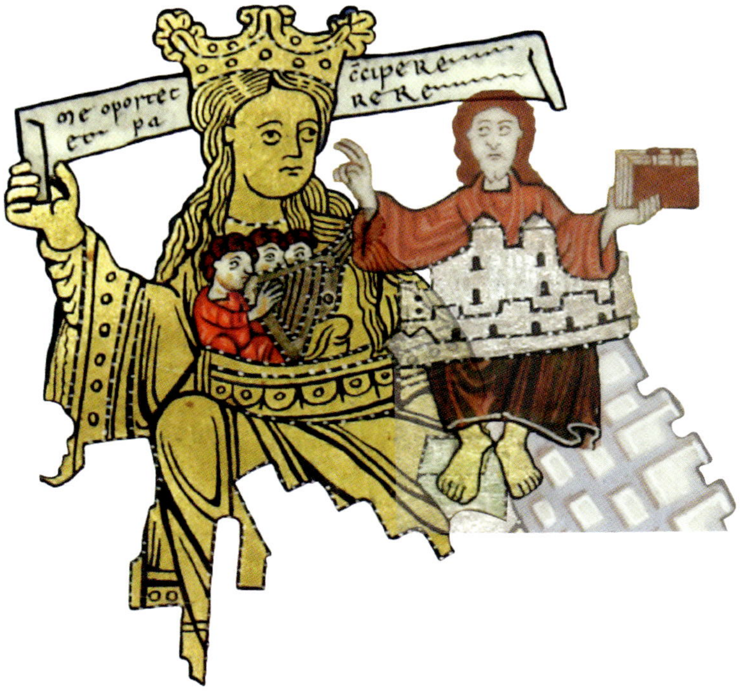

The song of the faithful
celebrates, in the bosom of the Church, the mystery of the aurora of the new day; in the breast of Christ there is the joy of the chosen ones who have reached the quietude of the city of God.

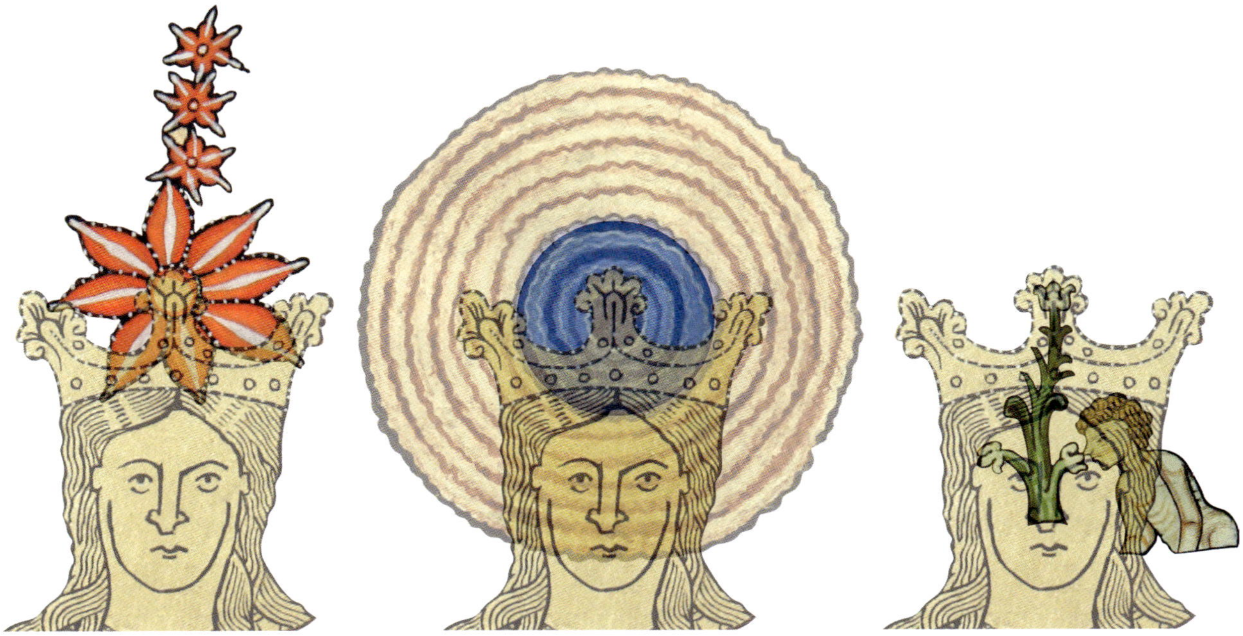

The bride's crown
coincides with the fiery red light of the sun and the sapphire blue flames of the Word, and blooms like the lily of the valley, pure white flower of obedience to the Word, offered to Adam.

The Flowering of Stars

And the soul flows through the body like sap through a tree. What does this mean? By the sap, the tree grows green and produces flowers and then fruit. And how is this fruit matured? By the air's tempering. How? The sun warms it, the rain waters it, and thus by the tempering of the air it is perfected. What does this mean? The mercy of God's grace, like the sun, will illumine the person, the breath of the Holy Spirit, like the rain, will water him, and so discernment, like the tempering of the air, will lead him to the perfection of good fruits (*SC* I.4.25, pp. 123–124).

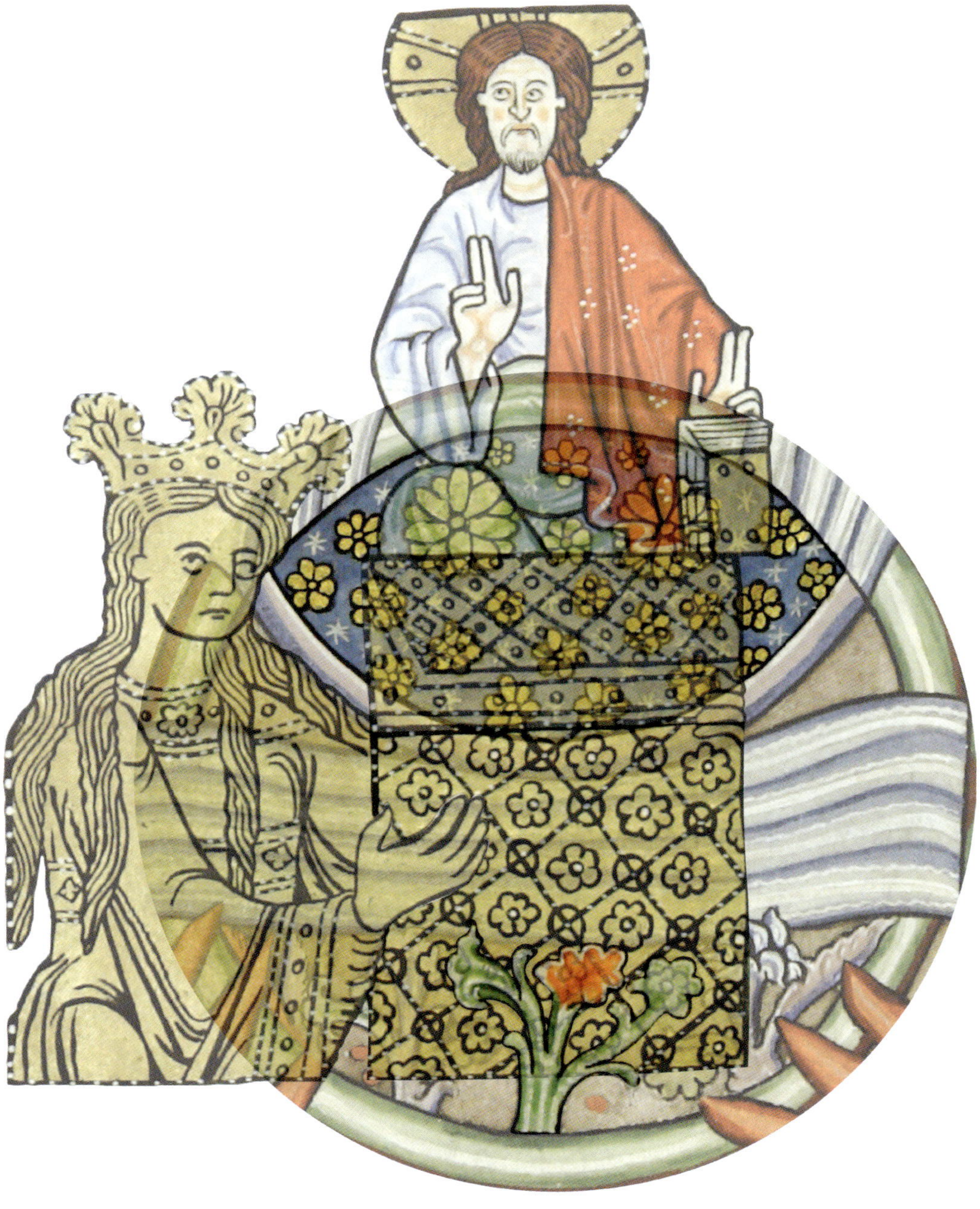

The offering of the bride, the Church, graces the altar with the virtuous works of the faithful, in the same way that flowers adorn the cloth that covers it. At the End Times, they will shine among the stars like flowers in Paradise.

The Journey of the Soul

I have received you, and you have recognized Me. Now, therefore, behold the two paths, one to the East and the other to the North. If you will diligently contemplate Me with your inner vision, as in faith you have been taught, I will receive you into My kingdom. And if you love Me rightly, I will do whatever you shall wish (*SC* II.3.D, p. 169).

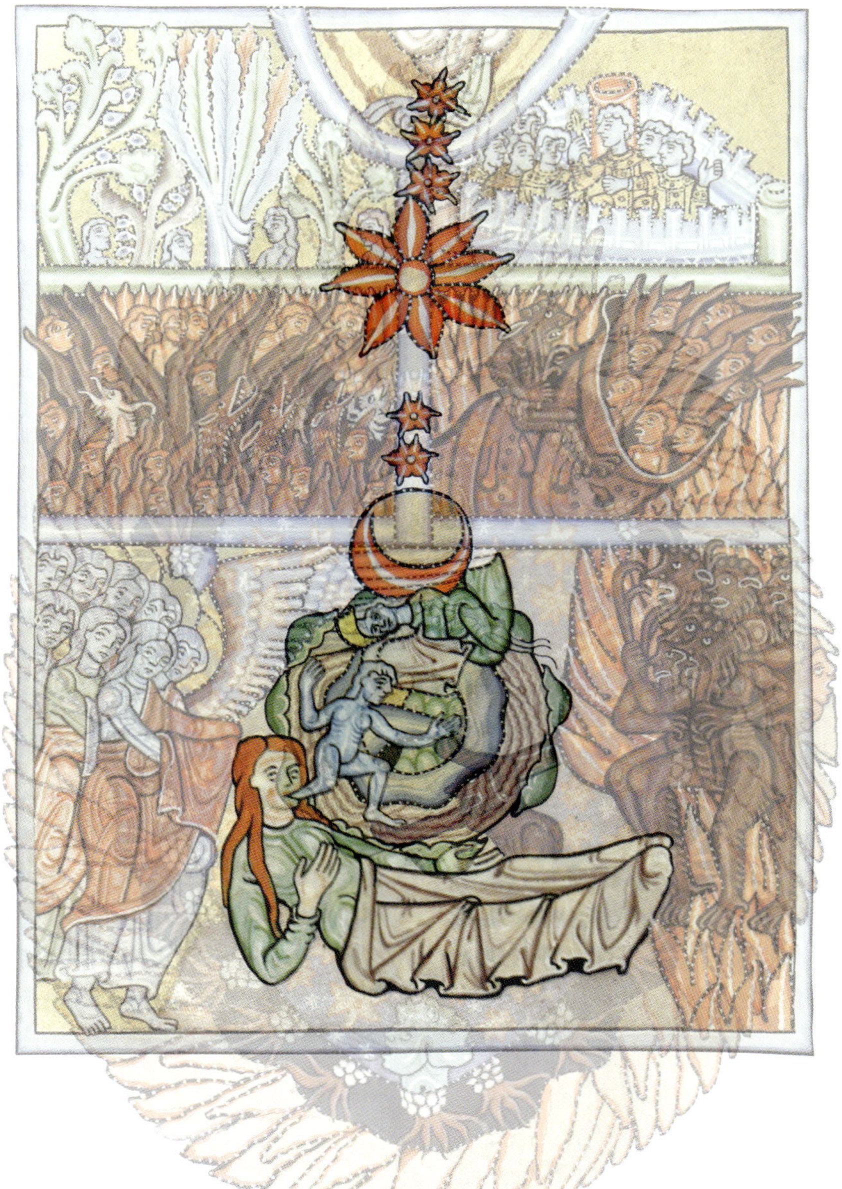

The way of the spirit that leaves the soul takes on a celestial aspect and arrives at the time of judgment. The human, earth, must choose the way of good and let himself be drawn toward heaven by the force of the stars.

"Behold, I stand at the door and knock; if any shall hear My voice and open the door, I will come in to him and will sup with him, and he with Me" (Rev 3:20). That is to say: O you who faithfully love Me, your Savior, look and see how, wishing to aid you, I wait at the tabernacle of your heart (SC I.2.25, p. 85).

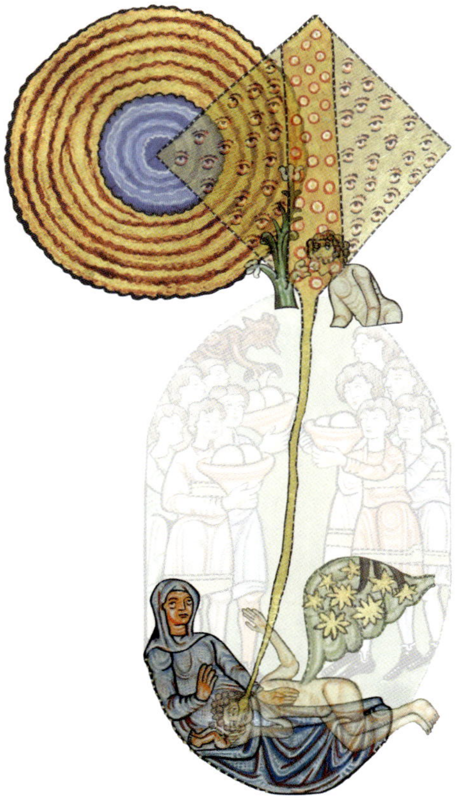

The genesis of the soul and the fear of Adam
the ensoulment coincides with the fall of Adam into the darkness.

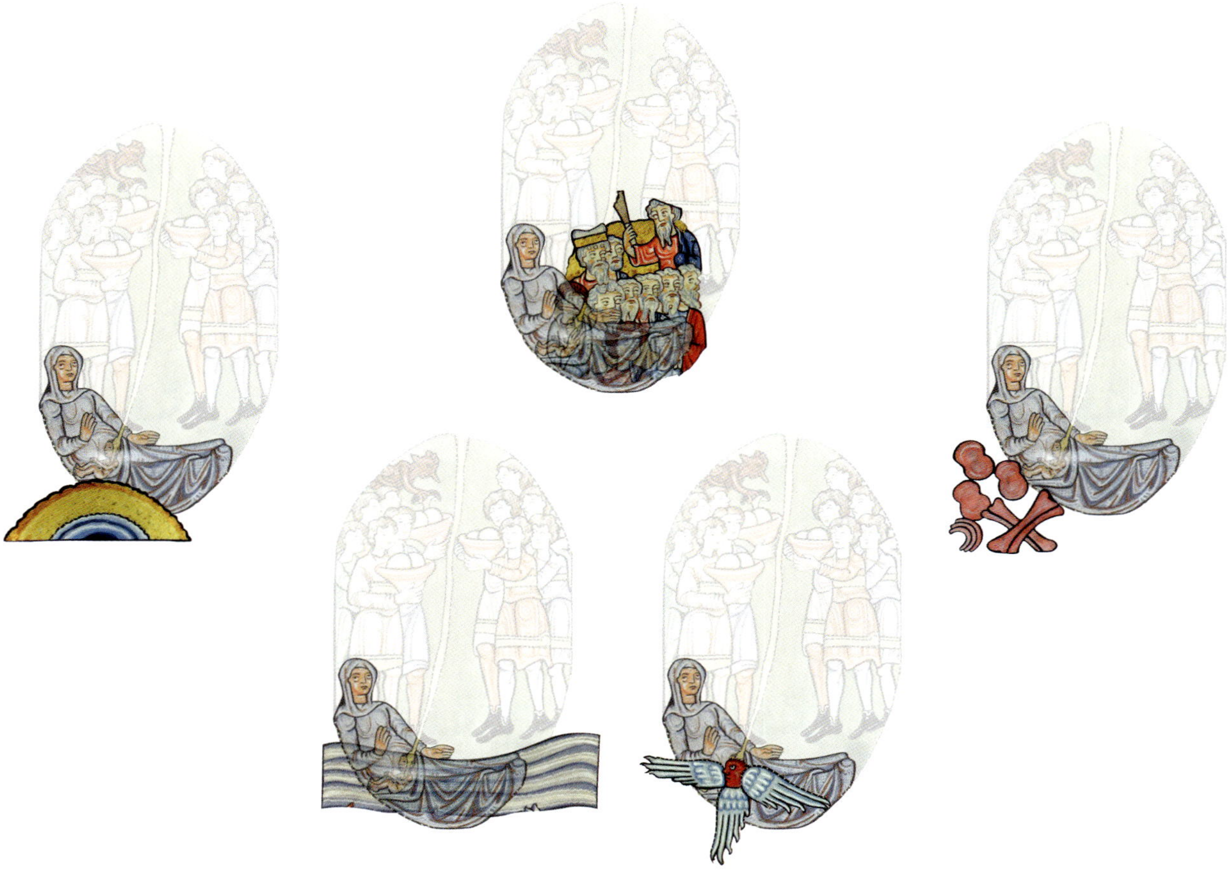

The soul and the story of salvation
show the waters of Paradise and the birth of the child; the zeal of God who safeguards the infant; the protection of the Marian aurora at birth; the soul animated by the word of the prophets; the sign of the pink bones indicating the hope that the soul will be reborn with the body at the End Times.

For God created the world, which he wished to prepare as a tabernacle for Man (*LDO* I.4.105, p. 256).

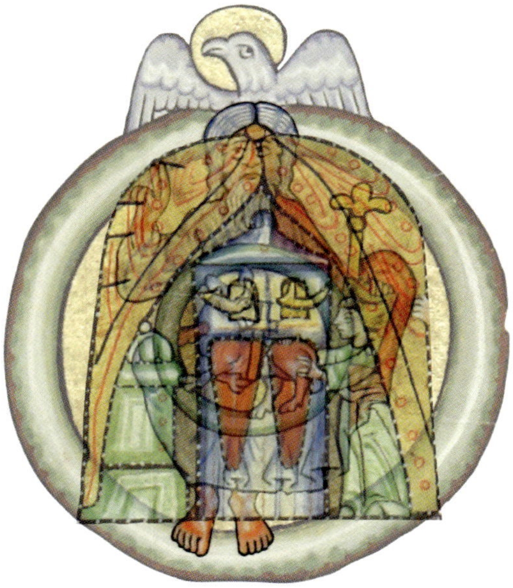

The tabernacle of the soul
in the heart of God.

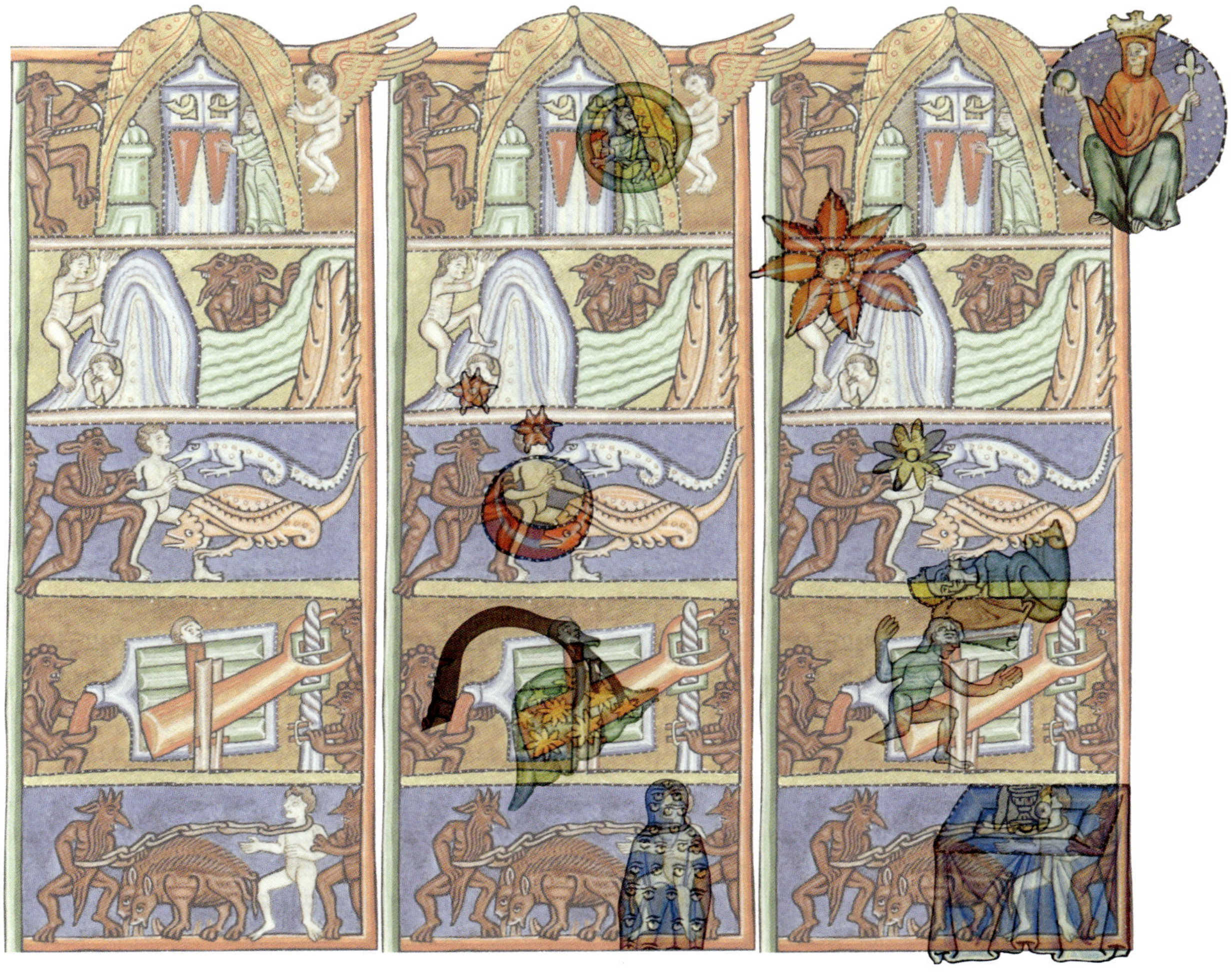

The journey of the soul
At the beginning, it assumes the strength of the virtue of the Fear of God and eats the bread of life; tempted by the serpent, then squeezed in the winepress, it frees itself and puts on the new garment; it starts along the path of edification, in the Moon/Church; illuminated by the star of the Old Testament, it receives baptism from the star of John the Baptist; through the second star, the Gospel, it rises until it is illuminated by the sun of Christ. The soul finds its tabernacle anew, spreads its wings, and like the Lamb born of Mary, returns to the heart of the Father.

From the Fragment to the Revealed Image

Thus therefore, O human, speak these things that you see and hear. And write them not by yourself or any other human being, but by the will of Him Who knows, sees and disposes all things in the secrets of His mysteries (*SC* Protestificatio, p. 59).

The final images explode with a magnificent beauty. Hidden in fragments of color and of the design, they require attentive contemplation and patient and thoughtful assembly to reconstruct each image in its entirety. Their wondrous revelation enables us to perceive the greatness and depth of the mystery. Hildegard and her collaborators inserted in the square of the Science of God filled with eyes, and in the central band with the seeds of the Word, a fragment of the design which, when placed in front of a mirror, reveals the complete image of the quadrilobate flower and of the cross. In fact, we read: *As that mirror also holds within itself very many hidden wonders, it broadcasts from itself a radiance of great breadth and height. This signifies that God's knowledge, which holds within itself many unknown mysteries, brings forth the showing of its wonders by opening out and lifting up, as it pleases.*

The recomposition of the fragments hidden in the backgrounds of the image of the symphony reveals the words of the song to the Virgin *O splendidissima gemma* (O splendid jewel) that opens the vision, where Christ is described as an offshoot of the Tree of Jesse, born from the leafy branches that represent Mary, and the humans who have journeyed in virtue are praised like perfumed flowers. The image on paper, reflected, translated, multiplied, and united generates the leaves and flowers, stirred by the gentle breeze of the spirit, and the beauty of the carpet of branches and flowers is revealed to our outer eye, so that we can almost smell their perfume: *In the nostrils, moreover, God shows the Wisdom that is the aromatic principle of order in all arts, so that a person recognizes through its perfume what Wisdom ordains.*

Lastly, Hildegard conceals in the lines of the green curtain and chalice on the altar a fragment of the design that in the mirror reveals an interwoven form combining the green of *viriditas*, the *candid* white of the light, and the *splendid* gold of the chalice. This design is reminiscent of Solomon's knot, representing wisdom and the union of the human and divine dimensions.

Eyes

The square of the Science of God (I.4) is constructed from two triangles and a central band with thirty seeds, image of the Word, within which there is an image of the face of the Soul in an embryonic state, prior to its descent to earth. Some eyes in the triangles form undulating lines. Taken singly, the two triangles—mirrored, combined and multiplied—show that those lines are not placed randomly, but delineate the fragment of an image that was conceived and designed previously, then deliberately hidden so that it might be discovered. It corresponds to the motif of a quadrilobate flower and of a cross, decorative elements that are also found on the altar cloth and the priestly robe (see pp. 58–61). The decoration is enriched by the red of the seeds of the central band (see p. 149).

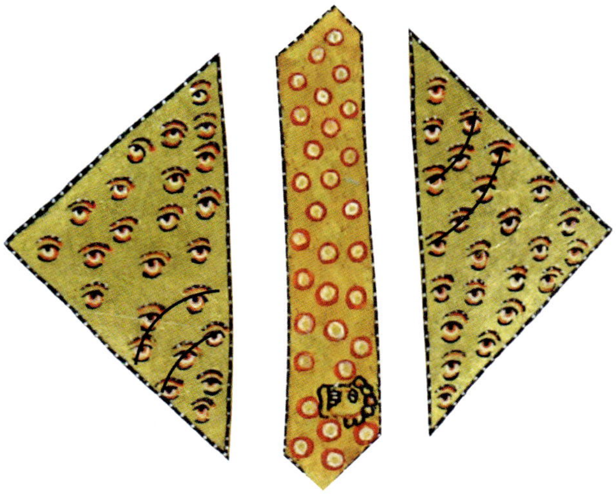

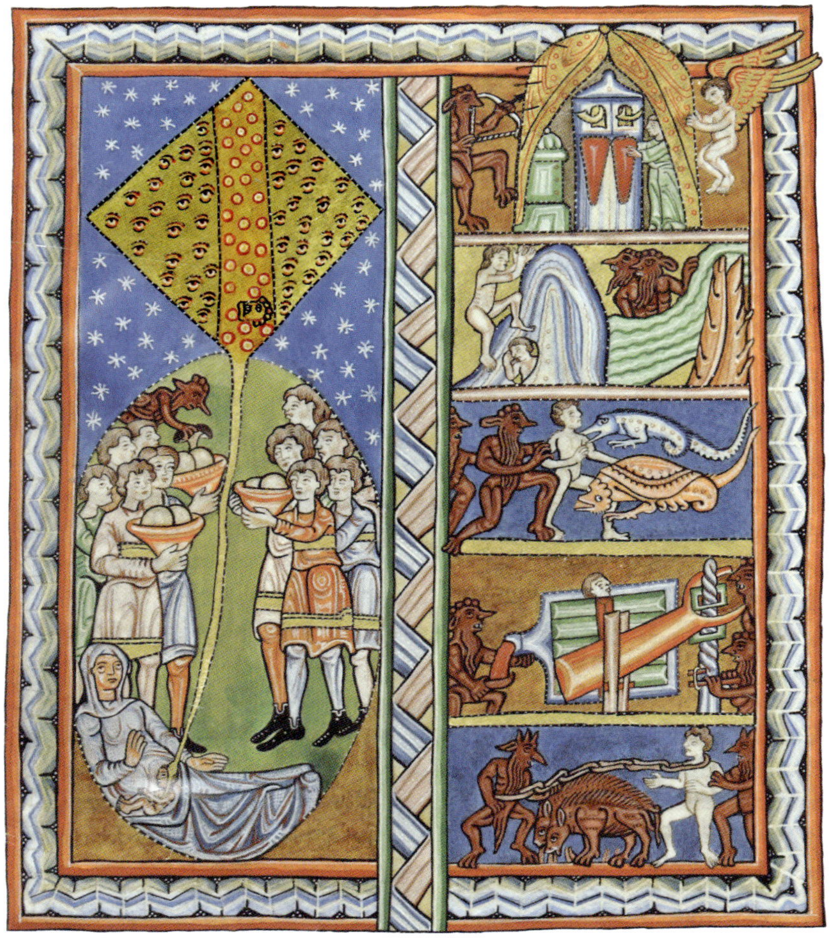

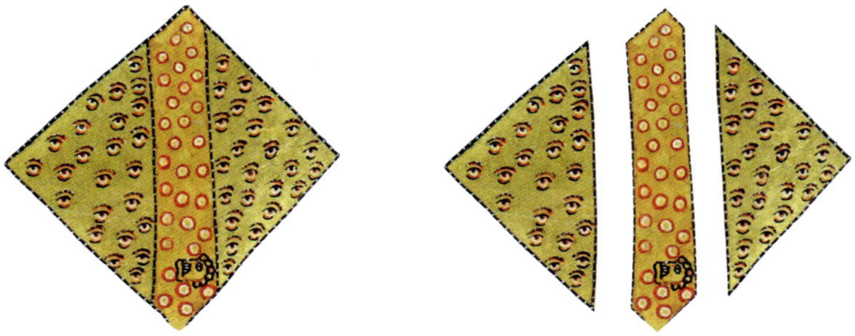

Construction process
the single figures of the two triangles and the central band are separated; each triangular figure is placed alongside its mirror image; the two parts are united to create the basic module; the module is replicated; the four modules are united to obtain the design of the two quadrilobate flowers and the cross.

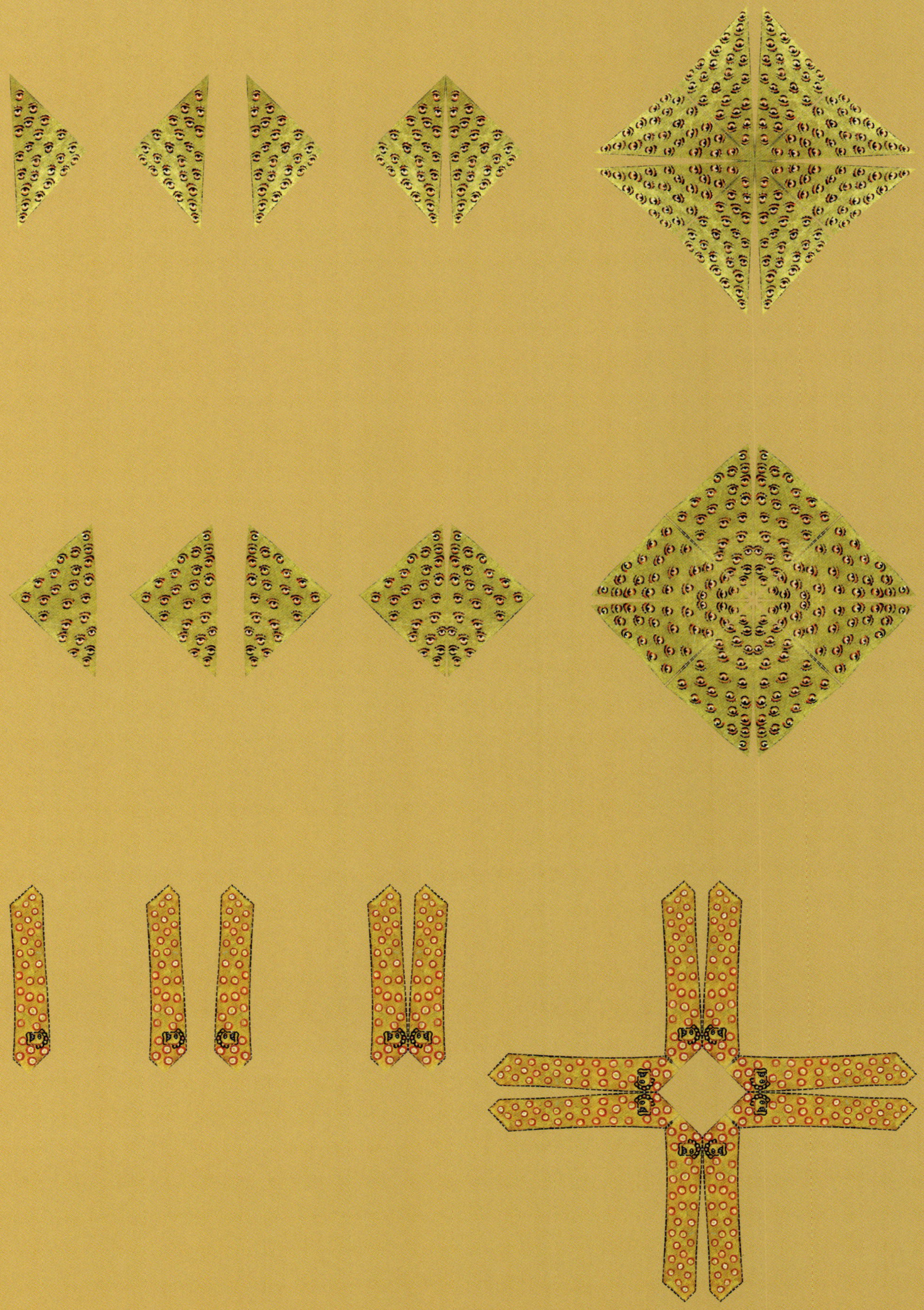

Mirror

For as all things shine in the mirror before which they stand, so in the holy divinity all his works appeared outside of the passage of time (*LDO* I.1.6, p. 38).

The use of the mirror immediately shows the formation of the figures and substantiates the reflected image as a form of knowledge.

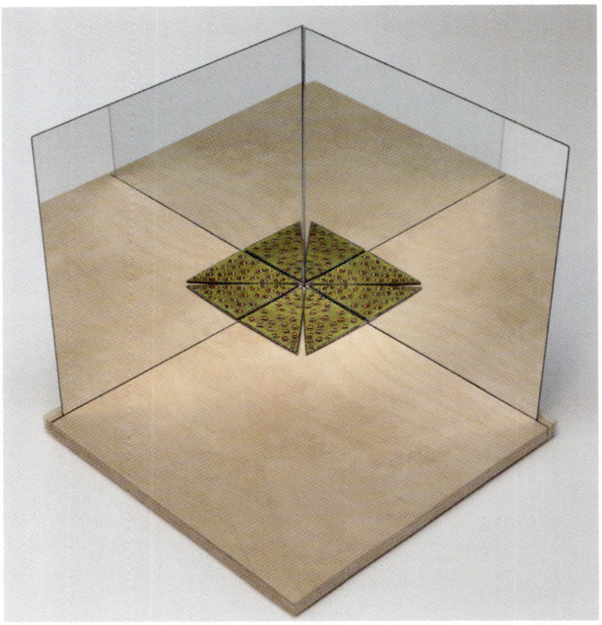

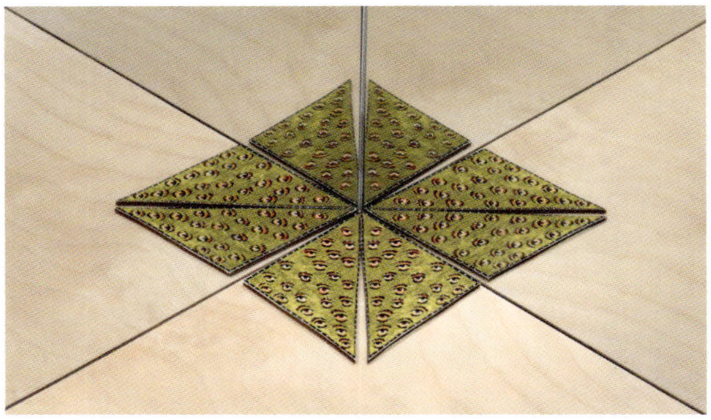

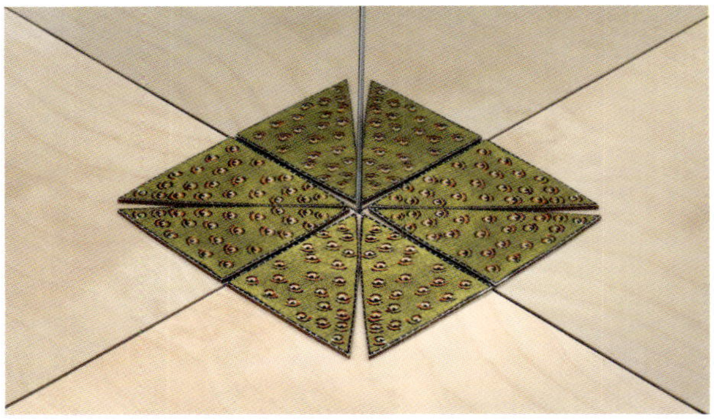

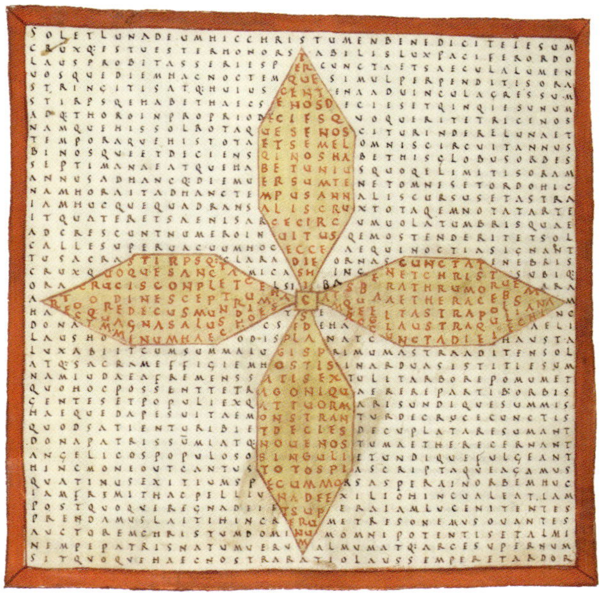

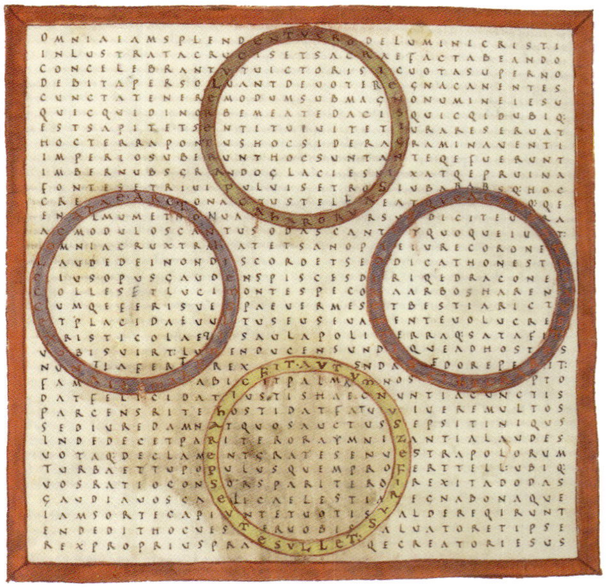

The images reveal a clear homage to *Carmina Figures* of Rabano Mauro (see pp. 173–175)

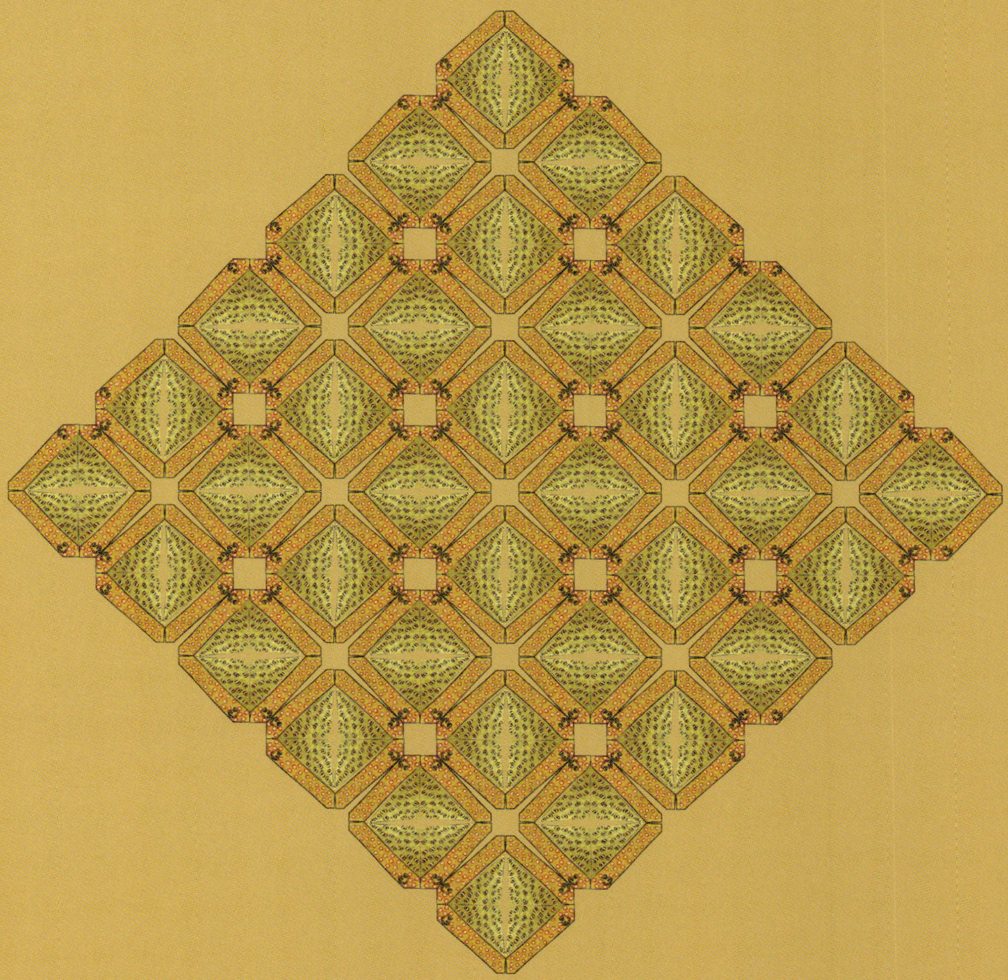

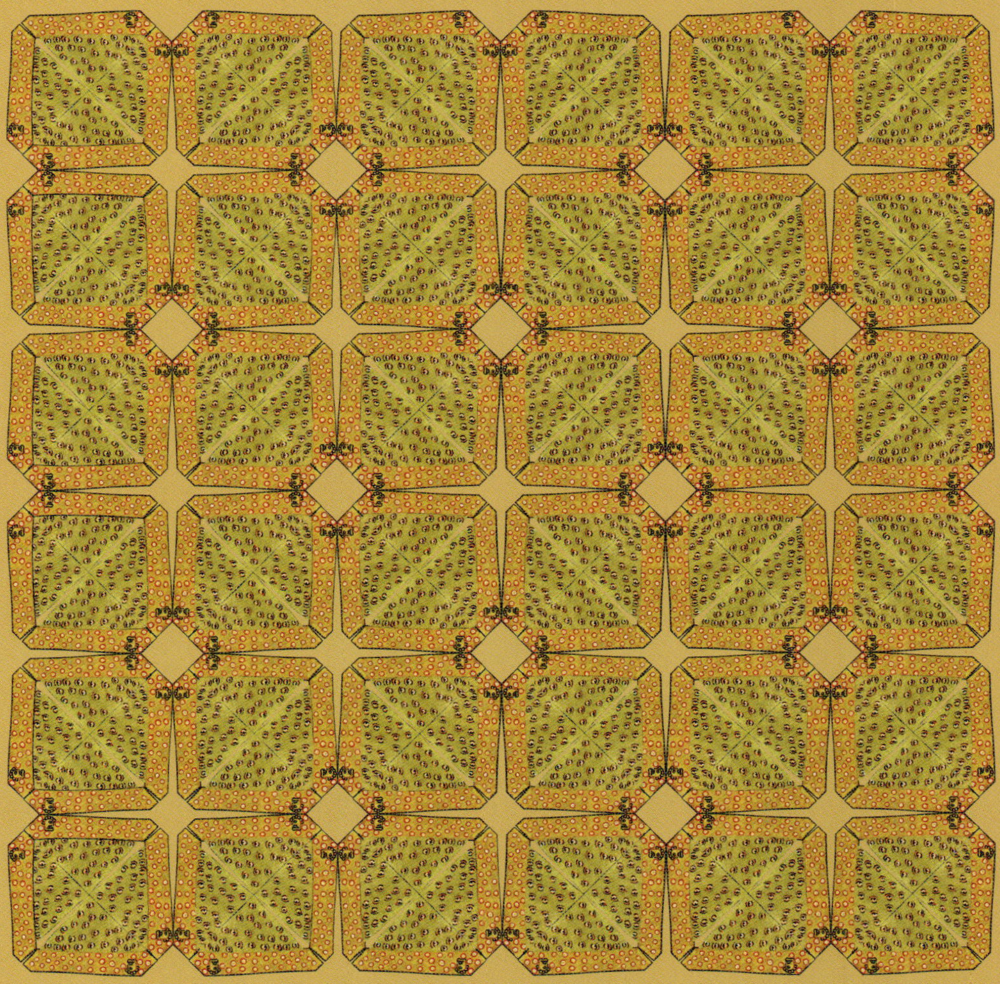

Leafy Branches

In the miniature, the forms of the scrolls and the three colors of the background appear to be meaningless. But if the image is rotated and placed next to the miniature in its correct position, we notice that the colors of the background are the shape of leaves, and compose the leafy branch of the Tree of Jesse. The foliage of the tree is created by the combination and intertwining of several branches to which the gentle breeze of the Spirit gives an undulating movement, thus forming the complete image as described in the vision (see pp. 68–69). The composition executed on paper enables us to see the movement in a three-dimensional form, which is not visible in digital reconstructions.

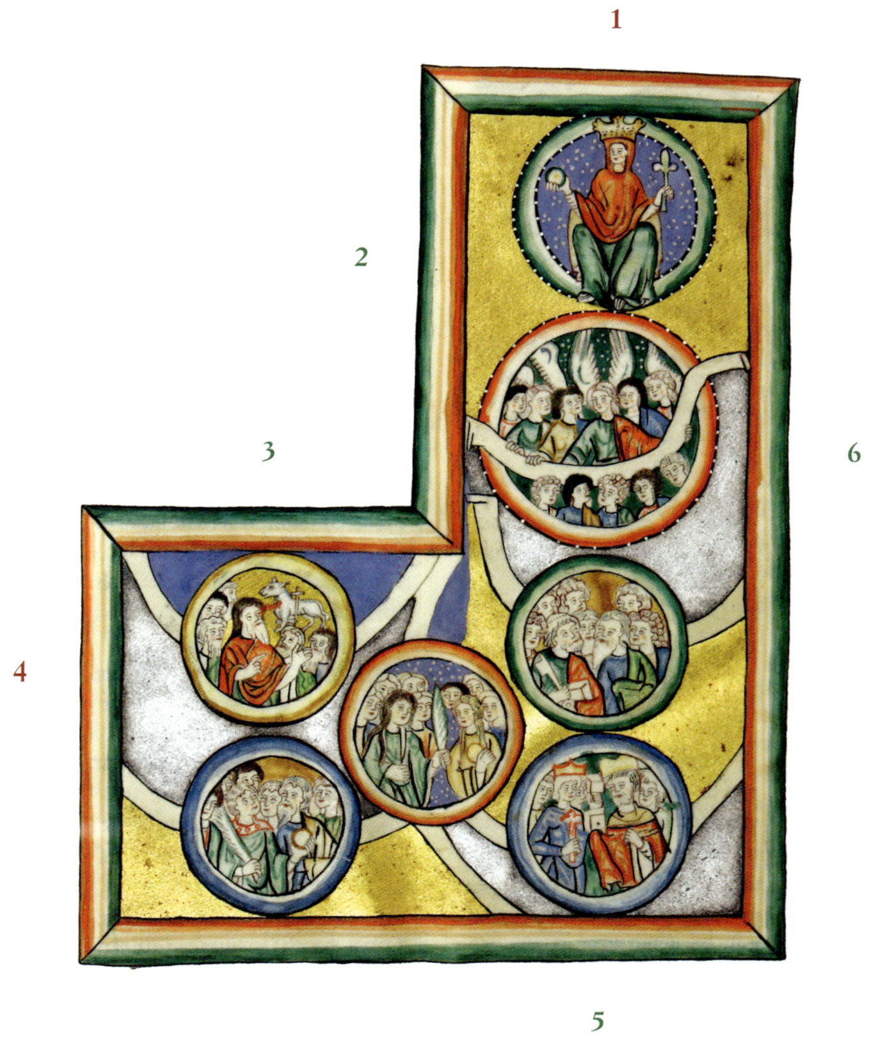

On the opposite page
Construction process
(from the top) the inverted image joined along the short side (no. 4) forms the first leaf; the inverted image joined along the long side (no. 6) forms the second leaf; the union of the four images, thus connected, creates the constructive module of the first leafy branch; the unframed branch; and the branch without the figure of Mary, who in the composition with several fronds, is placed below the design.

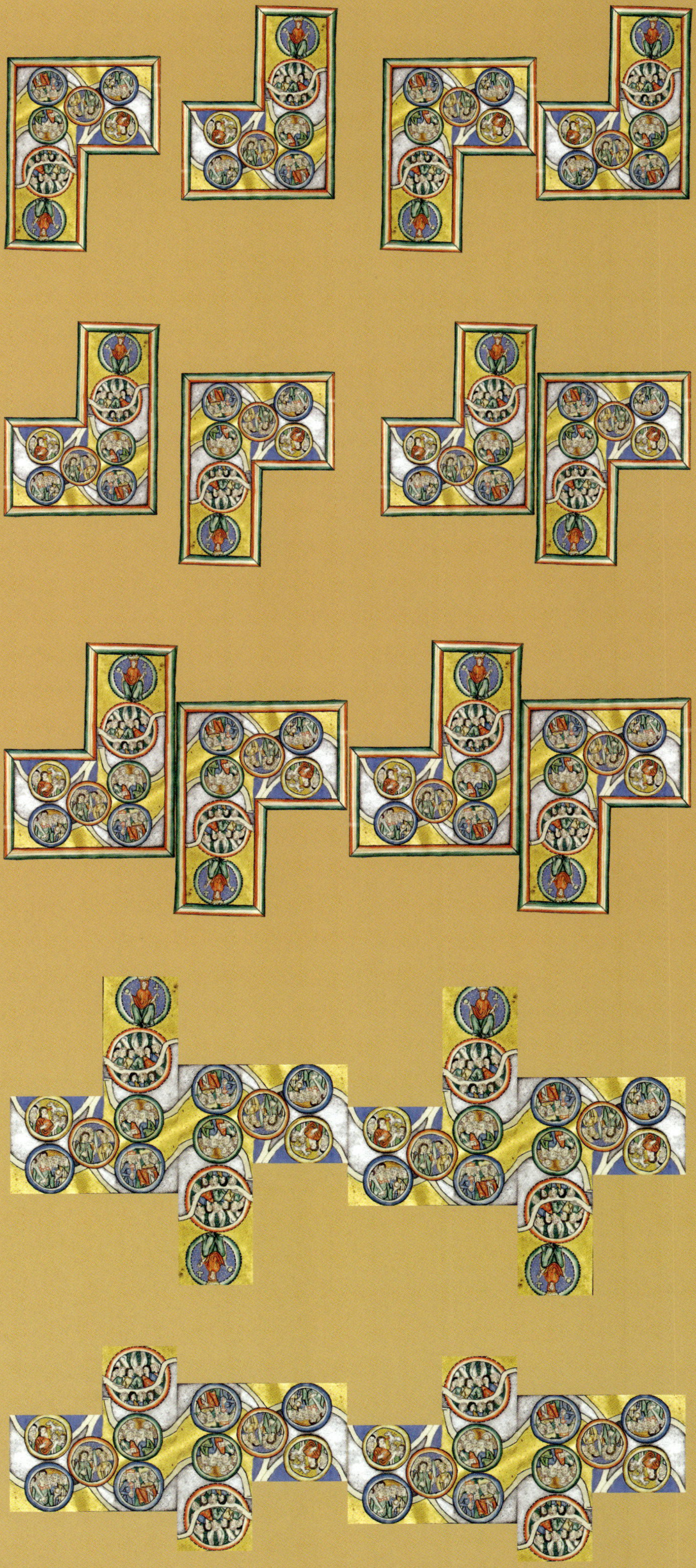

Flowers

The anonymous blue-violet fragments of the background form the flowers, which bloom on the leafy branches of the Tree of Jesse—image of the just ones—as flowers of the garden of Paradise (see pp. 70–71). The flowers, like the branches, become visible through a process of reconstruction and elaboration.

The inverted L-shape of the miniature lends itself to the dovetailing of the image, in its proper position, with an inverted replica. The particular arrangement of the three frames in red, white and green—where the green frame is innermost on sides 1 and 4, and outermost on the other sides—indicates how to proceed.

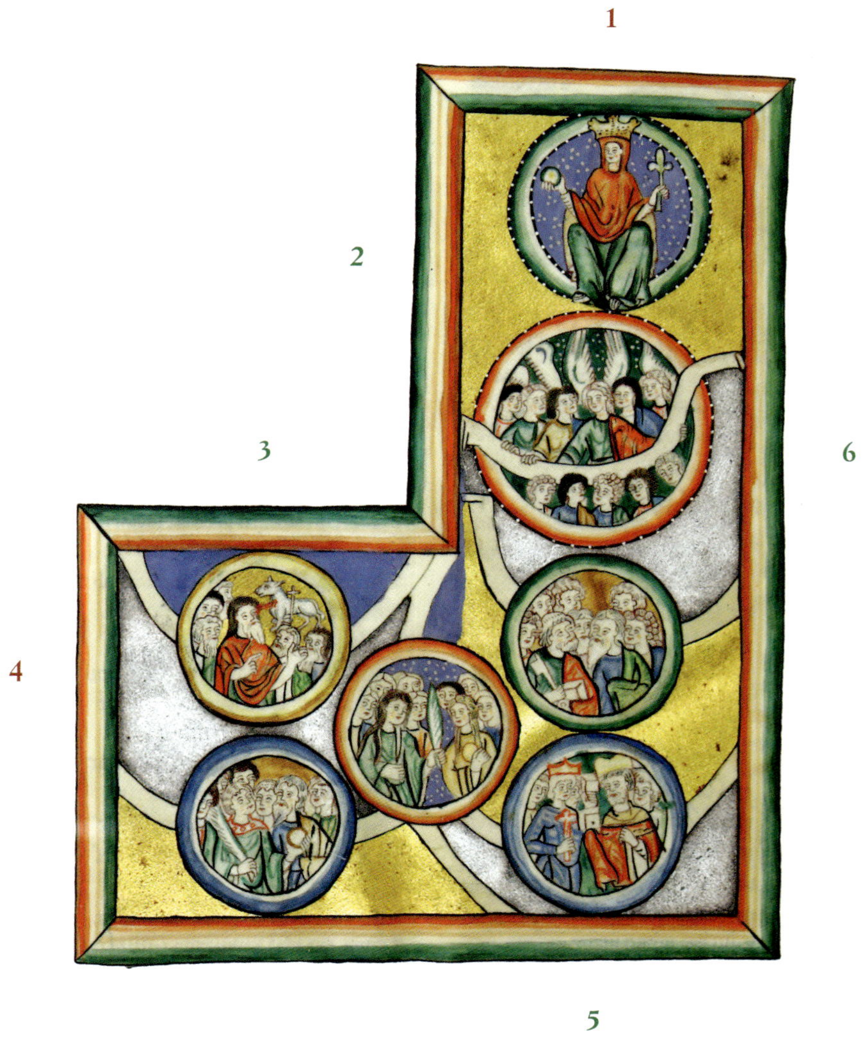

On the opposite page
Construction process
(above) the construction of the basic module, obtained by dovetailing the figure in its proper position with an inverted replica, by means of a vertical and a horizontal movement; (center) to the module thus obtained are joined two replicas of the images, appropriately positioned at the two sides by means of a horizontal dovetailing movement, so that the figures of Mary and the angels remain hidden beneath the figure; (below) the complete constructive module without the hidden parts: left, unframed; right, with the united parts that reveal the shape of the flower.

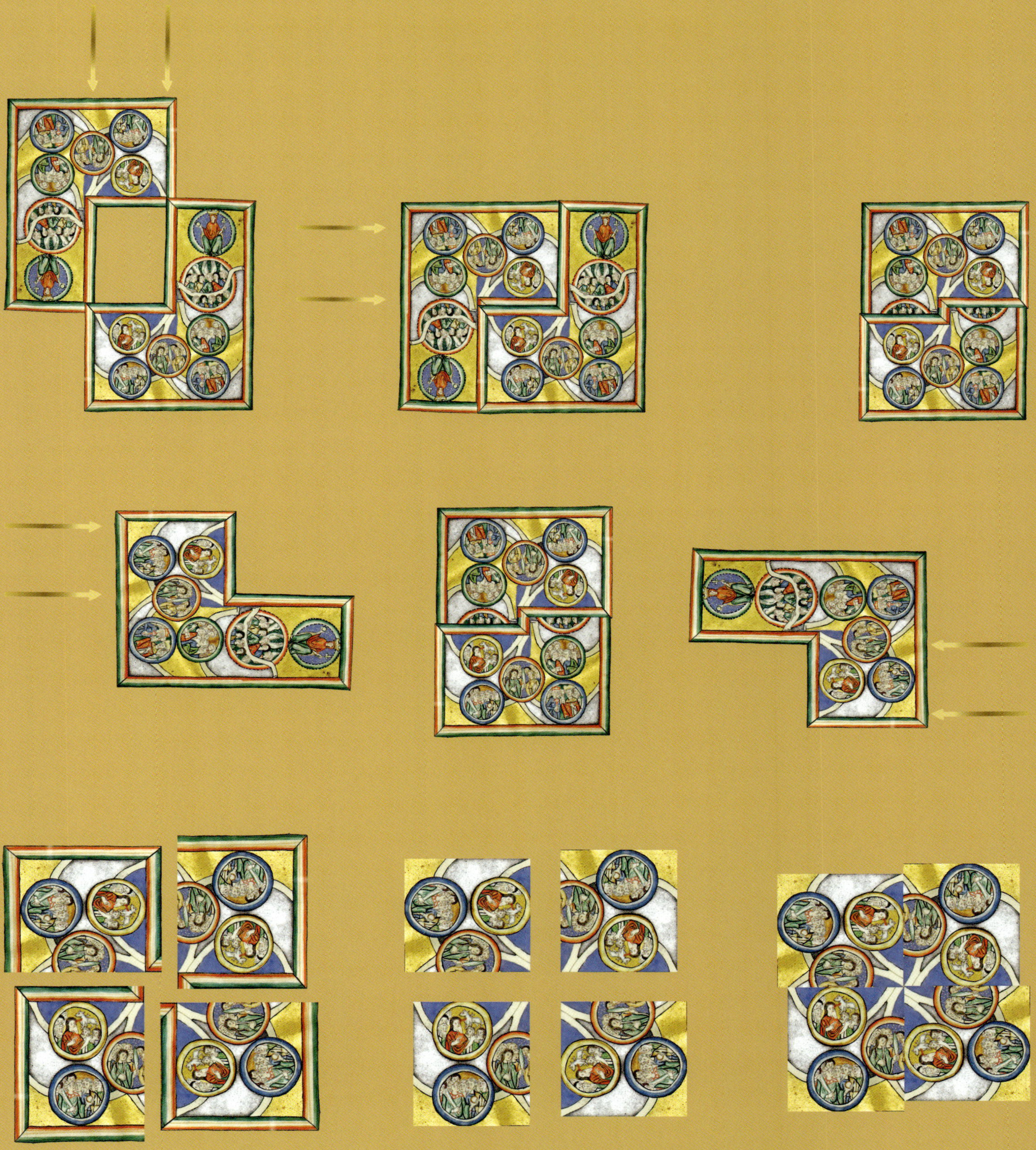

Viriditas

In the image of the Sacrament of the Altar (II.6b) the chalice and bread are kept under a green curtain, symbol of fecundity. Beside them is the open book of the Word, where we read the beginning of the Eucharistic prayer *te igitur clementissime Pater.* The chalice is revealed through mirroring and the curtain forms the letter "M" of Mary, which envelops the chalice. Through multiplication, a figure is formed that initially brings to mind Solomon's knot, symbol of the union of humanity with God, which is enriched by the book, creating a weave in which it is alternated with the quadrilobate flower (see pp. 72–73). As with the flowers and the leafy branches, the figure is recomposed through cutting along the dotted line and the interlocking of the paper.

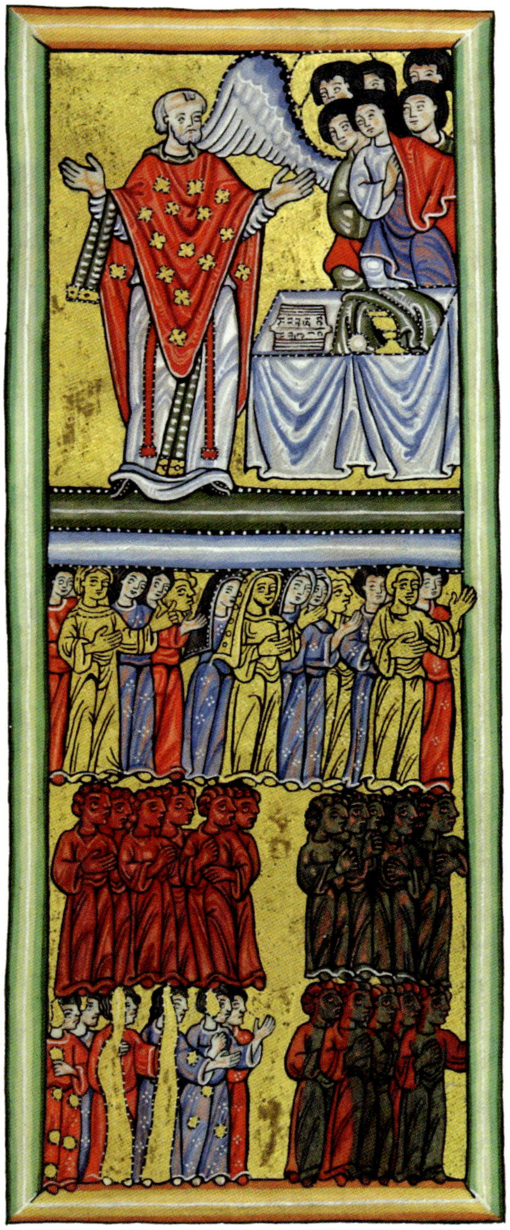

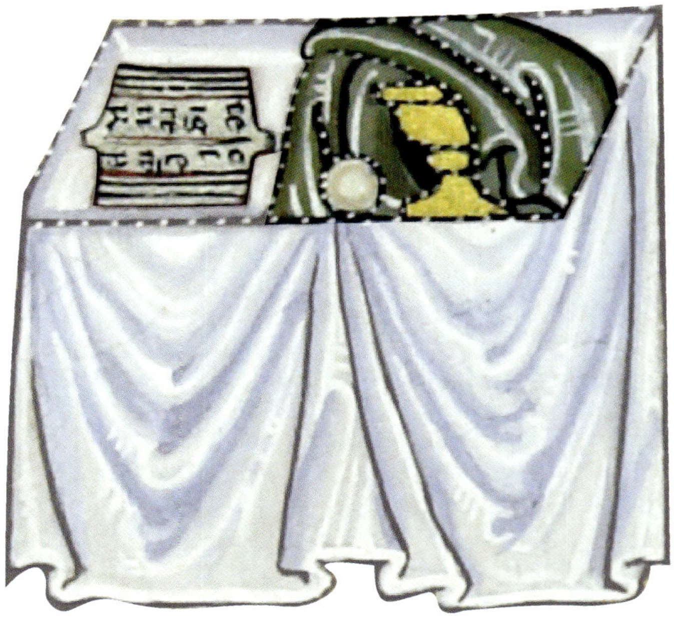

On the opposite page
Construction process
(from the top) the figure of the curtain in its real and mirrored positions; the union of the two figures creates the basic module; the multiplied module creates the complete figure; the process is repeated for the module incorporating the book.

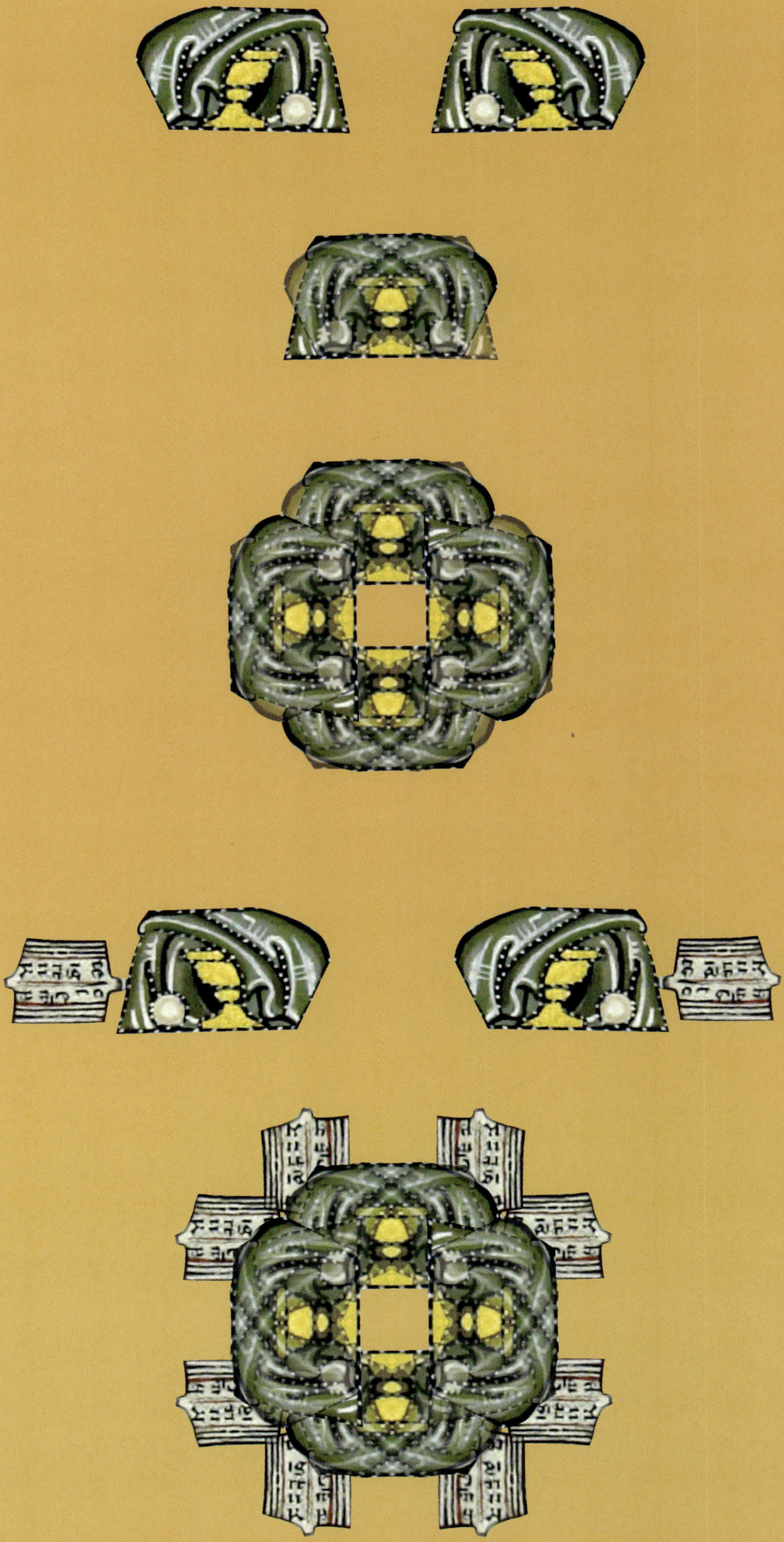

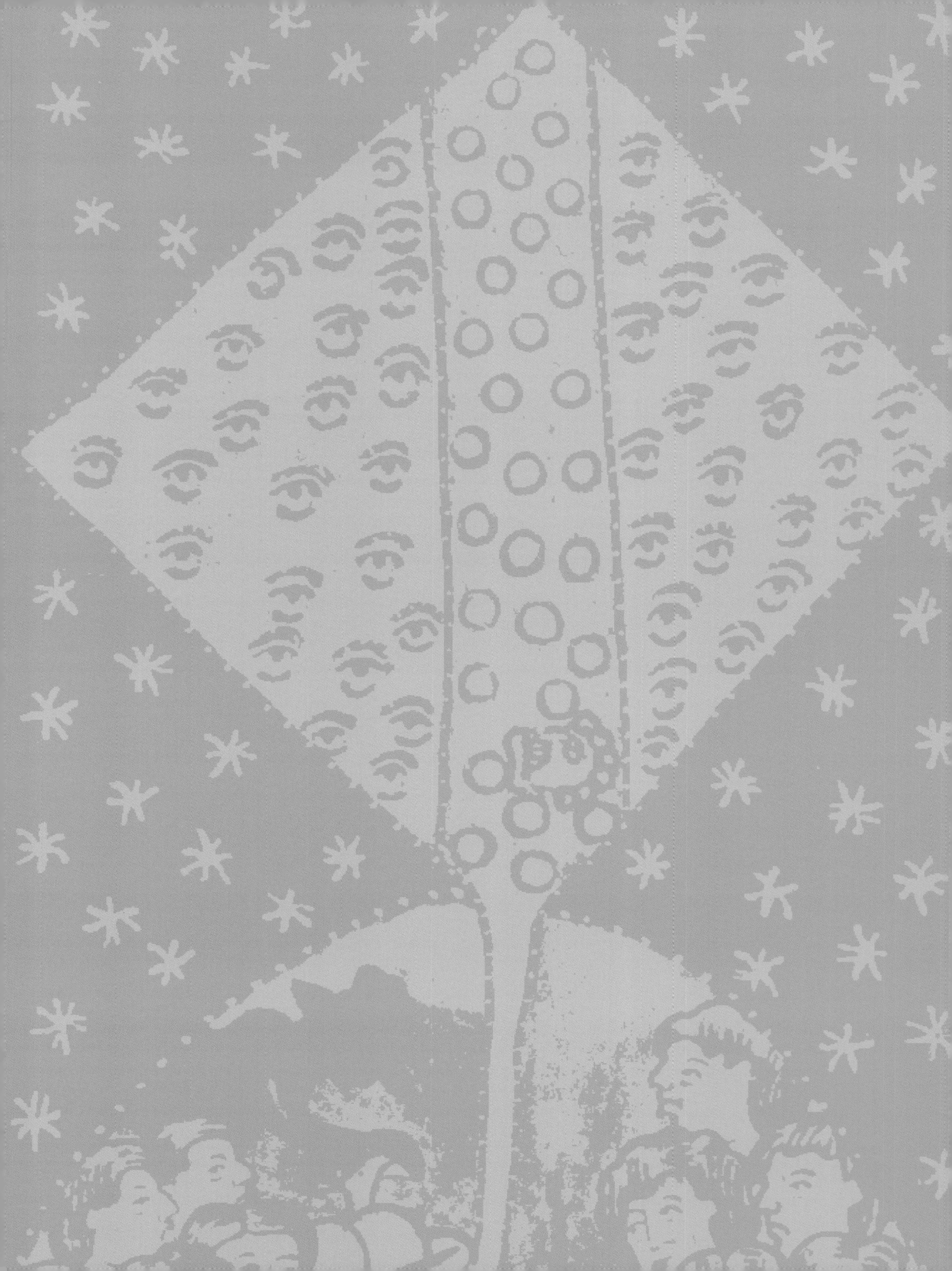

CHAPTER III

Quadrivium

Who has measured the waters in the hollow of his hand, or with the breadth of his hand marked off the heavens? Who has held the dust of the earth in a basket, or weighed the mountains on the scale and the hills in a balance? (Isaiah 40:12,14).

The harmony of creation is manifest in the perfection of its forms and in the balance of its parts. Through her visions, Hildegard experienced this extraordinary richness that speaks the language of wisdom, *number, weight and measurement*, and transcribed it into her entire work through the arts of the *quadrivium*. Rabano Mauro describes these in his treatise *On the Formation of the Clergy*, inspired by the wisdom of the Fathers.

Arithmetic [...] is the discipline of numbers—the Greeks call "number"(numerum)*"rithmon" [...] it needs no other discipline for itself. [...] it is necessary that those who wish to arrive at a knowledge of Sacred Scripture study attentively this art.*

Let us now come to geometry, which is the theoretical description of patterns and the visible proof of the philosophers [...]. For Holy Divinity practices geometry—if this is right to say—when He grants various appearances and shapes to His creatures [...] when His venerable power assigned the course of the stars [...]. Therefore, this discipline is preserved in the building of the tabernacle and of the Temple, where [...] linear measure and [...] the circle and the sphere and the hemisphere, and the orderly arrangement of the shape of the quadrangle and other shapes is used.

Music is the discipline that speaks about numbers in relation to what is found in sounds, as double, triple, quadruple, and other similar things that are said to be related to it. [...] For this reason, then, is musical discipline diffused through every deed in our life [...]. For whatever we say, or however we are moved inwardly by our beating pulse, is shown to be allied by musical rhythm to the powers of harmony [...].

Pythagoras testifies that this world is established through music and can be governed by it.

Astronomy [...] imbues our understanding [...] with great clarity. For how excellent it is to ascend to the heavens with the intellect and to examine the whole heavenly structure with our investigative reason and in some part to gather by the contemplative grandeur of the mind what the mysteries of such great scope conceal! For the world itself, as some say, is thought to be gathered into a spherical form so that the extent of its circumference may contain the diverse forms of things [...] astronomy is called in our language, "the law of the stars," because they do not know either how to move or how to stop in any other way than that prescribed by their Creator (Hrabanus Maurus 2023).

Knowledge gathered thus, through the contemplation of creation, and codified in numbers, forms, sounds, and measurements is the way to restore the wondrousness of divine order. In fact, the Creator has *disposed everything with his own hands* and watches over it tirelessly with love and care, *counting every hair on a person's head*. In the images, wisdom is guarded like a treasure in the temple. The beauty of its revelation thrills the soul and makes the heartstrings sing.

Arithmetic

I also made this work rational out of my own rationality, [...] just as human rationality comprehends with its skill all things by name and number (*LDO* I.4.105, p. 245).

The number describes the arc of Hildegard's three prophetic works: a hymn to the Trinity, marked by forty-two visions, and an eschatological symbol of the prophetic time of waiting for the Revelation.

Scivias opens with an invocation to the Holy Spirit, who shines with his seven gifts in the seven letters of the title. The three letters *sci* represent knowing God and God making himself known, and the four letters *vias* represent the earth with the ways to follow to return to the original source. The entire word *scivias* describes the form of a cross and multiplied ad infinitum generates praise and ceaseless prayer, drawing inspiration from Rabano Mauro's *carmina figurata.*

The architectural structure of the work can be compared to that of a great cathedral, image of God's unity, and its parts can be seen as representing the meeting between God and humanity. The three parts of *Scivias*, symbol of the Three Persons, describe the aisles. The twenty-six visions, symbol of God revealed to Moses, describe a Greek Cross plan. On the arms of the cross are arranged two groups of thirteen visions, symbol of the Son of God crushing the tempter. The thirty-five miniatures, image of the seven gifts of the Holy Spirit that meet the five human senses and enable the connection with the divine, describe the columns. Lastly, the seven hundred and six chapters that make up the account of the visions, images of the works of humanity, living stones, describe the plan of the celestial Jerusalem.

Thus, in the cathedral there are signs of the presence of the Trinity, of the manifestation of God in the burning bush, of the incarnation of the Son of God, of the gifts of the Holy Spirit received by humanity, and of the good works that form the Church, Christ's bride. The numbers inscribed within the architectural structure are openly revealed in the vivid forms of the images, giving profound meaning to the symbolic figures and setting the tempo of the song of wisdom.

Number and Architecture

GREEK CROSS
The number thirteen

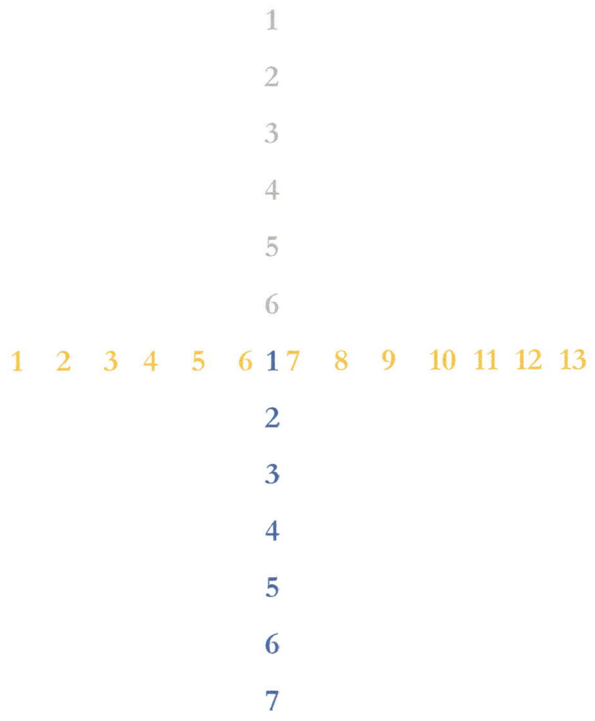

The three parts into which *Scivias* is divided, shown in the diagram below, are connected by a specific proportion. The number of visions in the third part, at the top of the diagram, is equal to the sum of those in the first and second parts. This relationship evokes the form of a Greek cross: on the vertical arm, thirteen visions—six from the first part and seven from the second—narrate the events from the beginning of the journey to the crucifixion and the passing through death; on the horizontal arm, thirteen visions from the third part narrate humanity's journey from the revelation of Christ to the last judgment and the peace of Paradise.

In the ancient Judeo-Christian tradition, the number thirteen symbolizes the name of God, *Ahod*, which means one, referencing the subsequent image of the Son of God. At the base of the cross, the last two visions of the second part show Christ crucified crushing the Ancient Serpent, thus emphasizing victory over evil as in traditional iconography (see p. 162).

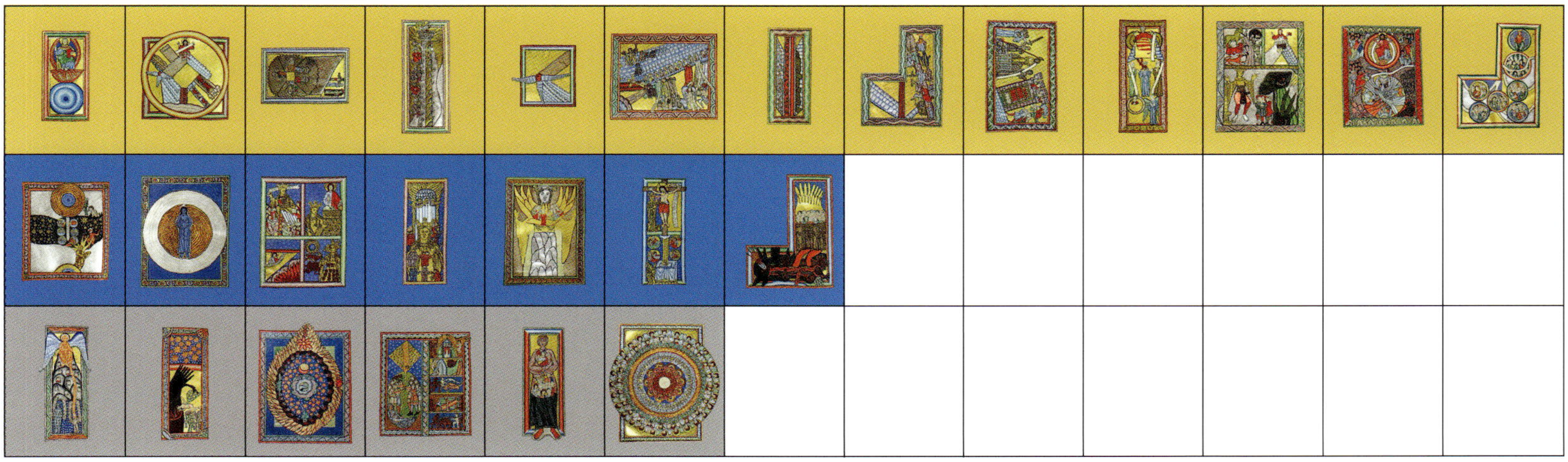

Because He was born of the Virgin, and so has the sweetest savor and the strongest unguent, which He distills like balsam; which is the resurrection unto life (*SC* III.8.18, p. 440).

At the intersection point of the cross, there are two overlapping visions, symbolizing the birth and death of the Son of God, the cornerstone. In the first image, The Word (II.1), the serene *man* born from the *aurora* appears, who with his brightness liberates man from the darkness and in infinite glory *wondrously irradiates the fullness of magnificent and fragrant fecundity*. In the second image, the three blades of the Column of the Trinity (III.7) are *three sharp swords* that penetrate the entire terrestrial globe and show the action of the Trinity on earth.

The death of the Son of God gives new life to the first human who *draws a sigh with all his heart and all his wisdom* and *opens up again* to the mystery, marking the way of the edification of humanity that leads toward a new heaven and a new earth.

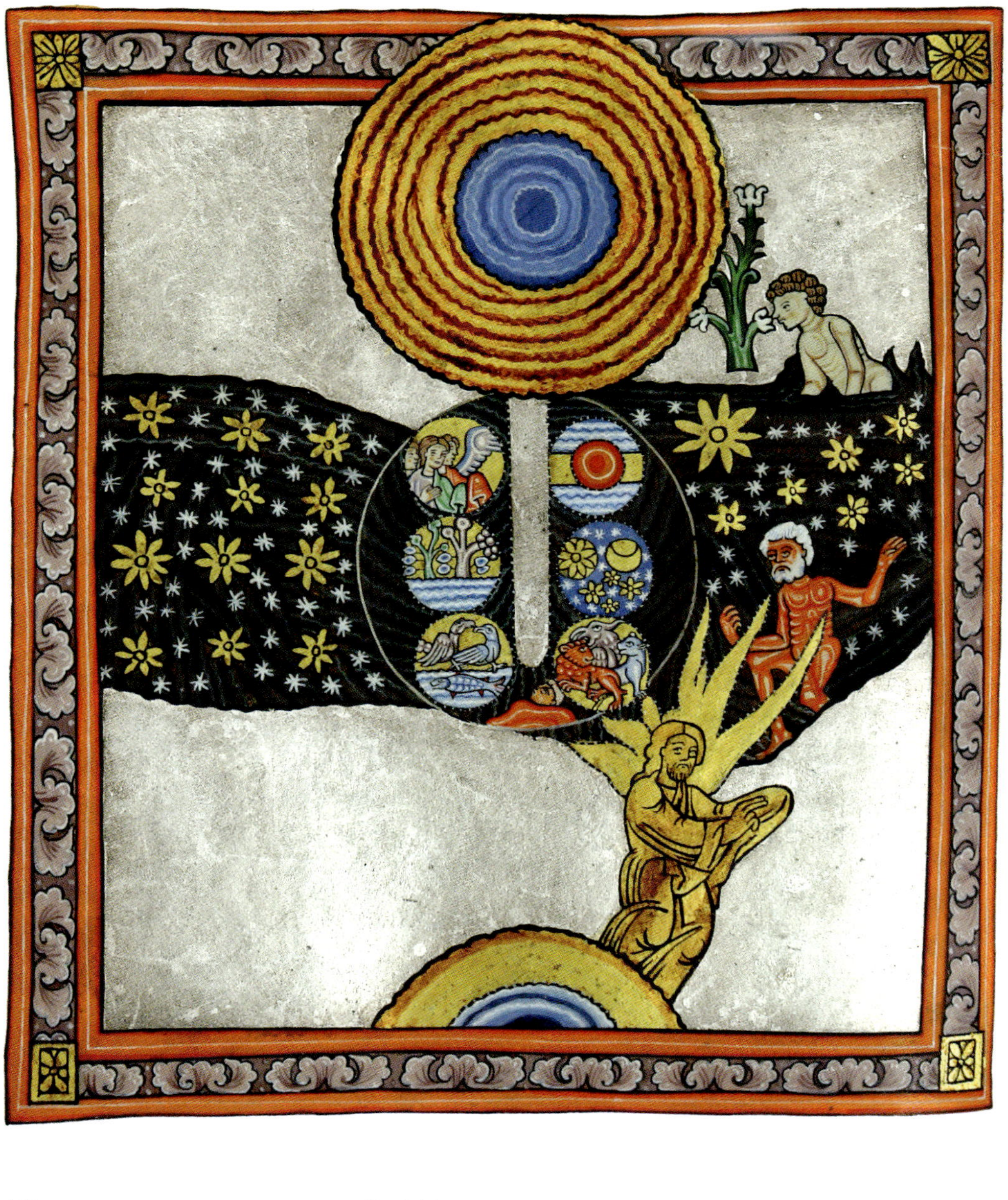

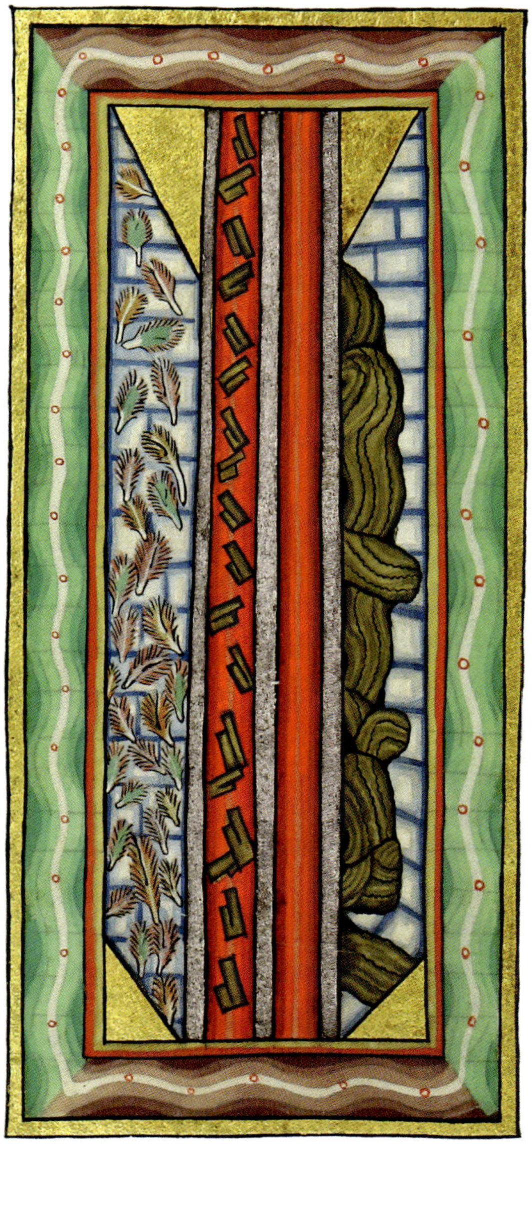

The Son of God and his Bride

The two three-by-three squares

Then I saw a bright light, and in this light the figure of a man the color of a sapphire, which was all blazing with a gentle glowing fire (*SC* II.2.D, p. 161).

[...] you see the image of a woman as large as a great city; this designates the Bride of My Son, who always bears her children by regeneration in the Spirit and in water (*SC* II.3.1, p. 170).

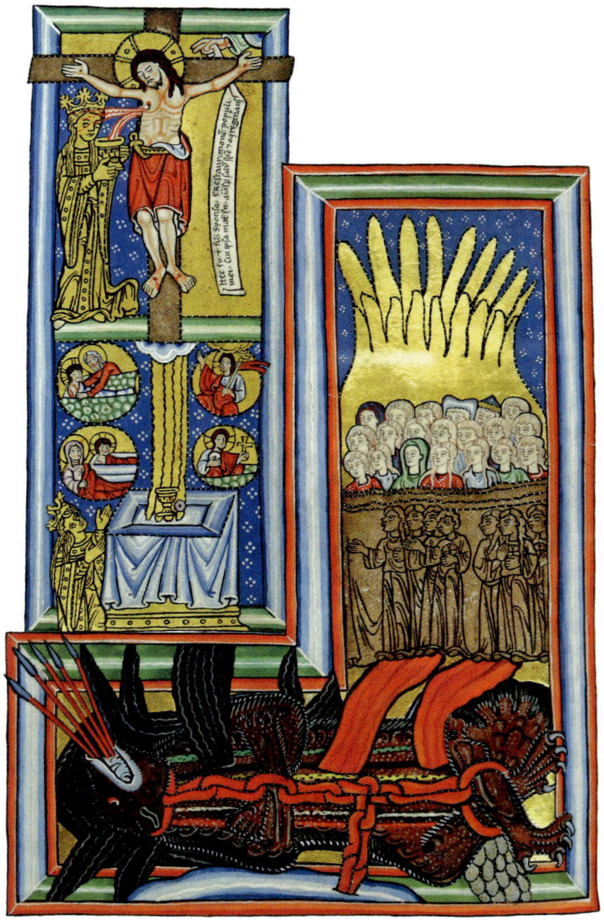

The spousal image of the Son of God (II.2), man of sapphire blue, and his bride, the Church (II.5), is revealed within the symbolic form of two squares, each containing nine visions, emblem of the Trinity (see opposite page).

This figure is created by reducing the number of visions on each axis to six, compared to the six, seven, and thirteen visions in the original arrangement. Hildegard constructs it by combining, in a single image, miniatures illustrating different aspects of the same vision (see diagram below). In fact, she combines the images of the Crucifixion (II.6a) and the Ancient Serpent (II.7a) at the end of the second part (in gray), and condenses in a single image of the map of the Building (III.2), the seven visions of the third part, which illustrate the architectural details of each element of the actual Building (in pink).

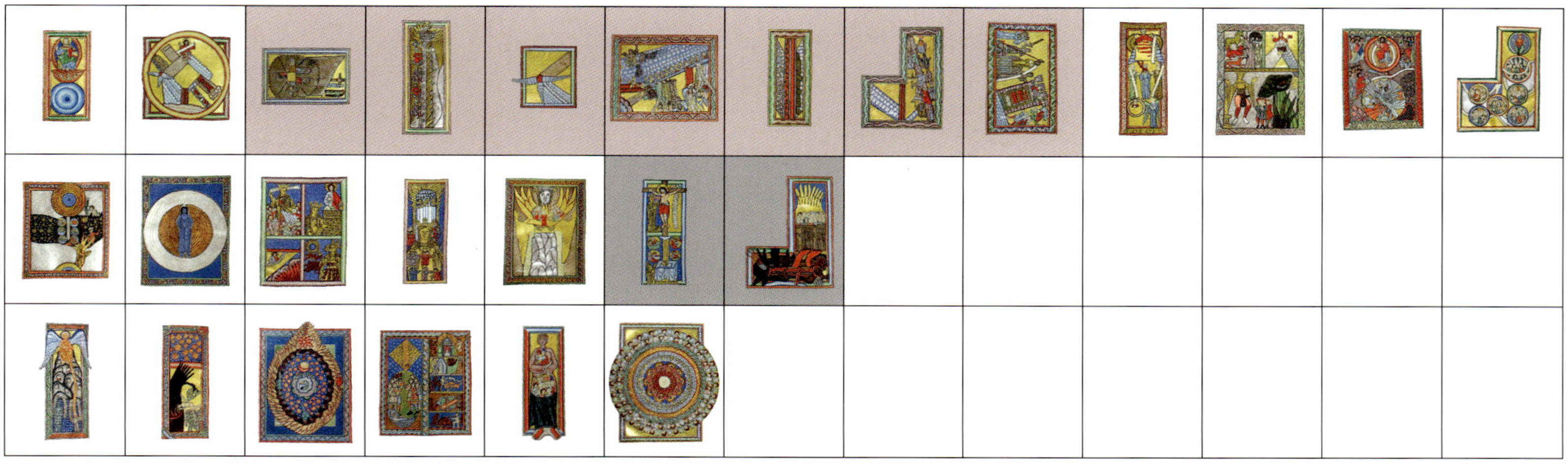

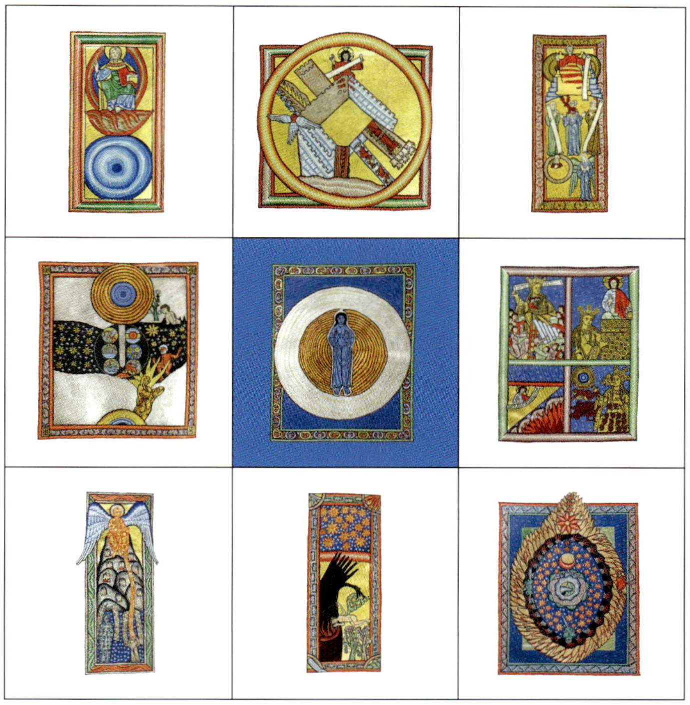
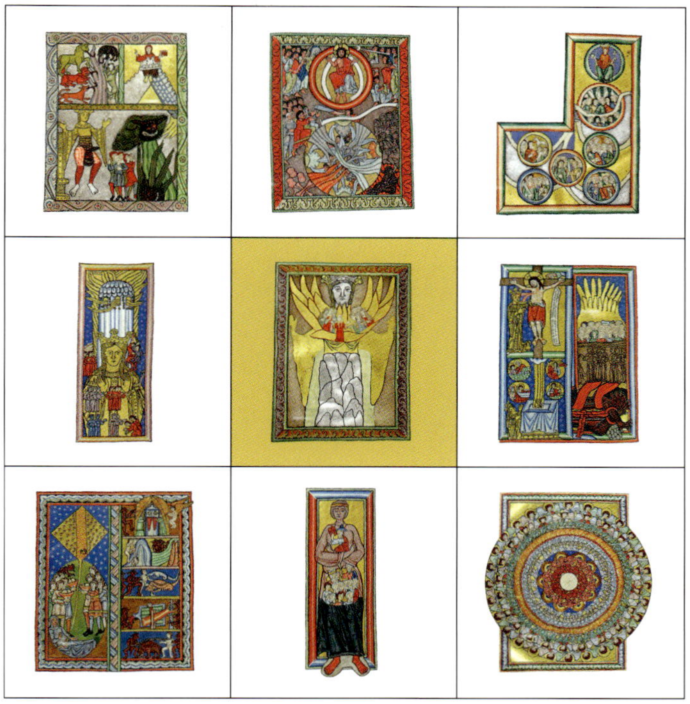
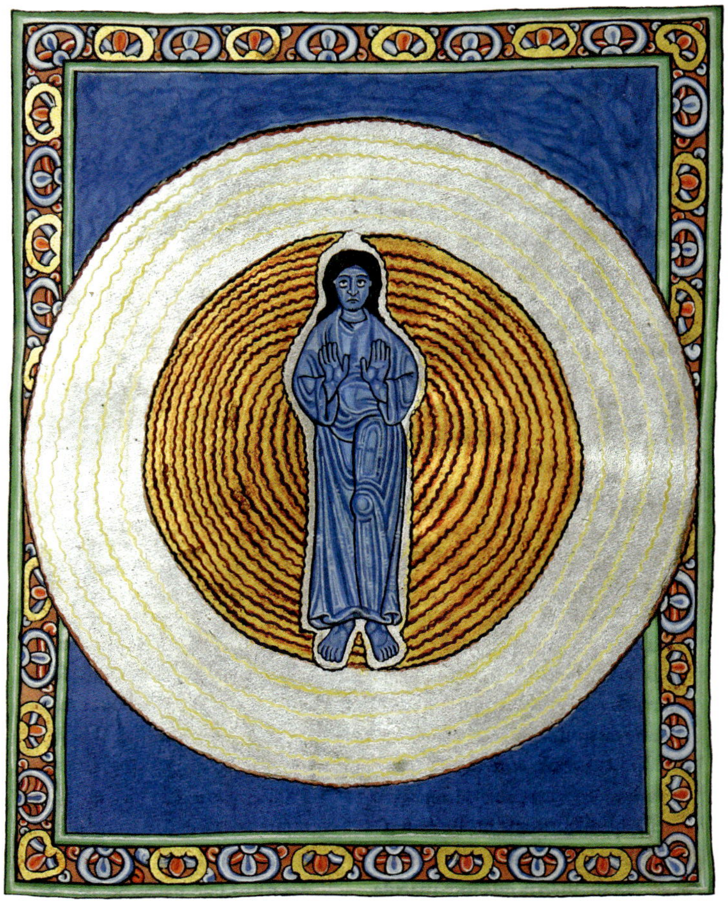
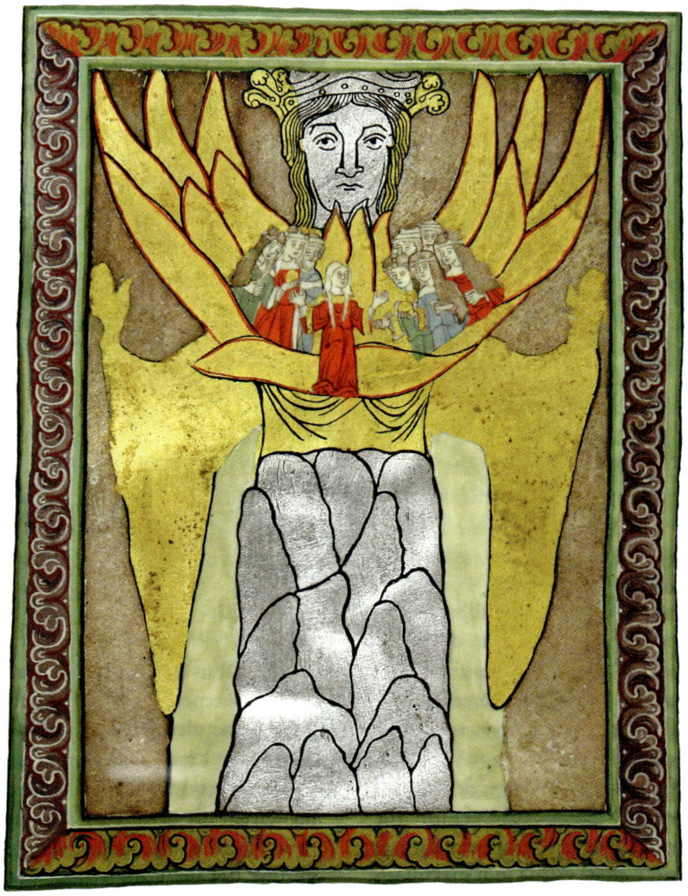

God Meets Humanity

The number thirty-five

Thus, with the seven gifts of the Holy Spirit and the five senses, a person begins and perfects all his works through the soul, as too the seventh month ripens all the earth's fruits (*LDO* I.4.98, p. 231).

There are thirty-five miniatures in the *Scivias* codex, which illustrate the twenty-six visions described in the text, as well as the introduction of the *Protestifiatio* (in red). The difference between the number of miniatures (35) and the number of visions (26) derives from the fact that, beyond the introductory miniature, seven visions are illustrated by more than one miniature (in gray). Hildegard makes this architecture to indicate the presence of God with the number twenty-six and the descent of the seven gifts of the Holy Spirit into the five senses of the human being with the number thirty-five, as represented in the diagram by the placement of seven miniatures on the horizontal axis and five on the vertical axis.

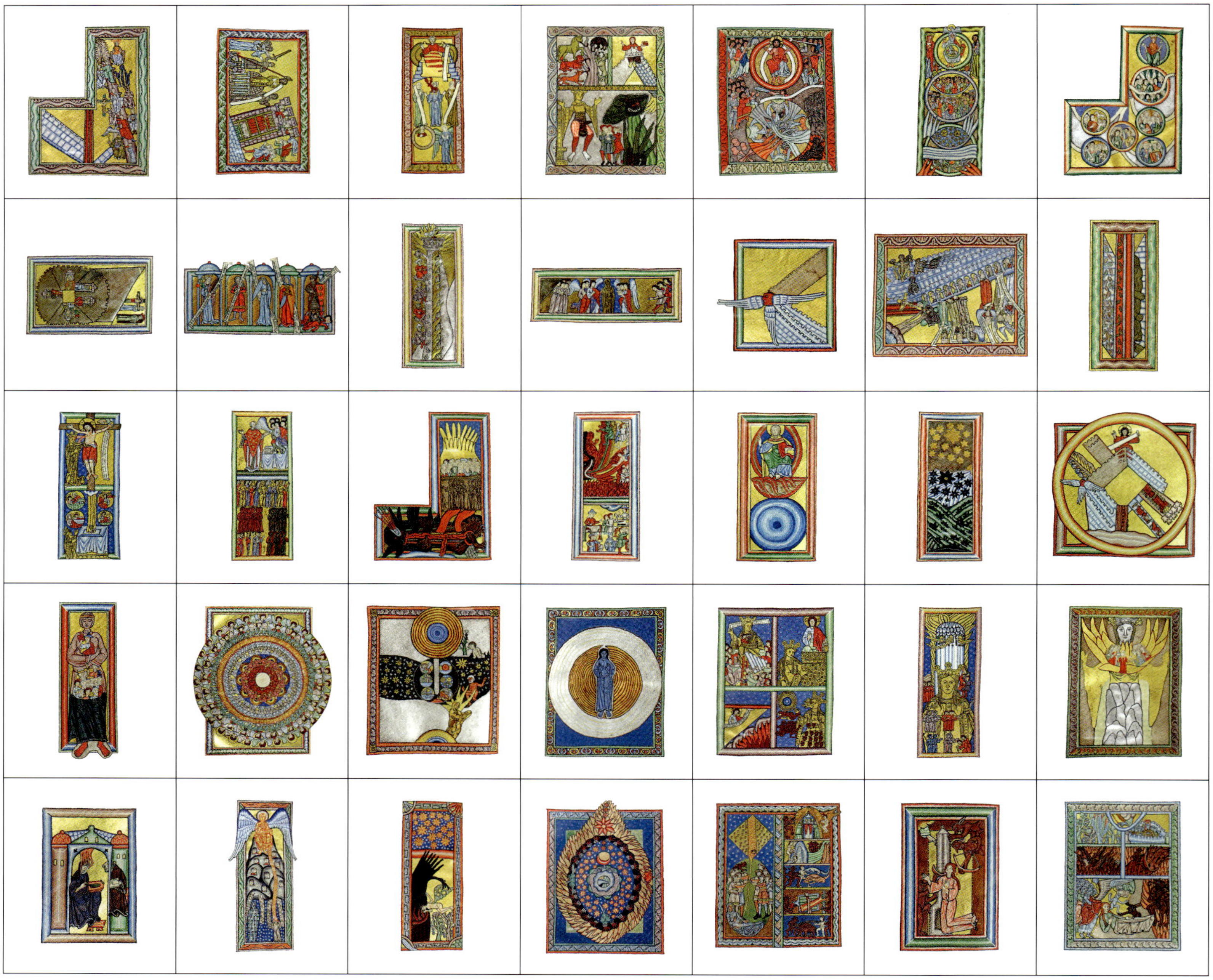

I Am

The number twenty-six

I who am without beginning and from whom all beginnings proceed, who am the Ancient of Days, I speak: "I am in myself the Day—I came not from the sun, but the sun was set alight from me. I am also Reason, which took its sound from no one else, but from which all rationality breathes" (*LDO* I.4.105, p. 244).

Twenty-six is the number of the visions and represents the *tetragrammaton*, YHWH, which, in the ancient Judeo-Christian tradition, indicates God's revelation to Moses: *I am who I am*. The path to salvation is depicted in the work through the number thirteen and its two multiples, twenty-six and sixty-five, which represent the three names of God: *Ahod, YHWH, Adonai*, visible respectively in the cross, in the number of visions, and in the design of the triple wall (see pp. 170–172).

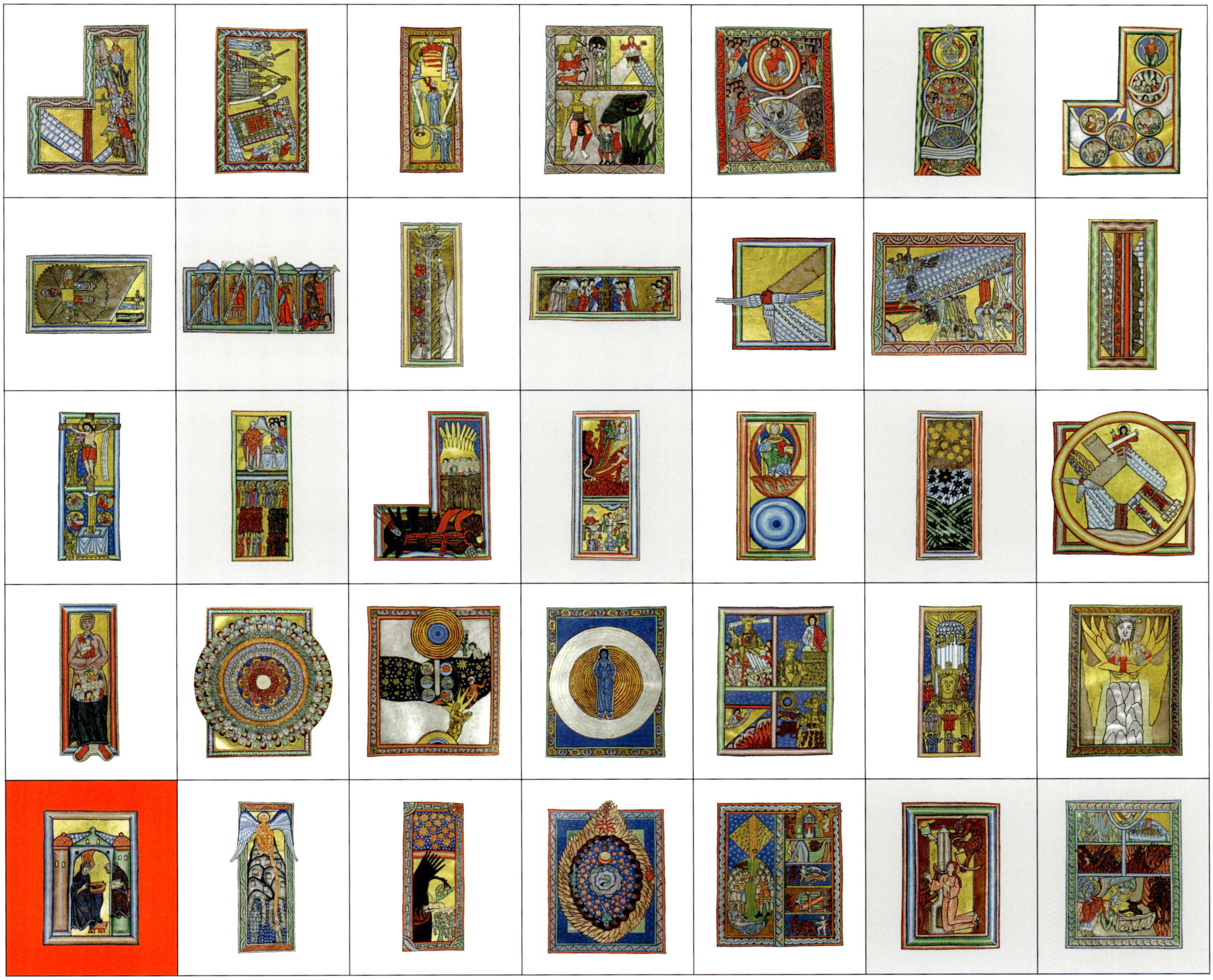

The Victory over Evil

The five-by-five square

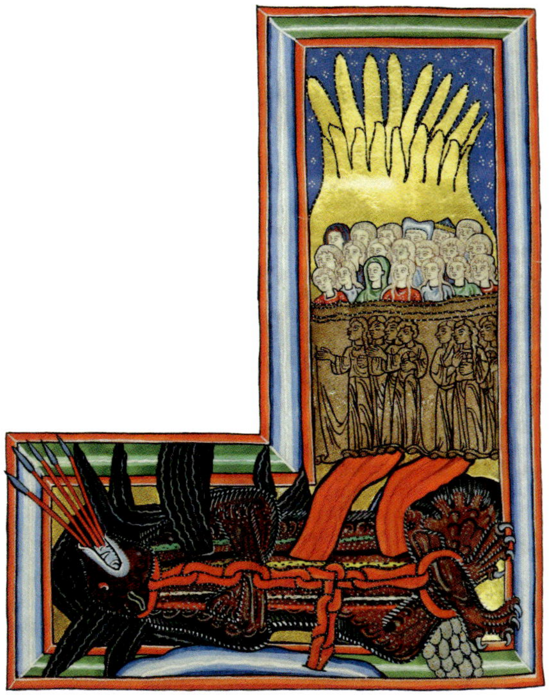

But it will not be so when time is transformed;
for then the shade of night will be put to flight and
its darkness will not appear from that time on
(*SC* III.12.16, p. 520).

The *Liber Divinorum Operum* describes the measurements of the human being, whose height is divided into five equal spaces, and equal to the width of his outstretched arms. Thus, the human body is inscribed in a five-by-five square, five being a *mystical number*. The twenty-six visions can be placed in the *mystical square* following the *boustrophedon* pattern used in sacred squares, by starting from the two opposite corners and proceeding to the center, with the thirteen visions of the first and second parts beginning at the lower left corner, and the thirteen visions of the third part, at the upper right corner. The ancient serpent is not visible since it is figuratively and symbolically crushed by the image of Mary in the center.

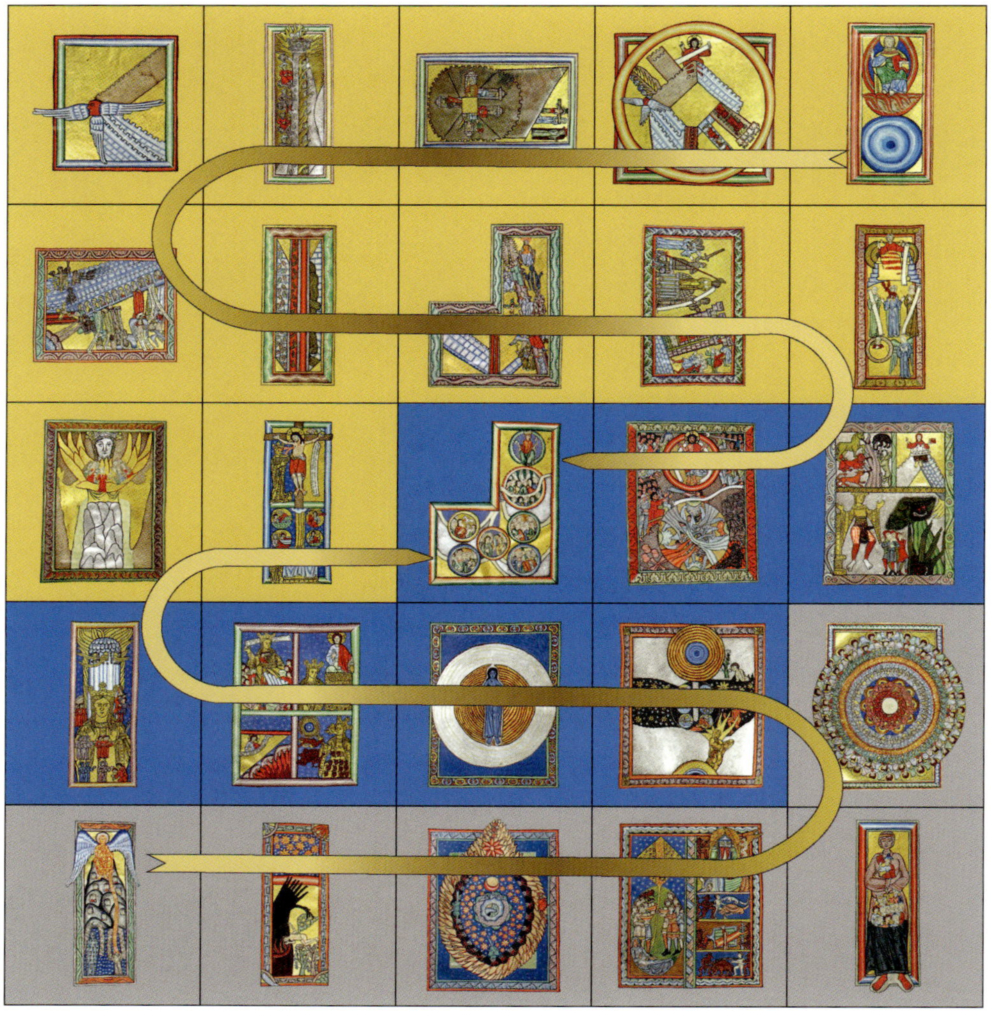

Song to Mary

At the center of the mystic square

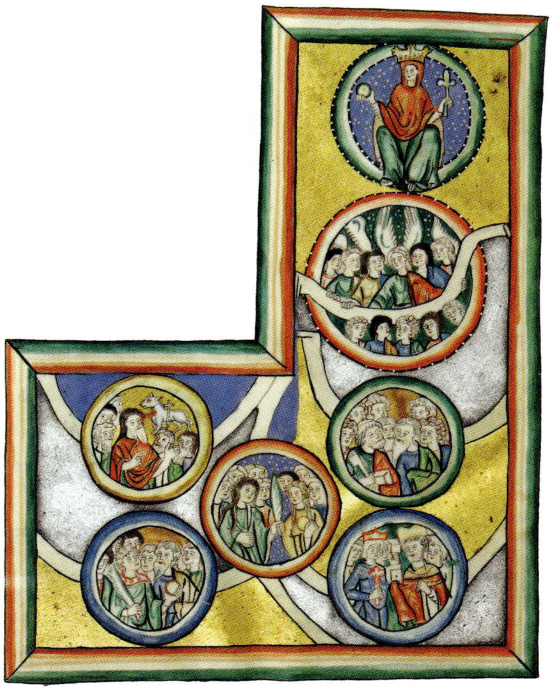

And their song, like the voice of a multitude, making music in harmony praising the ranks of Heaven, had these words: O splendid jewel, serenely infused with the Sun (*SC* III.13.D and 1, p. 525).

At the center of the square, in fact, there are two superimposed visions: the Ancient Serpent (II.7a), the thirteenth vision, and the Symphony (III.13), the twenty-sixth vision, in which Mary is visible in the uppermost circle, praised by the song of the blessed. The superimposition of the two images powerfully evokes the image of Mary the Holy Queen who crushes the serpent and banishes it from the world forever.

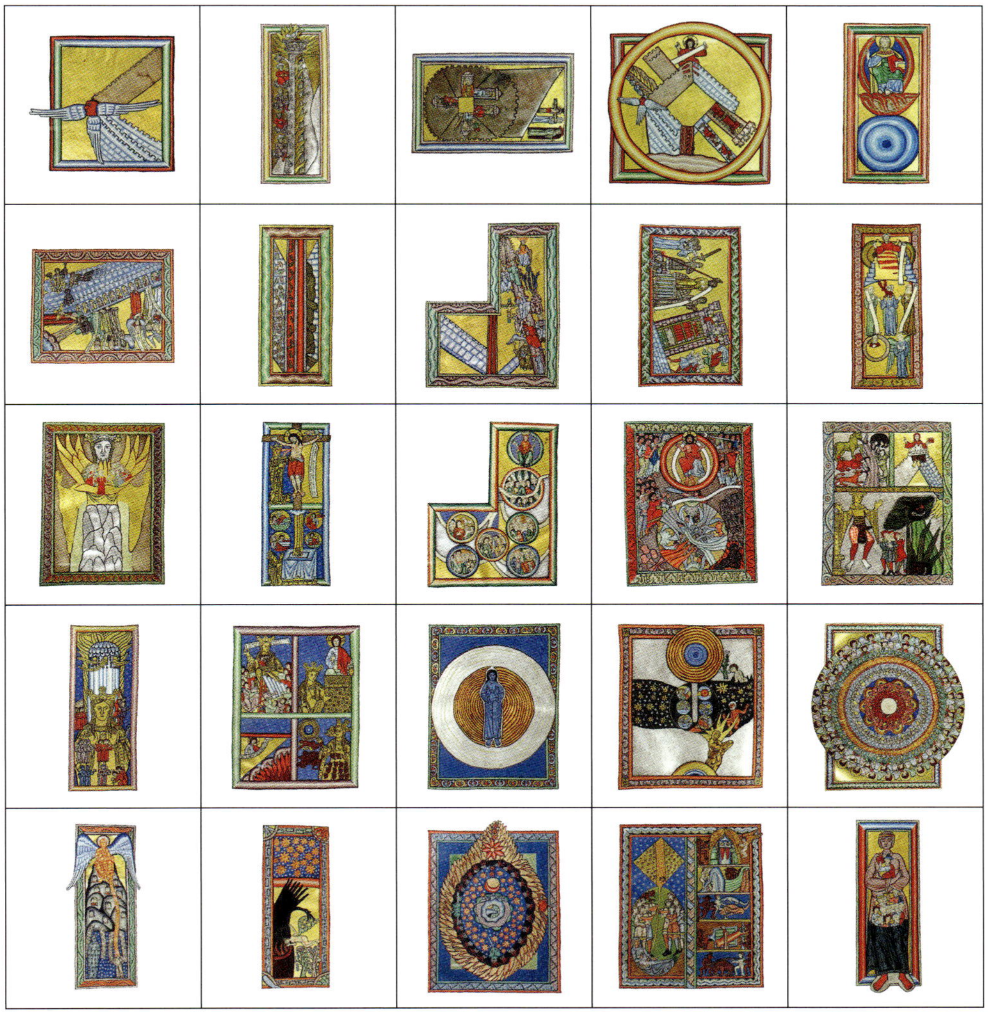

Living Stones

The number seven hundred and six

The city built of living stones directs its gaze through the origin of justice and amid God's protection to his judgment, glorifying him, for faithful souls continually praise God because he rightly orders all things (*LDO* II.1.11, p. 280).

The *Scivias* text is divided into seven hundred and six chapters, representing the living stones of the construction of the heavenly Jerusalem. There are a specific number of chapters for each vision, which when inserted into the five-by-five sacred square, reveal connections and create the design of the triple wall where the prayer of the psalms, the adoration of God, and the invocation of his name *Adonai* reverberate.

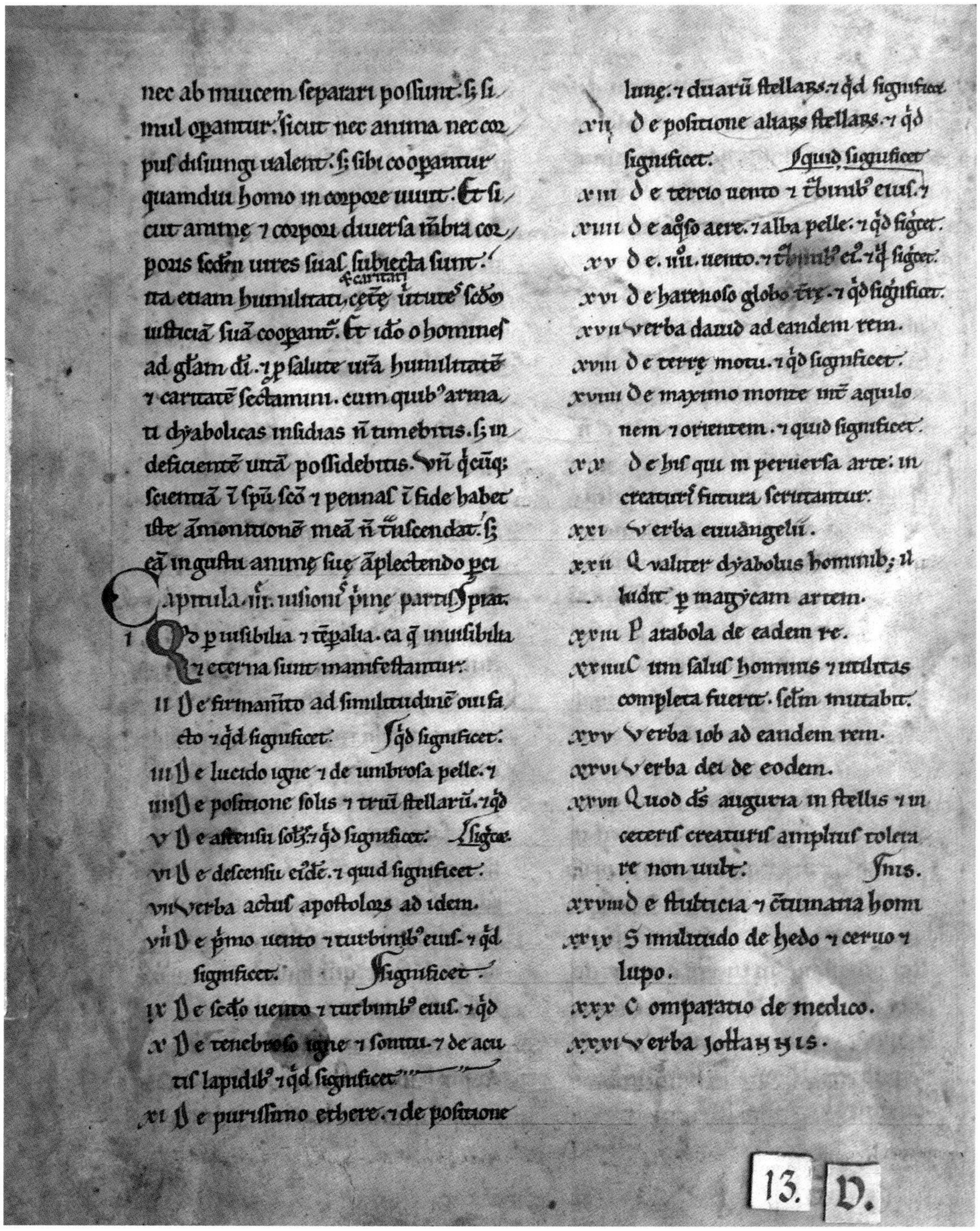

Photo of the original manuscript of *Scivias* Hs1 showing the chapter numbers

The number of chapters of each vision is inserted in the diagram below, directly below the image of the corresponding vision. Careful observation of these numbers, enables various considerations:

• the total number of chapters, 706, is formed by the numbers 7 and 6 whose sum is 13 and refers to the tripartite division of the work into six, seven and thirteen visions;

• the number of chapters into which the vision is divided symbolically illustrates the meaning of the vision itself. For example:

6 chapters are devoted to the first vision (I.1), image of the six days of the genesis that mark the beginning of the story;

9 chapters are devoted to the vision of the Three Persons (II.2), image of action embodying the power of the Trinity;

42 chapters are devoted to the vision of the End Times (III.11), image of the forty-two months of Revelation;

• the same chapter number identifies four pairs of visions that symbolically trace the four stages of the eschatological journey:

33 chapters are devoted to The Fall (I.2), from which Hell originates, and The Wrath of God (III.5), where the power of God opposes evil;

32 chapters are devoted to the Birth of the Soul (I.4a), which also celebrates the infusion of the Word in the body of woman, and to the revelation of the Son of God (III.10);

25 chapters are devoted to the Ancient Serpent (II.7a), in which Evil is vanquished, and to the Column of the Savior (III.8), when, following the death of Christ and the victory over Evil, the time of edification began.

16 chapters are devoted to the New Heaven and the New Earth (III.12) and to the Symphony (III.13), image of eternal blessedness, symbolized by the number sixteen.

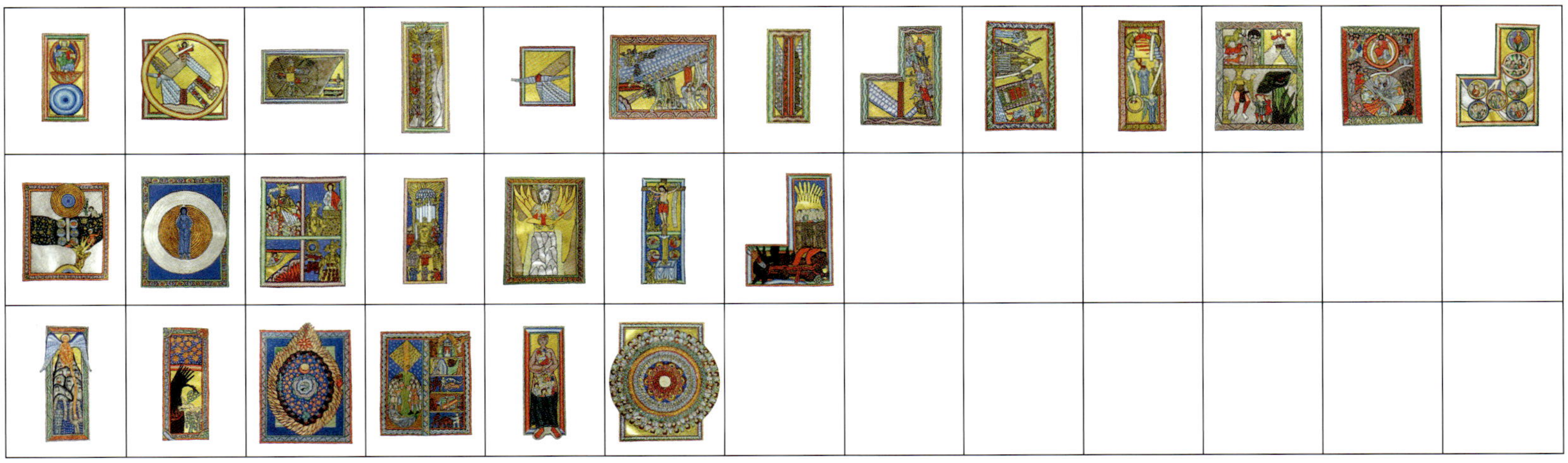

Visions		I	II	III	IV	V	VI	VII	VIII	IX	X	XI	XII	XIII	Total chapters
	III	18	28	13	22	33	35	11	25	29	32	42	16	16	320
Parts	II	17	9	37	14	60	102	25							264
	I	6	33	31	32	8	12								122
															706

Heavenly Jerusalem

The chanting of psalms, the prayer of adoration, and the invocation of God.
The journey toward the heavenly Jerusalem

The numbers of the chapters of each vision are placed in the five-by-five square, next to the image of the corresponding vision, and reveal the image of the heavenly Jerusalem in its symbolic form of the triple wall (see p. 172). The hidden design is formed by the union of five geometric figures generated by groups of numbers, which are cleverly positioned and connected.

The first three groups indicate the numbers of three psalms, according to the Vulgate: Psalm 138, *You have searched me, Lord, and you know me*; Psalm 104, *Praise the Lord. Give thanks to the Lord, for he is good*; and Psalm 18, *The heavens declare the glory of God.*

The three psalms delineate the path along the ways: praising God who knows everything about the human being and searches his heart to guide him in the ways of good, and praising divine creation, the beauty of forgiveness, and the manifestation of God as a strong rock.

The last two groups recall the tetractys and God's name, *Adonai*, through which they invite humanity to pray in adoration and to invoke God.

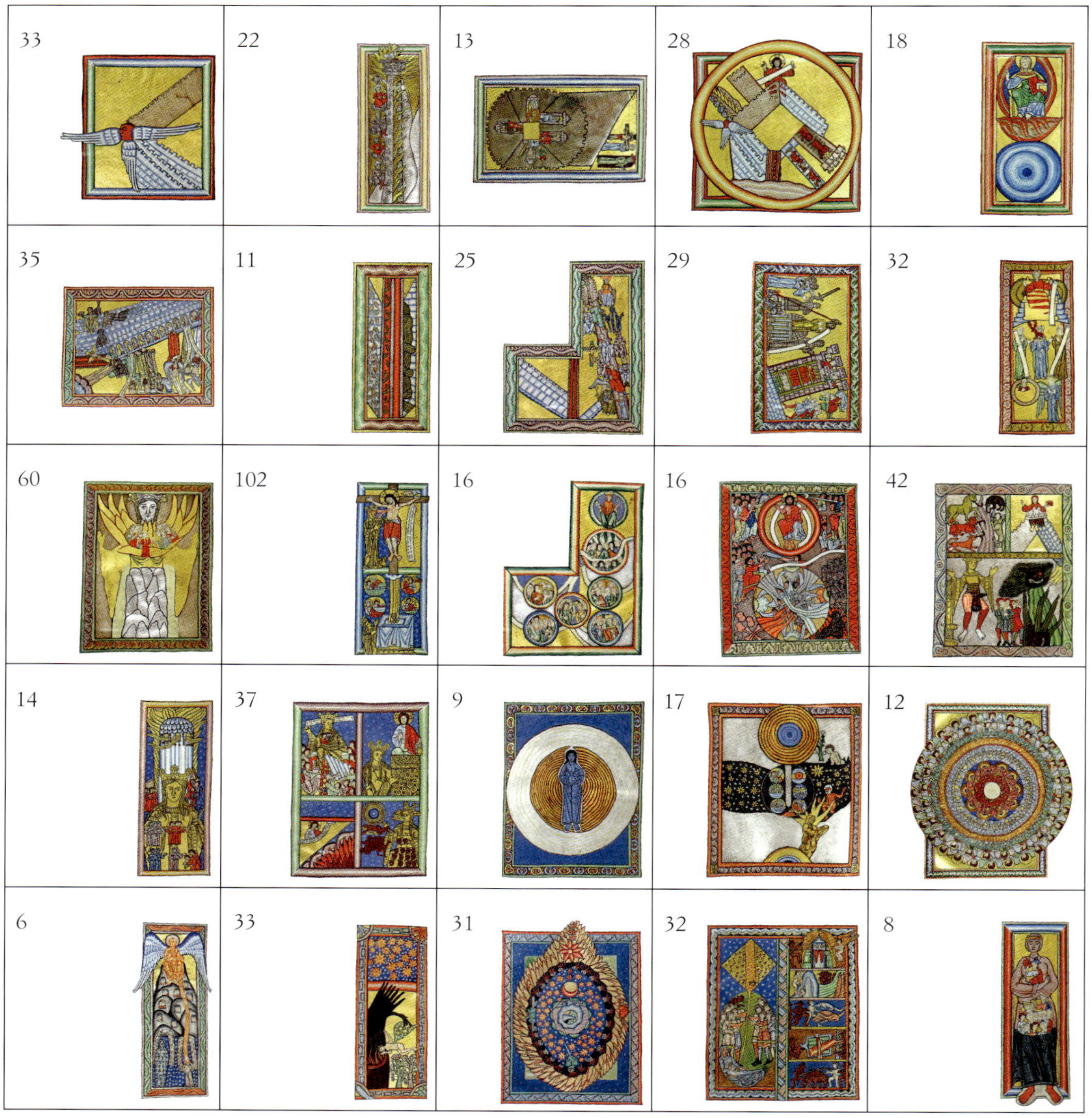

Psalm 138

You have searched me, Lord, and you know me

The number 138 is indicated by the sum of the numbers 11, 13, 29, 37, 31, 17: the only prime numbers in the square, which can only be divided by themselves and the number 1. The extension of the lines that join them creates the form of an oblique square.

33	22	13	28	18
35	11	25	29	32
60	102	16	16	42
14	37	9	17	12
6	33	31	32	8

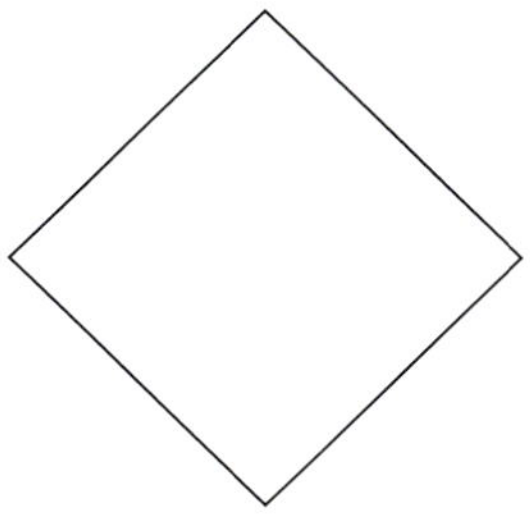

Psalm 104

Praise the Lord. Give thanks to the Lord, for he is good

The number 104 is indicated by the sum of the numbers 22, 35,14, 33, and of the numbers 28, 32, 12, 32. The extension of the lines that join them creates the form of a second, larger oblique square.

33	22	13	28	18
35	11	25	29	32
60	102	16	16	42
14	37	9	17	12
6	33	31	32	8

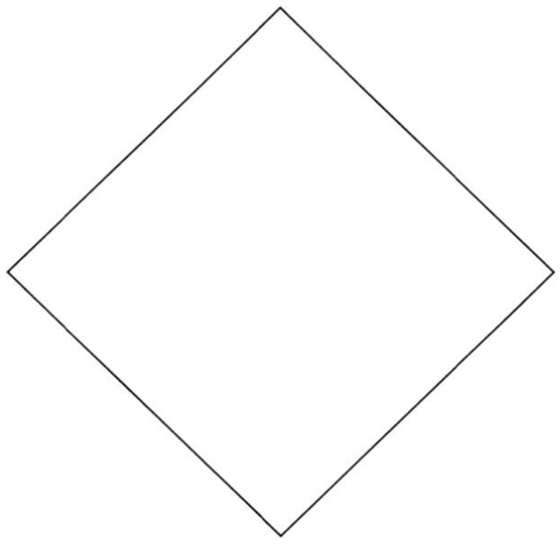

Psalm 18

The heavens declare the glory of God

The number 18 is indicated by the value equal to the difference between the numbers 60 and 42, and between the numbers 31 and 13. The two lines that join them create the form of a cross.

33	22	13	28	18
35	11	25	29	32
60	102	16	16	42
14	37	9	17	12
6	33	31	32	8

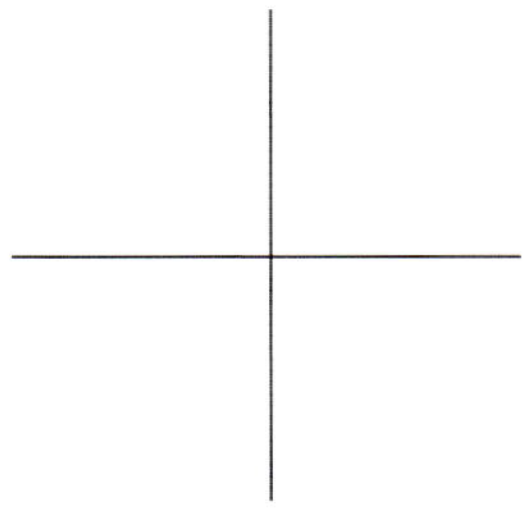

Tetractys

The numbers 9, 16, 25, in the center of the square, are equal to the square of the numbers 3, 4, 5 that form the first Pythagorean triple, image of the tetractys. They suggest the formation of three concentric squares with a side length, respectively, of 3, 4 and 5.

33	22	13	28	18
35	11	25	29	32
60	102	16	16	42
14	37	9	17	12
6	33	31	32	8

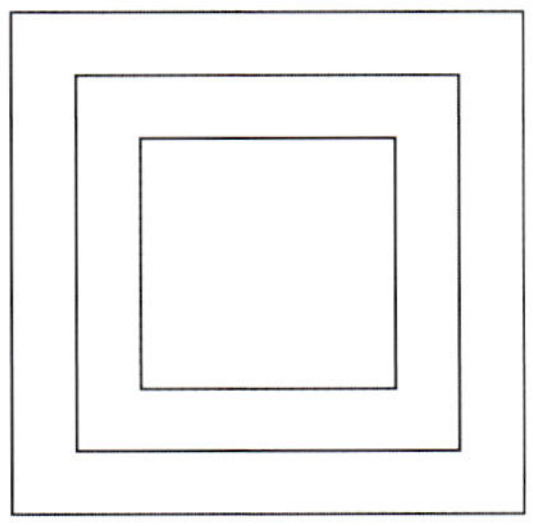

The name of God

Adonai

The number 65, which represents God's name, *Adonai*, is indicated by the sum of the four numbers 6, 8, 18, 33 placed at the corners of the square.

The line that joins them forms a square that circumscribes the other three, formed by the numbers of the tetractys.

33	22	13	28	18
35	11	25	29	32
60	102	16	16	42
14	37	9	17	12
6	33	31	32	8

"The great edifice of living souls, which is constructed in Heaven from living stones [...] encircles as a great city encircles [...] and blossoms with celestial virtues" (*SC* II.3.D, p. 170).

The union of the five geometric forms the numbers of the chapters (see previous page) creates the image of the triple wall, symbol of the celestial city.

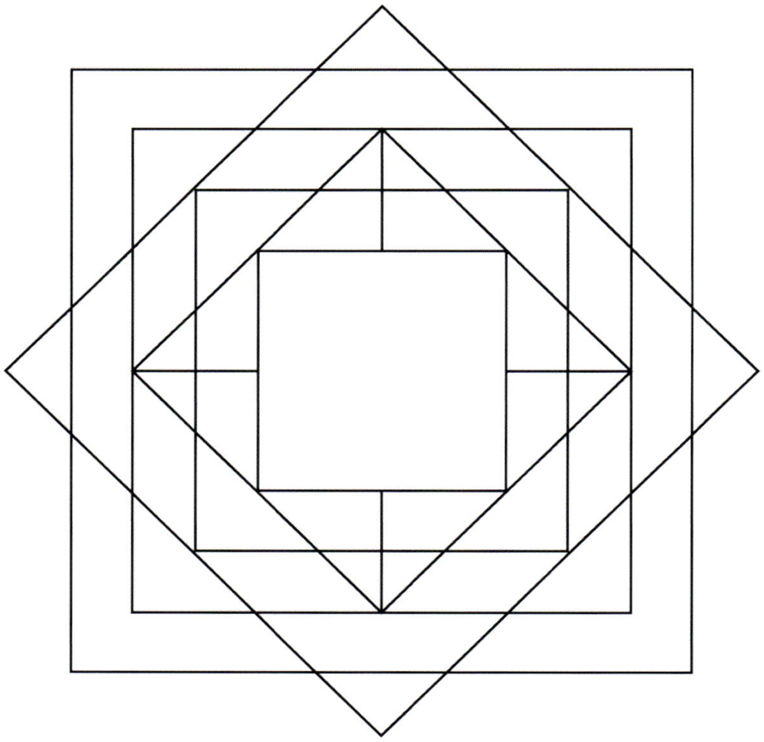

33	22	13	28	18
35	11	25	29	32
60	102	16	16	42
14	37	9	17	12
6	33	31	32	8

Psalm 118

Give thanks to the Lord because he is good

The number 118 appears twice, in the sum of the group of numbers 60, 16, 42 and of the group 102 and 16, which are alternated on the horizontal axis of the square. It references Psalm 118, hymn to the beauty of God's law. The psalm was chosen by St. Benedict as the foundation of Benedictine prayer, and recited at Lauds on the holy day of Sunday and at the Little Hours on Monday.

In Praise of the Holy Cross

Rabano Mauro (Hrabanus Maurus, 780–856) was abbot of the Benedictine abbey of Fulda— about two days on foot from Bingen—which he turned into a hub of medieval culture. His fame is acknowledged by Dante in Canto XII of *Paradise*, when the poet, finding himself in the heaven of wise spirits, simply says, *Here is Rabano*. Hildegard fully mastered the lessons of her teacher and from his work, *In Praise of the Holy Cross*, she learned the figurative art of drawing with letters, combined in different numbers and shapes, with which she created images that praised the different manifestations of God.

Hildegard composed the word *scivias* in a way that enabled her, through its particular structure, to imitate the *carmina figurata* devised by Rabano:

- formed from *sci* and *vias*, respectively of three and four letters, the word is the image of the trinitarian dimension of God and of the quaternary dimension of the earth on which humanity is called upon to travel the ways;
- the seven letters of *scivias* describe the cross (figure at the top), at the center of which there is the letter "V" indicating Christ, cornerstone of the human story, with an "I" on either side, which, together with the "V" form the letter "M" of Mary (see p. 174), mother of the new humanity. The cross of seven letters recalls the first flowered cross of Rabano, image of the seven gifts of the Spirit (see p. 175);
- the word is a semi-palindrome: the only unmatching letters are "A" and "C," which generate, at the center of the figures, groupings of nine "C"s around the letter "S," image of the centrality of Christ the Savior (see p. 174);

S
C
I
S C I V I A S
I
A
S

- repeated twice, the word creates a sequence of 13 letters, in which the last "S" of the first word becomes the first letter of the second, forming two groups of 6 and 7 letters that recall the numerical structure 6, 7, 13 of the three parts of the work (see p. 160); the cross thus formed of thirteen letters reprises Rabano's image of the green cross at whose foot he is prostrate in adoration (see following page).

3			4			
S	C	I	V	I	A	S

6						7						
S	C	I	V	I	A	S	C	I	V	I	A	S

7						
S	C	I	V	I	A	S

13												
S	C	I	V	I	A	S	C	I	V	I	A	S

S	C	I	V	I	A	S
	●				●	
S	A	I	V	I	C	S

13												
S	C	I	V	I	A	S	C	I	V	I	A	S
S	A	I	V	I	C	S	C	I	V	I	A	S

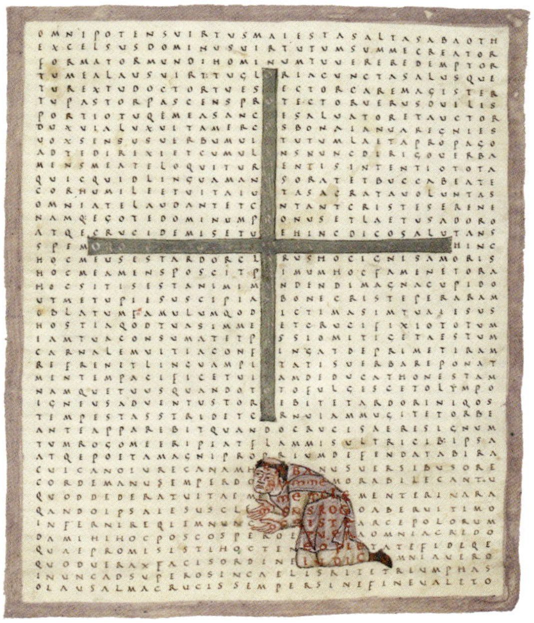

The adoration of the Cross

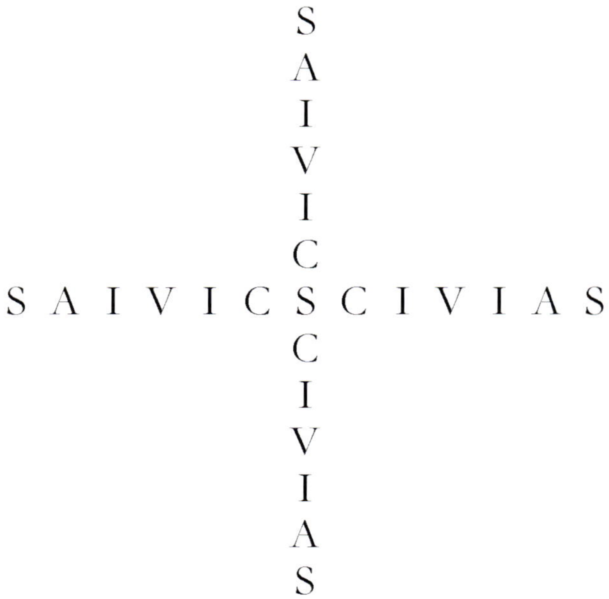

The characteristics of the word *scivias* have allowed us to create the designs on these pages and to compare them with those of the geometries delineated by Rabano. In our opinion, these designs in which numbers, shapes, and meaning merge and mark an explicit homage to the beauty of the master's figurative prayer, tellingly convey the constructive sensibility of Hildegard and her collaborators. Unlike the other images in this volume, they are obviously the result of a deductive process and therefore subject to verification.

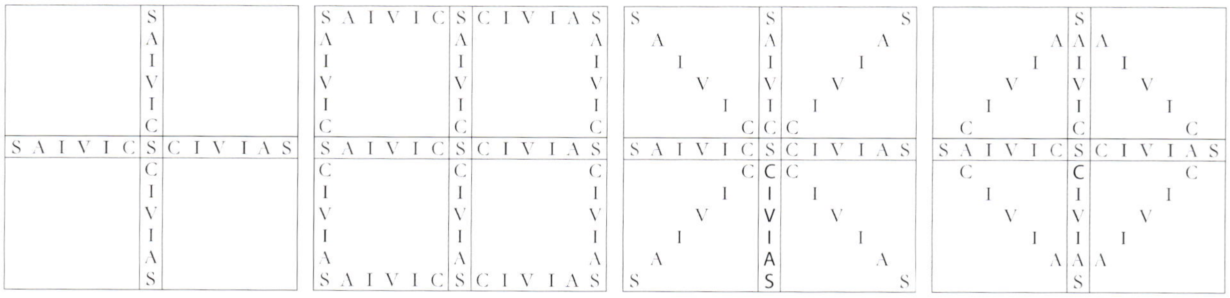

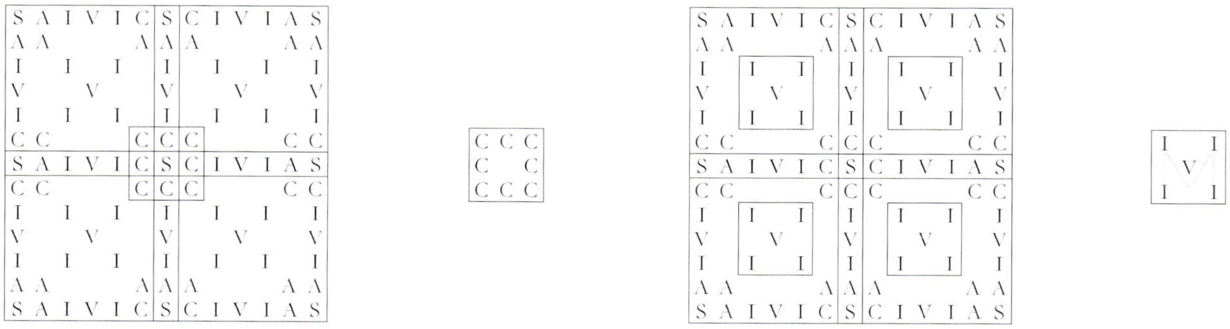

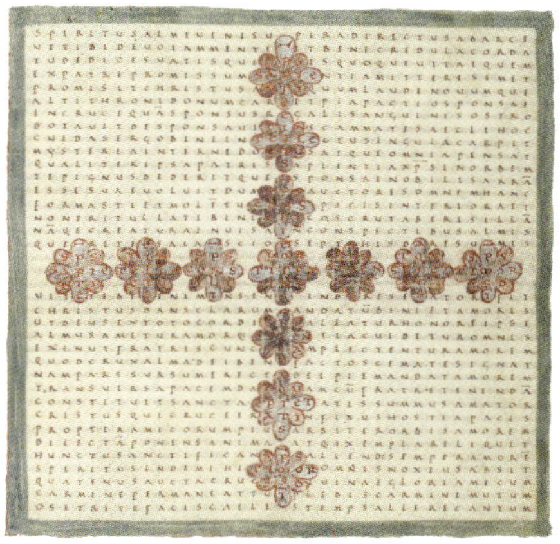

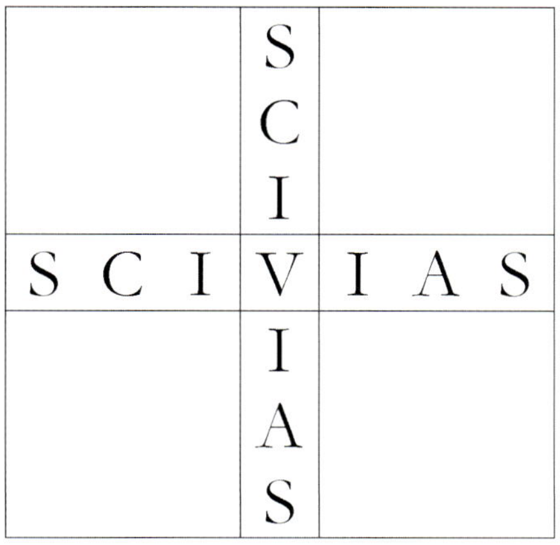

The seven gifts of the Holy Spirit

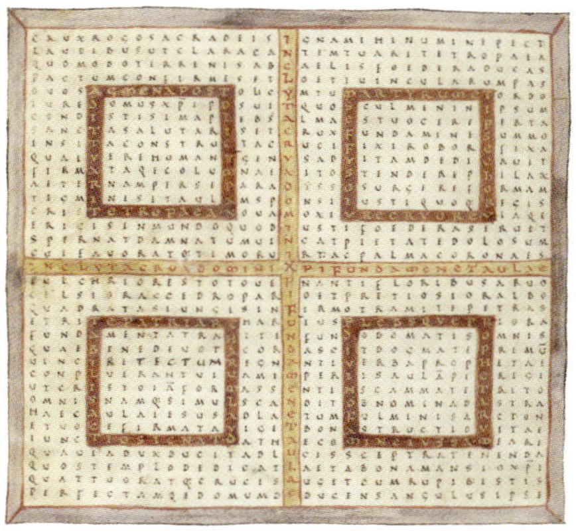

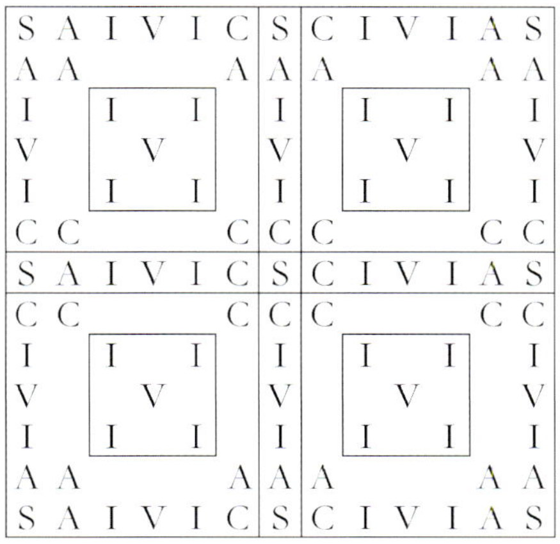

The House of God

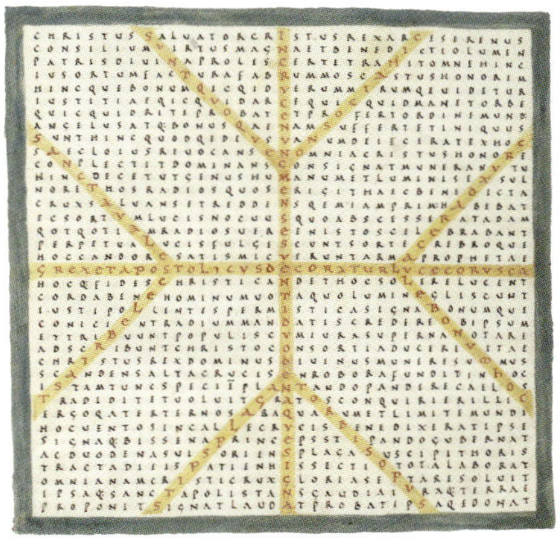

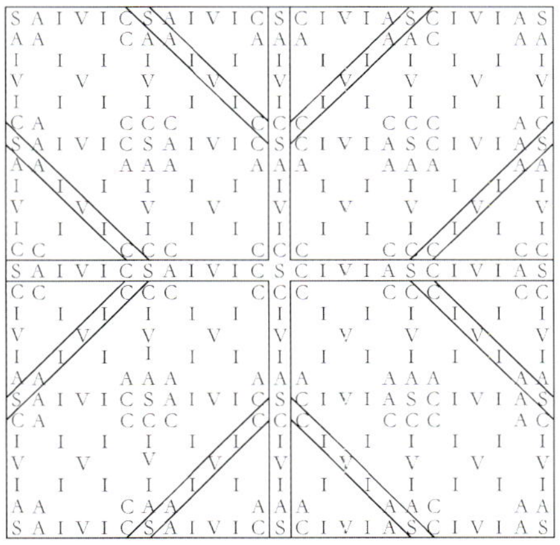

The twelve months, twelve signs, twelve winds and twelve apostles

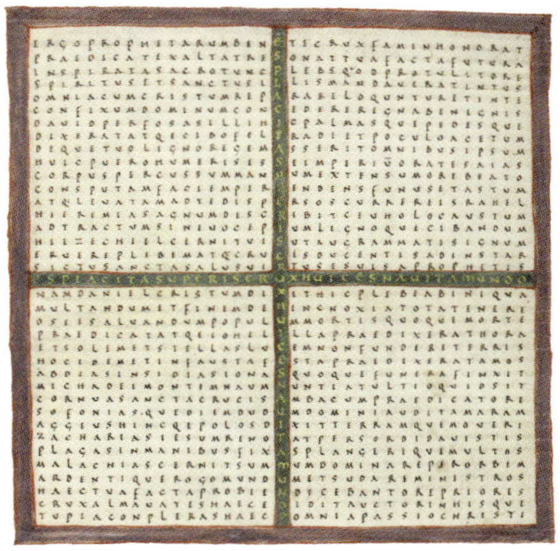

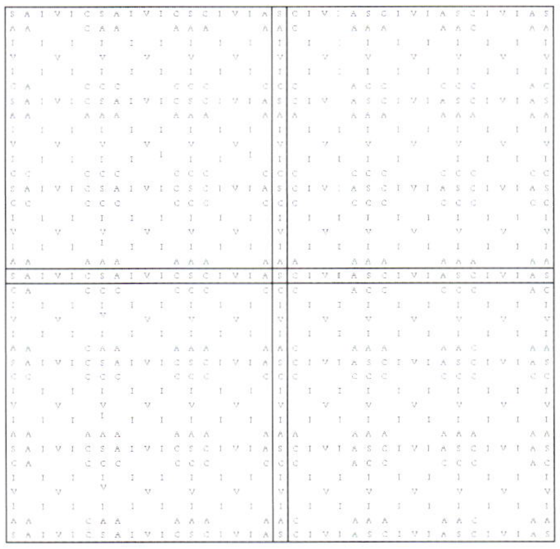

The Cross shows that everything is in God

Numbers and Symbols

In the images, numbers are present in the quantity of forms and the elements of the figures. The first ten numbers mark the story of revelation and are accented by the ten groups of circles present in the visions. These numbers are represented in the figures through the repetition of the same element, and generate all the other numbers.

Numerical symbolism represents the word of the Sacred Scripture, as in the case of the forty-eight eyes in the Science of God square, which in the two triangles derived from it are divided into two groups of twenty-four, image of the twenty-four elders in Revelation; or the thirty seeds in the square, a reference to the Trinity, image of the incarnation of the Word (see below).

In other cases, the number is used as a narrative thread to link different images. This is done directly, as in the nineteen *stars* that appear first as heavenly spirits (I.2) and then as prophets (II.1), with the former keeping vigil like lamps and the latter being sent as a light in the darkness; or indirectly, as with the forty-four eyes of the virtue of the Fear of God (I.1) that scrutinize humanity so that it may act with devotion and its works shine like forty-four *spheres* in the firmament (I.3) (see p. 215).

Another refined example of the figurative connections made through the number is found in the image of the Son of God seated on the throne. The steps are seven on one side and five on the other (see below), signifying that the human can only ascend to heaven by accepting the seven gifts of the Spirit through the five senses.

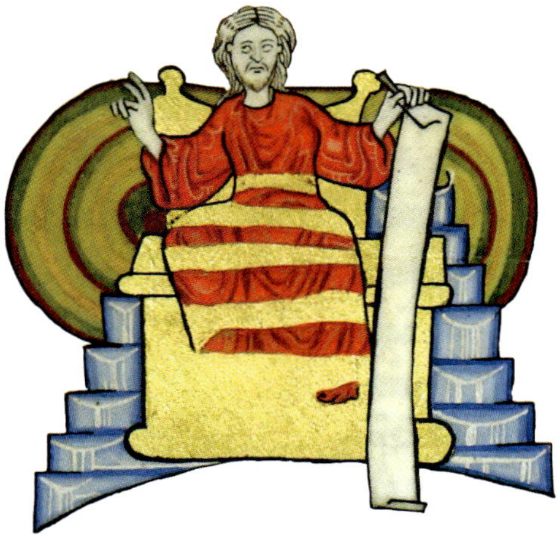

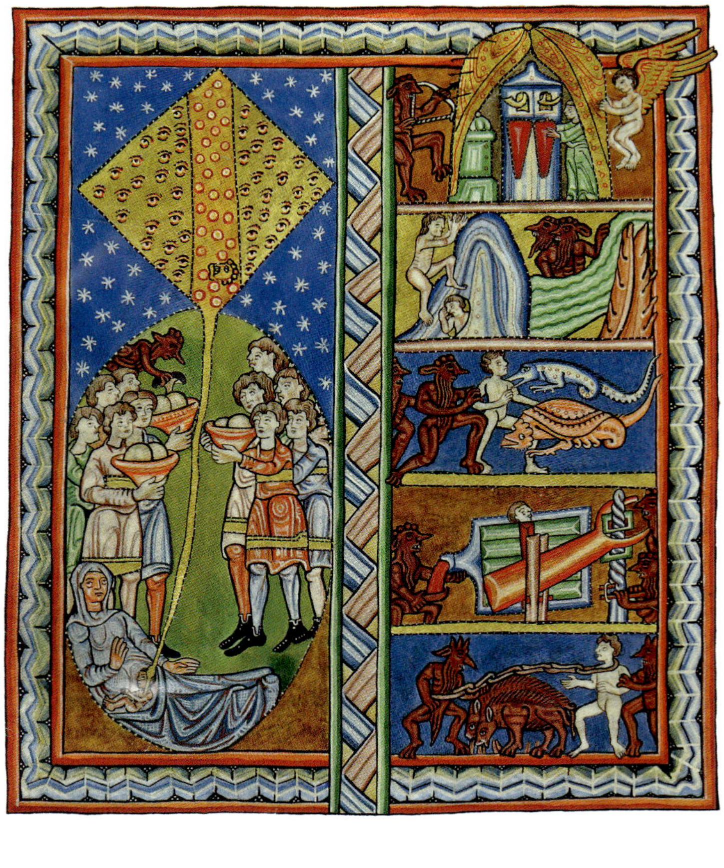

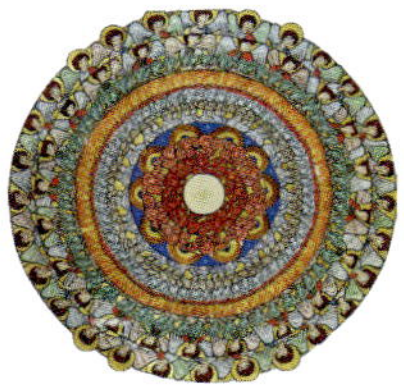

God is indeed the living Light from whom all lights shine; and so it is through him that a person remains a light alive, and fire too (*LDO* II.1.15, p. 284).

One is the divine light, God, adored by the Heavenly Hosts (I.6).

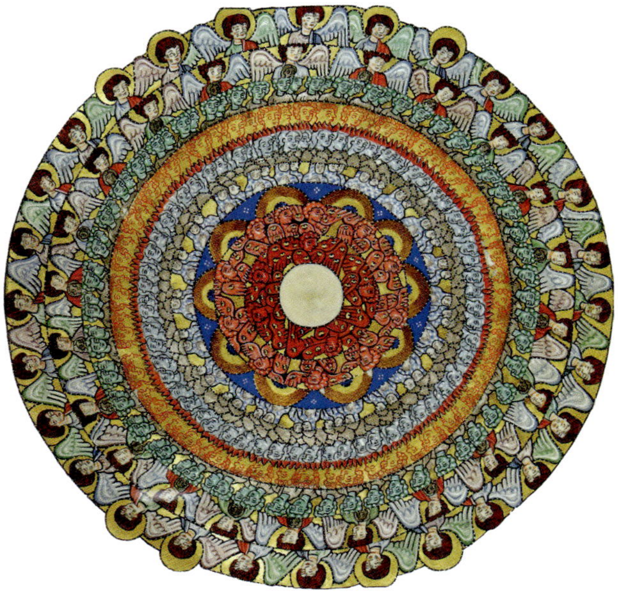

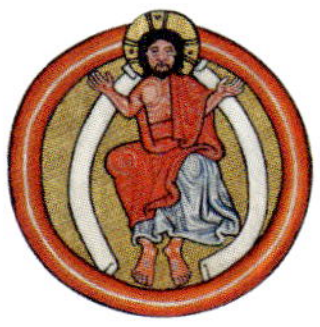

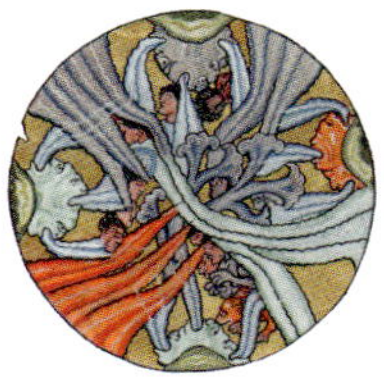

Therefore, O human, if you turn your eyes to the two roads, good and evil, then you will learn, for you will understand both great things and small (*SC* I.4.30, p. 126).

Two are the ways between which man is called upon to choose, thanks to the freedom bestowed on him by God. Two are the trees of the genesis (I.2), and two the children who come out of the mouth of the Church after baptism (II.3), one golden and the other dark. Two are the circles of the judgment miniature (III.12a).

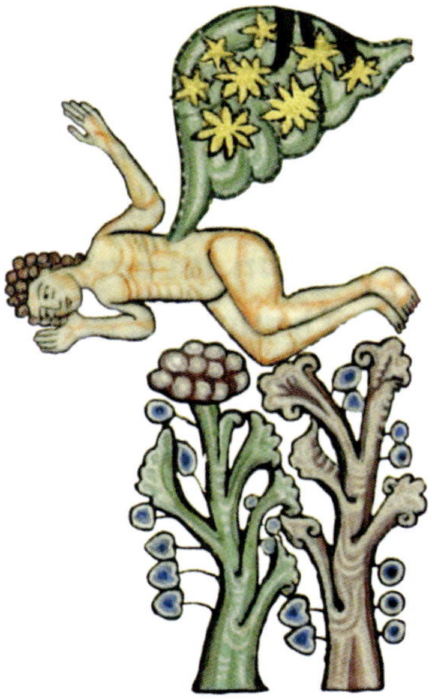

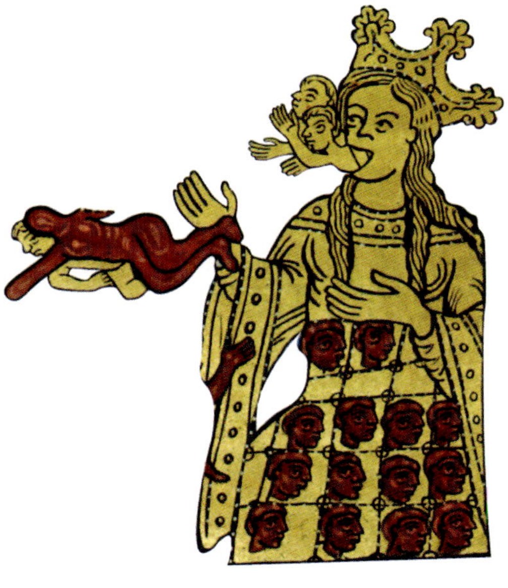

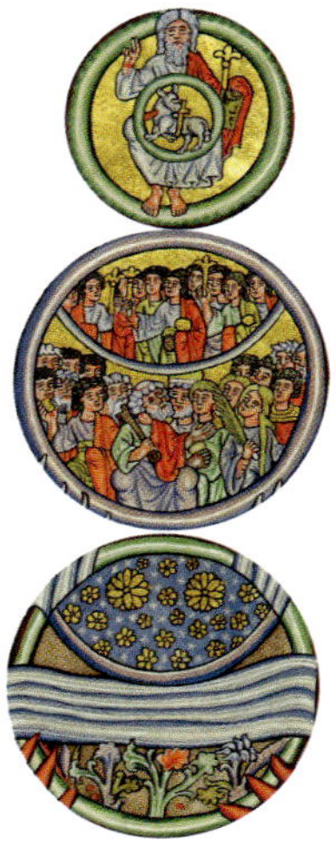

It had three wings of wondrous breadth and length, candid like a cloud [. . .] This symbolizes the expansion of the ineffable power of the Holy Trinity (*SC* III.5.14, p. 377).

Three are the petals of the flower of obedience to the Word offered to Adam (II.1) and three the petals of the flower that Mary holds aloft at the End Times (III.13), together with the body of the world, to signify the journey of the revelation of God, Three in One. Three are the circles in the Paradise miniature (III.12b).

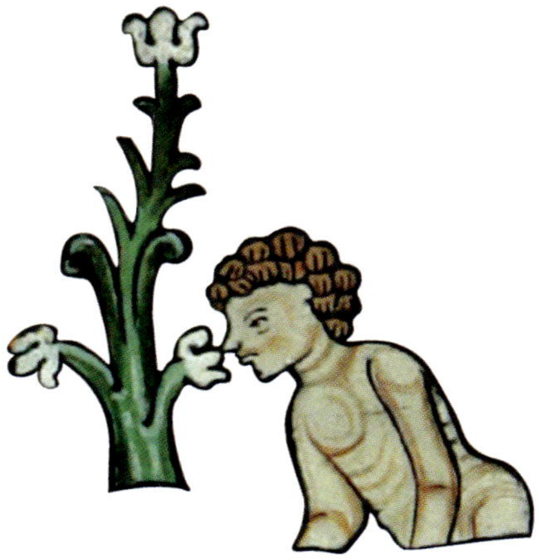

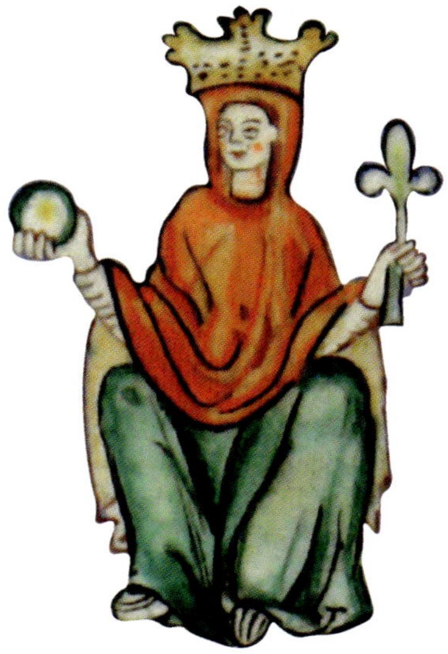

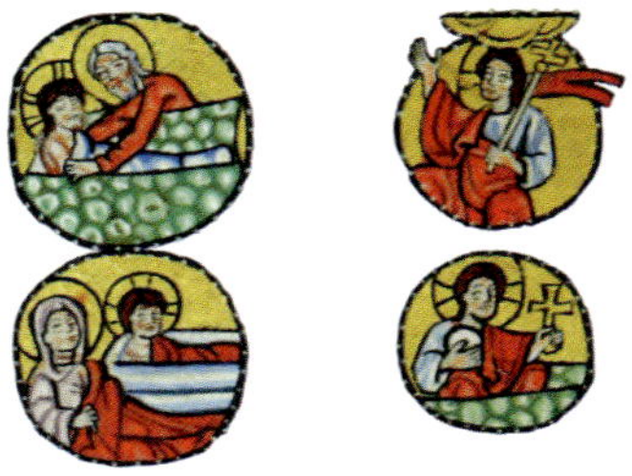

The soul indeed has four wings—sensibility, knowledge, will, and intellect (*LDO* I.4.95, p. 221).

Four are the flashes of light that rain down on the head of the Antichrist, witnessed by four human beings (III.11). It is the time of Revelation, announced by the four prophets (III.4). Four are the circles below the cross in the miniature of the crucifixion (II.6a): nativity, death, resurrection, ascension.

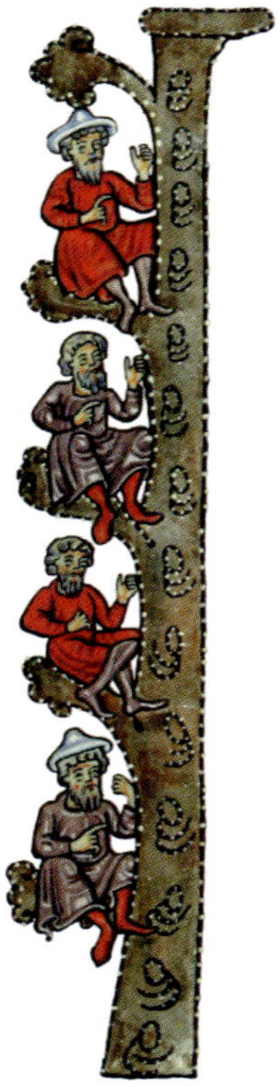

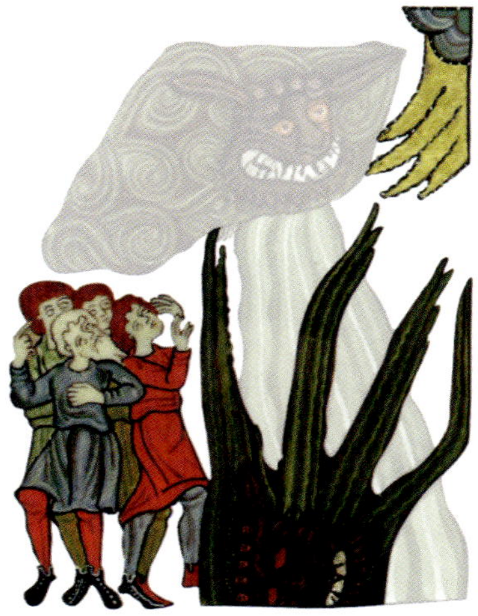

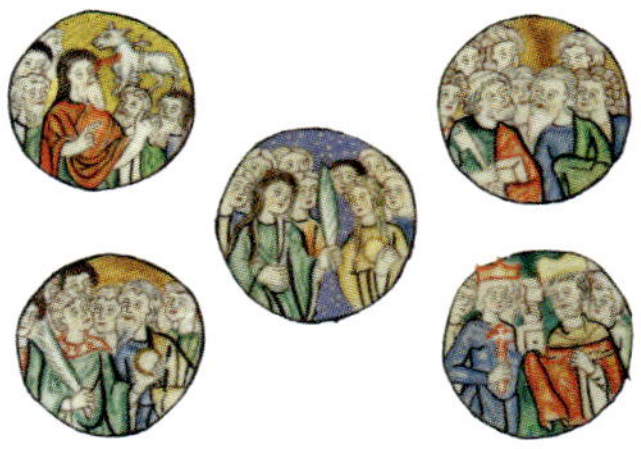

So too Man sits upon his seat—the earth—and rules the rest of creation, for Man is distinguished by the insignia of almighty God. Furthermore, these insignia are the five human senses (*LDO* I.4.102, p. 240).

Five are the virtues that accompany the final stages of humanity's journey (III.10) and five the ages of the kingdom, symbolized by the five animals (III.11). Five are the circles of the miniature of the Symphony with the virgins in the center, *blessed hearts in which the Most High would be manifest* (III.13).

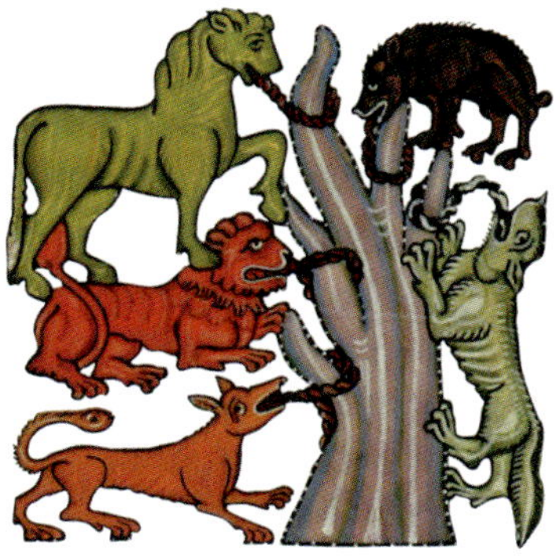

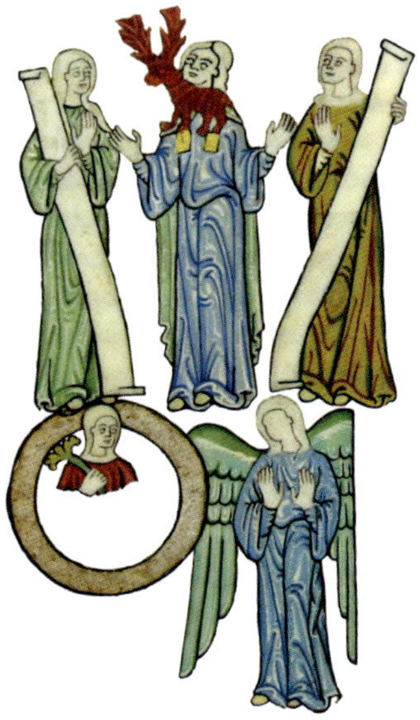

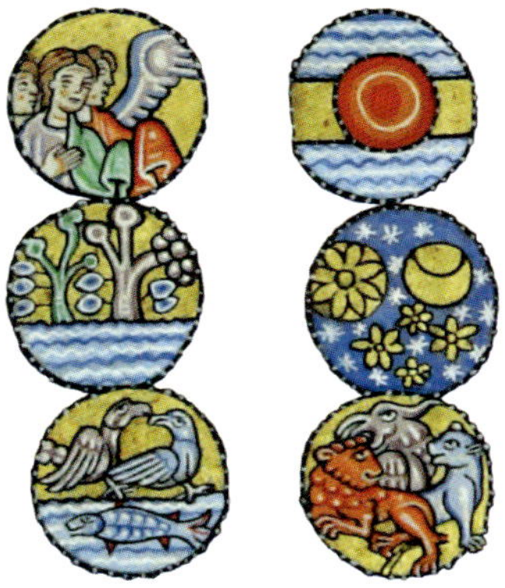

With the end of that beginning that God had made in creation and in Man, whom he had predestined in place of the fallen angel, the sixth day cast light upon Man perfected (*LDO* II.1.43, p. 334).

Six are the angels that surround the knowledge of God (III.4b) and six are the angels that approach the altar at the moment of consecration (II.6b). Six are the steps brought by the angels to build the Woman Church (II.3). Six are the circles, image of the six days of the genesis (II.1).

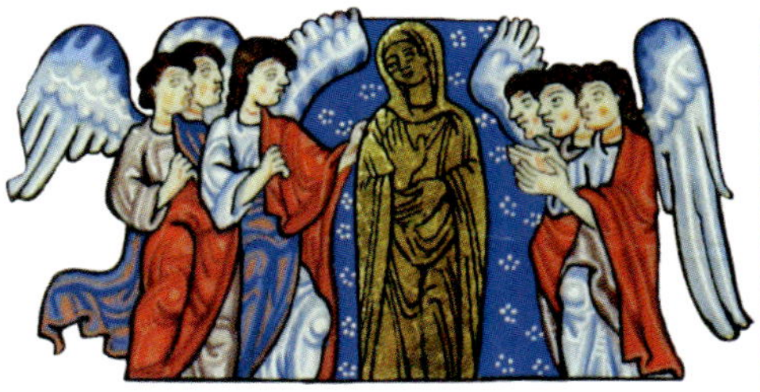

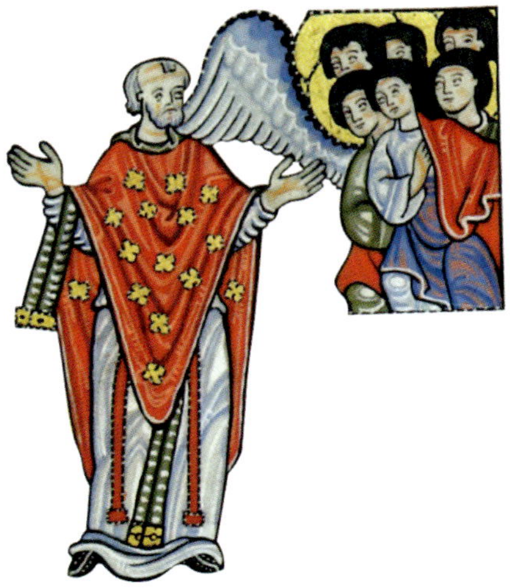

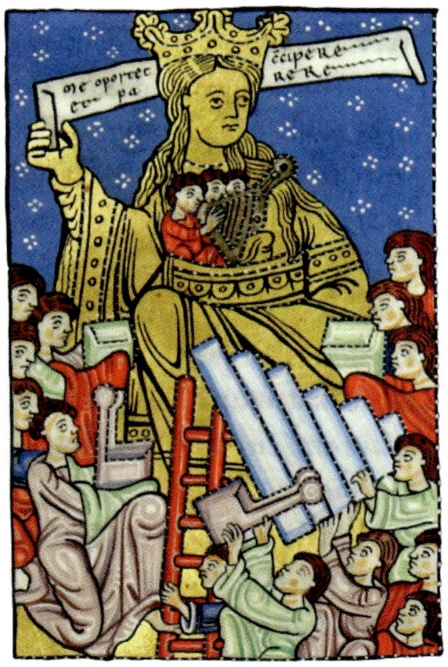

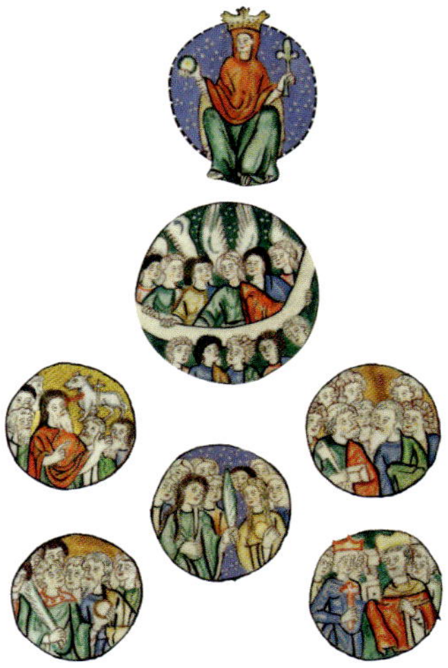

God blessed the seventh day with praise and hallowed it with an honorable solemnity, for all creation came forth fully created in him [...] the whole angelic host and all the hidden mysteries of divinity blessed God because of the finishing of God's work, and they praised him because he had perfected all his work with the seven gifts of the Holy Spirit (*LDO* II.1.47, p. 344).

Seven are the columns of light which, like a tower, protect the Church (II.4) and support the Temple of Wisdom (III.9); they represent the seven gifts of the Holy Spirit. Seven are the circles of the miniature of the Symphony (III.13).

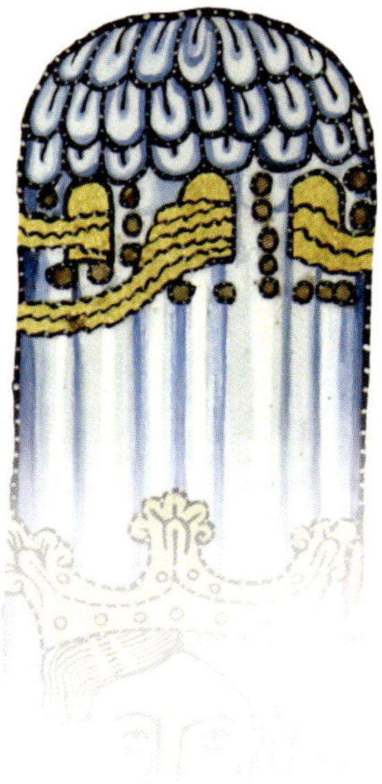

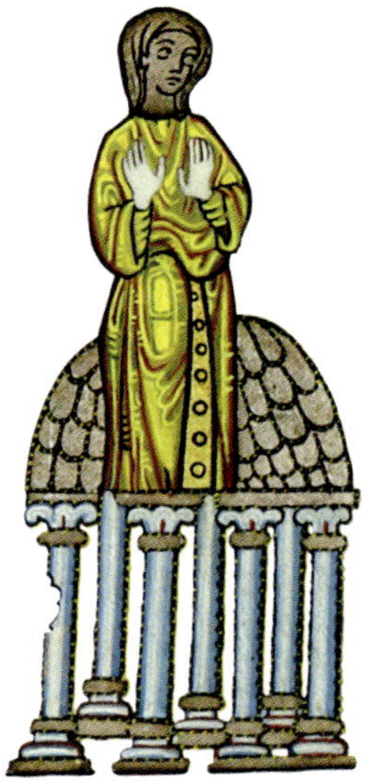

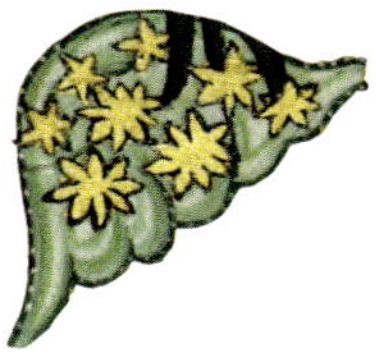

The eighth month, moreover, is in its powers like a great prince who has all things fully under his sway [...]
And so its qualities are shown in a person's hands, which accomplish very many works and have within themselves sway over the entire body (*LDO* I.4.98, p. 231).

Eight are the stars, image of the multitude of humanity, which shine in the womb of the candid cloud, Eve, tempted by the serpent, the eighth spire of smoke issuing from bottomless pit of Hell (I.2). Eight are the sides of the rock of the Fear of God (III.1a) which generates the octagonal base of the chalice of life. Life and new life.

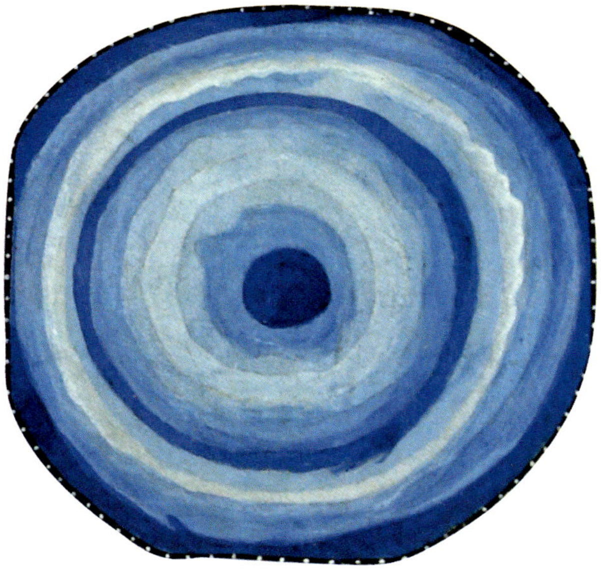

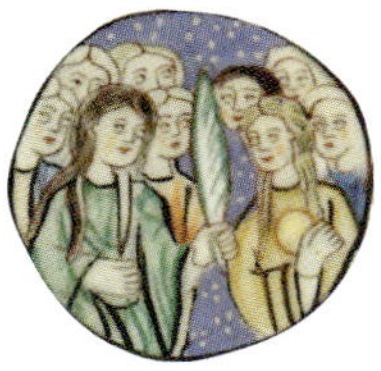

Furthermore, these insignia are the five human senses, through which by God's power a person understands and perceives that the Trinity in unity and the unity in Trinity ought to be worshiped in God through the right faith. This worship is the beauty of the nine orders of angels (*LDO* 1.4.102, p. 240).

Nine are the angels that receive the soul that leaves the body and puts on the celestial garment (1.4c); nine are the faithful who shine with auroral light within the Church (II.5); and nine are the virgins in the circle who sing in Paradise (III.13), image of the trinitarian presence and action of God.

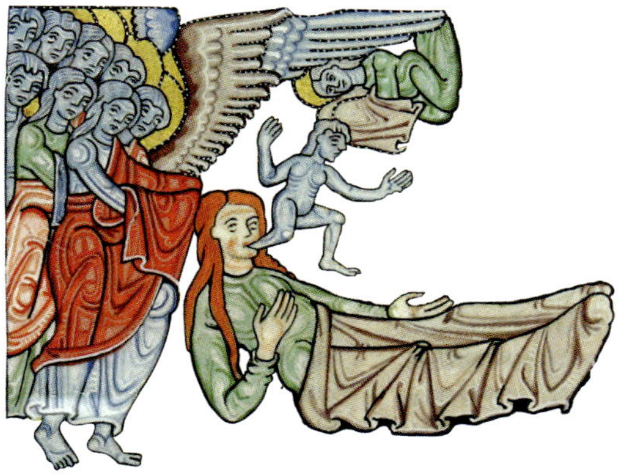

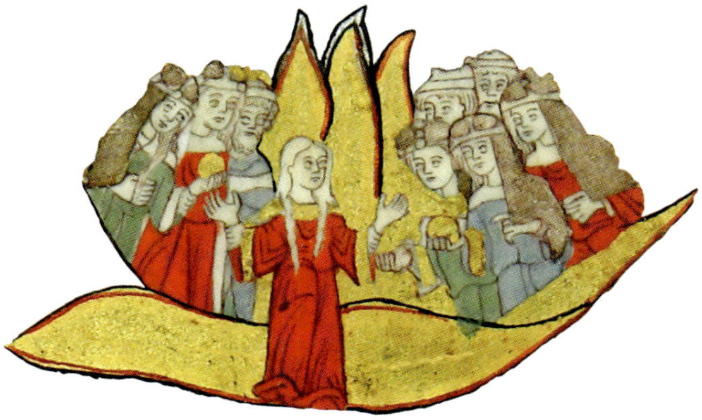

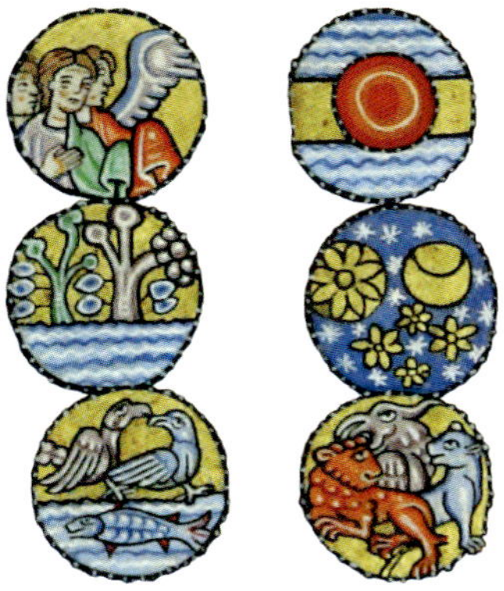

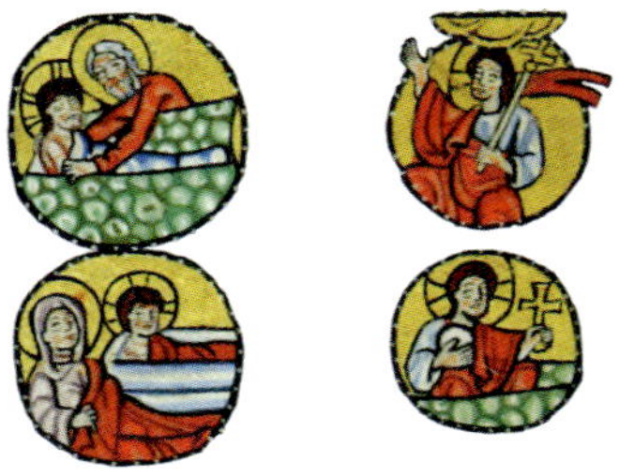

And so Man symbolizes the full number ten, perfecting these things by the power of God (*SC* III.2.19, p. 335).

Ten are the clouds that surround the seed of the earth (I.3) and ten are the auroras in the host of Thrones (I.6). They show the transition from Eve, green cloud, mother of humanity, to Mary, aurora, mother of the faithful, opening the way to the time of fulfillment when humanity will be able to take the place of the tenth host. The journey of salvation evolves and is completed in ten circles: the six circles of the genesis (II.1) and to the four circles of the life of Christ (II.6).

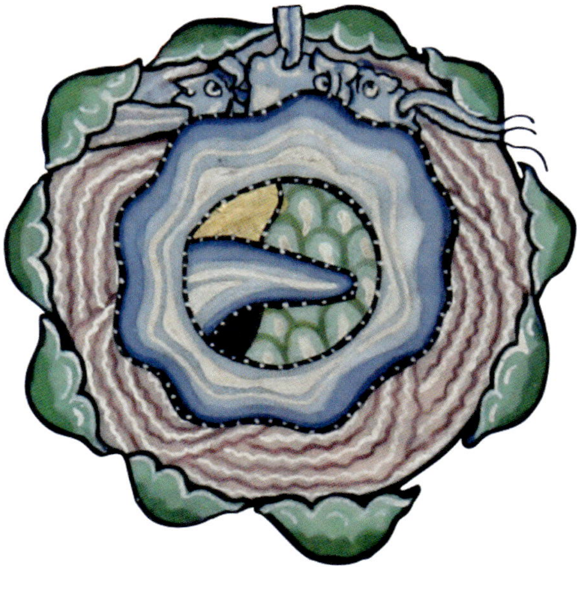

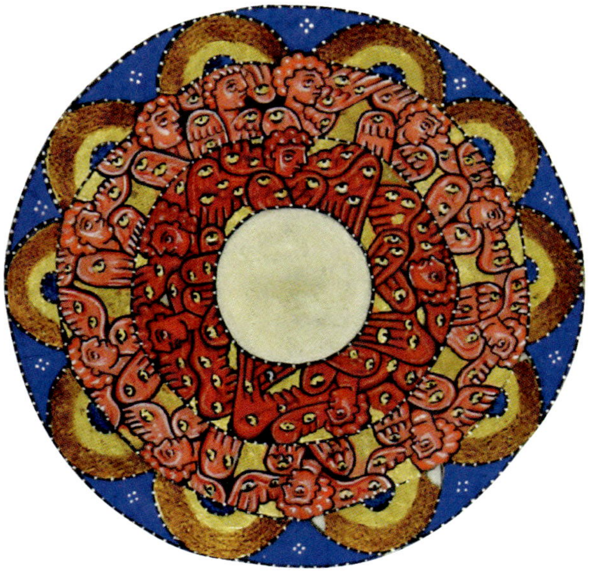

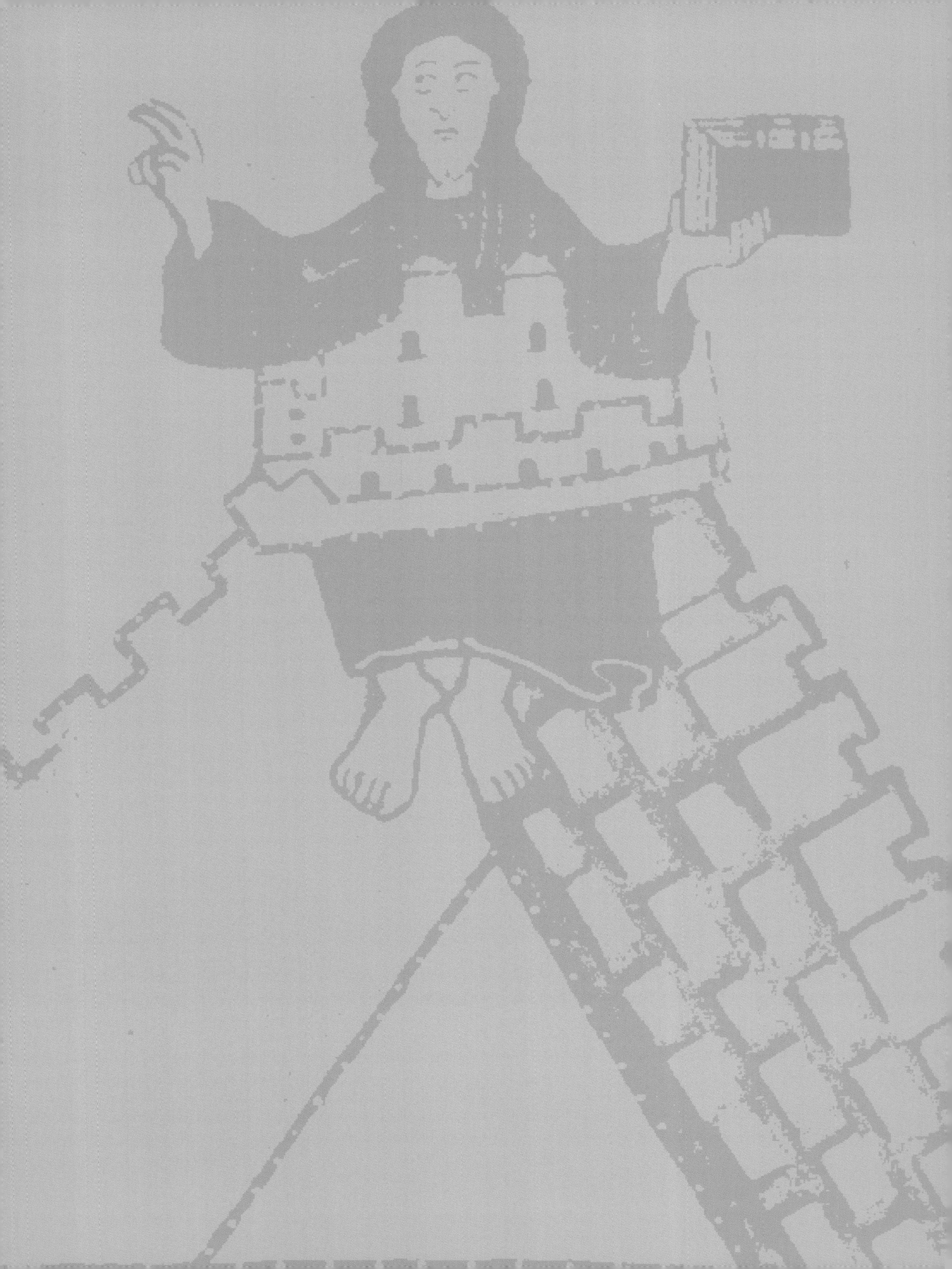

Geometry

And as a circle surrounds and contains all that lies inside of it, so holy divinity contains and exceeds all things infinitely, for no one can divide or overcome it in its power, or bring it to an end (*LDO* I.2.2, p. 55).

The number expands in space and describes geometric forms. Number one, symbol of God visible in the point of light, is extended and generates all forms of creation, represented by circles, ellipses, triangles, squares, pentagons, and the curved lines of spirals. The shifting of figures onto a different spatial plane, enlivens the three-dimensional forms of the polyhedra, culminating in the vision of the *whole, round, and whirling* sphere. Each form has a symbolic meaning, as did the numbers. God, Three in One, becomes visible in the circle and the triangle on the plane.

The circle is the figure present most often in the work and shows, through its increasing size, the journey of life from the bread of the Eucharist to the praising of the angels; through its colors, the path of transformation from the red fire of the action of God to the white light; through the joining of circles, the fertile form of the mandorla; through its diameters, the orbits of the stars and the sounds of the symphony; and lastly, through the fire of the concentric circles, the burning bush. The circle in the space describes, within it, the sphere and the double spiral of the winds and virtues; it animates the body of the world and kindles the body of man with the soul, a *sphere of fire*. On the other hand, the triangle, through the perfection of Pythagorean *tetractys*, enhances the figure of the heavenly city with the perfume of the blessed and the praise of music in the form of the *lyre*. The union of two triangles will create the square of the Science of God, mirrored in the square of the Building and the altar, symbol of the earth.

The pentagon is the geometric form associated with the *mystical number* five, and represents the union of the divine dimension, symbolized by three, and the earthly dimension, symbolized by two. Its form determines the starry image of the human body inscribed in the wheel, and enhances the doors of Solomon's temple. The definitive shift of the point of light on the spatial planes indicated by colors, orientations, dotted lines, and projection, enables the ultimate and definitive leap from the wheel depicted on the manuscript page to the vital center of the sphere, in the heart of man and in the heart of God.

The Golden Ratio

God acted in the creation of the Church, before he was to build her. For he began, starting in the beginning— that is, in his Son, whom he would send into the world through the golden gate of the Virgin (*LDO* II.1.18, p. 290).
The golden number's not yet full (*LDO* III.5.8, p. 429).

The Golden Ratio is the image of divine harmony inscribed by God in creation. Hildegard and her collaborators chose to use it in the images, as they had already done in the songs, to demonstrate the divine presence (Pozzi 1984).

The tabernacle of the soul, constructive model for the symbolic figures

The miniature of the *Protestificatio*, image of the tabernacle of Hildegard's soul, is based on a golden rectangle, which is used as a model for constructing all the figures in the work. For example, the figure of Hildegard is the same height as that of the Fear of God and of the Shining One in the first vision, and the same height as the shorter side of the rectangle, which corresponds to the side of the inner square, signifying that living in the virtue of the Fear of God helps us to rediscover our original dimension as a creature made in the image and likeness of God.

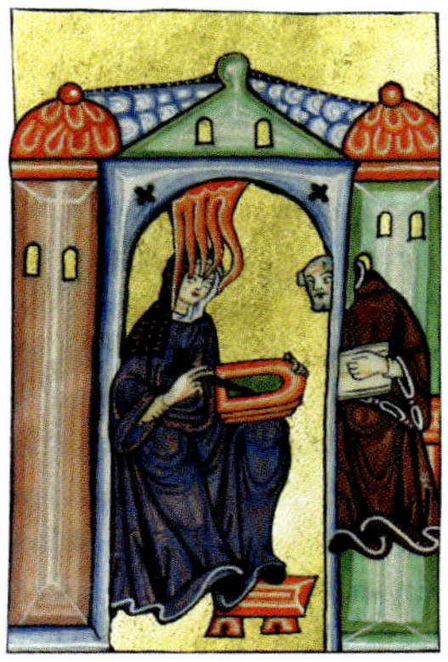
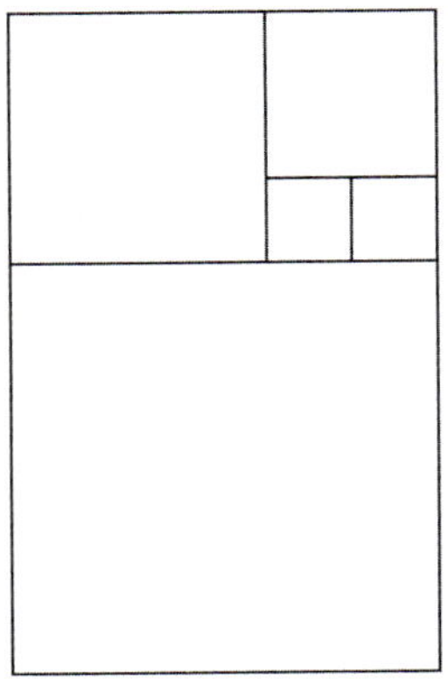
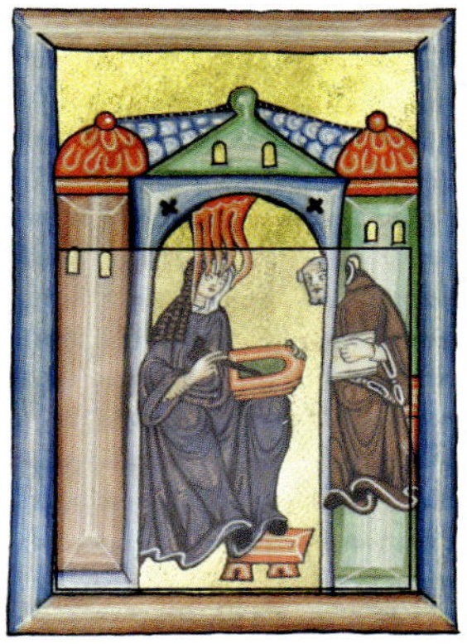
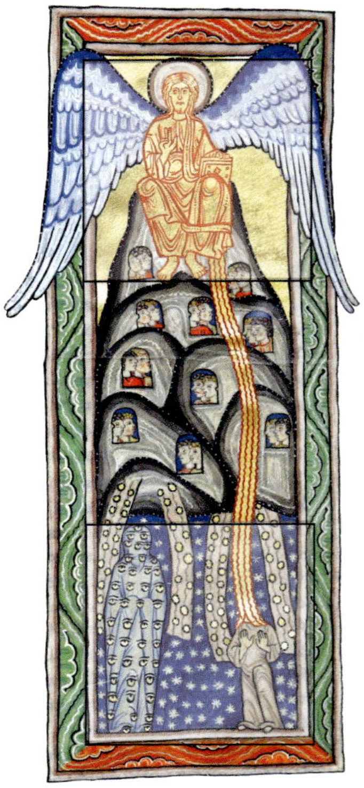

The work of God and banishment of evil

The number of chapters in the third and first parts of the work, respectively 320 and 122, corresponds to the measurements of a golden rectangle identified by the numerical series 320, 198, 122. The number of chapters in the second part, 264, exceeds the above measurement of 198 by sixty-six. The number 66 evokes the 666 of the beast of Revelation, which has nothing to do with the perfection of the divine plan of which the golden rectangle is an image, as was the case with the figure of the ancient serpent that was expelled from the sacred square (see p. 166).

The golden rectangle is determined by the proportion:
a:b=b:(a–b) = F
longer side (a) shorter side (b)
golden ratio (F)

Parts	Third	Second	First
Golden Ratio	a	b	a–b
Chapters and Golden Ratio	320	198	122
		264-198 = 66	

The map of the journey

The three images of the Ancient Serpent (II.7a), Column of the Savior (III.8), and the Symphony (III.13) are the only miniatures in the shape of a reversed "L." They are positioned, respectively, as follows: the first as the thirteenth vision from the beginning of the work; the second as the eighth image in the next section; and the third as the fifth image in the last section. Thus they mark on the map the turning points of the journey, which coincide with the corners of a golden rectangle whose sides measure, respectively, five, eight and thirteen units.

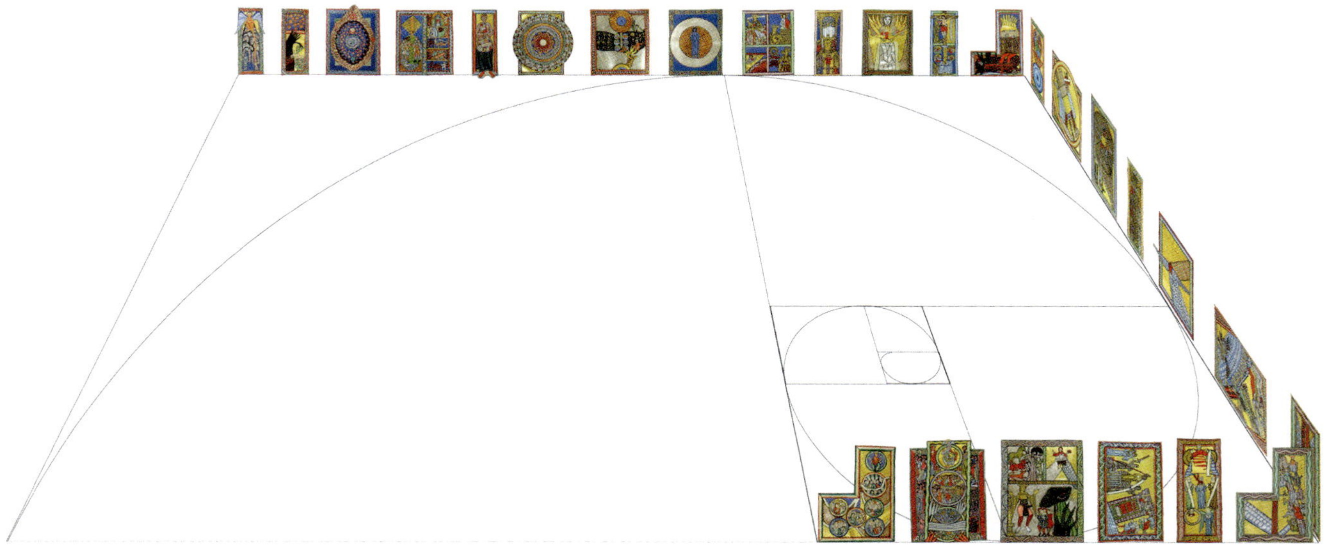

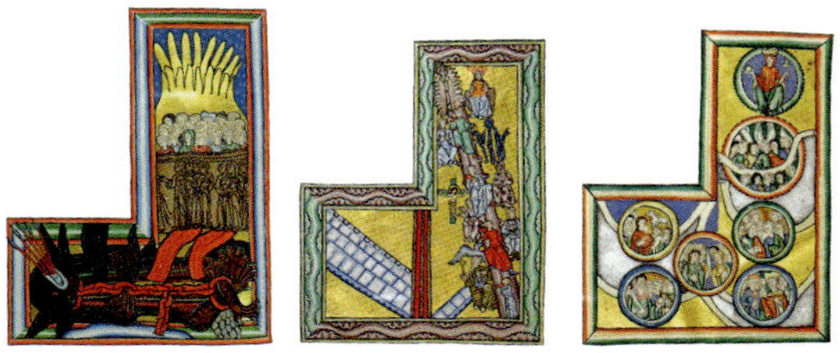

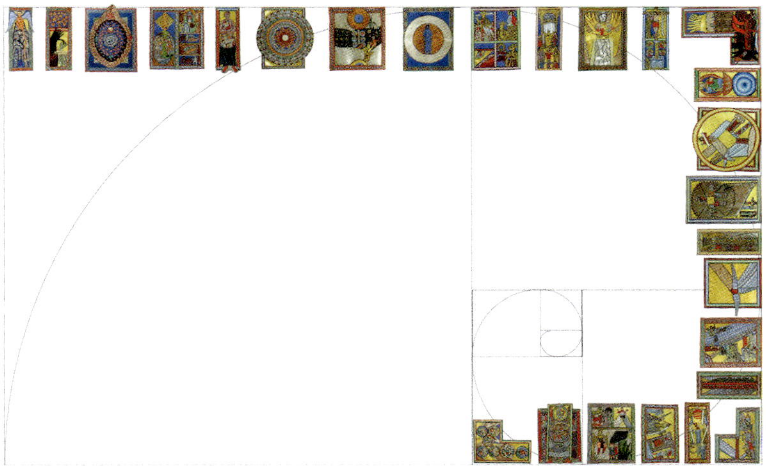

Circles

Thus God is round like a wheel as he creates all things, wills the good, and perfects the good (*LDO* I.4.105, p. 263).

The circle is the image of divine perfection, which surrounds and comprehends everything.

THE DIMENSION OF THE CIRCLES
From the bread of life to adoration

In the *Liber Divinorum Operum* Hildegard describes creation as a wheel that springs from the heart of God with a human figure in the center. The roundness of his face is a mirror image of creation that God infused with his rationality, giving man the possibility of knowing. In *Scivias* the journey of revelation has still only just begun and the circularity of the wheel is recognizable first in the shadow, then in the shape of the egg, and gradually in the circle.

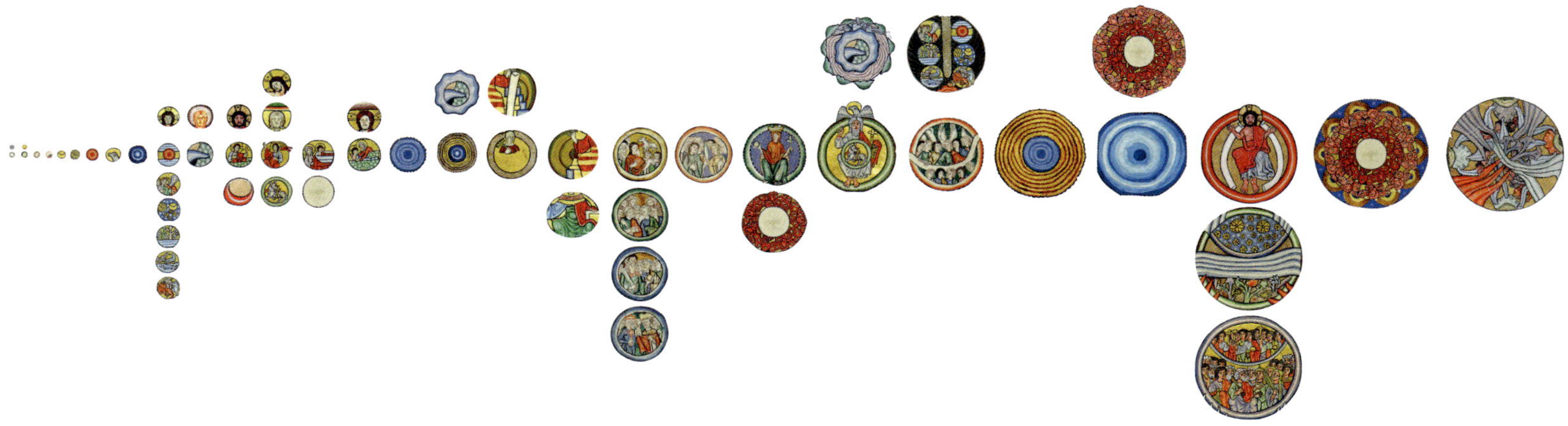

In the work, the form of the circle accompanies the journey in a steady and gradual crescendo, starting from the small circle of the Eucharistic bread on the altar to arrive at the large circle of the Heavenly Hosts that embrace the divine light. The aim is to remind humanity that receiving the bread of life rekindles the memory of the divine light infused in the body, with the soul, sphere of fire, being called on to shine again, amidst the stars, in the heavens.

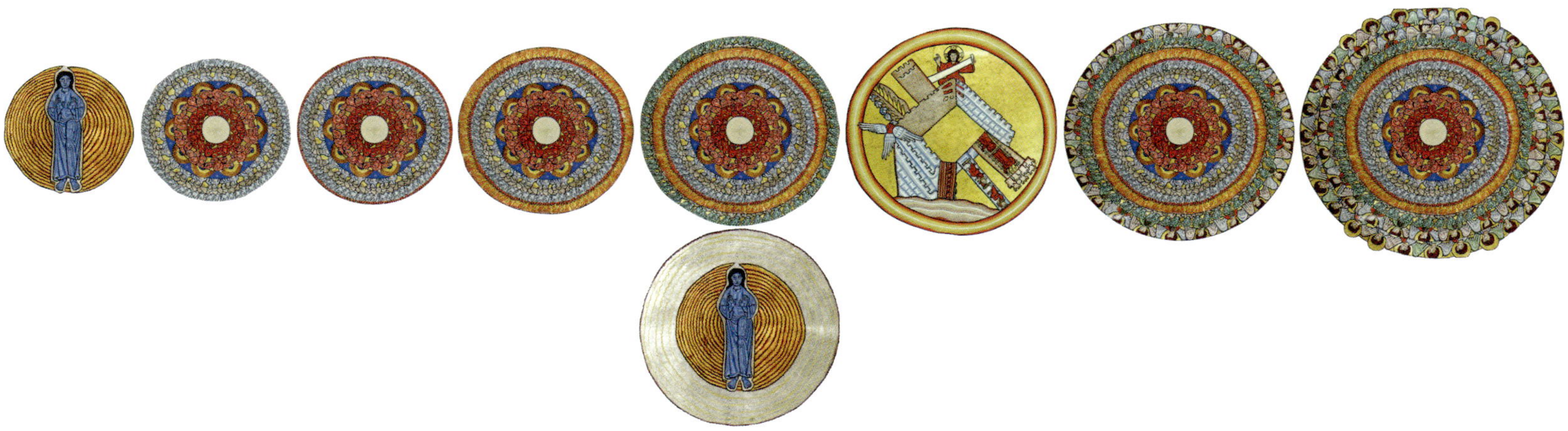

THE COLOR OF THE CIRCLES
From the white of the light of God to the silver, gold and sapphire blue of the Three Persons

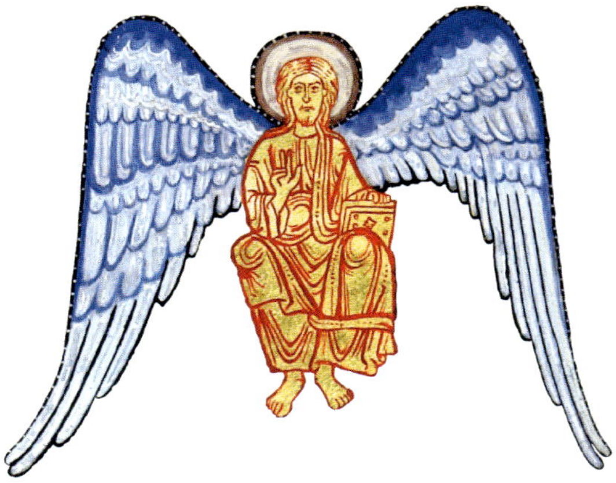

The circle of white light, adored by the angels, is the image of God. Within it, the Three Persons are shown in different colors: the Father in silvery white; the Spirit in reddish gold; and the Son in sapphire blue. This image appears at the beginning of the journey, when the white light of the aureole of the Luminous One seated on the mountain permeates the soft shadow of his wings, the color of air, and the reddish gold of his robe.

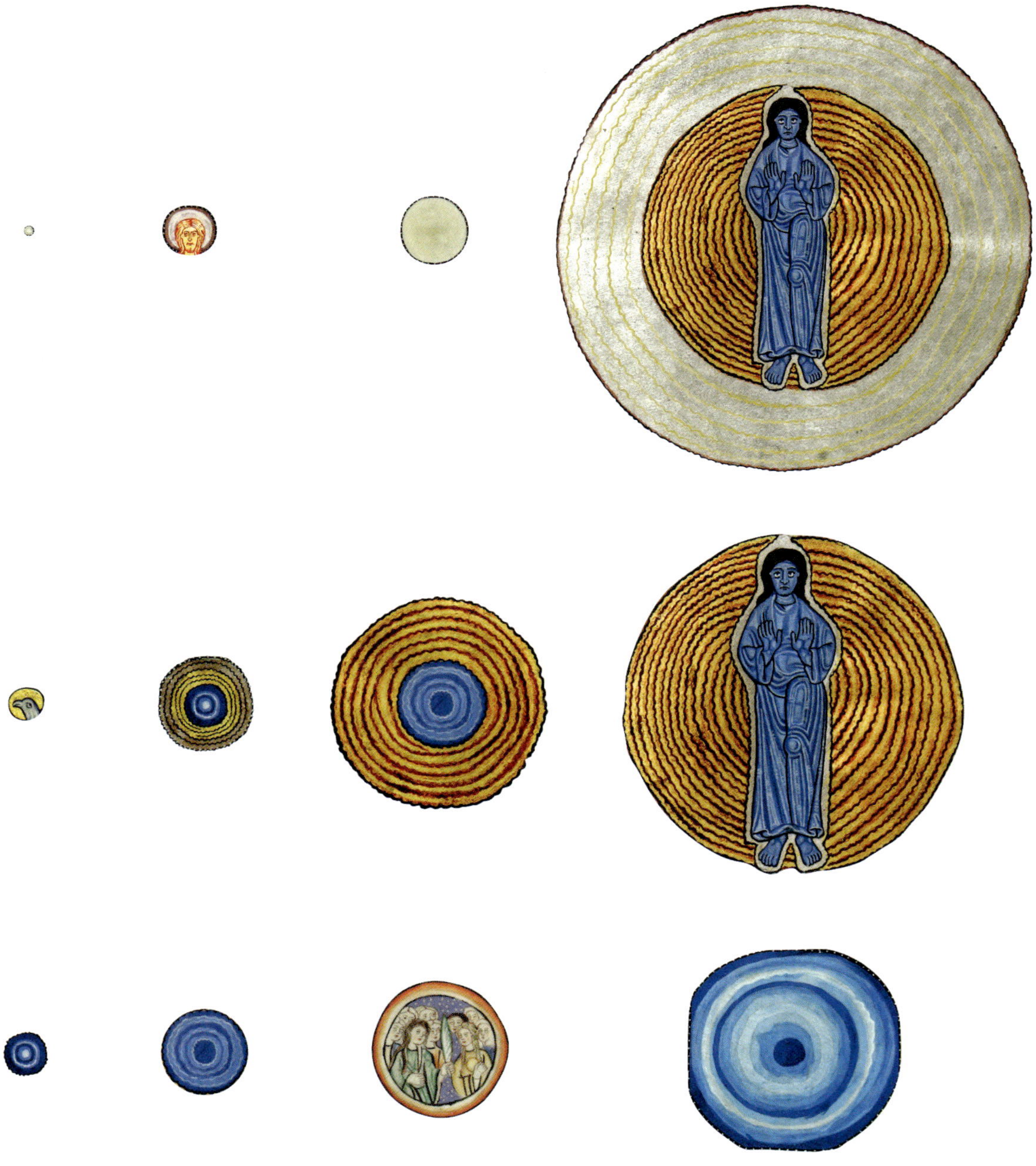

From the black of darkness to the white of light

The transformative journey passes through three stages marked by the red of God's fiery power, the fertile green of the *viriditas* of the garden of Paradise, and the white of the original light. Those who live in faith and entrust themselves to God survive the crucible of the furnace and the turmoil of the elements of the time of judgment and, leaving darkness behind them, are received in the heavenly city.

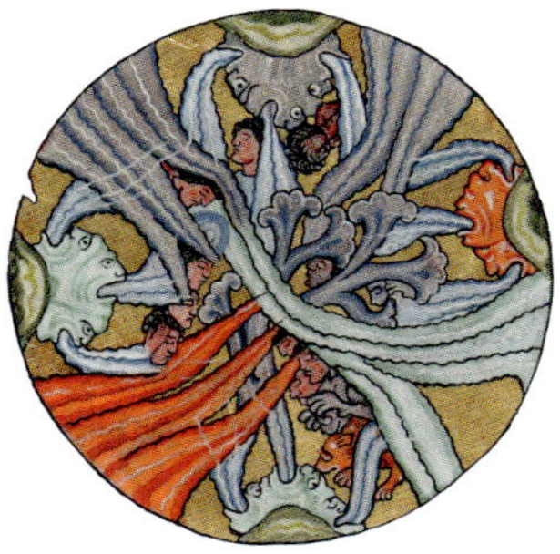

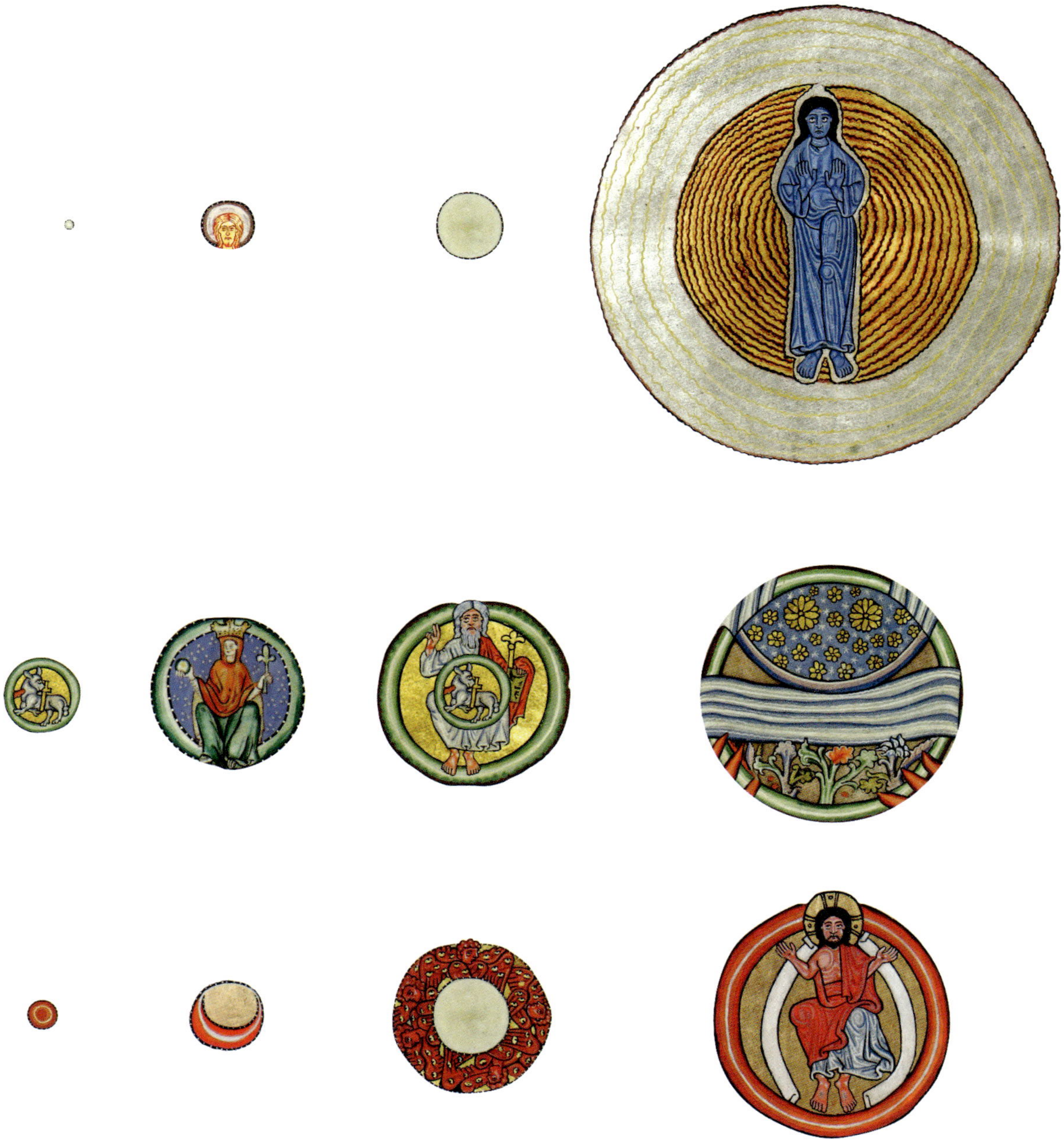

CONCENTRIC CIRCLES
The burning bush

And, as you see, when all these things are over the elements will shine out with the greatest brightness and beauty, and all the blackness and filth will be removed from them. And fire, *without its raging heat, will blaze like the dawn* (*SC* III.12.15–16, p. 520).

The seven superimposed circles in red and the reddish gold of the aurora create a concentric image reminiscent of the flames of the burning bush, revelation of the strength of divine love, which burns but is never consumed.

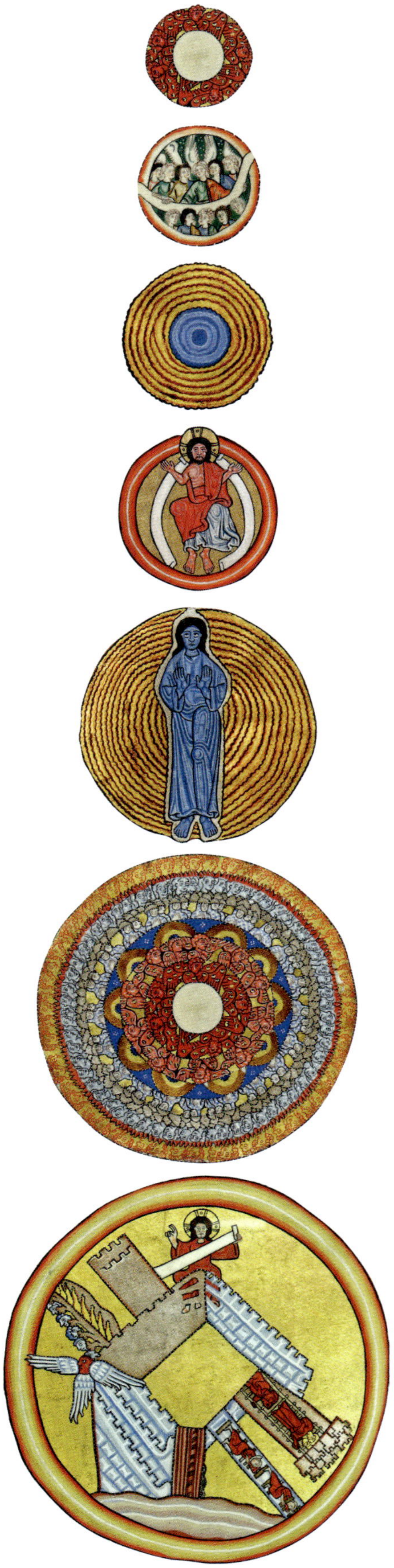

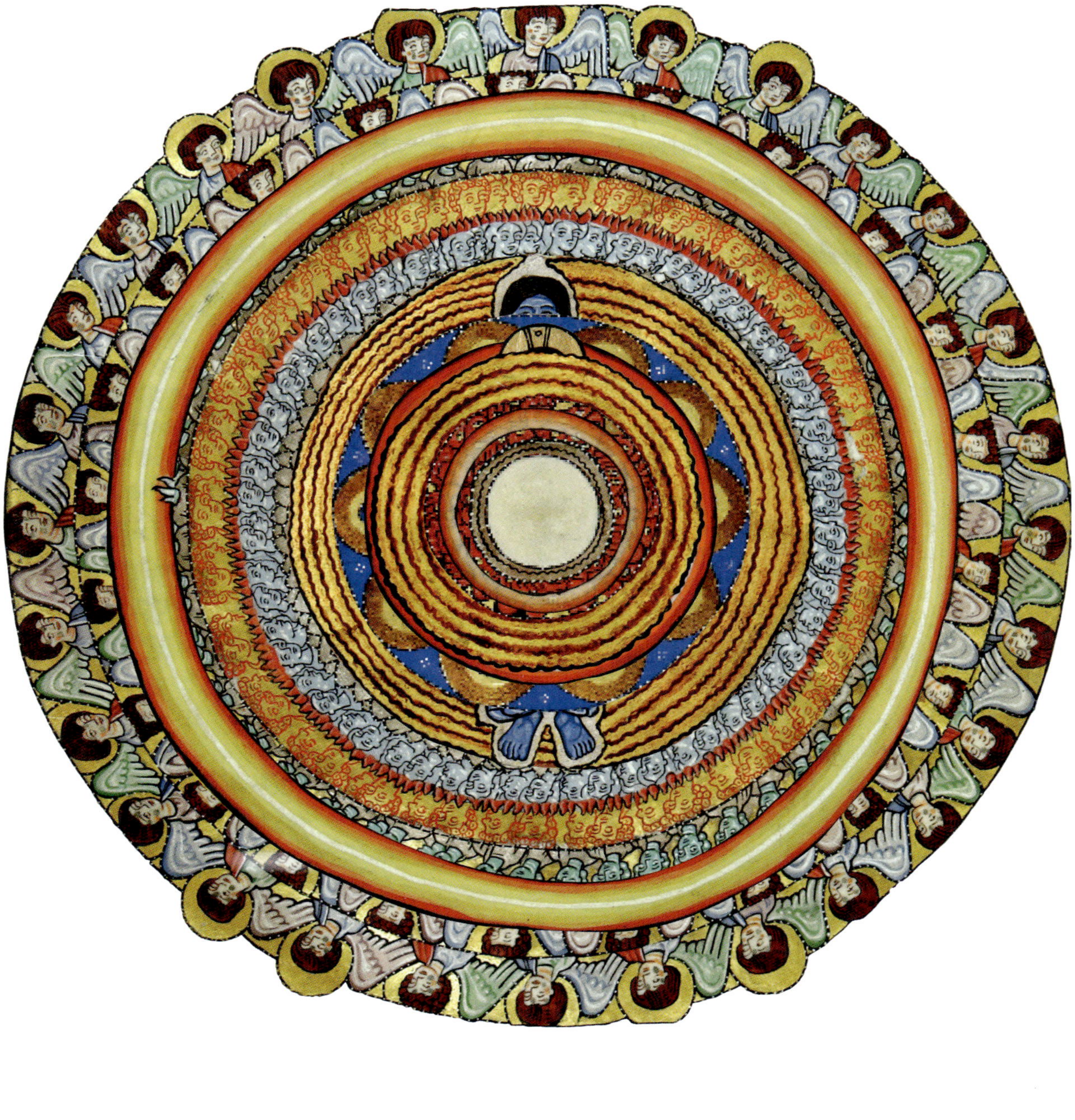

Mandorlas

The song of the angels and the revelation of creation

The mandorla, known as *vesica piscis*, is the symbol of life. The perfection of its design derives from its geometric construction based on the intersection of two circles the same size, with the center of one located on the circumference of the other. In the work there are six mandorlas, each created by the intersection of two circles the same size as one of the circles of the Heavenly Hosts. Thus, the mandorlas and Heavenly Hosts are symbolically linked. For example: the circle of the Thrones, witnesses of the birth of Christ from Mary Aurora, forms the mandorla that surrounds Christ Enthroned, image of Almighty God (see image opposite at top). The last mandorla, that of the egg, is created by the circle of the orbit of the Star of the Trinity (not visible in the figure).

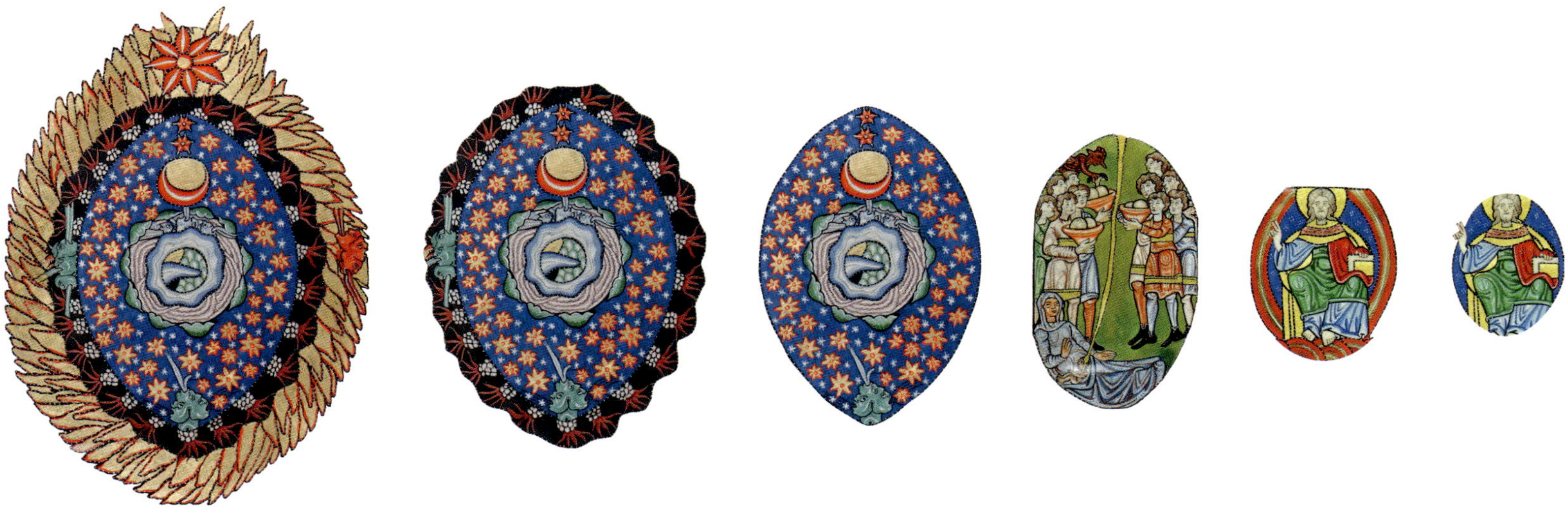

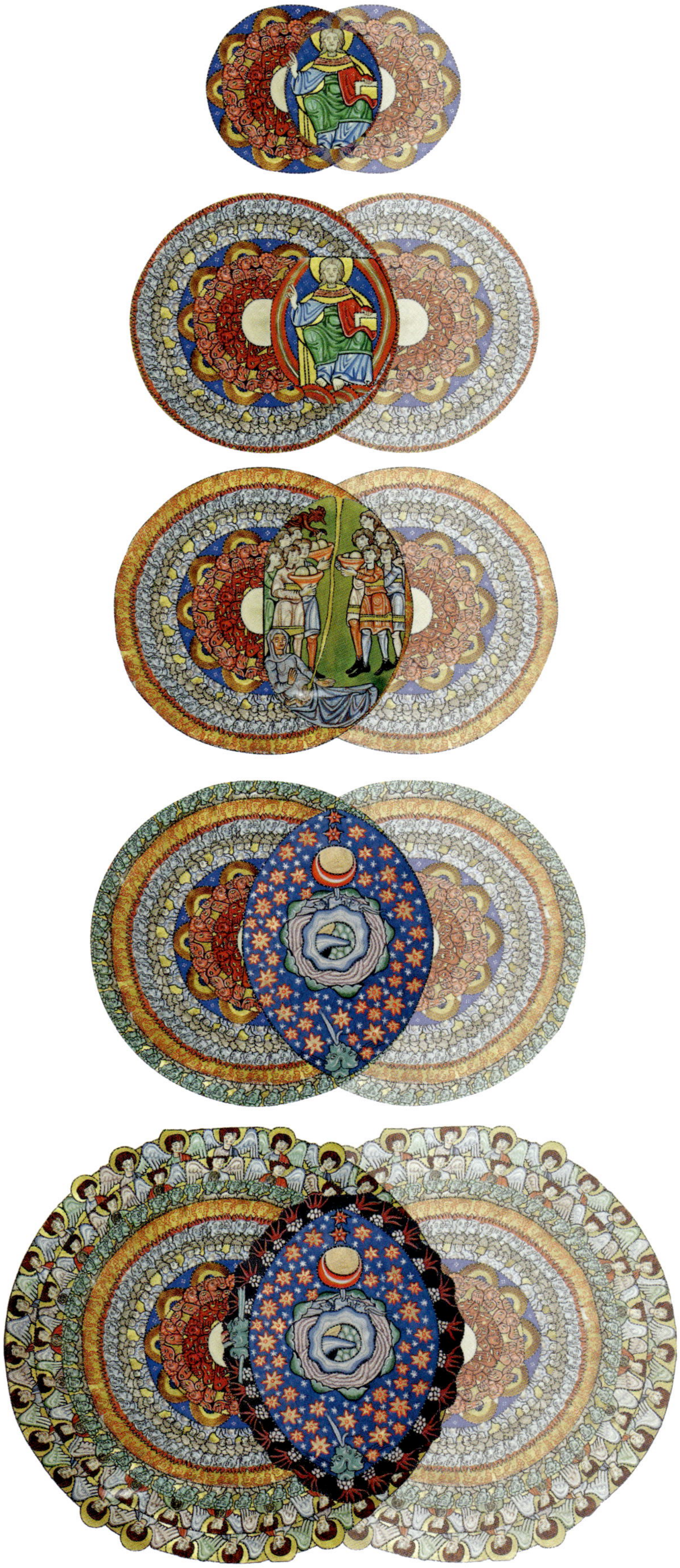

Spirals

The strength of the winds and the virtues

With the airy wind I quicken all things with some invisible life that sustains them all (*LDO*, I.1,2, p. 139).

And when out of the wicked he made the righteous, as when he made Paul from Saul, so that they might fly upon the wings of the winds, that is, upon the heavenly harmony (*LDO* I.1.11, p. 41).

And now that you are freed in My Only-Begotten from that oppression, go from strength to strength (*SC* II.6.27, p. 254).

The winds, represented by four faces and each with three heads, are placed in the four cosmological elements of the firmament. The imaginary line that connects them is reminiscent of a spiral, which expands outward from the center, moving in a clockwise direction from the watery air to the ether and the black fire, to arrive at the shining fire.

The virtues depicted inside the Building are located next to individual architectural elements (Salvadori 2019, pp. 202–203). As in the case of the winds, the imaginary line connecting them evokes the shape of a spiral, but one that moves from the outside to the center, counterclockwise, from the virtue of the love for heaven to the last of the thirty-five virtues, winged Concord.

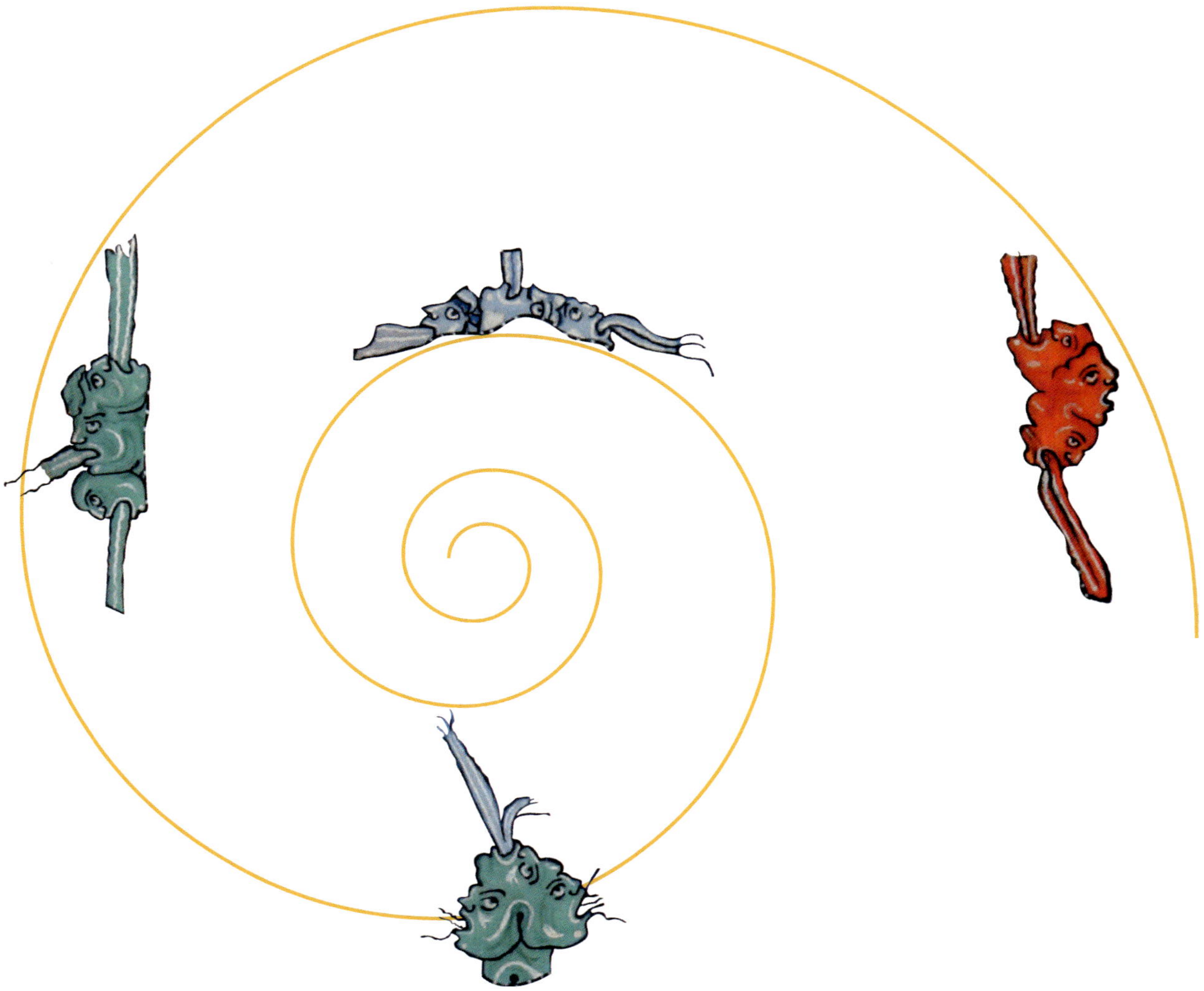

The two spirals move within the three-dimensional form of the sphere, creating a double spiral that leads from the center to the outside, and back to the center. They represent the energies that move the firmament, the winds, and the energies that likewise move the soul, the virtues. In the wheel of the *Liber Divinorum Operum*, in fact, the images of the winds coincide with those of the virtues, evidencing, once again, the specular relationship between the firmament and the human being.

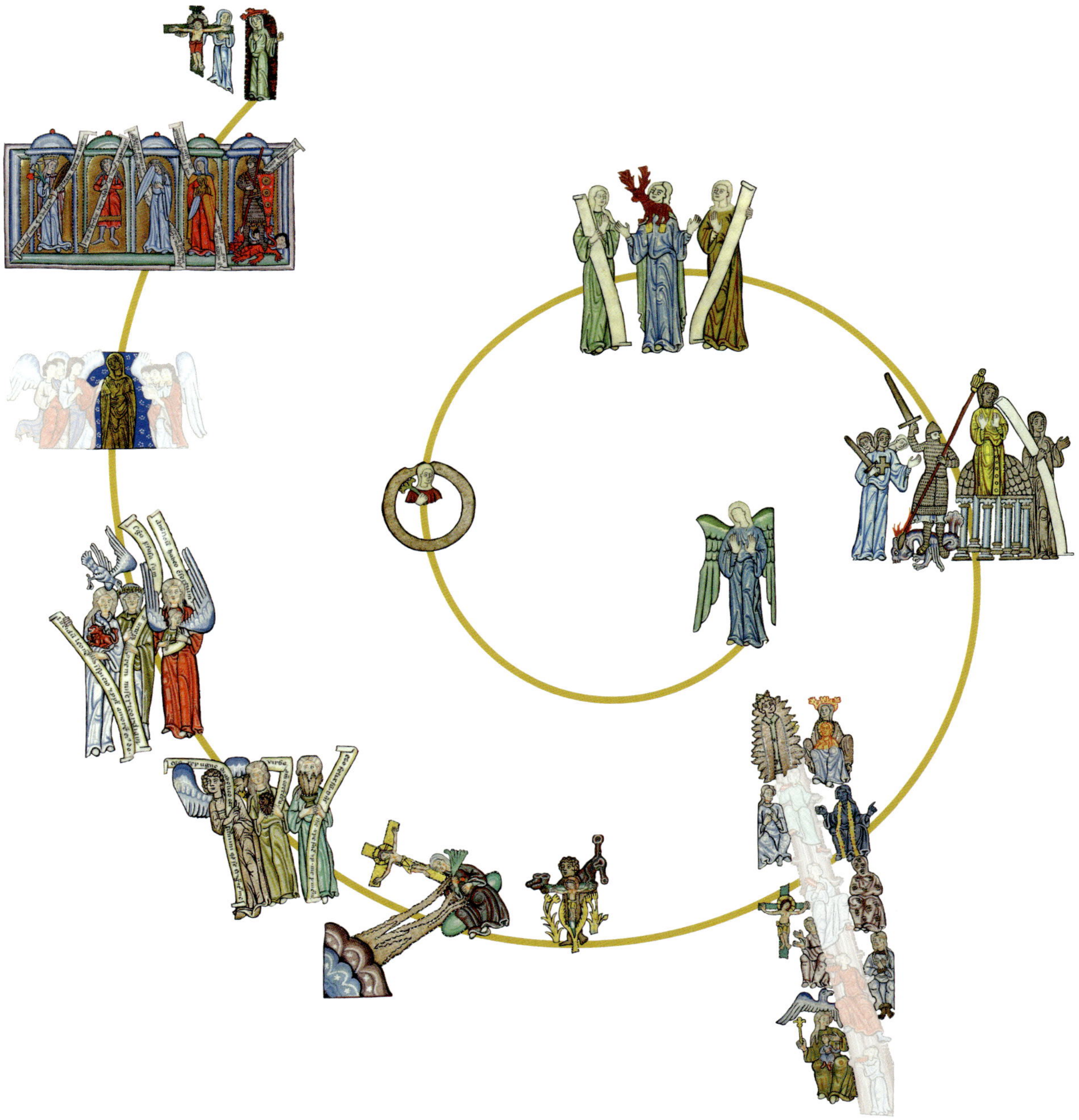

Triangles

So the first figure designates Humility […]. Thus she wears a gold crown on her head, with three higher prongs […] The crown is triangular, for the Trinity is in the Unity and the Unity in the Trinity; the Son with the Father and the Holy Spirit is One True God, excelling all things in the height of Divinity (*SC* III.8.18, p. 442).

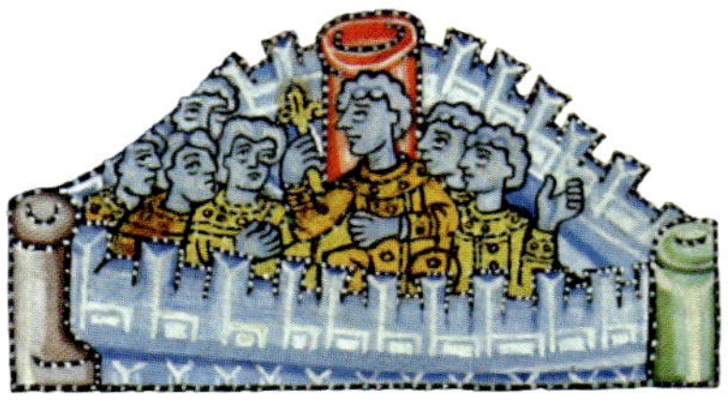

From the tabernacle of the soul to the heavenly Jerusalem.
Perfume and music

The triangle is an image of God. It is visible on the top of the column of the tabernacle of the soul where fragrant aromas, image of divine protection (I.4b) (see image below), are burned; in the heavenly city, through the three columns, image of Paradise (I.4c); in the lyre in the bosom of the Church, an image of harmony and praise of the saints (II.3); in the golden triangle framing Christ, who in the vision is fighting the flames of darkness, thus representing God's power (II.3); and at the moment of the revelation of the Son of God, image of fulfillment (III.11).

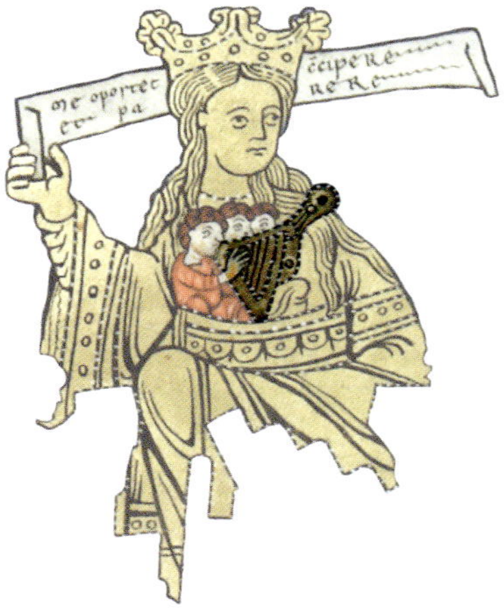

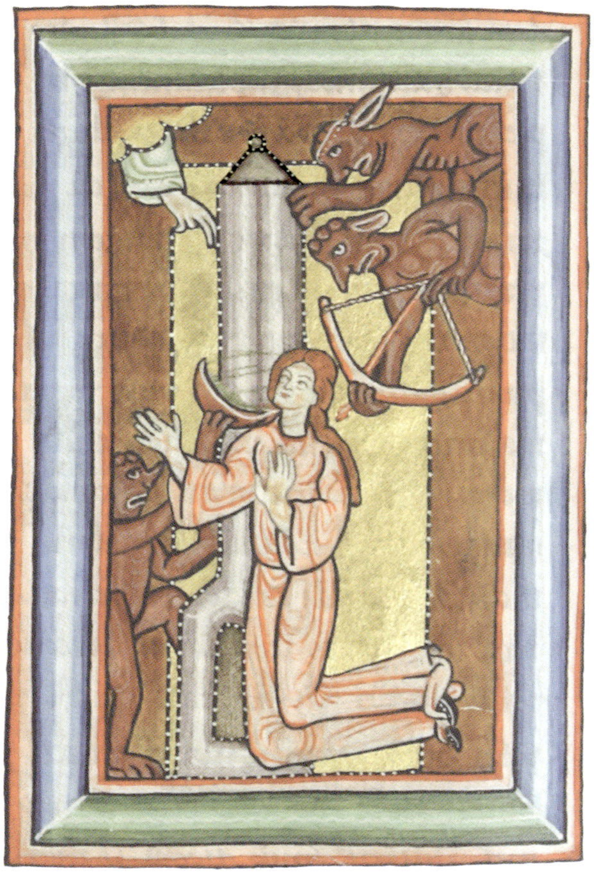

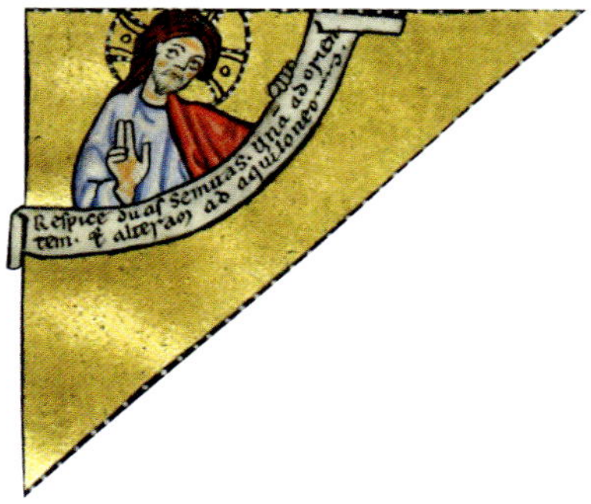

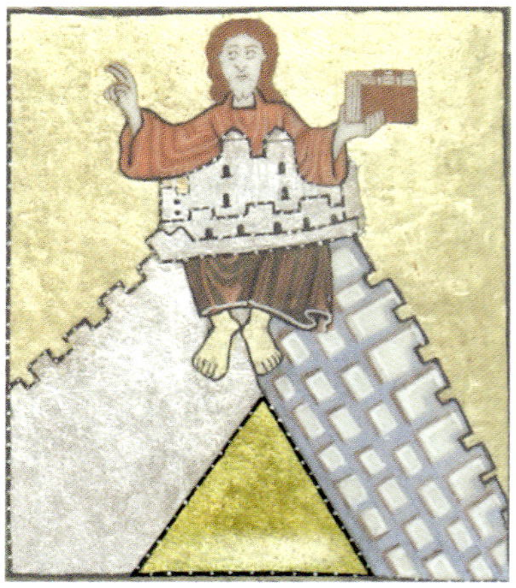

Tetractys

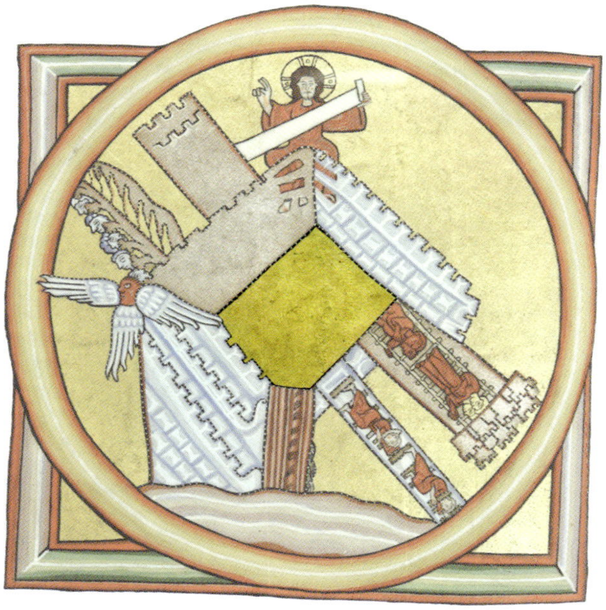

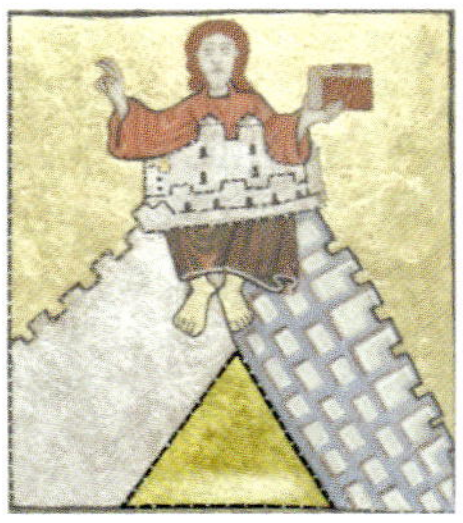

The Son of God appears seated in the eastern corner of the Building at two different moments in history: the first time at the end of the journey of edification, when he is only partially visible, while the golden quadrangle of the building can be seen below him (III.2); the second time, following the victory over the Antichrist, when he is fully visible and the quadrangle below him has been transformed into an equilateral triangle (III.11).

The perfection of the geometric figure of the equilateral triangle represents God and recalls the figure of the Pythagorean *tetractys*. In the *Liber Divinorum Operum* this triangle is concealed in the measurements of the face and neck of the human being, as an image of the virtue of discernment, which gives us the capacity to make choices (Salvadori 2021, pp. 93–94).

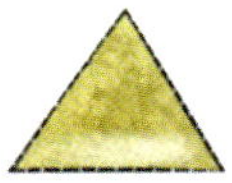

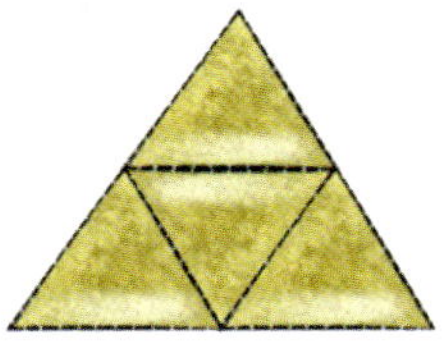

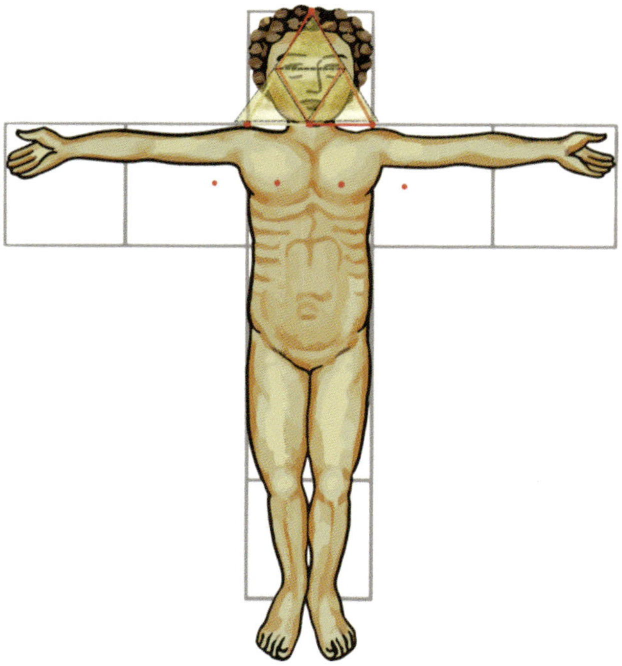

Squares

The tower is four cubits wide; for these virtues, by God's will, are brought about in people by placing them in the world of the four elements, from which, while they are in the body, they get physical nourishment (*SC* III.3.2, p. 345).

The eyes of the golden square of the Science of God turn their gaze in the four directions of the world from which they summon humanity (I.4a), so that it may enter the Building (III.2) through the gates in its four walls and complete the journey of salvation. A journey that unfolds around the square of the altar (II.3), prefigured by the Tower of the Law (III.3a).

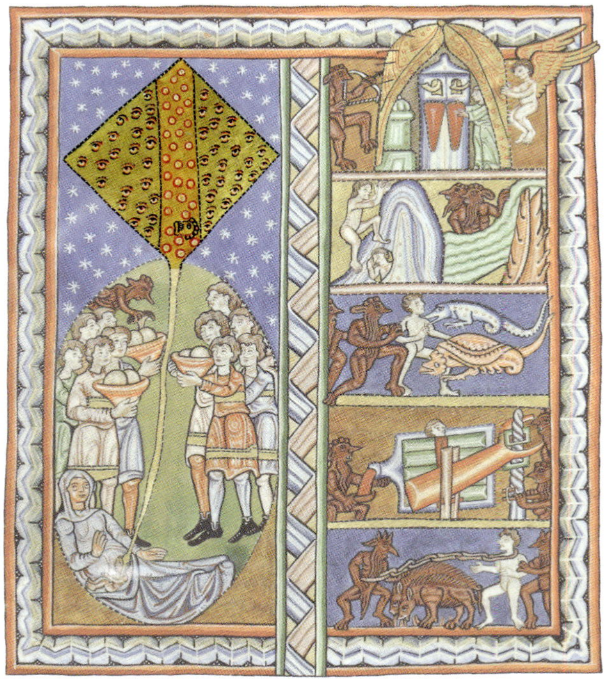

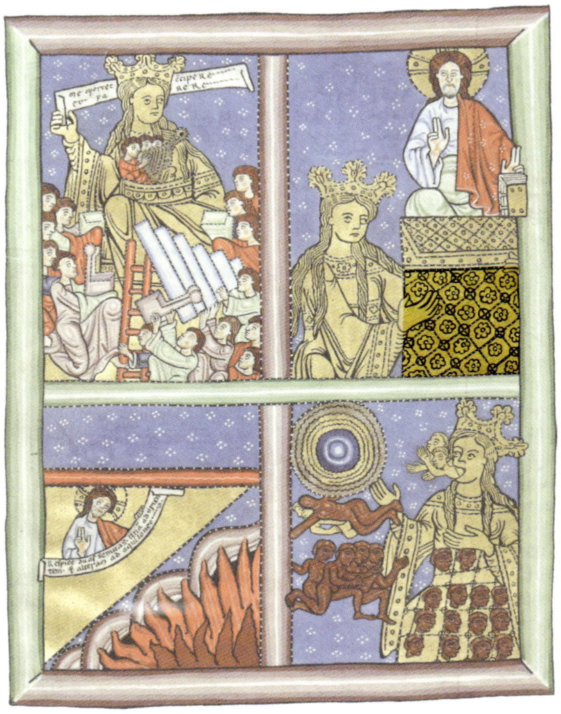

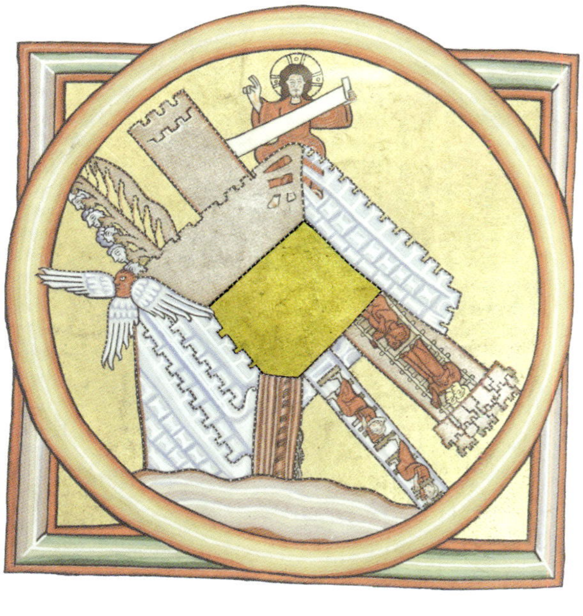

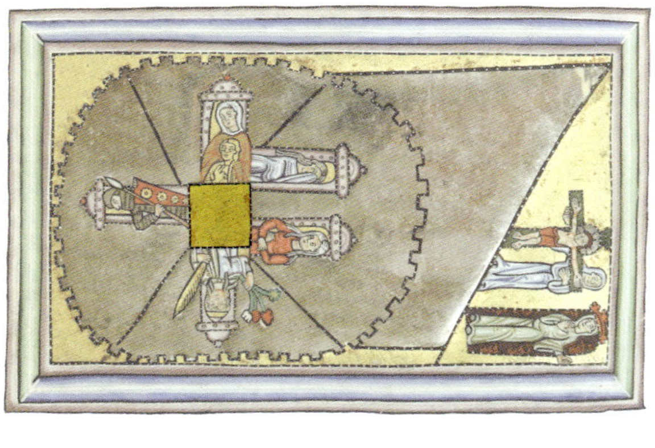

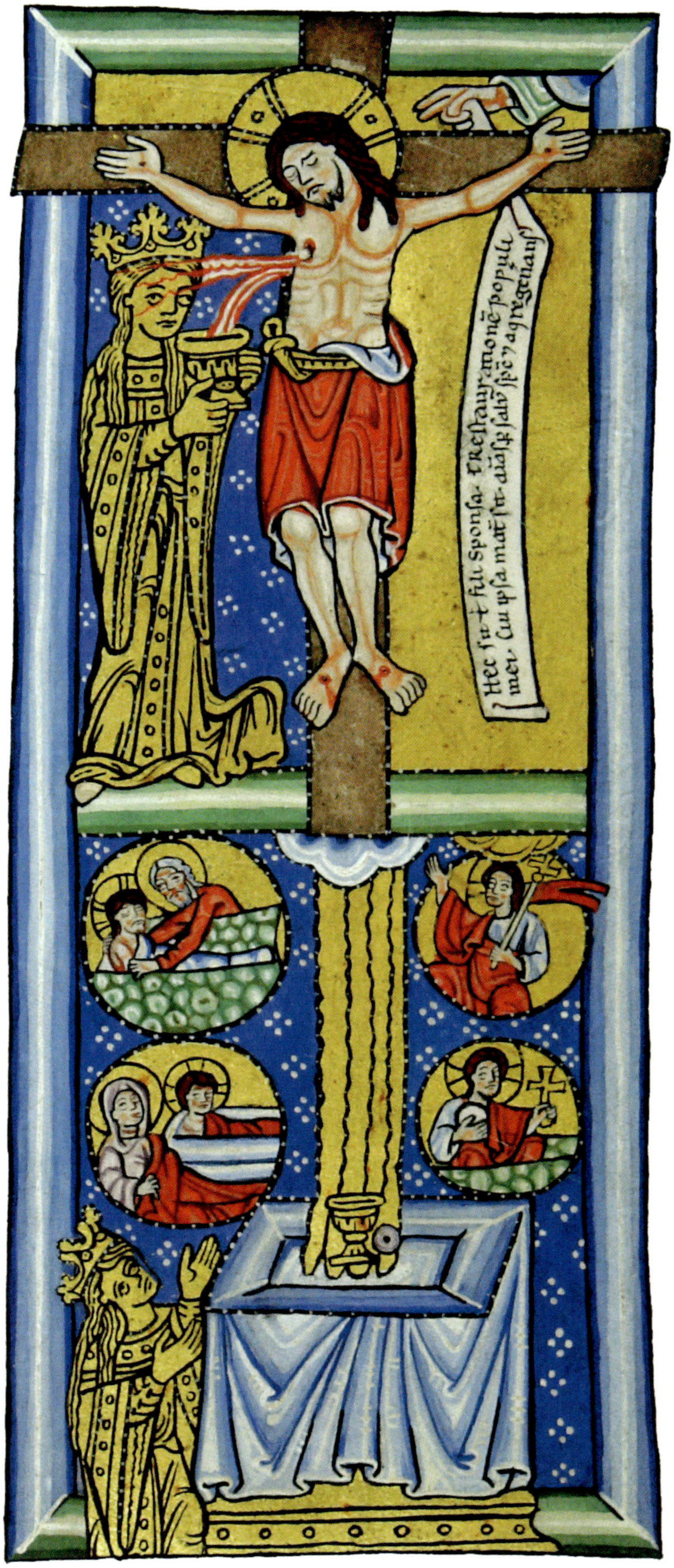

Pentagons

For I [Soul] should have had a tabernacle adorned with five square gems more brilliant than the sun and stars (*SC* I.4.1, p. 109).

And on the two wings that stretch down to the top of the aforementioned head there appear five mirrors. For in the Old and New Testaments, which look to the dignity of the ancient counsel, there are shown five luminaries of the various ages: first in Abel, second in Noah, third in Abraham, fourth in Moses, and fifth in the Son of God (*LDO* III.4.6, p. 402).

The walls of the Building form a pentagon, which evokes the doors of the Temple of Solomon (Salvadori 2019, p. 177). Five is a *mystical number* associated with fulfillment and revelation.

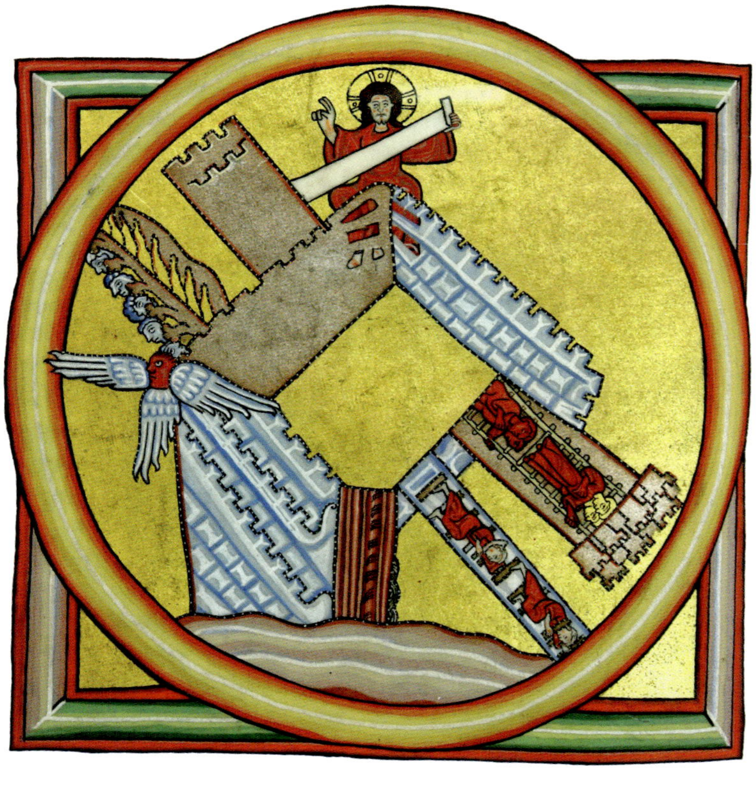

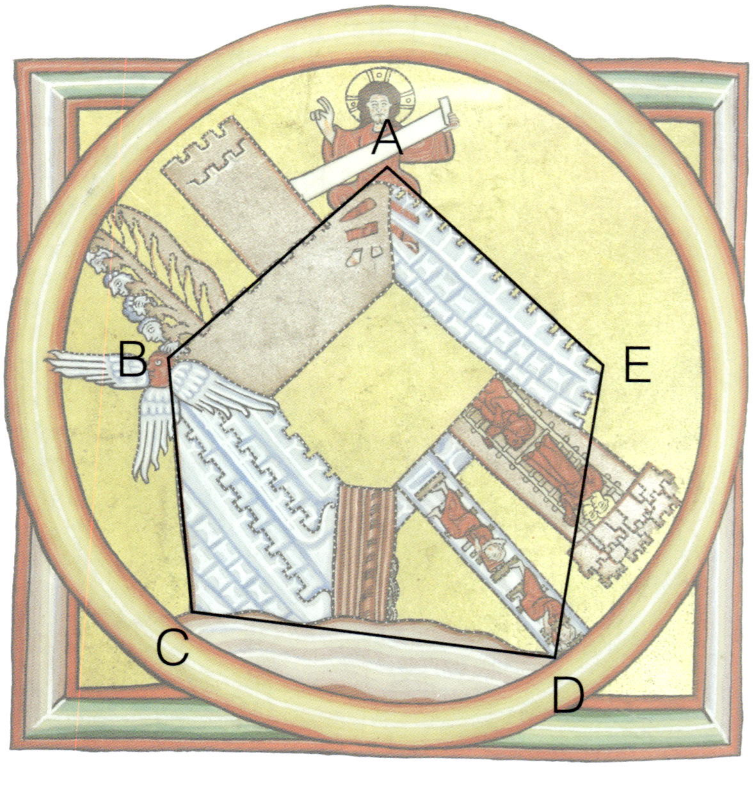

Toward the Third Dimension and Beyond

A vision occupies a multidimensional space. Hildegard renders it in words, when she indicates the size of spaces or directions of movement, and in images when she utilizes figurative elements like colored frames, orientation, dotted lines, and light projections that guide us in the reconstruction of the complete scene of the vision, transcending the two-dimensional space of the page.

The colors of the frames. The different perspectives

At the beginning of the journey, humanity finds itself at the foot of the mountain and God invites it to look upward (I.1). After the revelation of the cross, God is seen as he looks down on man from his throne (III.1a). The frames of the two images are tinted with the red of God and the green of the earth, revealing the different perspectives of the gaze: from earth to heaven in the first image; from heaven to earth, in the second.

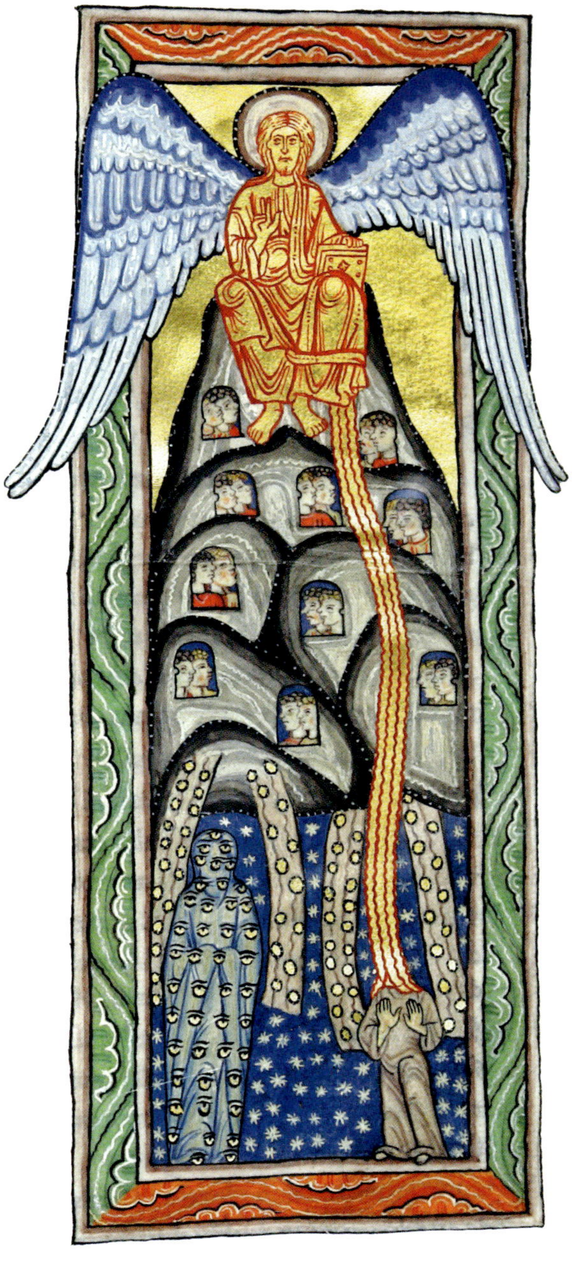

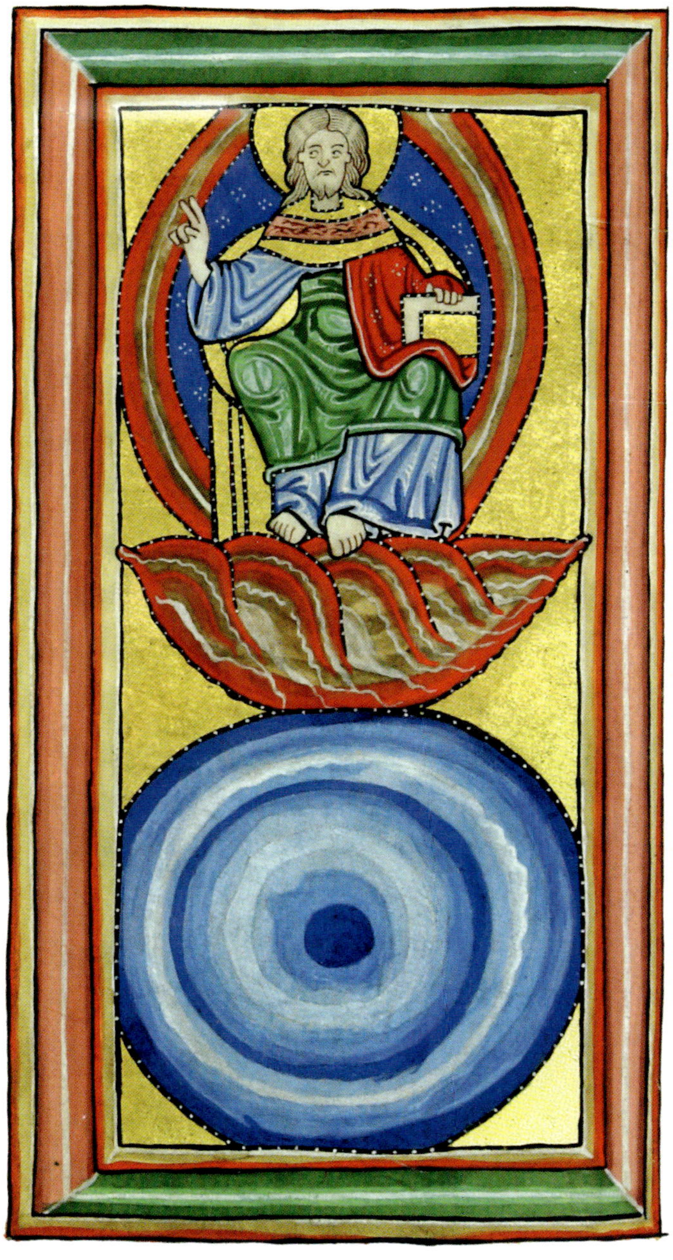

Orientation of the Figures

God manifests himself in creation in the form of an egg in which, in the upper part, the sun guides the way and, at the center of the earth, the mountain, seen horizontally, separates the light from darkness. If the image is rotated, the egg-shaped figure assumes the shape of an eye, God's eye watching over humanity's journey. The mountain, previously horizontal, is now in a vertical position, becoming a physical place where human beings find refuge and resume the journey back to their origins (see pp. 36–39).

The change in position reveals a new image and visually represents the inner transformation that enables us to interpret reality with a new vision and awareness.

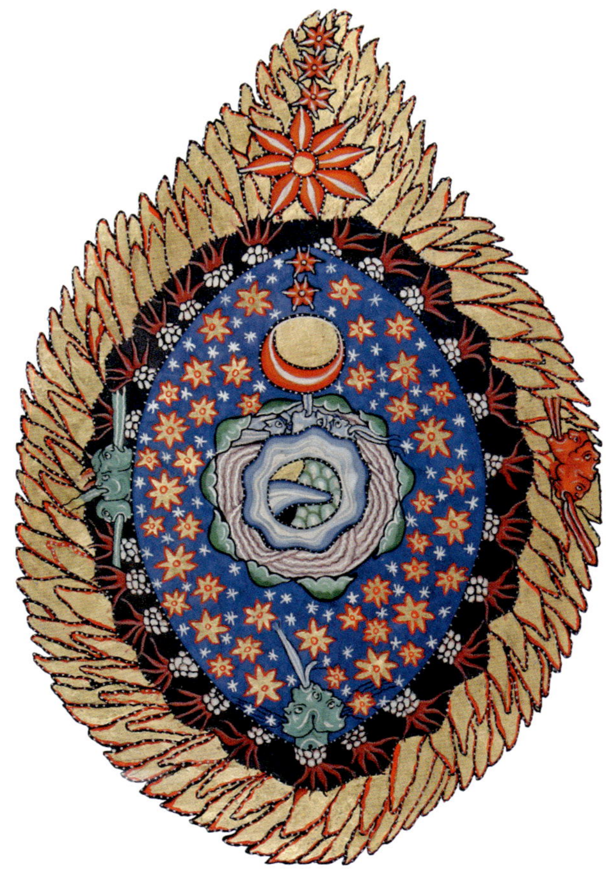

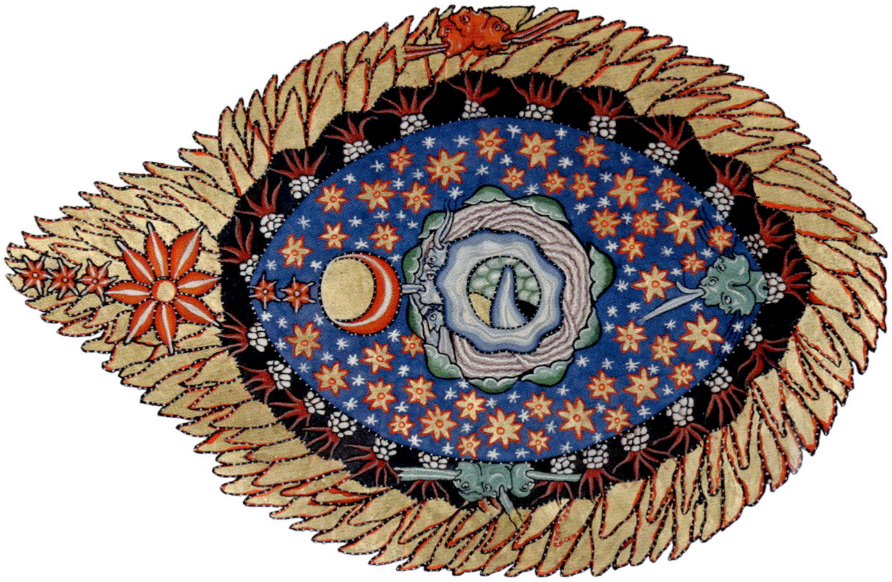

The Dotted Line and the Architecture of the Visions

The nimbus around the heads of saints sparkles like the divine light. Artists of the period represented this scintillating effect with a dotted line. Hildegard and her collaborators used the iconographic element to accentuate the lines of the design to be followed in cutting and folding the paper support, to create the three-dimensional images representing the scene of the vision. Hildegard followed the three-step process described by Vitruvius in *On Architecture*, starting with the design of the map to arrive at the elevation and the construction of the scene (Salvadori 2019, p. 175, and 2021, p. 114). The clearest example of this is the transition from the map of the Building (III.2) to the three-dimensional model.

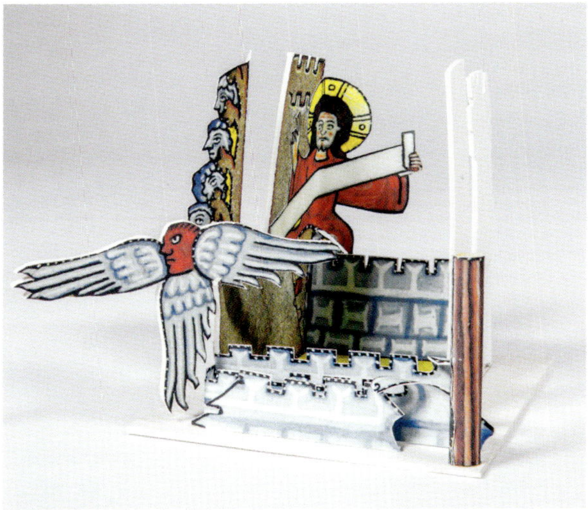

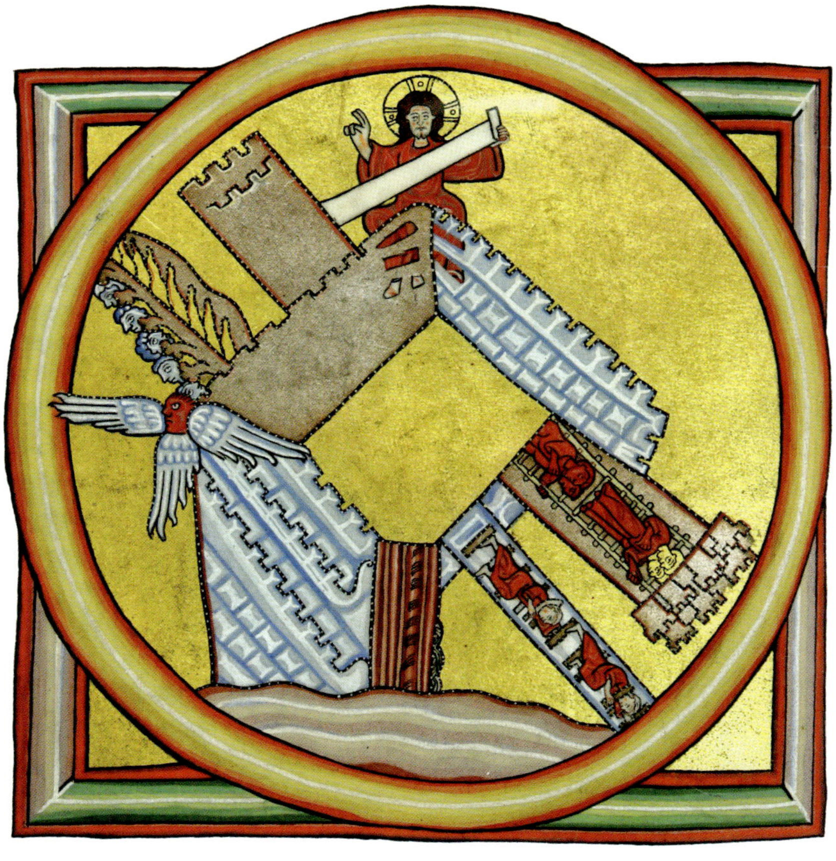

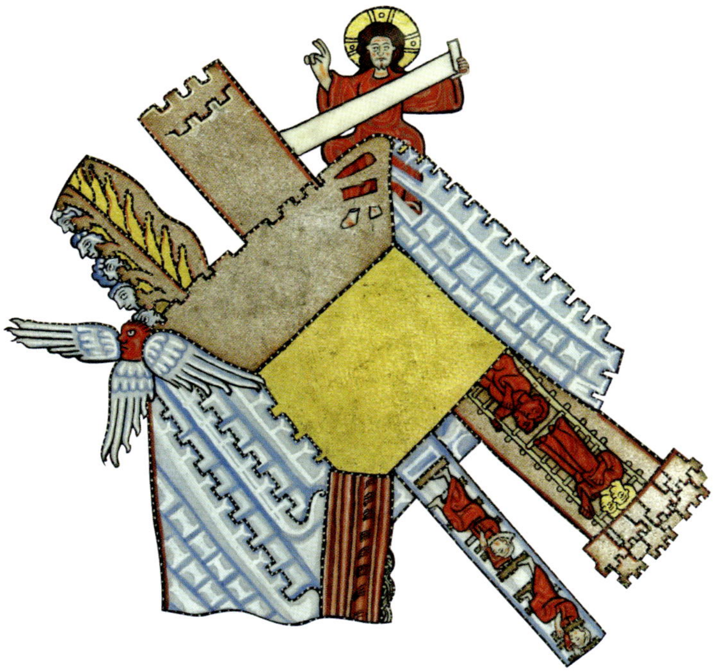

The Projection of Light

Light illuminates a form and projects its shadow onto the plane, creating different forms according to the angle. Thus, the divine light reveals to the human gaze images of the same reality that are visible according to different levels of knowledge.

The shadow of the wheel of creation describes the form of the egg/mandorla of the firmament.

The shadow of the mandorla of light emanated by the Shining One describes the circle colored reddish gold like the aurora, which surrounds the building (Salvadori 2019, p. 174).

From the wheel to the mandorla, from the mandorla to the circle of light: everything is an image of the sphere, an image of God.

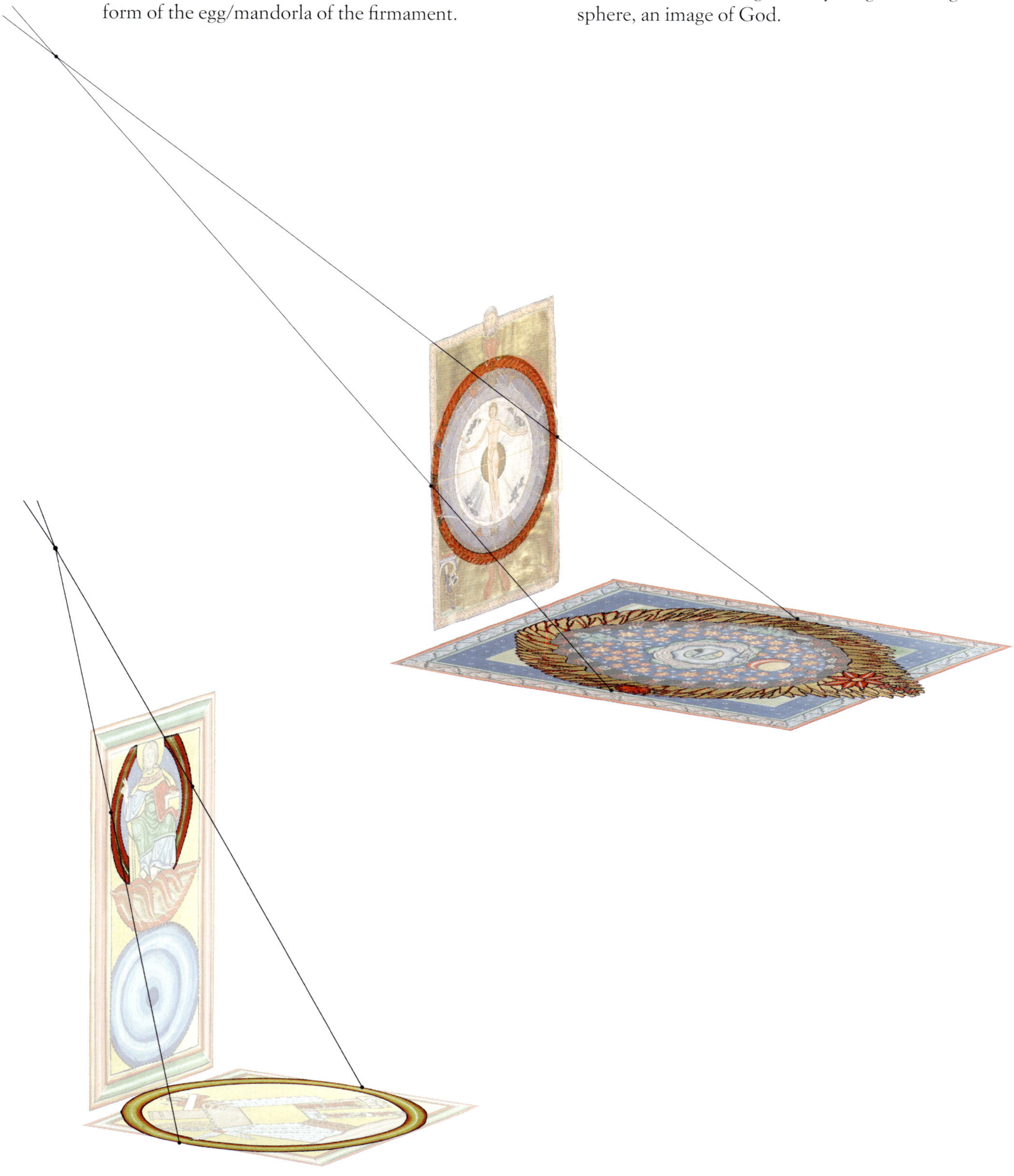

The Vision in the Space

The globe in constant movement is revealed in the egg of the firmament, inside which the three globes of the sun, moon and earth are in orbit. Three globes in one globe, hovering in the space, like a *honeycomb amid the honey*.

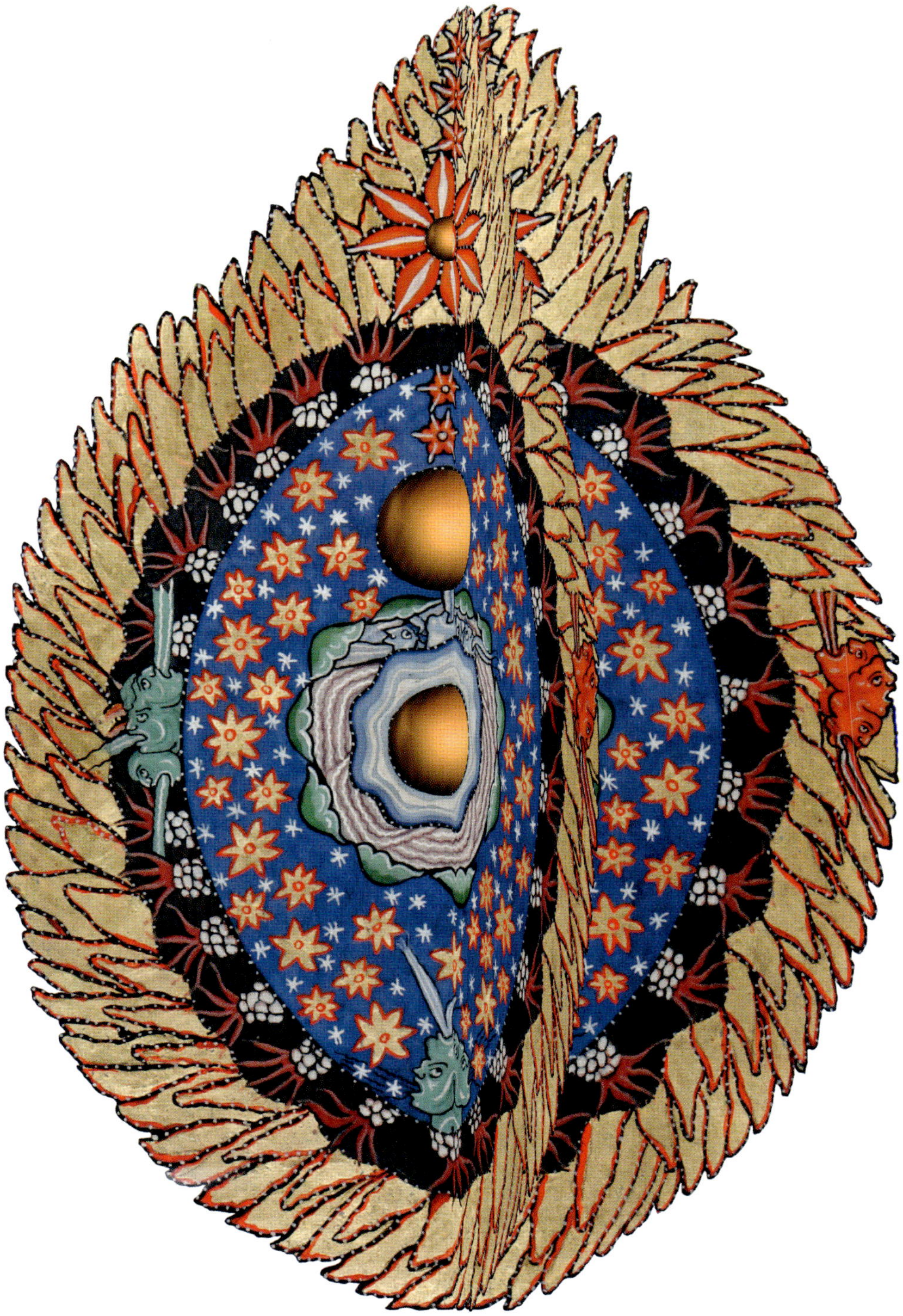

From Sphere to Circle

The sphere of divine light surrounds, and is surrounded by, the flight and song of angels.

Its light projects the luminescent image of the circles of Heavenly Hosts onto the manuscript page.

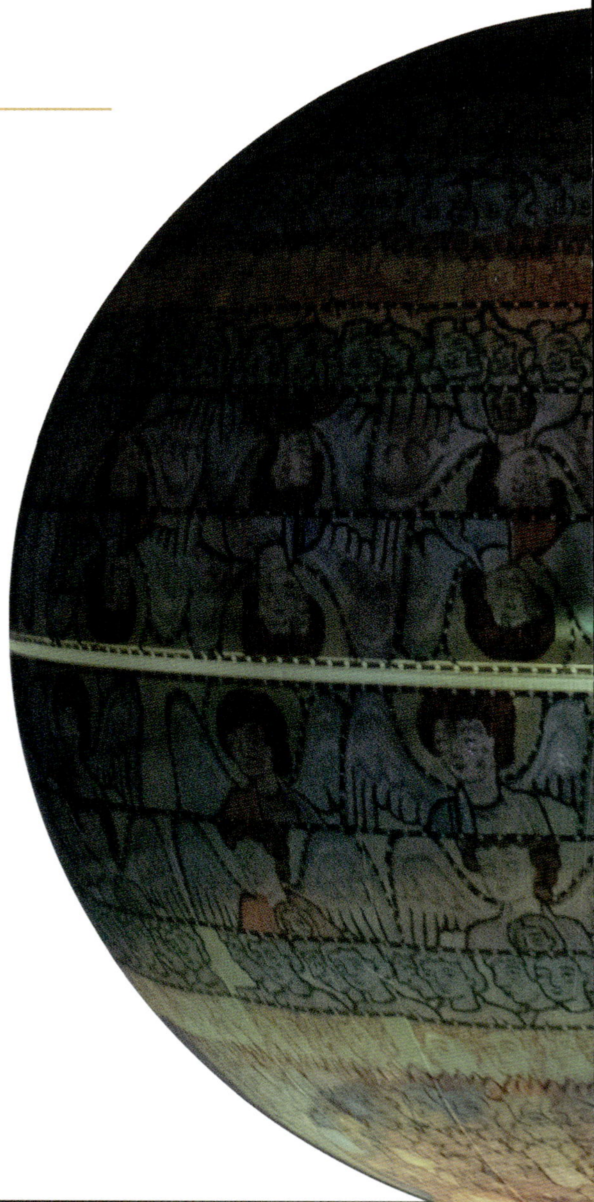

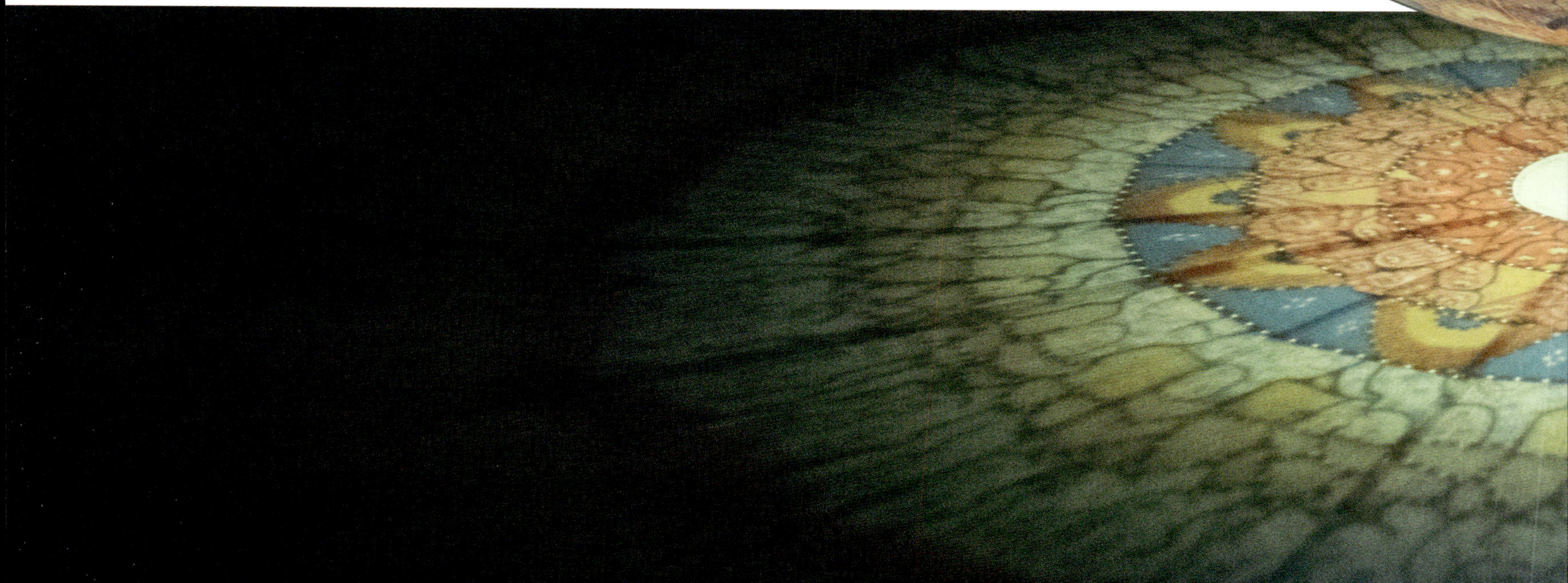

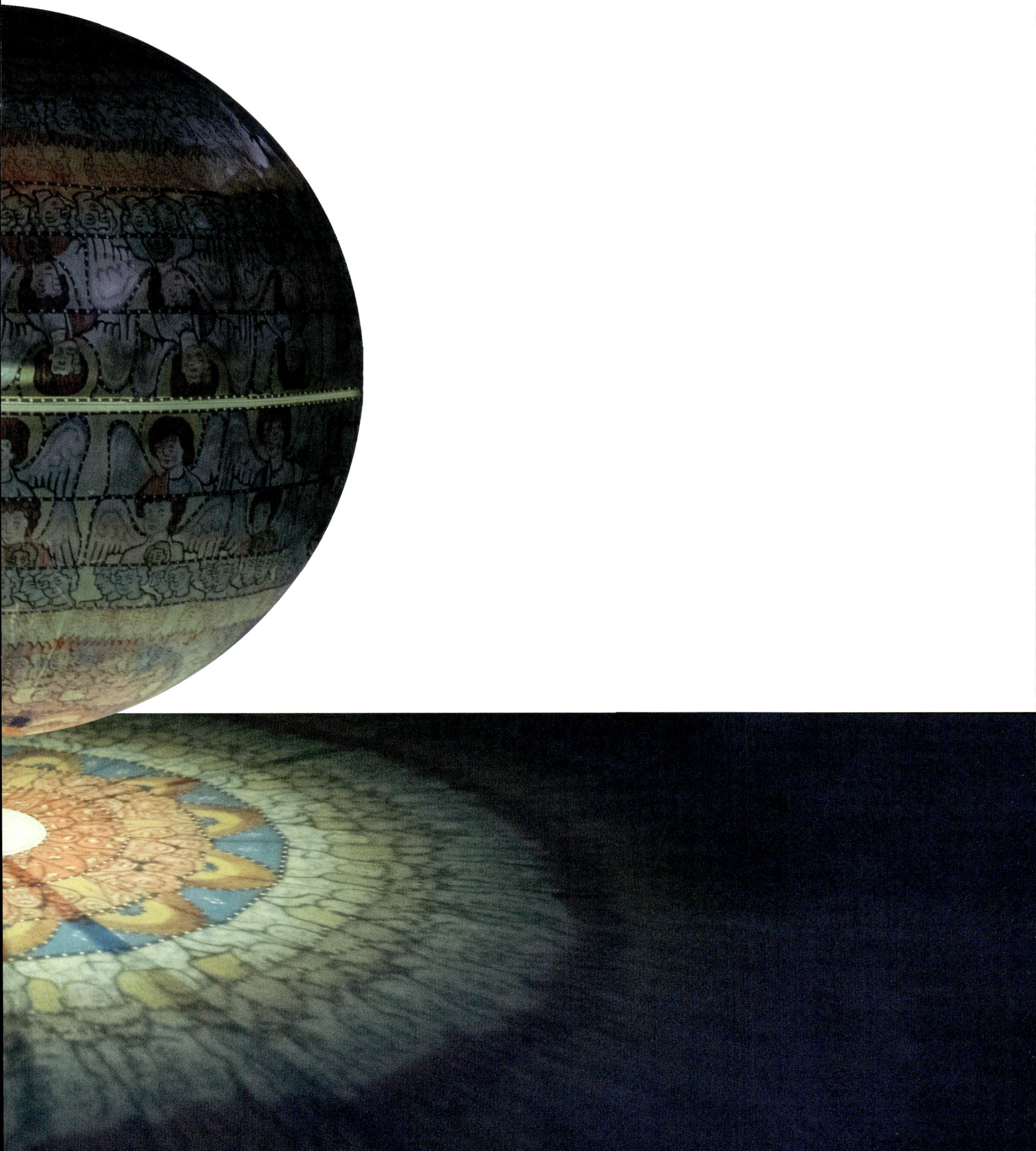

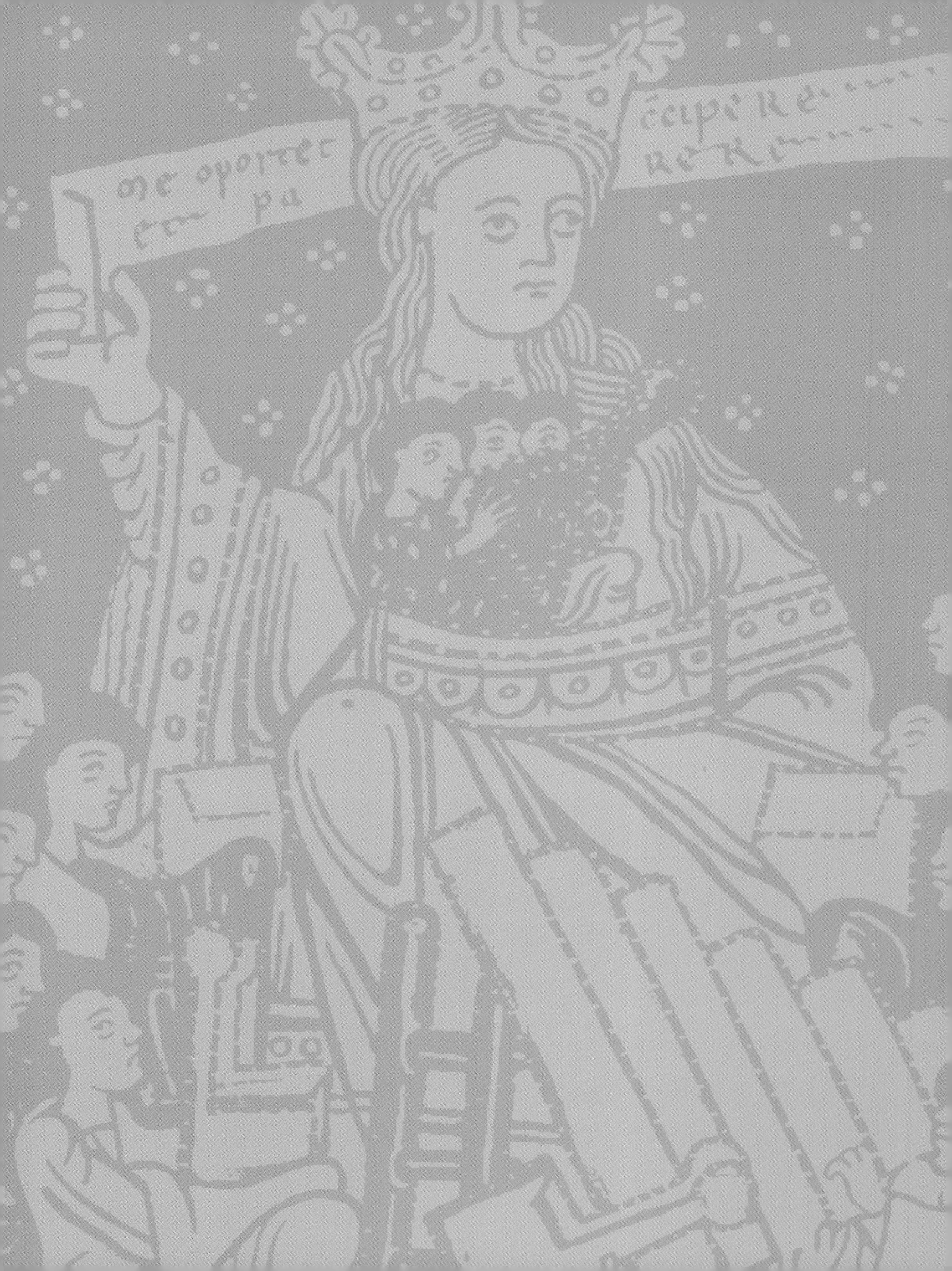
me oportet
et pa
ccipe Re
re R

Music

For the song of rejoicing softens hard hearts, and draws forth from them the tears of compunction, and invokes the Holy Spirit (*SC* III.13.14, p. 534).

In the *lucent air* of Paradise *the word representing the body gives way to music that reveals the spirit.* It is the time of the symphony, of music, and dance. It is the time of the joy of the blessed choir and of humanity that has dissolved all its burdens in tears. The words of the last psalm ring out: *Praise him [the Lord] with the sounding of the trumpet, praise him with the harp and lyre, praise him with timbrel and dancing, praise him with the strings and pipe, praise him with the clash of cymbals, praise him with resounding cymbals.* The trumpet is an image of rationality, the psaltery of angels, and the other instruments of *prophets, apostles, martyrs, doctors, and virgins*, gathered in the circles of the final vision of the symphony. Everything converges in the light and sound of the beginning, in *praise of the Trinity, sound and life*, which, expanding in waves of circles, gave life to creation, informing it with sound.

The soul recognizes its origin in the harmonic waves of the fiery cloud of human wisdom, receives the divine gift that *from the sound of the word* allows it to complete its works with music, voice, and song, and imitates the voices of the angels and virtues, until it achieves the chorality of concord.

Hildegard experienced this dimension profoundly through her visions, in which she saw the circular movement of the stars and Heavenly Hosts, and heard the *symphony of the harmony of celestial revelations*. She transcribed the sound experience with neumes in songs and with circles in images. The proportional relationships between the sizes of the circles produces a score with chords in perfect consonance. Sound is thus the divine seal inscribed in the constructive matrix of the work.

Through the contemplation of the heavens and the gift of wisdom, humanity is once again able to see itself as an instrument, *a trumpet played by someone else or a string of a lyre*, to discover anew its symphonic being, *symphonialis est anima*, and reverberate in harmony with the vital breath of the sound sphere of creation.

Waves of Sound and Life

For when the Word of God resounded, that Word appeared in all creation, and its sound was life in all creation (*LDO* I.4.105, p. 247).

The sound of the *logos* is propagated in the purest ether and gives life to creation through the expanding waves of concentric circles.

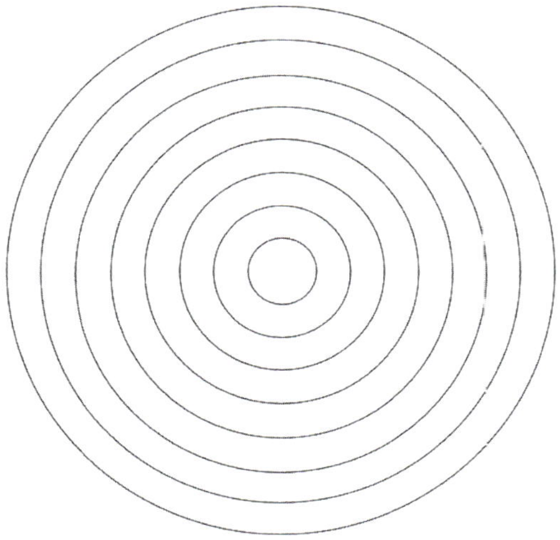

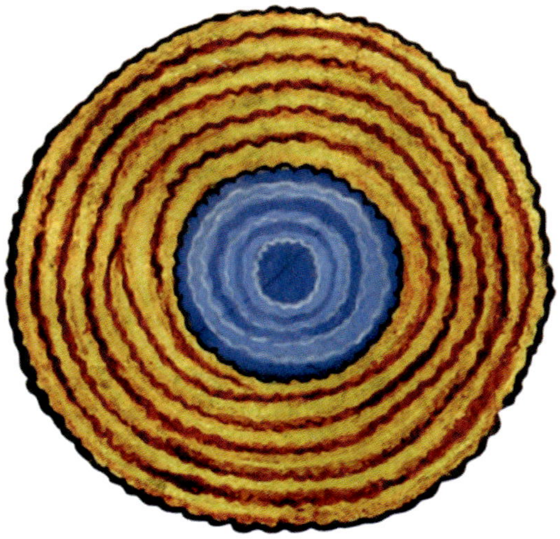

The Harmonious Cloud of Wisdom

And so the words symbolize the body, and the jubilant music indicates the spirit; and the celestial harmony declares the Divinity, and the words show the the Humanity of the Son of God (*SC* III.13.12, p. 533).

Humanity receives the *logos* and sees it mirrored in the soundwaves that float through and glow in the candid cloud of wisdom. They are generated by a point and spread through the space in the form of harmonious superimposed waves.

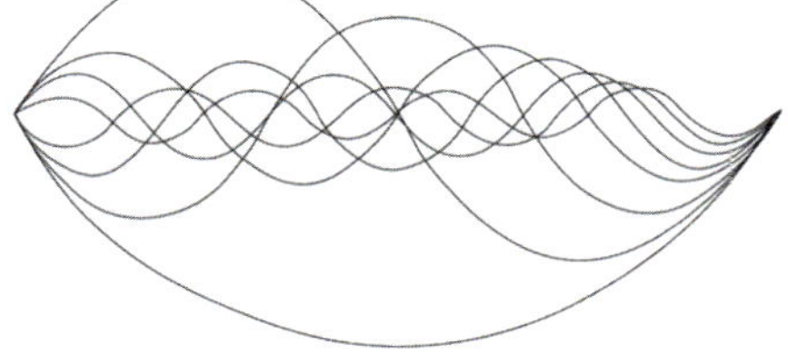

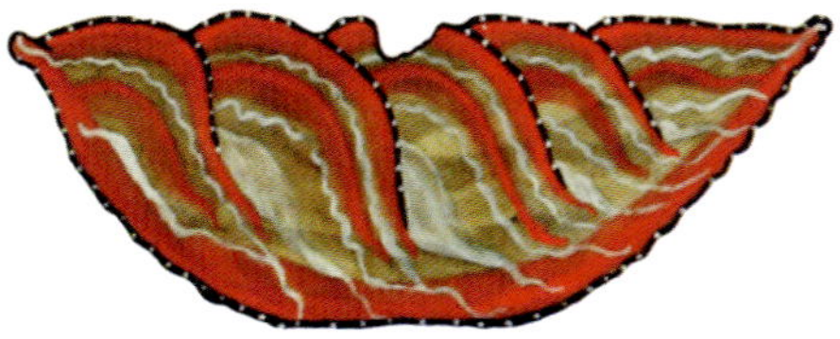

Circles and Measurement Ratios, Forms of Sound

Pythagoras used the monochord to demonstrate that the tonic, or base note, produced by a stretched string has a specific relationship with the increasingly higher-pitched sounds produced by the same string divided into two, three, four, five parts, etc. The intervals thus determined are: half the length, octave interval; third, fifth interval; fifth, upper octave; and so on until all the intervals of the scale are identified.

The diameter of the circles in the images of *Scivias* represents the length of the sounds. The relationship between their measurements represents the intervals; for example, the seraphim, cherubim, and light at the center of the crown of the Heavenly Hosts are related to each other as a whole, a half, and a third, where one is the measure of light. The cherubim have the same frequency as God at the lower octave and the seraphim at the fifth. The three sounds are in perfect consonance and show that the angels' role is to convey to humanity the perfection of the love of the divine light.

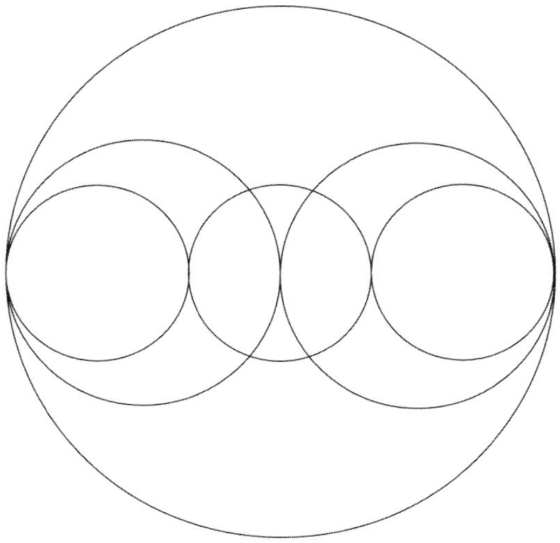

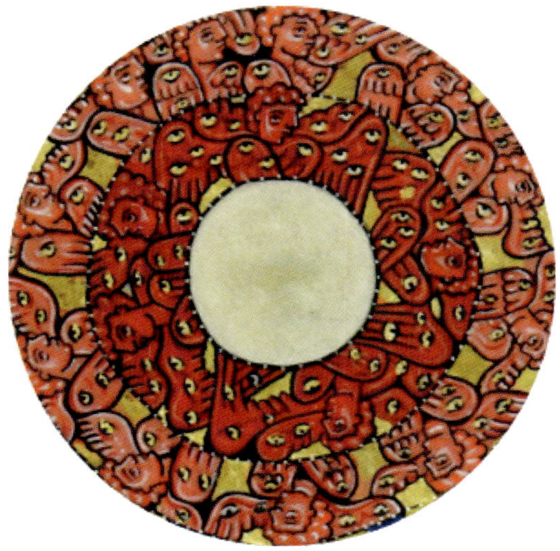

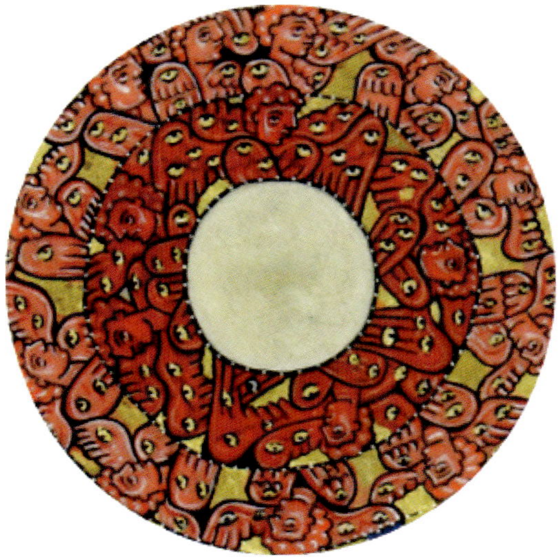

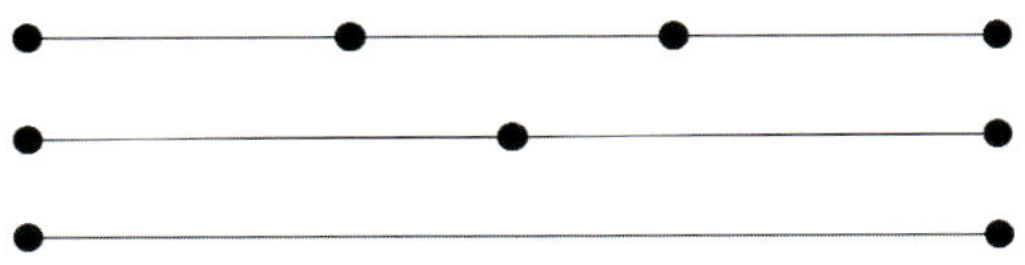

The Symphony of the Harmony of Celestial Revelations

The measurement of the diameter of the circumference of the third star, the largest in the whole work, can be taken as the fundamental note of the monochord. The measurement of the diameter of the five circles placed within it—of the circle of the star of the Gospel, of the Father, of Mary, of the Lamb—correspond precisely to the measurements of the sections into which the string is divided, respectively: a half, a third, a fourth, a fifth, and a tenth. The measurement of the largest circle corresponds to the *tonic*, the base note, and that of the other circles to the sounds of the eighth, fifth, upper eighth, third, upper third. Together they create the greatest accord, perfect harmony and consonance. The same happens with the other circles whose diameter can be taken as the measurement of the entire string and the measurements of the diameters of the inner circles of its subdivisions, creating different music, image of the *symphony of the harmony of celestial revelations.*

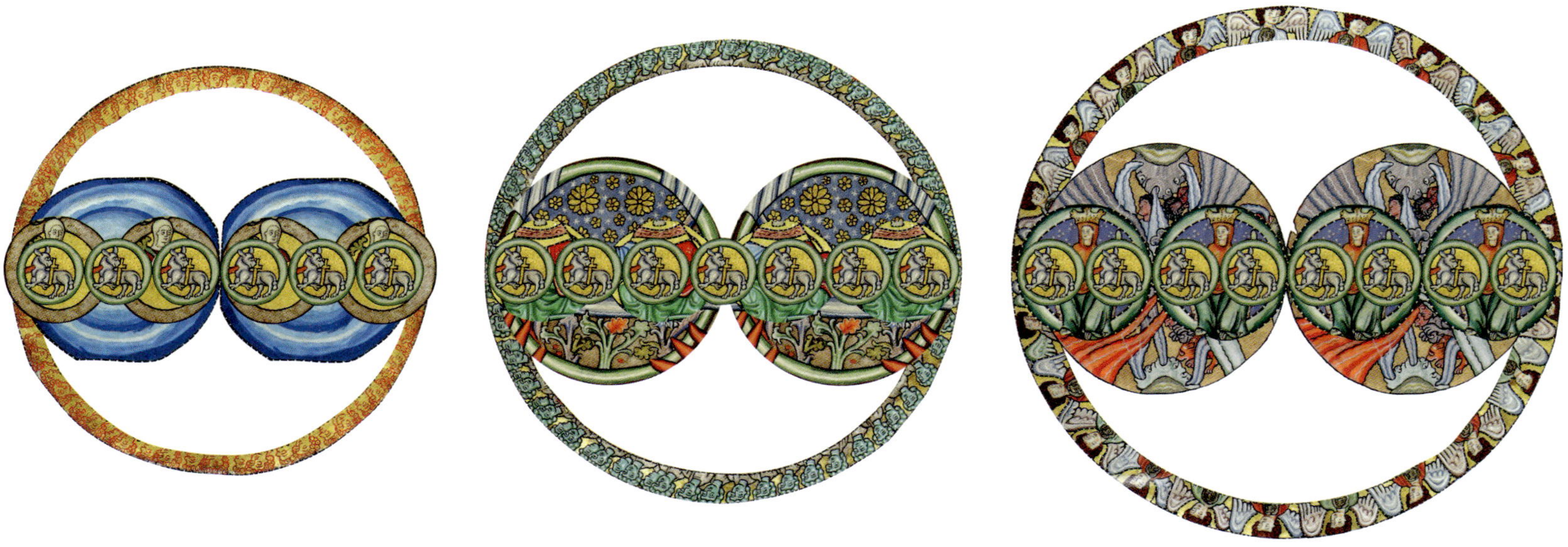

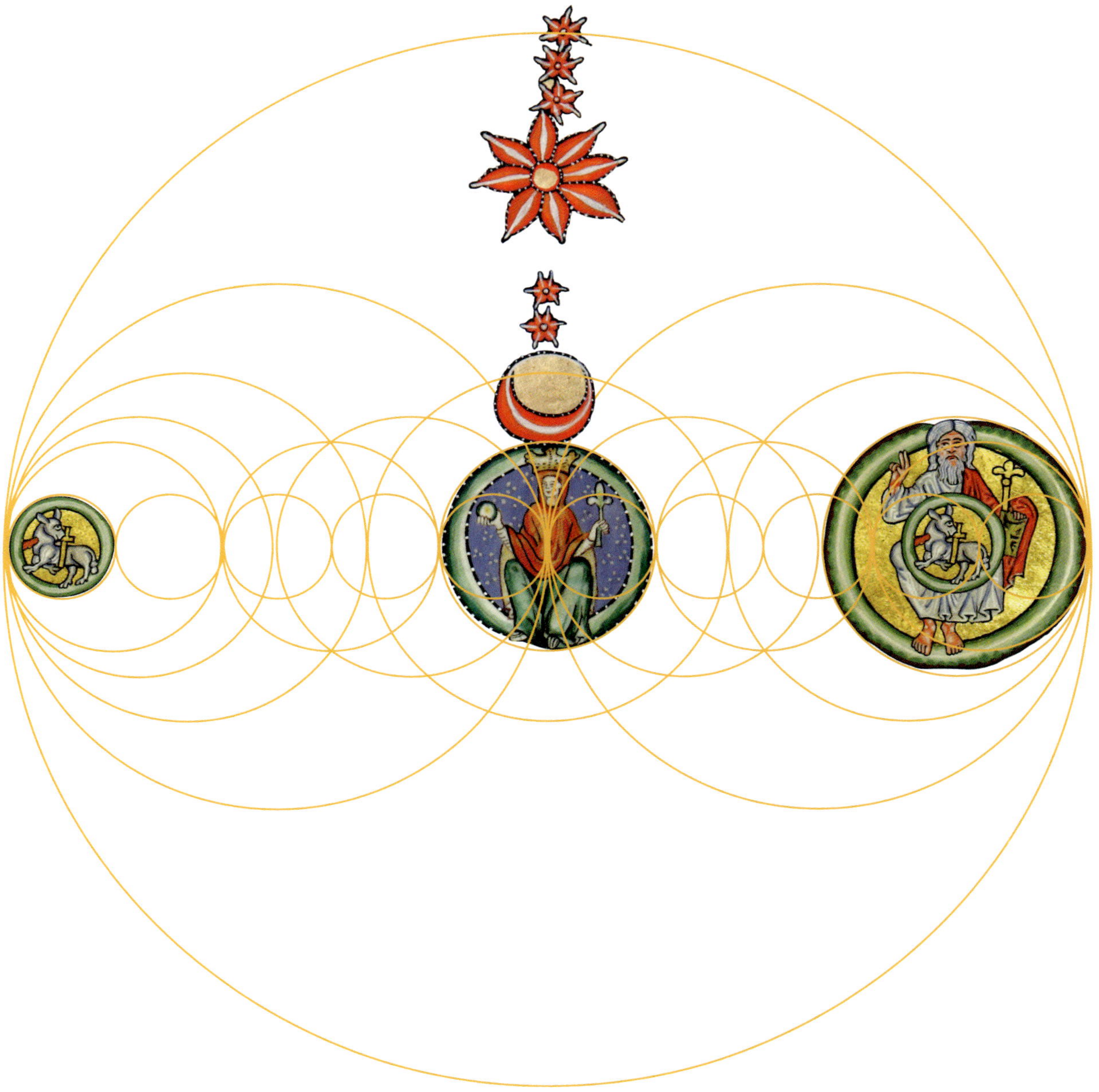

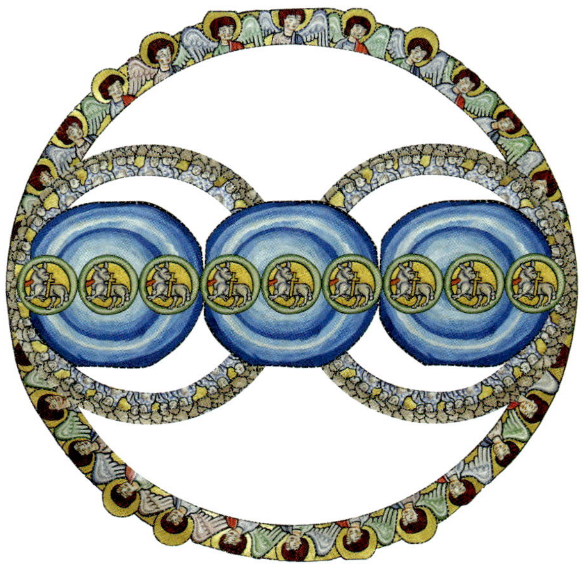

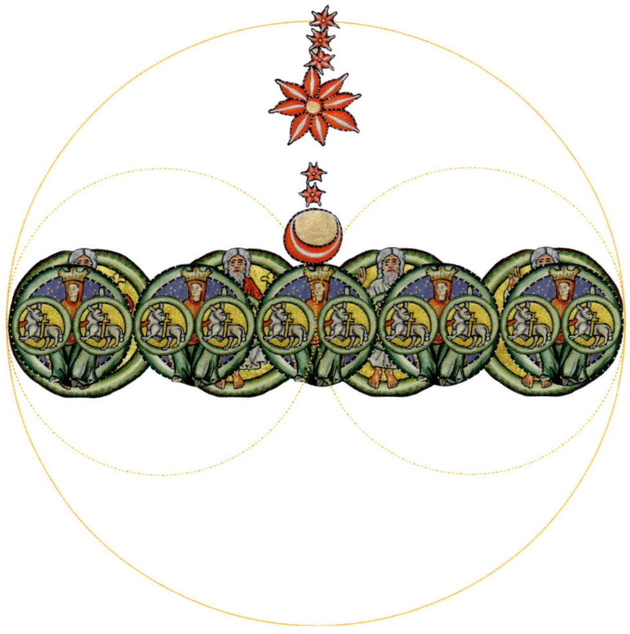

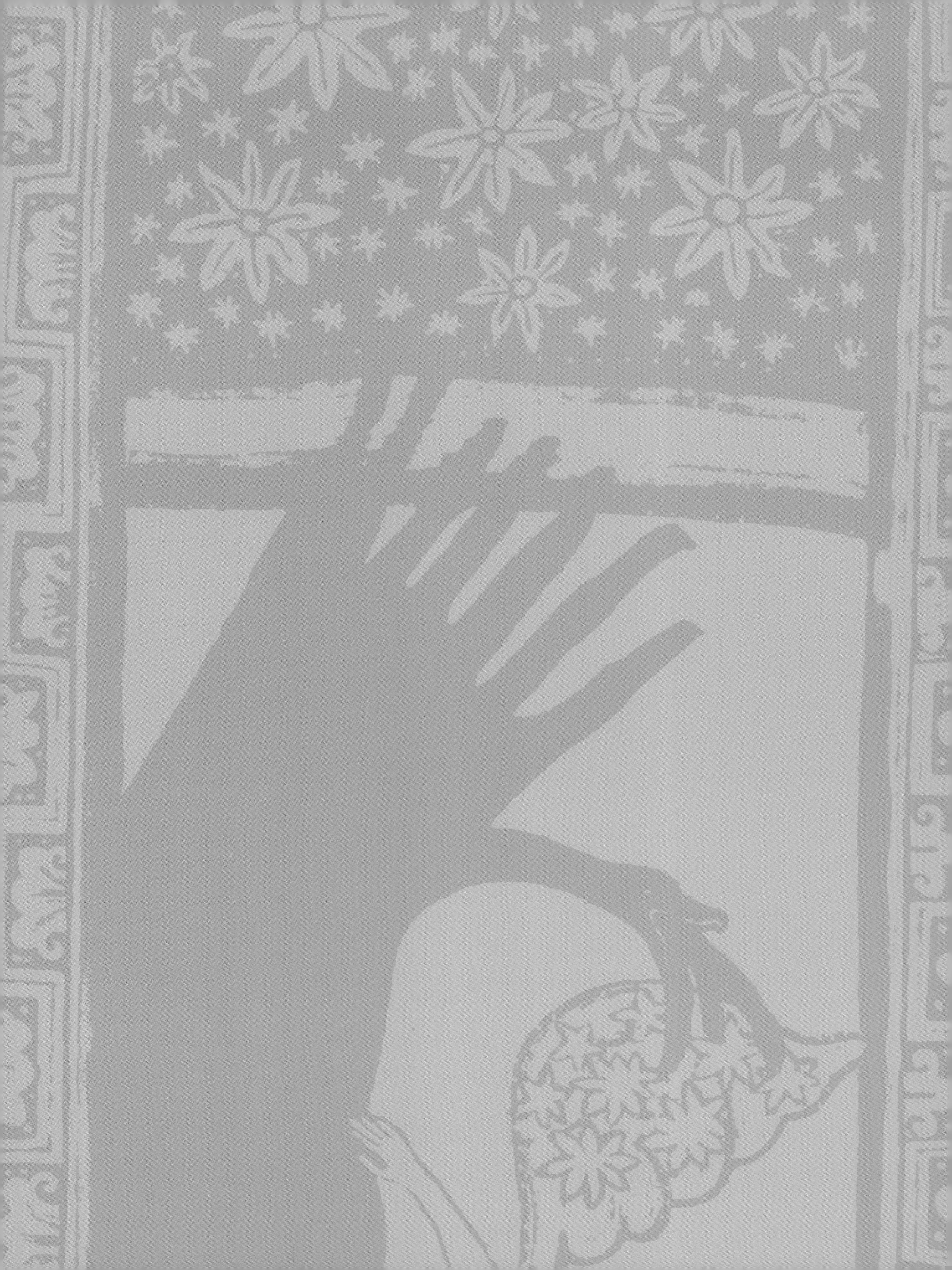

Astronomy

And, in a region of brightness [. . .] a candid cloud [. . .] had come forth from a beautiful human form and contained within itself many stars (*SC* I.2.10, p. 73).

At the beginning of the *Liber Divinorum Operum* the voice of the living light urges humanity *to observe the rising and setting of the sun, moon, and stars [. . .] to recognize in all of them how great an honor it is to be created*, and concludes with: *whoever does not do this scorns God and knows neither the human creature nor himself*. In the work, the accurate description of the movement of the earth and the stars, of the solstices and equinoxes created by the revolution of the earth around the sun, and of the movement of the winds that, like columns, support the firmament, and the symbols they represent, is a profound hymn of praise to creation and the Creator.

In the images of *Scivias*, instead, Hildegard chose to represent the trinitarian vision of the sphere divided into three spheres—an image described in the *Divine Comedy* by Dante and in the theories of contemporary physics. Within the sphere, the planets move in their orbits in a series of concentric circles. The circle with the widest diameter, that of the third star, image of the Trinity, surrounds creation and the Heavenly Hosts. The diameter of this circle is ten times that of the diameter of the divine light adored by the angels, and thirteen times the diameter of the earth, signifying that the cross, symbol of the humanity of the Son of God, is inscribed in the circle of divine perfection. Lastly, the measurements of the circles mark the harmonious rhythm of creation, from which the proportions of the figures and the music derive.

Lastly, Hildegard uses the image of stars to recount the journey along the ways. At the beginning of creation the human multitude represented as eight stars—eight being the number associated with infinity—is deposited in the womb of the cloud Eve. After the fall of the progenitors the heavenly spirits, living lamps, are separated from the earth to illumine the pilgrim souls from on high. On this journey of redemption human beings are invited to follow the angelic light and to do good; their acts of faith adorn the skies of the firmament like bright spheres. At the same time, God sends to earth the stars of the prophets to rend the darkness with light and to announce the coming of the new life and the future flowering of souls in the serene light of eternity. The driving force behind humanity's journey is its *desire* to be reunited with the *sidera*, stars of the heavens, fragments of the light of the divine sphere.

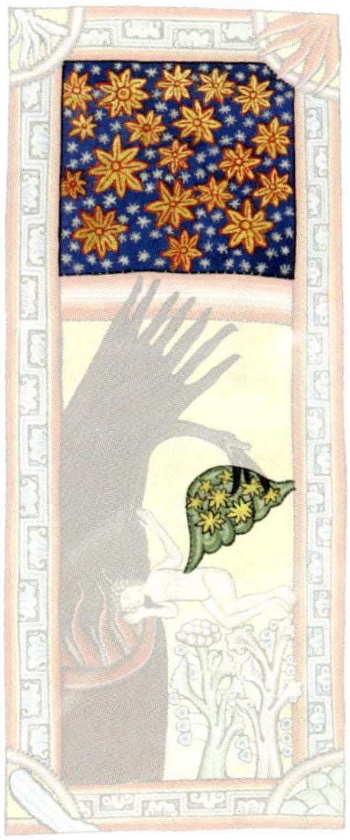

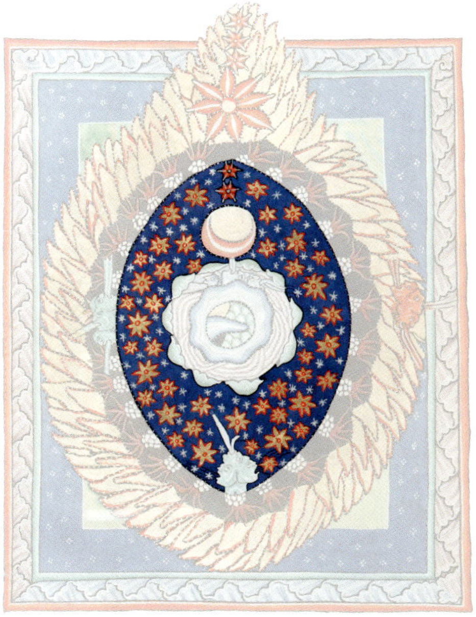

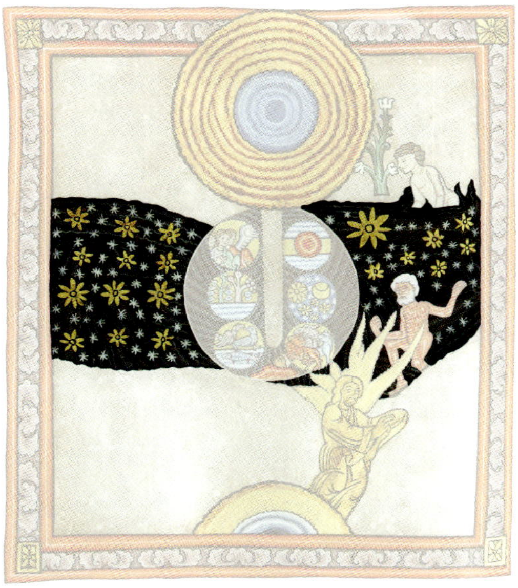

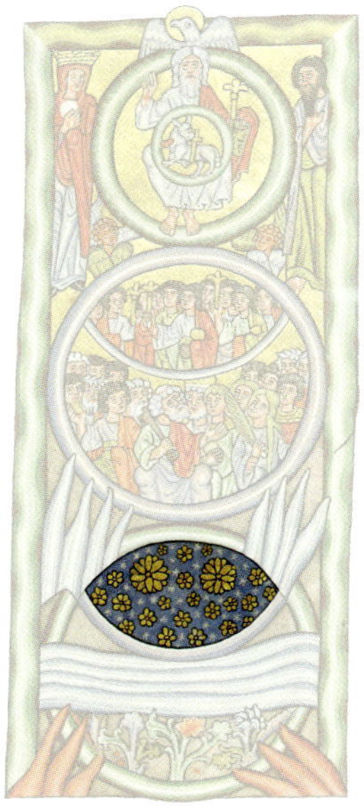

The Orbits of the Planets and the Circles of the Angels

For the above-mentioned celestial bodies are carried around from west to east against the firmament (*LDO* I.2.32, p. 89).

Here are marked out above the head of this image seven celestial bodies [...] These signify that the seven gifts of the Holy Spirit surpass all human understanding in the three time periods of the world (*LDO* I.2.33, p. 90).

The outer circle of the sphere coincides with the orbit of the third star from the bottom and encompasses the firmament and the Heavenly Hosts. Its diameter is ten times that of the circle of light (see p. 122), image of divine perfection. The seven planets within the sphere describe a vertical axis, indicating the path that leads the Earth/humanity, illuminated by the light of the Moon/Church and the two stars of the Word, to meet the warmth of the Sun/Christ, finally reaching the light of the divine Trinity of the three stars at the top. The distance between the planets is determined by the diameter of the circle of the earth at the center of the firmament. The axis of the planets describes the upper part of the cross inscribed in the sphere and the measurement of its arms is thirteen times the measurement of the earth. As we have seen, the number thirteen is the symbol of Christ.

The diameter of the divine sphere and the arms of the cross coincide: the measurement of the former is ten times that of the light; the measurement of the latter, thirteen times that of the earth. This is determined by the fact that the size of the diameter of the earth is slightly smaller than that of the circle of light adored by the angels, signifying that the human creature is similar but not equal to his Creator. The two measurements indicate the following: the number ten is the perfection of the circle, image of God; the number thirteen is the image of the Cross, symbol of the journey from heaven to earth and from earth to heaven of the Son of God. A journey that every soul, sphere of fire, is called upon to make during its incarnation in the life-giving space of the sphere of creation.

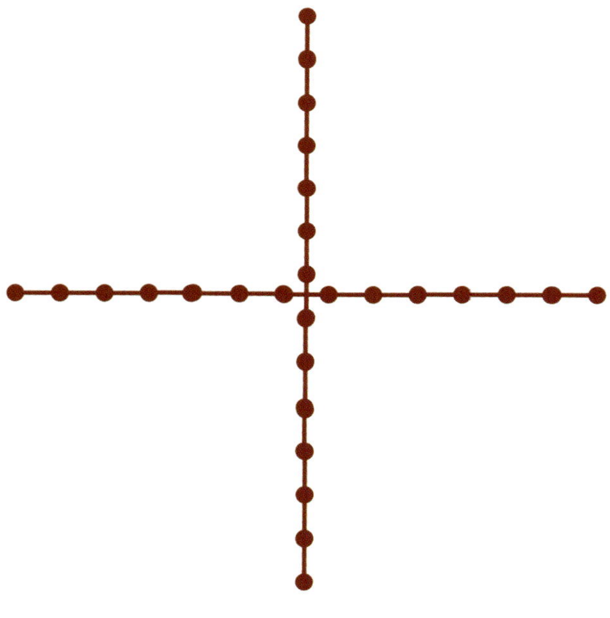

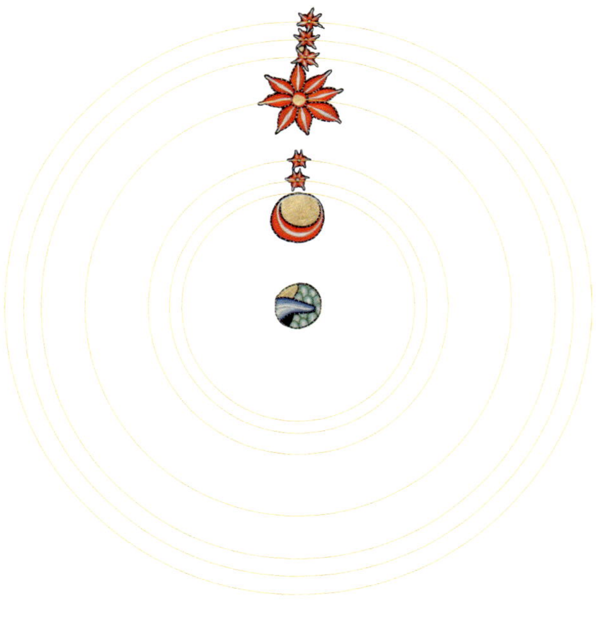

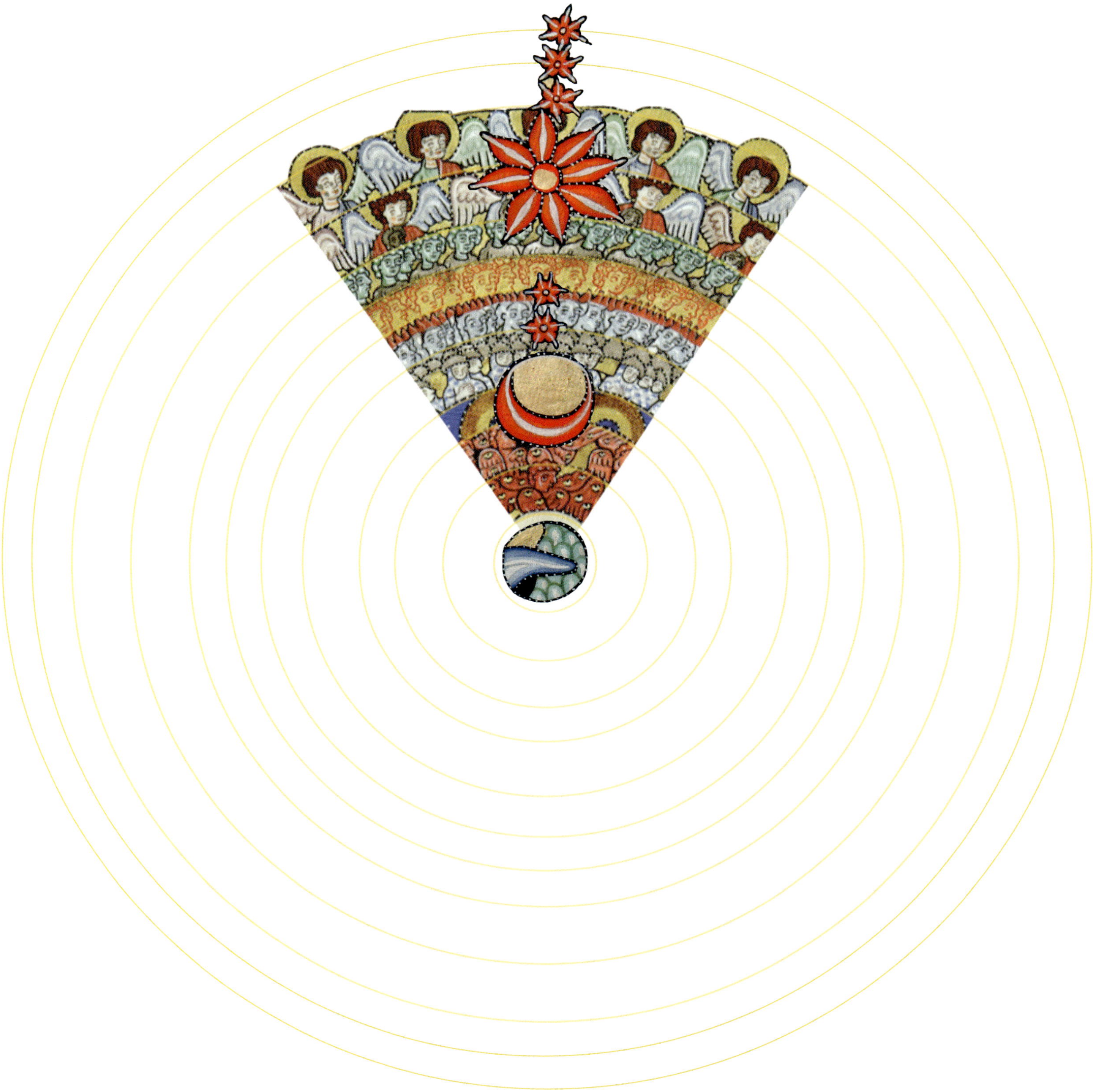

One Sphere in Three Spheres

After this I saw a vast instrument, round and shadowed, in the shape of an egg, small at the top, large in the middle and narrowed at the bottom (*SC* I.3.D, p. 93).

And God said, "Let there be light". And there was light. God, the inextinguishable light that can be darkened by no one [...] adhered the living spheres, the angels (*LDO* II.1.17, pp. 288–289).

Above them, as if sculpted on the veils, is the likeness of the glorious and ineffable Trinity as it was represented to you earlier (*SC* II.5.7, p. 205).

The sphere of the fire of the soul makes its journey within the sphere of creation, passing through the elements of the firmament, the waves of sound and of the gazes of the angels, and the lights of the divine flame, until it crosses the space-time threshold of the divine door of sapphire blue in the form of man. And it is then that the soul shines in the shared chorality, a living spark of eternal light, a wave of sound and life, a breath of the whole, complete, and whirling globe held in the heart of Divine Love since the beginning of time.

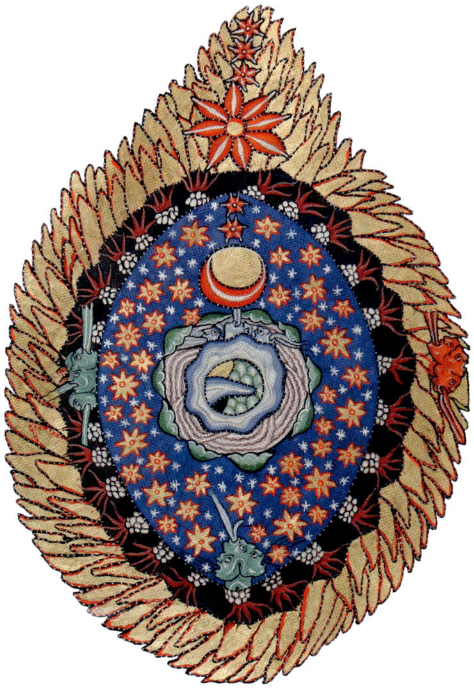

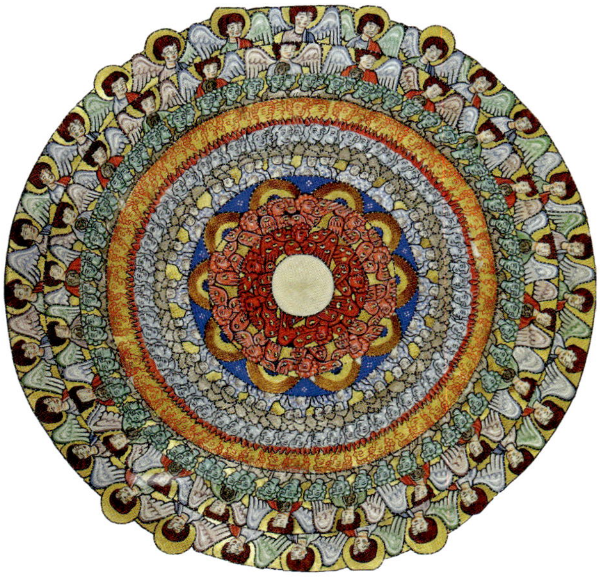

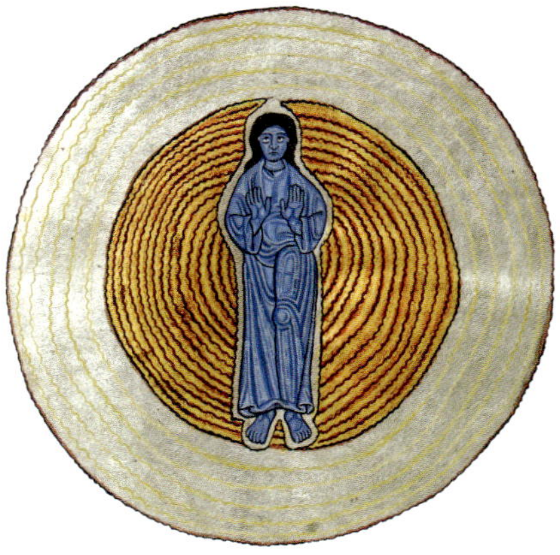

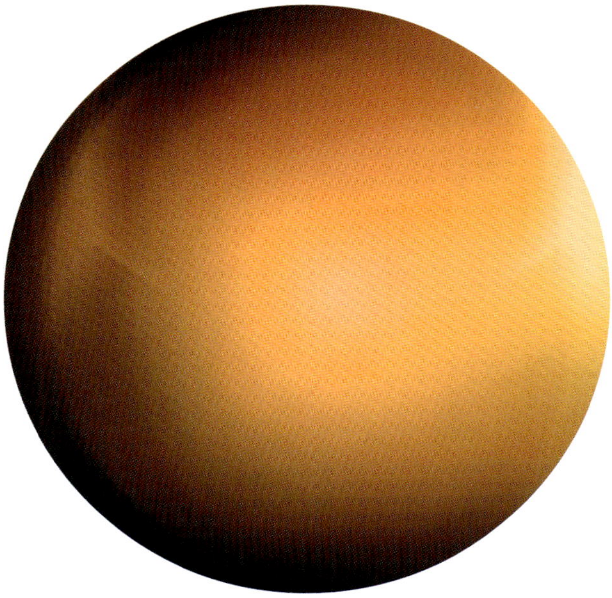

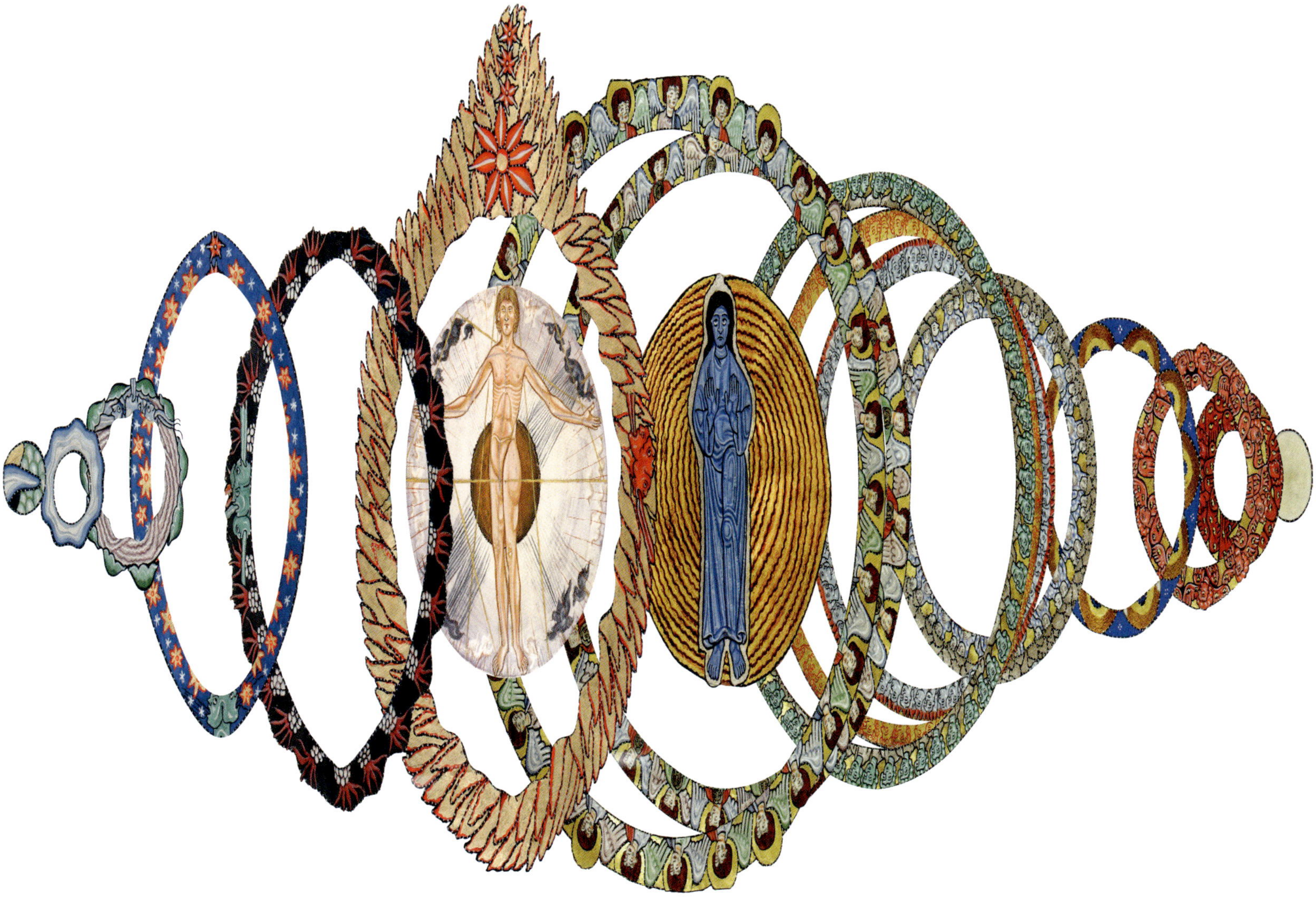

Appendix

Summary of the Images

Bibliographical Note

Works by Hildegard von Bingen

Scivias, edited by A. Carlevaris OSB and A. Führkötter OSB (Corpus Christianorum – Continuatio Mediaevalis [CCCM] voll. 43, 43A), Brepols, Turnhout, 1978 (anastatic edition 2003).

Liber Divinorum Operum, edited by A. Derolez and P. Dronke (CCCM vol. 92), Brepols, Turnhout, 1996.

Opera minora I, edited by H. Feiss, C. Evans, B. M. Kienzle, C. Muessig, B. Newmann, P. Dronke (CCCM vol. 226), Brepols, Turnhout. 2007.

Il libro delle opere divine, edited by M. Cristiani and M. Pereira, Mondadori, Milan, 2003.

The Book of the Divine Works, translated by Nathaniel M. Campbell, The Catholic University of America Press, Washington D.C., 2018.

Symphonia, introduction, translation and commentary by Barbara Newman, Cornell University Press, New York, 1998.

Manuscripts

Hildegard von Bingen
Scivias

Wiesbaden, Hess. Landesbibliothek, Hs I, 1165 (Rupertsberg, XII sec. ex.), lost since 1945.

Two reproductions exist:

- Eibingen, library of the Abbey of St. Hildegard, black and white photographs (1927), https://www.kulturelles-erbe-koeln.de/documents/obj/4004935
- Eibingen, library of the Abbey of St. Hildegard, facsimile perg. (1927–1933), https://www.abtei-st-hildegard.de/die-scivias-miniaturen/.

The images we used in the book are reproduced from the parchment facsimile of the Wiesbaden codex, realized at Eibingen Abbey between 1927 and 1933; the 1927 black and white photographs attest to its fidelity to the original.

There is another illuminated manuscript, with different characteristics:

- Heidelberg, Universitätsbibliothek, Cod. Zwiefalten e Salem X,16,1220 (XII sec.), http://digi.ub.uni-heidelberg.de/touch/salX16/#page/8.

For these and all the other codices of *Scivias* see A. Carlevaris' and A. Führkötter's introduction to the critical edition, XXXII-LVI.

Liber Divinorum Operum

Lucca, Biblioteca Statale di Lucca, ms. 1942, https://www.internetculturale.it/it/41/collezioni-digitali/26271/hildegard-von-bingen-della-biblioteca-statale-di-lucca

Rabano Mauro (Hrabanus Maurus)
De laudibus sanctae crucis

Paris, Latin 2422, Bibliothèque nationale de France. Département des Manuscrits, https://gallica.bnf.fr/ark:/12148/btv1b8490076p#

Works on Hildegard von Bingen

The Hildegardian bibliography is extensive and somewhat dishomogeneous. For an introduction see Michela Pereira, *Ildegarda di Bingen. Maestra di sapienza nel suo tempo e oggi*, Gabrielli Editori, San Pietro in Cariano (Verona), 2017 (with a large bibliographical section). Also useful are the constantly-updated sites www.hildegard.society.org and www.hildegard-akademie.de.

Baillet, Luis, "Les Miniatures du Scivias de Sainte Hildegarde," in *Monuments et Mémoires publiés par l'Académie des Inscriptions et Belles Lettres*, 19, Paris, 1911.

Bain, Jennifer (edited by), *The Cambridge Companion to Hildegard von Bingen*, Cambridge University Press, Cambridge, 2021.

Calderoni, Masetti, Anna Rosa, Dalli Regoli, Gigetta, *Sanctae Hildegardis Revelationes. Manoscritto 1942*, Cassa di Risparmio, Lucca, 1973.

Caviness, Madeline, *Hildegard as the Designer of the Illustrations to her Works*, in C. Burnett, P. Dronke (edited by), *Hildegard of Bingen. The Context of her Thought and Art*, The Warburg Institute, London, 1998.

Cirlot, Victoria, *Hildegard von Bingen y la tradición visionaria de occidente*, Herder Editorial, Barcelona, 2012.

Dronke, Peter, "The Four Elements in the Thought of Hildegard of Bingen: Cosmology and Poetry. *Cause et cure* and the Berlin Fragment," in *Studi medievali*, LIV/2, 2013, 905–922.

Fassler, Margot, E., Cosmos, *Liturgy, and the Arts in the Twelfth Century: Hildegard's Illuminated "Scivias,"* University of Pennsyilvania Press, Philadelphia, 2022.

Gutjahr, Hiltrud and Zatonyi Maura, *Geschaut im Lebendigen Licht. Die Miniaturen des Liber Scivias der Hildegard von Bingen*, Beuroner Kunstverlag, Beuron, 2011.

Pereira, Michela, *Vedere nell'ombra. La conoscenza profetica nelle opere di Ildegarda di Bingen*, in *Profezia, filosofia e prassi politica*, edited by G. Garfagnini, A. Ridolfi, Edizioni ETS, Pisa, 2013.

Pozzi, Escot, "Hildegard von Bingen: Universal Proportion," in *Mystics Quarterly*, 19, no. 1 (March 1933), pp. 34–39, Penn State University Press, Pennsylvania 1984.

Pozzi, Escot, "The Gothic Cathedral and Hidden Geometry of St. Hildegard," in *Sonus* 5.1 (1984), pp. 14–31, Sonus Edizioni Musicali, Cambridge, 1984.

Rabassó, Georgina, *L'univers vivent d'Hildegarda de Bingen: perspectives filosòfiques*, Diputació de Barcelona-Institut d'Estudis Catalans, Barcelona, 2018.

Rainini, Marco G., *Ildegarda, l'eredità di Giovanni Scoto e Hirsau. «Homo medietas» e mediazioni*, in Reiner Berndt and Maura Zátonyi (edited by), *Unversehrt und unverletzt. Hildegards von Bingen Menschenbild und Kirchenverständnis heute* ("Erudiri Sapienti"), Aschendorff, Münster, 2015, 139–165.

Salvadori, Sara, *Hildegard von Bingen. A Journey into the Images*, Skira, Milan, 2019.

Salvadori, Sara, *Hildegard von Bingen. In the Heart of God*, Skira, Milan, 2021.
Santos-Paz, José Carlos, *"Tabulae capitulorum de las obras proféticas" de Hildegarde de Bingen. Diagnostica testuale. Le «Tabulae capitulorum»* (ed. L. Castaldi-V. Mattaloni) (223–260), SISMEL-Edizioni del Galluzzo, Florence, 2019.
Saurma-Jeltsch, Lieselotte, *Miniaturen im "Liber Scivias" der Hildegard von Bingen*, Reichert Verlag, Wiesbaden, 1998.
Tabaglio, Maria, *Carmina*, Gabrielli Editore, Verona, 2014.

Other works

Cirlot, Juan Eduardo, *Il dizionario dei Simboli*, Adelphi, Milan, 2021.
Davy, Marie-Madeleine, *Il simbolismo medioevale*, Edizioni Mediterranee, Rome, 1998.
De Champeaux, Gérard, and Sebastien Sterckx, *I simboli del Medioevo*, Jaca Book, Milan, 1998.
Eco, Umberto, *Arte e Bellezza nell'estetica medioevale*, La nave di Teseo, Milan, 2016.
Hrabanus Maurus, *Figurae*, edited by Perona, Josè and Artium, Magister, Universidad de Murcia, Murcia, 1995.
Bl. Hrabanus Maurus, *On the Formation of Clergy*, in Gregory F. LaNave, *The Fathers of the Church. Mediaeval Continuation, Volume 21*, translated by Owen M. Phelan, The Catholic University of America Press, Washington D.C., 2023.
Jung, Carl, *Psicologia e Alchimia*, Boringhieri, Turin, 1981.
Leonardi, Claudio, *Luce e tenebra del Medioevo*, Sismel Edizioni del Galluzzo, Florence, 2014.
Marco Vitruvio Pollione, *De Architectura*, Edizioni Studio Tesi, Rome, 1990.
Pozzi, Giovanni, *La Parola dipinta*, Adelphi, Milan, 1981.
Rabano, Mauro, *La formazione dei chierici*, Città Nuova, Rome, 2002.
Schneider, Marius, *Pietre che cantano*, Se Srl, Milan, 2005.
Schneider, Marius, *La musica Primitiva*, Adelphi, Milan, 1992.